T0317438

POWER AND POSSESSION IN THE
RUSSIAN REVOLUTION

HISTORIES OF ECONOMIC LIFE

*Jeremy Adelman, Sunil Amrith, Emma Rothschild, and
Francesca Trivellato, Series Editors*

Power and Possession in the Russian Revolution

ANNE O'DONNELL

PRINCETON UNIVERSITY PRESS

PRINCETON & OXFORD

Published by Princeton University Press
41 William Street, Princeton, New Jersey 08540
99 Banbury Road, Oxford OX2 6JX

press.princeton.edu

All Rights Reserved

Library of Congress Cataloging-in-Publication Data

Names: O'Donnell, Anne, 1980– author.
Title: Power and possession in the Russian Revolution / Anne O'Donnell.
Description: Princeton : Princeton University Press, [2024] | Series: Histories of economic life | Includes bibliographical references and index.
Identifiers: LCCN 2023026800 (print) | LCCN 2023026801 (ebook) | ISBN 9780691205540 (hardback) | ISBN 9780691255897 (ebook)
Subjects: LCSH: Right of property—Soviet Union. | Eviction—Soviet Union. | Government ownership—Soviet Union. | Soviet Union—Economic conditions—1917–1945. | Soviet Union—History—Revolution, 1917–1921—Confiscations and contributions. | BISAC: BUSINESS & ECONOMICS / Economic History | POLITICAL SCIENCE / Political Ideologies / Communism, Post-Communism & Socialism
Classification: LCC DK265.9.E2 O36 2024 (print) | LCC DK265.9.E2 (ebook) | DDC 323.4/60947—dc23/eng/20230728
LC record available at https://lccn.loc.gov/2023026800
LC ebook record available at https://lccn.loc.gov/2023026801

British Library Cataloging-in-Publication Data is available

Editorial: Priya Nelson, Emma Wagh, and Morgan Spehar
Production Editorial: Nathan Carr
Production: Danielle Amatucci
Publicity: William Pagdatoon

Jacket/Cover Credit: The Russian Photographic Society, c. spring 1921. Photograph taken by B.N. Maklakov. Courtesy of TsAGM

This book has been composed in Arno

Printed on acid-free paper. ∞

Printed in the United States of America

10 9 8 7 6 5 4 3 2 1

For my mother

They saw the spectre of socialism and became afraid; nor is this surprising, for they have something to lose, something to be afraid of. But we are not in that position at all . . .

Europe is sinking because it cannot rid itself of its cargo—that infinity of treasures . . .

In our case, all this is artificial ballast; out with it and overboard, and then full sail into the open sea!

—ALEXANDER HERZEN

CONTENTS

Illustrations

Tables

ACKNOWLEDGMENTS

IT IS A DELIGHT to acknowledge the many debts I have accrued in the course of writing this book. I gratefully acknowledge funding for research and writing from the American Council of Learned Societies, the U.S. Department of Education, Harvard University's Center for History and Economics, the Mellon Foundation, Princeton University's History Department and Institute for International and Regional Studies, and the Social Science Research Council. A grant from the Princeton University Press offered through an innovative program for first-time authors was crucial to getting this book over the finish line. I am deeply indebted to the archivists at the State Archive of the Russian Federation, the Manuscript Division at the Russian State Library, the Russian State Archive of the Economy, the Russian State Archive of Socio-Political History, the Russian State Historical Archive, the Central Archive of the City of Moscow, the Central Historical Archive of Moscow, and the Central State Archive of St. Petersburg, all of whom provided important guidance to the papers of a jumbled time, during which standard filing systems did not always obtain.

As it is with great teachers, I will never be able to repay what I owe to Stephen Kotkin. Nevertheless, I register my abiding gratitude here for all he has taught me, for the rigor and empathy he brings to study of history, for his unwavering support, dedication, and optimism. Ekaterina Pravilova taught me new ways of thinking about Russian history and new methods for accessing the history of the material world. She has been an essential interlocutor throughout my work on this book and generously agreed to read several of its chapters. Michael Gordin's clarity of mind and collegiality have helped me at many turns and I am grateful for his encouragement over the years. At Berkeley, I benefited from seminars with John Connelly, David Henkin, and Yuri Slezkine, who posed questions about Soviet history and what neighbors should expect of one another that left a deep impression. As an undergraduate, I received a summer stipend to work at a nonprofit on the South Side of

Chicago directed by Sokoni Karanja, who suggested a project: that I interview the residents of apartment buildings owned by the city, which the city planned soon to demolish. The questions raised in these encounters continue to guide my research and teaching, and I am deeply grateful to Dr. Karanja for welcoming me into his work. When I returned to school, I enrolled in a one-of-a-kind course on the history of housing and urbanism taught by the late Robert Guttmann, which provided an enriching foundation for my later inquiries.

This book began on Kazakova Street, in the company of an antique dining table that miraculously survived the turmoil described in these pages, and of the family who gathers around it. I am one of many travelers to have found respite in the Zhivovs' magical apartment; given its inhabitants, I am probably one of many to have found a dissertation topic there. In the best tradition of their parents, Lina Zhivova and her siblings have not only fed and housed me all these years, they have brought me along on their lives. My gratitude to them all is boundless. In the archives, it was a privilege to work alongside so many erudite and welcoming historians, including Seth Bernstein, Miriam Dobson, Sylvain Dufraisse, and James Heinzen. Katja Bruisch shared her capacious knowledge of RGAE as well as her friendship. Juliette Cadiot helped me get my footing intellectually and practically as I began this project, and has been a role model in the art of thoughtful and generous scholarship ever since.

Not everyone wants to spend their twenties in a small town in New Jersey. But in the company of Ryan Davis, Mayhill Fowler, Jamie Kreiner, Kyrill Kunakhovich, Elidor Mëhilli, Dael Norwood, Jamie Reuland, Chris Shannon, and Fadzilah Yahaya, Princeton always felt like a big place, rich with ideas and companionship. At Harvard, I had the good fortune to talk the history of real estate with Alexia Yates, and to absorb the fascinating scholarship on offer at the Center for History and Economics, where Emma Rothschild exercises her unique gift for cultivating scholarly connections across disciplines and fields. I have profited greatly from conversations and conferences with these scholars, at the Center and now in other spaces, especially those organized by Rohit De and Catherine Evans. Seth Bernstein and Elidor Mëhilli generously read drafts of the introduction, each with characteristic lucidity.

At New York University, I have been fortunate to join a thriving community devoted to the study of Russia. Anne Lounsbery and Eliot Borenstein have provided advice, encouragement, and good humor at every step. Thank you to Leydi Rofman for making everything run smoothly, Alla Roylance for incredible skill and speed in tracking down obscure sources, and Evelina Mendelevich for company. In the history department, Stephen Gross, Monica Kim (now at Wisconsin-Madison), Tatiana Linkhoeva, Andrew Needham, Susanah Romney, and Andrew Sartori read draft chapters with acumen. Karl Appuhn, Ayşe Baltacıoğlu-Brammer, Jane Burbank, Rossen Djagalov, Stef Geroulanos, Becky Goetz, Ilya Kliger, Yanni Kotsonis, Kim Phillips-Fein (now at Columbia), and Brandon Schechter served as sounding boards, suggested readings, and posed questions that sharpened my thinking. Robyn d'Avignon did all this and more; her camaraderie, wisdom, and careful readings of much of this book have been invaluable.

This book has benefited from the opportunity to present it at a number of institutions and other forums. I spent a fruitful month as a visiting scholar at the École des hautes études en sciences sociales, where I benefited from seminars with Juliette Cadiot, Sabine Dullin, and Alessandro Stanziani. For invitations and enjoyable visits over the years I am grateful to Jeff Hardy, Charis Marantzidou, Stephen Norris, Benjamin Schenk, and Melissa Stockdale, and to audiences at Brigham Young University, the Miami University of Ohio, The University of Oklahoma, the Penn Economic History Forum/Russian History and Culture Workshop, Georgetown University, and Sciences Po. Conversations at these and other meetings with Rachel Applebaum, Betty Banks, Xenia Cherkaev, Franziska Exeler, Anna Ivanova, Boris Kolonitskii, Eric Lohr, Clara Mattei, Liudmila Novikova, Alex Oberlander, Bhavani Raman, Aaron Retish, and Anna Safronova stimulated new ideas about the entangled histories of revolution, law, and economic life. Michael David-Fox and Peter Holquist offered incisive critique and useful suggestions at the very earliest presentations of my research, and have continued to do so on many occasions in all the years since then. Trevor Perri brought an ideal balance of rigor and sensitivity to this manuscript, and I am grateful for his clarifying interventions. I am grateful to the incredible staff at Princeton University Press, not just for bringing this book to fruition, but for supporting my work on it in so many different ways. Priya Nelson steered the manuscript through every stage of this process with an awe-inspiring combination of intelligence and skill. Emma Wagh has kept the manuscript, and me, in line with enthusiasm and efficiency. I am grateful to Nathan Carr for guiding production, and especially for matching this text with Anna Badkhen, whose skill in improving it has been matched only by her good humor. My thanks are due to the two anonymous readers of the manuscript, for their thoughtful engagement with this work. I am grateful to all the series editors for the confidence they showed in the manuscript, especially Emma Rothschild, who shepherded it through the first steps, and Jeremy Adelman, who offered clarifying advice when I most needed it.

April Williams made it possible for me to write this book, taking care of my children with skill and superhuman reliability amid a global pandemic. My thanks to Neva Durand, Charlotte Walker-Said, Johanna Winant, and Alexandra Shaw for their companionship in writing and life, and to Chris and Jay LeGore, Judith Grace, and Jeffrey Mabee for making life in Maine the way it is. I am grateful to my family, Chuck and Karen Whisler, Bill Whisler, Carrie Lee, George Lee, Rachel Levy, Catherine Hinman, Francesca O'Donnell, and Nicholas O'Donnell for their constant encouragement and generosity, and especially to Roger Lee, for making Belfast my home, and to my brother Colin, for looking out for me even still. My husband Ben vowed that, if it meant I finished this book even one moment sooner, I did not have to thank him in these acknowledgments. Combined with his steadfast love, encouragement, wit, and the long days he spent alone with our children, this made all the difference. In my wildest dreams I could never have conjured up children as wonderful as Henry and Vivian. I marvel every day at my incredible good fortune to be their mother. This book is for my mother, Gail, who died as I was just beginning it. I could never have started, let alone finished, without her bottomless well of confidence in me, her example of diligence, her joy in our lives together, her curiosity about the world—in short, without her great love.

NOTE ON USAGE

RUSSIA ADHERED to the Julian calendar through February 1918, after which it switched to the Gregorian calendar, which ran thirteen days ahead. The dates given in this book reflect the calendar systems in use at the time. Where a publication or document makes use of both dates, as was common during the transition, I include them, following the practice of giving the Gregorian date followed by the Julian (in parentheses). Transliterations generally follow the Library of Congress system, with the exception of common English versions of Russian proper names.

Institutional Abbreviations

Central Committee	Central Committee of the Communist Party
Cheka/VChK	All-Russian Extraordinary Commission for the Battle against Counterrevolution and Sabotage; changed in 1918 to the All-Russian Extraordinary Commission for the Battle against Counter-revolution, Speculation, and Abuse of Power
domkom	residential building committee
MChK	Moscow Cheka
Gokhran	State Depository of Valuables, department of Narkomfin
gorprodukt	municipal provisioning agency
Goskon	People's Commissariat of Government Control, succeeded by the Worker-Peasant Inspectorate (Rabkrin)
IEI	Institute for Economic Research, unit of Narkomfin

kvartkhoz	block economic unit; neighborhood-level administrative unit responsible for registry of built space in Moscow
Mossoviet	Moscow Soviet of Workers', Peasants' and Red-Army Soldiers' Deputies (subsequently People's Deputies)
MUNI	Moscow Directorate for Real Estate, successor to TsZhZO
Narkomfin	People's Commissariat of Finance
Narkomiust	People's Commissariat of Justice
NKVD	People's Commissariat of Internal Affairs
NKVT	People's Commissariat of Foreign Trade
partkom	Communist Party Committee at an enterprise or institution
Petrokommuna	Petrograd City Consumers' Commune, city provisioning body in Petrograd
Petrosoviet	Petrograd Soviet of Workers' and Soldiers' Deputies
Rabkrin/RKI	Worker-Peasant Inspectorate, successor to the People's Commissariat of Government Control
RSFSR	Russian Soviet Federated Socialist Republic
Soviet raionnykh dum	Council of Neighborhood Dumas, municipal administration of Moscow after the February Revolution, incorporated into the Mossoviet in spring 1918
Sovnarkom	Council of People's Commissars
TsZhZO	Central Housing-Land Department of the Mossoviet, succeeded by MUNI
VSNKh	Supreme Council of the National Economy
VTsIK	All-Russian Central Executive Committee
ZhZO	Housing and Land Department, unit of a local soviet

Units of Measure

Arshin	2.3 feet or 71.12 cm
Sazhen'	3 arshins
Desyatina	2,400 sazhens
Funt	0.9 lbs or 409.5 grams
Pood	40 funts

POWER AND POSSESSION IN THE
RUSSIAN REVOLUTION

An Infinity of Treasures

IN FEBRUARY 1917, the monarchy that had ruled the Russian Empire for three hundred years collapsed. For the next eight months, this empire's many peoples embarked on a search for freedom and democracy until, at the end of October, the more radical branch of the Russian Social Democratic Party, the Bolsheviks, seized power in the capital city, with the aim of bringing about a global communist revolution. Sometime between these two revolutions, a new language began to be heard in city streets, in shops and offices, markets and homes.[1] Some of the words making up this new language were entirely new: "*sovdep,*" to indicate a local institution of government; "*domkom,*" for a committee elected by residents of an apartment building to administer it; "*narkhoz,*" to denote an important new object of governance, the "people's economy." Some of the words in this language were familiar, but, as countless newspaper articles, diaries, and memoirs would attest, they were now being used in new ways. Many of the words described different kinds of loss. The simultaneous loss of one's home together with the movable property inside of it, for instance, was called "eviction" (*vyseleniye*). "Concentration" (*uplotneniye*), a technical term formally referring to the density of chemicals and other materials, rather suddenly came to mean the packing of an apartment with additional residents. "Valuables" (*tsennosti*), in addition to its general meaning, now specifically denoted a material object that was made of precious gems or metals but which lacked an ineffable quality that would elevate it to the level of "art."

The new lexicon grated on the ears of Moscow's feuilletonists, who mocked it in their last columns before the Bolshevik government shuttered their newspapers for good.[2] But in truth, even the people who embraced the language sometimes found it vexing. "These are sharp sounds, unpleasant for the ear, 'Goskhran,'" a trade official commented on one new institution's proposed name at a meeting. His boss, the People's Commissar of Foreign Trade, curtly informed the group that, in fact, "it will be called 'Gokhran,'" a clarification met by general silence.[3] No less an authority than Vladimir Lenin, the leader of the Bolsheviks and of the postrevolutionary state, can be seen diligently working to master and incorporate the new terms. Several weeks after seizing power, Lenin composed a set of "theses" on the fate of urban real estate, in which he proposed the "alienation" of "all (urban) buildings systematically rented out" by their owners. But upon reflection he scratched out, by hand, the prerevolutionary word, "alienation." In its place, he wrote a new one: "confiscation."[4]

These difficulties in no way hampered this lexicon's explosive spread. People used these words whether they wanted to or not, because they described something new and specific taking place all around them, a process that was not only violent—violence, however unwelcome, already had a place in the language—but more precisely, one that was aimed at dismantling basic features of material life. It was a lexicon of inversion, created to capture the unmaking of property and the hierarchies of social life, law, and political power it sustained, to express the undoing and revaluing of the material world. In short, it was a lexicon of dispossession.

———

In the weeks and months after Bolshevik revolutionaries seized power in October 1917, they declared themselves and the dissolving state they inherited to be the masters of a dazzling array of resources. Nationalization decrees asserted ownership over major industries, transport infrastructure, and the imperial banking network. Local governments claimed the rights to dispose of everything that trailed behind, from bakeries and apartments to hats and coats. In the blink of an eye, the revolutionaries asserted themselves as the rulers not only of the land and the people, but also of material things, becoming purveyors-in-chief of Russia's material wealth. This book is a history of this unprecedented quest to abolish private property and the search for an alternative system of political economy—socialism—that grew out of it. While prerevolutionary ideologies of socialism in Russia and abroad had trained their sights on the abolition of private property rights in land, factories, and other pieces of major infrastructure as the key precursor to socialist development, dispossession in the Russian Revolution burst far beyond these conventional landmarks, seeping into the nooks and crannies of daily life. It thus subsumed not only great industrial objects of significance to the whole society but also tiny, wholly unproductive ones, of significance to no one but their owners. Revolutionary dispossession therefore bore a double character, as a mechanism for rearranging the building blocks of economic production that, at the same time, held out the promise of rearranging the basic rhythms of daily life and the social relationships that engendered them.

It was in cities where these two aspects of dispossession most sharply collided.[5] This book examines the seizure and statization of the immovable and movable properties—buildings and their contents—that organized daily life in Russia's dense, bustling capitals. A vast confiscatory project was unfolding at the same time in the Russian countryside, where, in the summer of 1917, peasants seized land and estates, sometimes destroying houses; soldiers fighting in the First World War raced home from the front to participate and share in the spoils.[6] The war sharply expanded the possibilities for state seizure as well, as first the tsarist government and then its short-lived successor, the Provisional Government, made new use of "requisition" and "confiscation," forms of alienation introduced in 1914 to seize the property of enemy aliens, and, eventually, grain from Russian subjects.[7] The story told here, rooted in urban property, intersects with these other strands of seizure, while also illuminating distinctive problems in governance and economy connected to the modern city.

The outlines of this story have been dramatized in great works of literature and revolutionary satire. Although the Bolsheviks would quickly go silent on revolutionary dispossession and eschew its memorialization, they were among the first to caricature it. In 1918, Anatoly Lunacharsky, the new Commissar of Enlightenment himself, wrote the script for a film called "Concentration" and cheekily performed an uncredited cameo to boot. The plot was simple, if surprisingly heartwarming given the social conflict at the root of the process: after revolutionary authorities force an elite professor to cede space in his apartment to a working man and his grown daughter, the professor is unexpectedly drawn into their milieu. His younger son falls in love with the worker's daughter, while his villainous older son is exposed as a class enemy. The so-called communal apartments that resulted from their encounter, and from the hundreds of thousands of other "concentrations" carried out across Russia in real life over the next three years, became enduring symbols of Soviet socialism that were, at the same time, artifacts of how it came into the world—through the redistribution of built space.

I narrate this unmaking of private property in cities during the Revolution across two different stages of "dispossession," a term I employ throughout the text, together with "seizure," to indicate the generic act of removing a thing from somebody's possession. Both the specificity and the politicization of the language of seizure that developed during the Revolution make such a term necessary for distinguishing my analysis of dispossession from the rich lexicon of property-breaking and property-making contemporaries used to characterize it. The first part of the book examines the unmaking of the legal, cultural, and political infrastructure of private property in buildings and movable goods between 1917 and 1920. The seizure and redistribution of people's homes and belongings came to appear as a natural, indeed essential, element of the transition to socialism. As these chapters detail, however, it was in key respects a surprise—to the revolutionaries no less than the population. The book asks not only how this extraordinary unraveling happened, but also how the revolutionary state sought to remake the seized bounty of the city into a new kind of thing—socialist state property—and to remake itself into a nonmarket proprietor of seized things.

For nearly three years, the seizure of both real estate and movable property occurred largely in the absence of specific, central authorizing laws. But in the spring of 1920, the revolutionary government promulgated its first "Decree on Requisition and Confiscation," introducing new dynamics of property and power in the Revolution. The second part of the book follows seized things across this divide, as the revolutionary state sought to master its immense material inheritance in the city. These chapters ask how the revolutionaries tried to determine quite literally what there was and what they, as authors of a socialist revolution, ought to do with this trove: how to know and document the material world without the administrative apparatus of private property; how to find the value of material things without markets; and finally, after 1920, how to rebuild bonds of possession without erasing the great transformations that dispossession had wrought.

This story connects the phenomenon of revolutionary dispossession in Russian cities to other episodes of mass dispossession that played out across the twentieth century, both in Europe and beyond it: in the context of communist revolutions, population exchanges, and projects of social extermination. Material dispossession went hand in hand with the cataclysmic violence of these events, yet for much of the century, as one scholar of the Holocaust has written, it attracted comparatively little attention in either public discourse or scholarship, overshadowed by the loss of human life. In Europe, this began to change in the late 1980s and early 1990s—that is, with the end of Soviet power. The collapse of communism in Eastern Europe triggered a broad reckoning with the two interconnected episodes of dispossession on which the Soviet satellite states were built: of Jews in the Holocaust and of the new subjects of communist rule after the Second World War. The opening up of eastern European states as sites for specific claims of restitution in the 1990s produced a surge of interest in calculating and documenting dispossession on an individual and collective scale, a surge so powerful that it spread even beyond Eastern Europe, to France, Germany, and other western European countries with their own histories of Nazi occupation and collaboration. In all these places, in addition to the work of scholars, government-sponsored reports on the techniques, laws, and experiences of dispossession wielded against Jews and others in the service of "aryanization" began to appear, giving rise to court cases and petitions for restitution that are still wending their ways through the legal system in the present day.[8]

Paradoxically, the end of the Soviet Union did not have a similar impact on the study of dispossession inside the Soviet Union itself, particularly when it came to the Revolution.[9] The reasons for this difference are connected not only to the original conditions of dispossession in Russia and the longevity of the political economy that grew out of it, but also to the frenzied politics of the Soviet Union's exit from communism. A major stimulus to revisiting the wartime aryanization of property and postwar campaigns of state seizure in the 1990s was, after all, the pursuit of restitution. This stimulus was absent in post-Soviet Russia, where the privatization of state property, for a variety of reasons, did not involve a focus on prerevolutionary claims of ownership.[10] Ten years after the fall of communism in Russia, wrote the Belarusian historian Konstantin Kharchenko at the turn of the twenty-first century, amid the opening of "a great many topics once closed," there had been no serious opening in the topic of dispossession among scholars in the former Soviet states or abroad. Kharchenko, author of the first and, to date, still one of the few monographs on the topic, attributes this fact to a special reticence around the "property cataclysm" among former Soviet subjects, particularly as it concerned the types of property that are a central interest here—people's homes and their contents—connected to "the minimal social sanction for the alienation of this form of property" both before and after the Soviet collapse.[11] More broadly, as the historian Boris Kolonitskii writes, the "implosion of the communist experiment" dealt a body blow to the study of the Revolution in Russia, tearing down old "interpretive frameworks" and leaving nothing in their place.[12]

The interpretive emptiness, Kolonitskii contends, allowed the political figures and geopolitical fantasies of the Revolution to persist in contemporary Russian political life. In the West, the politics of the collapse were different, but the outcome for the Revolution as an object of study was much the same. "Nothing fails like failure," the eminent historian of the Revolution Sheila Fitzpatrick mused on the occasion of its centenary, describing the twinned loss of political import and scholarly interest in 1917.[13]

And yet, whatever the end of Soviet power has meant for the fate of communism, few moments have as much to offer conceptually to the study of the Revolution and the political economy to which it gave rise as does the Soviet collapse. Like the Revolution, the end of communism was attended by profound transformations in the concepts of property, value, and the state; by a vast project to redraw boundaries between public and private spheres that was embedded in material resources; and by the simultaneous labor of building new institutions and a new kind of economy. This book takes inspiration from studies of how the Soviet project unraveled, not because revolutionary dispossession and subsequent "statization" perfectly mirrored the collapse, but rather because, if the political economy of Soviet socialism lived and died as this literature contends, then there are new stories to tell and questions to ask of the Revolution.

My focus is on the fate of property in what was an avowedly socialist revolution, as one of many institutions that revolutionaries associated with capitalism and sought to eliminate in the expectation that eliminating private owners would pave the way to social justice and material abundance. Whether formal or informal, rooted in law or custom, property systems mediate the relationships between people through things. However they are constituted, the legal scholar Carol Rose contends, the most important function of a property system—what separates property from mere possession—is that of enabling "legibility, making clear what belongs to whom," and why.[14] Property systems, that is, do more than bind particular people to particular things; they are ways of knowing and valuing the material world. They assign certain kinds of powers and rights to things but, more than this, they identify and define who can bear these powers, and to what kinds of things.

After the fall of communism in Eastern Europe, writes the anthropologist Katherine Verdery, everything about the post-Soviet property landscape appeared "fuzzy." The fuzziness of this moment sets it apart from other major episodes of dispossession, nationalization, and privatization, in which particular enterprises, or even entire sectors, moved between state and private ownership. Here, the relative sizes of the public and private spheres did not merely grow or shrink; the spheres themselves and the division between them had to be wholly reconstituted. The architects of privatization in the 1990s assumed the existence of private landowners and found instead people who continued to limn themselves into collective bodies.[15] The would-be objects of property rights were no more distinct. Comprehensive state ownership had scrambled what were, in the liberal order, conventional boundaries between public and private infrastructure.[16] Even physical boundaries turned out to be muddy. In preparation for privatization, it was not uncommon to find the officials of two neighboring institutions pacing the land between their respective buildings, trying to establish where one parcel should end and the other should begin.[17]

The subjects and objects of a property relationship, then, are not given a priori—they are made. And critically, as this book shows, this was as true for the Soviet state, as the chief bearer of astonishing new powers in material life in the revolutionary era, as it was for private owners at the Soviet collapse. This book thus investigates the seizure and statization of urban infrastructure as, among other things, a process of state-making: of building (or not building) the institutions that would hold and manage the staggering array of material resources nominally flowing into state possession, and of articulating the boundaries within and among these institutions, inside and outside this vast new state domain. As will be seen, the Bolshevik abolition of private property in land and factories triggered a broad cascade of seizure, in some instances decreed by the revolutionary government and in many others not. The speed of dispossession as it ripped through revolutionary society came as a shock to the people who lost things and also to those put in charge of securing, redistributing, and managing them. Dispossession, that is, preceded the existence of a state that could govern it. If this was partly by design on the part of Bolshevik revolutionaries—who welcomed the demise of the "bourgeois" property order and, as need be, its proprietors—it also plunged them, together with the erstwhile proprietors who lost things, and the people who gained them, onto unfamiliar terrain. In eliminating private property in general and dispossessing "bourgeois" owners in particular, the Bolsheviks conceived of seizure in the cities as a blow against those private owners, the so-called nonlaboring element, in favor of their opposites, the laboring element. But as this book shows, dispossession did not cease action at the borders of the bourgeoisie or others targeted as enemies of the new order. It ricocheted through Russian society from top to bottom, thrusting losers and winners alike, up to and including the institutions of the revolutionary state, into a general condition of propertylessness—not in the sense of having or not having things, but in the sense of knowing how, why, and who could possess what.

Documenting Dispossession: Property, Law, and Socialism

Dispossession is a process that, quite often, destroys things: material objects, intangible valuables—and also the paper records that would allow us to trace the action of dispossession itself. The difficulty of documenting dispossession is a constituent part of the phenomenon, one that was amplified in 1917 by the anti-law instincts of the Bolsheviks, the coincidence of dispossession with political revolution, and by a widely shared sense that the act of dispossession represented not simply the transfer of a given piece of property from one owner to another, but a fundamental change in the nature of property itself, obviating the need for the old system's recordkeeping. This book recovers an archive of revolutionary dispossession, but it does not find it in the conventional legal documents sustaining the property order in prerevolutionary Russia or other places. Rather, this archive of dispossession grew up squarely in this order's absence.

The documentation of dispossession varies widely across episodes in place and time, making its format an important indicator for the nature of the process. Documentation is historically most robust when dispossession has been preemptively sanctioned by legal order, and when those doing the seizing anticipate being able to solidify their grip over seized things through recourse to existing property law, such that they have an interest in ensuring proper records of the transfer. In order to assuage investors' fears of trucking in stolen property, for instance, some Nazi-occupied and collaborating governments erected "extensive legal and administrative frameworks to legitimize" the aryanization of Jewish property, with correspondingly large bases of transfer records.[18] These records would later become the basis for restitution claims and histories of dispossession after the Second World War.

The Soviet case lacks this sort of documentary basis. This absence derives from two basic features of revolutionary dispossession: the ambition to eradicate capitalism of which it was a part, and its slippery relationship to law. The fact that the Bolsheviks set out to destroy capitalism changed the character of their engagement with the paperwork of economic life. The architects of aryanization under Nazi occupation sought to preserve the economic value of the resources they seized, not only material assets but also paper instruments of credit. To that end, they created fictional banks—with real account books—into which Jews were required to transfer assets. They profited on the forcible takeover of businesses by falsifying (lowballing) the value of brand names, intellectual property, and other intangible resources—but they kept the markets that told them what the value of those assets was.[19]

By contrast, the Bolsheviks purposefully scrambled the economic value of entire asset classes after the Revolution, nullifying government bonds (while in theory allowing smallholders to cash out) and seizing firms and invalidating stocks in them (although sometimes keeping former owners on the hook for debts). Amid a countrywide paper shortage, some officials recycled the credit papers of seized firms, turning them over to use the blank sides as stationery.[20] Some of these papers made it out of Russia; according to a former merchant in Petrograd who kept up ties with his foreign trading partners after 1917, there were lively speculative markets in the stock papers of nationalized Russian firms in European cities into the 1920s.[21] But inside Russia, it would have been hard not to see the paperwork of value revealed as a fiction—if not metaphysically, as the Bolsheviks might have hoped, then simply in a practical sense. A mind-boggling quantity of paper wealth went up in smoke, with repercussions that were in no way limited to the wealthy, particularly in the case of the canceled war bonds.[22] Again and again, people wrote to Moscow from the provinces asking where to send the physical remnants of this value: the canceled papers, and, later, canceled currencies.[23] It was hard to imagine, at first, that so recently valuable things were now not only worthless but a matter of indifference. The documentation of property and the changes in it were part of the transformation brought about by the Revolution. Indeed, this was one of the many ways the Bolsheviks made their vision of a world without capital a reality.

Revolutionary dispossession in Russia cannot be traced through the conventional records of a liberal property order, then, not least because the revolutionaries had no interest in sustaining that order. Although it was not uncommon for the transfer of a building from its private owner to the new state to be accompanied by a formal walk-through (often with a janitor or superintendent accompanying a representative from a state institution), such handovers were virtually never accompanied by prerevolutionary property records, such as titles, leases, or other documents. The Bolsheviks forbade notaries from validating property documents of this sort not long after seizing power. (Although there is evidence that many continued to do so even after transactions between individuals were banned, for obvious reasons these papers were generally not saved).[24] If these transfers did occur in the "munici-palization" of real estate, it was in a vanishingly small proportion of cases. When it came to movable goods, of course, the likelihood of owners who had written proof of ownership was that much smaller; few people had written attestations for any but the most remarkable of household possessions, a fact they frequently lamented after the Revolution, when petitioning for the return of seized goods. At first, petitioners were sometimes told by local soviets and other institutions involved in seizure that the return of "improperly seized" things was possible if they could produce written record of prior possession. Later on, as will be seen in the book's final chapter, those who sought the return of things taken from them during the Revolution were instructed to provide clear evidence of an object's "theft," on top of the already-required evidence of prior possession. Needless to say, they never could. In a way, this was the Bolsheviks invoking a fictional version of the liberal property order, in which all possessions of all kinds left paper trails—or perhaps, more accu-rately, it was their vision of a new socialist property order peeking through, an order in which all possessions of all kinds really did leave paper trails, at least in theory, because they were allocated by the state.

And yet, there is a voluminous paperwork of dispossession, documenting the wounds it inflicted on people and that they inflicted on one another in searing detail, like an autopsy of revolutionary events. Symptomatically, while made during the Revolution, this is a paperwork of retrospection rather than instigation, in which those who have witnessed dispossession and perhaps been party to it recount what happened, and what they think should have hap-pened, in the great labor of parsing people and things that the Revolution brought about. This paperwork grew out of documents that began to appear simultaneously with revolutionary dispossession itself, bearing witness to the coming of the Revolution at home, in the places where people lived. These accounts were composed by individuals or collectives, typically in the after-math of a dispossessive encounter. They tell of nighttime searches and violent evictions, cases of mistaken identity, sealed rooms, and power-hungry janitors. Sometimes, these narratives were written for a reason beside or on top of the material losses of dispossession, reflecting the embedded quality of seizure during the Revolution, a constituent part of arrests, inspections, "concentra-tions," and other common revolutionary events. But often, seizure was the main event. People wrote these accounts not simply when they lost things, but especially when they sensed some kind of error in their loss: in how it was performed, in the reasons that were provided, and, less commonly, in the very premise of seizure itself.

These accounts were just the beginning of the archive of revolutionary dispossession, the seeds from which it grew. They landed in the mailboxes of a wide array of revolutionary authorities, including local soviets, powerful individual officials, and major institutions, particularly the Council of People's Commissars (Sovnarkom). When, due to their large number, this became too cumbersome, they were concentrated in the hands of a new institution, the People's Commissariat of Government Control—heir to the office responsible for auditing the tsarist state—which in turn created a special department to manage them, the Central Bureau of Complaint.[25] No matter which institution handled them, such accounts commonly underwent thorough processes of review, which involved gathering witness testimonies, auditing account books, and reviewing official correspondence. In the hands of revolutionary officials, that is, these accounts of dispossession, narrating the experience of it from within, entered into a second life as a "case"—a problem or a question about the Revolution and its design or operation no less than about an individual petitioner, deserving of inquiry and investigation.

Through this trove of documents, this book marries the lived experience of the Revolution with an inquiry into problems of political economy and state-making more commonly narrated through theoretical tracts, decrees, and political speeches. This perspective offers an unusually intimate vantage onto the conceptual, political, and practical dilemmas that revolutionaries and ordinary people encountered as they struggled to bring socialism, variously conceived, to life. Petitions that developed into "cases" typically revolved around questions about the new order that lacked obvious answers, either because they reflected situations that existing Bolshevik ideology, governing practice, or common mores had not yet encountered, or because they could be answered, according to these same guiding frameworks, in multiple ways. How to apply norms, identify "parasites," manage material life without markets and property rights—all these questions and more coalesced in the explosive flash of an eviction or a seized possession. While the book ultimately relies on a wide variety of sources beyond these cases—published and unpublished memoirs and diaries, the painstakingly preserved records of Vladimir Lenin's personal administration at the Sovnarkom, the barely preserved records of neighborhood housing departments, Communist Party personnel files, meeting transcripts, audits of the political police, and more—the questions these cases pose orient my analysis around distinct problems of power and possession in the revolutionary era: from the onset of dispossession, through the elaboration of tools of governance suited to a material world without legal markets or property rights, to attempts to close out dispossession and erase its revolutionary signature.

To the frequent surprise of petitioners, these experiences and the cases built around them circulated at the highest levels of the Soviet state. They were saved in its archives, not only those of the People's Commissariat of Government Control and its successor, the Worker-Peasant Inspectorate, but also, in the state's earliest days, those of the Sovnarkom, as well as the local soviets. As the book shows, these cases provided the source material for revolutionary governance; they inspired decrees, orders, and practices that would define core elements of socialism during the Revolution and after it.[26] In addition to its substantive value, then, this paperwork is significant as an artifact in itself of the revolutionary process. In the course of investigation, these petitions and complaints were sometimes reviewed by half a dozen different institutions, at all levels of power. The resulting case files could run to dozens of pages long, reflecting weeks or months of investigation. The richness and depth of this documentation presents a curious paradox—and with it, an important point of entry into the investigation of the revolutionary state.

What is lawlessness during a revolution? How did law and lawlessness change in the hands of revolutionaries who saw themselves as the heralds of socialism? One of the chief aims of the October Revolution was to sever the connection between law and property, to place the disposal of material resources under the control of rational economic plans rather than the vicissitudes of property law, thereby displacing law—cudgel of the bourgeoisie that it was, in the Bolsheviks' view—from its seat as arbiter of who got what.[27] The history of dispossession and the statization of economic life after the October Revolution nevertheless often appears as a story of law, narrated through Bolshevik decrees that began with the "Decree on Land," issued on October 26, 1917, and continued in fits and starts through the following summer, when the Sovnarkom released orders seizing the last privately held branches of major industry.[28] This framing does not do justice to the process of statization in several respects—particularly when it comes to the objects at the heart of this book, which were generally excluded from this raft of central orders. The seizure of buildings and their contents—the stuff of urban material life—became an archetypal feature of the revolutionary process and a benchmark of socialist political economy, but the central government did not regulate it in a meaningful way for nearly a year after the Revolution, and then only in the case of buildings. As for movable goods, no central decree at all arrived until the Sovnarkom's "Decree on Requisition and Confiscation" of April 1920, which, rather than instigating the process of seizure, was intended to put a stop to it.

The absence of central laws regulating dispossession in urban life has had several important effects on our understanding of its history and that of the Revolution (in addition to the documentary effects described above). On the one hand, the absence of law has lent itself to an interpretive displacement of revolutionary dispossession into lawlessness—a manifestation of the collapse of the state's monopoly on violence and an expression of ahistorical thuggery and disregard for the law that was, depending on one's view of the Bolsheviks, either peripheral or central to the main revolutionary event. This perspective finds reinforcement in the fact that revolutionary society was, indeed, afflicted by a surge in violent crime that dispossession nourished, and which it resembled in any number of ways.[29] Like thieves, the revolutionaries eschewed regular business hours, working primarily at night; like thieves, the revolutionaries sometimes took and kept for themselves.

At the same time, the absence of central laws regulating dispossession has also manifested simply as absence: the seizure of buildings and their contents, because it does not appear in the raft of central orders on statization, has been left out of statization and revolutionary political economy analytically.[30] This is a missed opportunity, insofar as the revolutionary economy was in key respects one of "redistribution" rather than "production," as the historian Mary McAuley has noted.[31] The seizure, redistribution, and attempted statization of buildings and their contents—the things with which people lived and were forced to make do in the absence of new production—in fact made up an important site for developing tools of revolutionary governance in economic life, to which the second half of this book is devoted. But the absence of central laws, particularly when combined with the fact that these objects did not classically belong to the "means of production" in Bolshevik ideology, meant that, dating back to the early days of Soviet rule, they were not treated as part of socialist economic development.

The earliest Soviet accounts of the Revolution acknowledged freely that the seizure of apartments and movable property had been a surprise, noting even that, to the extent that the expropriation of buildings had been imagined before 1917, it was by "bourgeois" reformers, not Russian Social Democrats who, like their peers in Europe, disdained the "gas and water socialism" of municipal political life.[32] But Stalin-era histories glossed over the spontaneity, diversity, and extent of dispossession during the Revolution, taking credit only for what had, by then, become the linchpin of the Soviet welfare offering—the promise of housing, precisely as Hoovervilles began to rise in the United States—while effacing the seizure of movable goods.[33] Indeed, as John Hazard observed in his 1945 classic on Soviet property law, by the start of the first Five-Year Plan in 1928, the Bolsheviks had begun to attribute their success in seizing and retaining power, "and the defeat of their colleagues in other countries, in considerable measure to the manner in which the property problem was handled." By this, they meant that their Revolution had struck the necessary balance—destroying private ownership of the means of production while retaining it in the "consumer sphere"—a reference to the protections built up around so-called personal property that would be ensconced in the Constitution of 1936.[34] As a result, many of the most consequential accounts of dispossession during the Revolution appeared not in its histories but in its great literature—Mikhail Bulgakov's *White Guard*; Boris Pasternak's *Doctor Zhivago*—and in the recollections of those who fled from it, landing penniless in Istanbul, Prague, and Paris. These renderings colored revolutionary dispossession in a distinctively aristocratic hue, to which the Bolsheviks hardly objected. On the contrary, they enjoyed sparring with the impoverished nobles and statesmen on the pages of émigré publications.[35]

The petitions and cases that I rely upon here exist precisely because the revolutionary state did not provide an authoritative legal footing to dispossession—or, for that matter, to possession. Local regulations announced routinely changing prohibitions on the possession of particular categories of things, by particular categories of people—objects associated with vice, such as narcotics, but also ordinary things above fixed quantities, and objects deemed precious or "counterrevolutionary." The problem in revolutionary society, that is, was not simply that illegal behaviors exploded, that crime flourished, that the revolutionary state failed to tamp it down, as the narrative of lawlessness emphasizes; it was that the very conditions of possession as well as dispossession had become indeterminate, a situation enabled and perpetuated, purposefully and otherwise, by the revolutionary state.

This book follows the absence of central laws about possession and dispossession into its significant administrative and interpersonal aftermath, in local governments and at the center, illuminating the creation of entire institutions to manage the fallout in social and material life—not only the Central Bureau of Complaint, but also dedicated offices in the All-Russian Extraordinary Commission for the Battle against Counterrevolution and Sabotage (Cheka, later the Extraordinary Commission for the Battle against Counterrevolution, Speculation, and Abuse of Power), housing departments, so-called conflict commissions, and special-purpose "*troikas*," all charged with resolving the disposal of material things. Through these agencies, the disorder of dispossession was documented meticulously, although not comprehensively. Some of these bodies did not retain records of their decisions as a matter of routine— even offering their files to interested petitioners—precisely because they did not intend the allocations they made to constitute legal property. Still, thanks to the constant second-guessing that pervaded decision-making about allocation, relevant records frequently appear in the files of more than one institution, making it possible to reconstruct a number of cases in detail.

The conflicts and questions captured in these accounts reveal the absence of central law during the Revolution to have produced something more than lawlessness; they reveal a feverish search for meaning even within chaotic dispossessive encounters, a surfeit of new words to describe possession and loss and a surfeit of "property sentiments" and routines that flooded into the vacuum of authoritative legal order.[36] The revolutionary state's insatiable curiosity about its subjects, and its openness to learning from the solutions they devised to bumps on the road to socialism, elevated these documents from a form of public outreach to a sustained inquiry into the nature of this new political economy. Most important, these sources uncover the perspectives and property stories not only of erstwhile owners who lost things—a framing imported from studies of liberal property orders and favored in accounts of the period's lawlessness—but also those of people who gained them, and of collectives and bodies within perhaps the most significant and nebulous subject of property rights to take shape during the Revolution: the revolutionary state. They reveal an essential dilemma of the socialist Revolution—the dilemma of recreating large swathes of material life as the property of the state.

Making state property and making the new state, this book contends, went hand in hand. Rather than conceiving of the revolutionary state exogenously, as something that came into people's lives whole, my aim here is to illuminate the practices, concepts, and tools of governance that gave shape to revolutionary institutions as they sought to rule through new spheres of material life.[37] Like a ship retooling itself while at sea, the revolutionary state came into being through the process of taking on this material cargo—this infinity of treasures that Alexander Herzen, the spiritual father of Russian socialism, had so earnestly hoped Russia to be without.[38] This revolutionary state's nominal agents and institutions were summoned to witness, negotiate, and rule on dispossessive encounters by the people living through them, even when it did not order them directly.

To assert that statization was a process of state-making implies no normative judgment of the revolutionary state's capacity.[39] The ideal-type standards on which such judgments depend are ill-suited to revolutionary states in general, and the Soviet state in particular.[40] The Revolutions of 1917 augured a violent reimagining of the possibilities for state power, during which time the locus of power was not confined to formal institutions. As Boris Kolonitskii notes, "specific forms and methods of exercising power that differ greatly from those practiced during 'normal' times" characterize all revolutionary periods; "the operation of laws, for example, is rather limited." In place of law, a constitution, or some other enabling framework, the idea of the Revolution itself authorizes popular action, crystallized in particular institutions, symbols, flags, language, and behavior, which competing political forces seek to master.[41] Indeed, the emergence of this exceptional, "self-reflexive" authority, wielding power during the caesura between constitutionally defined periods of rule, is a hallmark of the modern phenomenon of revolution.[42] Whatever its ideological coloration, revolutionary authority derives its power in part from its affiliation with lawlessness; William Sewell pinpoints the birth of the modern revolution to the taking of the Bastille precisely because it was an infraction of law, an action that "in any other circumstance would have been deemed criminal," subsequently embraced by the deputies of the national assembly as "unlawful and legitimate at once."[43] Its connection to lawlessness, Dan Edelstein suggests, is part of what makes it difficult for state institutions to capture the élan of revolution for themselves; instead, they come up with workarounds—calling themselves extraordinary commissions, temporary bodies—to make themselves appear more irregular, and thus, more revolutionary.

In Russia, of course, this was not the hurdle that it had been in France. The Bolsheviks embraced lawlessness to a greater degree than other revolutionary movements, viewing it not merely as a tactic but as the aim of Marxist transformation. Their first months in power were marked by a distinctly "anti-law" stance, a reluctance to consider adopting a legal code of their own, even in the service of socialism. In the fall of 1918 this began to change.[44] The central government announced that henceforth, tsarist-era laws that were not explicitly repealed by revolutionary orders should be considered still in force. Theft, then, would have a legal grounding, even in the socialist revolution. But signally, the legal grounding for theft was not accompanied by an equivalent framework for possession—or for the legitimate versions of revolutionary dispossession, known as "requisition" and "confiscation." As a result, while the criminal iteration of dispossession could be identified and known, the non-criminal variants of it could not. In the spring of 1920, the People's Commissariat of Justice (Narkomiust) declared that in order to relieve citizens from the "incorrect and inexpedient deprivation of that property [*imushchestvo*] necessary to sustain a normal capacity for labor and psychological energy, which has been gradually drained from the entire population" over the previous three years, it was necessary at last to codify revolutionary dispossession, practiced without law these long years.[45] Even then, however, in setting "requisition" and "confiscation" to law, Narkomiust expressly declined to make similar provisions for possession, thereby avoiding what had been before 1917, in Russia as elsewhere, the basic state function of defending private property.[46]

The changes in the property regime brought about by the Revolution therefore affected not only peoples' lives and destinies, but also formed the foundation of the Soviet state, which defined itself in the management of this lawlessness and in the abandonment of what, in other places, was the state's traditional role as defender of private property rights.[47] This book identifies that state not through firm institutional or policy criteria, but through the eyes of its subjects and its employees, through the mechanics and practices of government that they witnessed and ascribed to it.[48] It traces the degradation of clear boundaries identifying and delineating the state precisely through the breakdown of property relations, in spaces such as warehouses and apartments, where people confronted them on a daily basis. Rather than merely weak, the revolutionary state was indeterminate, both in the sense of who precisely represented it, and also, at a moment when the legal order of private property had ceased, in the sense of the limits between the state as a material domain and what was beyond it.

The indeterminacy of the revolutionary state fueled the process of dispossession far beyond what Bolshevik ideology had envisioned, indeed far beyond what state institutions could manage. In this sense, dispossession was broadly participatory. Urban residents from many walks of life involved themselves in the seizure and disposal of material resources, for a host of different reasons. Because dispossession could visit people more than once, they might also experience it in different registers: as state agents and as residents; as seizers and dispossessed. While this book identifies people in the social roles they occupied at the time, it eschews the assignment of rigid social categories, which risk occluding the social dynamism so essential to the revolutionary process. This was especially so in Moscow, where the new state was concentrated, where tens of thousands of people were transformed into state employees in the first few years of Bolshevik power, and where few of these people were members of the Bolshevik party.[49] As the literary theorist Viktor Shklovsky insisted at the time, fighting the prevailing headwinds of "partification" and social categorization, they were all "people."[50] It was a point to which he returned again and again, telling stories of people who, in the crucible of Revolution, were forced to make choices—choices that changed them. "And you and I are people," Shklovsky wrote. "So I'm writing what kind of people we were."[51]

Inventories and Estrangement:
The Management of Seized Things

In its earliest days, the whirlwind of dispossession created just one kind of problem for people caught up in its movement—a problem of loss. But as it went on, dispossession created other kinds of problems as well. Some months in, a new complaint began to appear in official mailbags. Rather than describing the loss of things one needed or cherished, this complaint described being made to live with things one did not want. One household reported having moved into a new room that was ideal in almost every way, save for the existence of a large cabinet packed with the belongings of the room's previous inhabitant, which now stood behind an imposing wax seal. The new inhabitants begged local officials to intervene, as they "lived in fear" of what might happen should they accidentally rupture the seal—would they "lose materially" in the event of damage? Could they be held criminally responsible for it? Their complaint drew a representative from the police precinct that placed the seal originally, who performed an inventory, replaced the seal, and—to their dismay—left.[52] In another building, the building committee chairman wrote to inform local authorities that a large stock of dishware and café furniture belonging to a shuttered pub stood in a storage area in his building. "Unidentified thieves" visited the unsecured storage area regularly. The building committee had already contacted the Moscow Cheka (MChK) about the matter, as well as the local police precinct—they had visited and set "protocols," but had not removed the dishes from the building. The chairman therefore formally declared that henceforth, the building committee "removed responsibility from itself" for the dishes, which it "lacked the means" to "defend."[53]

Commonly identified as a period of material dearth, these years were also a time of profound alienation, as people lost connections to particular objects and to the manners of conduct and care for material things to which they had long been accustomed. Shklovsky described how a group of his old friends in Petrograd lived in a house "on a very aristocratic street," in which they burned first the furniture and then the floorboards, before moving into the next apartment. In Moscow, the members of a military unit he knew settled onto the lowest floor of an apartment building, burned through its contents, then moved one story up, cutting a hole through the floor and locking the lower apartment to fashion a toilet. "It wasn't so much swinishness as the use of things from a new point of view, and weakness," he explained.[54] The abolition of private property in the urban environment took things from some people and deposited them with others. But the changes it wrought in the material landscape and in the relationships between people and their things cannot be measured purely as a matter of quantity lost or gained. Seizure and statization altered the bonds of possession, introducing distinctive logics into people's relationships with material things, and leading to situations like the one encountered by the building committee chairman or the household with the sealed cabinet—situations in which people sought loudly to distance themselves from things nearby, because they could not "defend" those things or because they feared they would suffer from them.

At the root of these encounters was the question of state property—whose was it and what should they do with it? Factories and agricultural land had long histories of being owned by a state in Russia and abroad, but the same was not true of apartment buildings, to say nothing of sofas.[55] For several decades before the Revolution, European progressives had debated whether and how the state might directly own housing on a large scale, a question that was troubling because it involved recasting the private and privately enjoyed space of the home as a public good. Not long before the First World War, municipal authorities in Great Britain had provided proof of concept, in the form of state-built and state-owned apartment blocks for the "deserving" poor.[56] But these debates offered little guidance to the sorts of situations unfolding in apartments across Russian cities, where people lived with things they wanted but that were not theirs, and also with things they did not want, from which they sought estrangement. The advent of state property coincided with these palpable demonstrations of estrangement from material things, and from what had seemed, until recently, basic principles of husbandry in material life. Shklovsky narrated another story, about milk brought to a collection point as a tax in kind, poured for transport into barrels that previously stored herring. "They poured in the milk, hauled it off, got it there and then had to pour it out. Even the smell made them sick."[57] Waste, like destruction, is a constituent part of the dispossessive phenomenon, no matter where it occurs. Leora Auslander has remarked upon its prevalence in the aryanization of Jewish movable goods in Paris, where seized things, while intended for redistribution into "Aryan" hands, more commonly languished in warehouses (even after the war ended) or were taken by neighbors.[58] But what Shklovsky described was different from mere waste, which functioned within recognizable logics of utility and profit. What Shklovsky described was the lived experience of becoming estranged from material things, in the course of which these logics seemed to disappear.

The second part of this book examines the earliest installments of a longer story of state property and socialist management. The revolutionary political economy is often set apart from the main event of socialism, the command economy.[59] But the history of the Revolution belongs in this narrative—not because the solutions identified before 1922 necessarily endured, but rather because they sought answers to what became enduring questions. When staging the Revolution, the Bolsheviks had anticipated that, in its earliest days, they would be able to rely upon capitalist tools of management—most notably accounting—in order to take charge of economic life. These expectations almost immediately imploded after the Revolution, under the pressure of confounding new circumstances in economic life. Like dispossession, the search for alternative methods of economic management was not restricted to formal institutions or theoretical tracts; it too was a part of the revolutionary experience.

The scale of transformation embedded in these techniques can be easy to miss. Some of the showiest exemplars of nonmarket management—material (nonmonetary) budgets; a "labor unit" currency—bottomed out in 1920, succeeded by the more familiar categories of "profit," "economic accounting," and conventional money under the New Economic Policy (NEP) introduced the following year.[60] Yet, as in the case of dispossession, continuities in language could mask significant underlying change. Continuities in terminology between capitalism and socialism, the anthropologist Caroline Humphrey observes of a later period, have tended to obscure "the historic difference between capitalist and socialist economies."[61] The Soviet economy owed itself a new terminology, Humphrey argues, but its theoreticians avoided creating one, because doing so would require acknowledging the plethora of new phenomena actually developing in economic practice, in violation of ideological commitments to the idea of fixed laws of economic development. This feature of Soviet socialism makes it imperative to examine what content filled up the lexicon of economic life, as I do here through two essential concepts in the revolutionary economy: inventories and valuation.

Inventories were an unremarkable part of material life before the Revolution, a seemingly straightforward component of the more sophisticated double-entry bookkeeping practice in broad use by the turn of the twentieth century. After the Revolution, however, they emerged as a locus for defining what kinds of things mattered in the new economy—what should be counted, how to measure it, what the assets flowing into state coffers truly were. Pre-revolutionary records were often of little help in this endeavor, as they failed to capture the attributes of material resources most important to their new keepers. In their place, in keeping with the materialist spirit of the times, revolutionary authorities elevated comprehensive physical measurement and allocation according to fixed norms as the baseline of rational nonmarket management.[62] This analysis shows not only how the *methods* of inventorying changed with the elimination of private property and other circumstances of the revolutionary economy, but also how the *objects* of account did, depending on the optics employed to visualize them, like a kaleidoscope bringing different attributes into focus depending on how it was turned. More than a transfer from one owner to another, this book contends that state seizure entailed a process of transformation: in which powers were available to exert over material resources; in who or what could wield them; and in which material resources were available for manipulation and control.

It is undoubtedly true, as Shklovsky ruefully attested, that people did strange things with objects during the Revolution. But it is also the case that objects wielded strange powers over people in this same period. In a satire of everyday life in the 1920s, the writer Vyacheslav Shishkov described a couple who resolved to divorce, only to have their decision unravel when, unable to find separate rooms, they continued to sleep in the same bed and were drawn back together by it—as if the bed itself overturned the intentions of its occupants.[63] In real life, too, people spoke about objects as if they wielded exceptional power. When confronted by a demand to return a typewriter, a sub-department of Supreme Council of the National Economy, or VSNKh, extravagantly claimed that ceding the typewriter "would mean a complete halt of our work, and the death of our department."[64] This declaration was self-serving, of course; but it also struck at something true.[65] Literary scholars have noted the intense and enduring symbolic powers wielded by particular objects under socialism.[66] During the Revolution, people encountered this strange power vested in material objects for the first time, and we can see them grappling with it, uncertain of its source—scarcity? Political symbolism? In a stream-of-consciousness letter begging help from Vladimir Bonch-Bruevich, Lenin's Administrative Director at the Sovnarkom, a woman in Moscow recounted the dawning realization that her husband had been re-imprisoned on the very day he was to be freed from detention by the Cheka, due to the incorrect appraisal of a piano in their apartment. She had not paid careful attention to the appraisal, she explained, a mistake she would never repeat. "Being in such a state of horrible worry, I did not even look at how they were valuing the things, I did not give meaning to that act, b.c. [because] I thought that this was all a mistake, it would soon be clarified. . . . Can this possibly be the reason my husband is still in prison," she stated flatly. The piano did not belong to her; it was rented. But now it seemed the cause of her undoing. "How to get out of this horror," she continued, as if working it out for herself. "What else to do, I don't know, I could write a statement like this to the Extraordinary Commission [Cheka]. Would it be read. . . . After all it could happen that tomorrow people would come and take the last things I have."[67]

Many others would be arrested over the value of seized objects before the appraisals were through. The Bolsheviks forbade the free exchange of many things during their first five years in power, eliminating legal markets and with them, the existence of broadly shared, officially recognized market prices. And yet, the act of appraisal formed a routine step in the process of dispossession, either in situ at the moment of seizure, or later on, upon the physical entry of seized things into state coffers. Appraisals served a number of purposes during these years: they were a weapon in the class war, a source of identifying information, a control on thieving warehouse workers, and a means of extracting revenue. What all these uses of appraisal shared was a sense that prices in the nonmarket economy, as well as the "true values" on which prices were meant to be based, were now the product of purposeful decision-making.[68] As such, appraisal was a site rich with political intrigue, the search for ideological fidelity, and the complex mechanics of governing a purportedly closed economy. Some of the problems that would-be appraisers encountered when handling seized goods stemmed from the nature of the objects themselves: How, if at all, did the experience of seizure affect the value of seized things? Others stemmed from the absence of legal markets, while still others stemmed from the years of deepening economic disorder, disrupting the expected equivalencies between things. The search for "normal" values drew early Soviet appraisers into contact with foreign markets and black markets, as well as into the recesses of their own memories. It drew them back to the year 1913, which was generally agreed to be the last "normal" time, and which was elevated in official use as the last "normal" market—the best distillation of what capitalism had been, and therefore, the ideal benchmark against which socialism could be judged.

————

The chronological focus of this book falls in the years between 1917 and 1922, with forays into earlier and later events in the book's prologue and conclusion. The advent of the NEP in 1921 is not the key turning point here, although its effects are a focus of the last chapters of the book. Rather, dispossession is bisected by the events of 1920, when revolutionary authorities embarked on efforts to restrict seizure and put seized things to use in new ways. Geographically, the emphasis is on Moscow, an epicenter of seizure and nonmarket statemaking in this period. Stories from other cities in the Russian Soviet Federated Socialist Republic (RSFSR) supplement those situated in Moscow, documenting the spread of the dispossession outside the capital. Dispossession in many of these places was inspired by texts, orders, reports, and people from the center, but it also incorporated eclectic methods and aims, generated isomorphically, at the same time in different places, in response to shared ideas and challenges as much as concrete orders. As in the capitals, dispossession in other cities also occurred in violation of directives; as in the capitals, that is, "legal" and "lawless" dispossession occurred not as separate processes but as different and often complementary aspects of the same process, the tensions between which served as a wellspring of power in the revolutionary era. Attending to these stories exposes the creativity of local attempts to use law to codify dispossession—the great diversity of lawfulness after the Revolution—which saw regional, municipal, and village soviets anticipate central decrees, revise them, and violate them in the service of their own dispossessive pursuits. Beginning in 1920, the central government would take aim at this diversity, which it sought to stamp out together with any lingering remnants of the bourgeoisie.

Because these other stories are told through documents that arrived in the center, they do not ever swing the perspective entirely out of the capital. At the same time, this book relies upon unusual archival points of access to Moscow's story, due to the fact that the location of the files of the Moscow Soviet, on which a book like this would ordinarily depend, is unknown for the years between 1917 and 1928.[69] Like other histories of Moscow in this period, this one necessarily reconstructs the city's past through alternative sources, depending most of all on documents from the central state on the one hand, and the neighborhood soviets on the other.[70] Thanks to the parallelism of the early Soviet state, many central institutions hold extensive runs of Mossoviet meeting protocols as well as communication with the Mossoviet; the files of the neighborhood soviets likewise contain a wealth of information about the granular, and often independent, seizure programs pursued by neighborhood authorities.[71] The result is not a political history of particular institutions, but rather, a history of intersecting problems of property, everyday life, and urban governance in the revolutionary era.

The Bolsheviks and others would later claim their takeover of the urban built environment as an obvious and essential component of Soviet socialism, but, as the book's first chapters show, the incorporation of buildings into state property after the Revolution was a surprise, the unexpected byproduct of overlapping crises in the built environment precipitated by the First World War and the tsarist government's unwillingness to curb the rights of private owners in city life. The prologue of the book explores prerevolutionary ideas about "municipalization," or alienation by the city government, situating Russian approaches to urban infrastructure within the landscapes of European progressive thought and Russia's revolutionary tradition. Apartment buildings emerged as flashpoints in political life during the war, even in places that lacked the markers of the housing crisis seemingly driving the turmoil. The summer of 1917 saw a sharp escalation in popular antipathy toward landlords, on the one hand, and in the willingness of officials in local and central government to consider the possibility of "requisitioning" built space for state use on the other. But these prospects were held in check by, among other things, a deference to the physical integrity of the buildings themselves—one the Bolsheviks would not share.

The Bolsheviks abolished the private ownership of land within days of seizing power; over the next six months, orders seizing banks, factories, and other types of property followed in rapid succession. But as the first chapter shows, these decrees did not control the whirlwind of seizure whipping up across Russia in 1918 so much as they fed and inspired it, fueling local processes of dispossession that sought out ever-smaller, more intimate targets—including apartment buildings, apartments, rooms, and their contents. The abolition of private property rights in buildings and their creation as state property was known as "municipalization," a process that fused elements of property ownership with governance in pursuit of class war. The state, on behalf of the proletariat, was the supposed beneficiary of this process, and its victims were the "bourgeoisie," "parasites," and other class enemies. But this chapter reveals that the abolition of private property could not be contained at the borders of these enemies. It yielded propertylessness for all, including those newly endowed with stuff, as well as the state institutions charged with managing the people's bounty.

This gargantuan task, the overnight absorption of urban infrastructure into municipal governments, blurred the edges of the state, and presented it with a number of familiar and unfamiliar obstacles. The extent to which the socialist state could or would bear property rights for itself or as a stand-in for a collective subject over large and productive objects was a topic of sustained debate in fields ranging from industrial and agricultural management to cultural production. But nowhere were the challenges of sustaining the state as owner greater than in the seizure and disposal of things that belonged in the home.[72] The second chapter examines the effort to create state property out of what were generally known before the Revolution as "movable things," and what came to be known in the Soviet Union as "personal property." The revolutionary state found it virtually impossible to own these things in most conventional senses of the term. This was due in part to pervasive mismanagement, a symptom of the state's poor defenses against those inside and outside its ranks who would seek to profit off the Revolution's project of social leveling (the redistribution of material things in service of social justice). Lenin and others spoke about the violations in the familiar language of theft and corruption. But this rhetoric sold the Revolution short, undervaluing the magnitude of its project to refashion the possession and allocation of intimate household goods, which sought to eliminate individuals as the owners of movable property and destabilized basic attributes of ownership in the process.

The third and fourth chapters shift the book's focus from the seizure of material things to their management. The creation of information about the built environment was envisioned as a cornerstone of rational, nonmarket management, one that would facilitate the transformation of buildings into an abstract, fungible new resource known as "living space." The third chapter shows how, in the process of use, this accounting utopia was turned on its head. In place of the transparent inventory of the built environment, revolutionary housing authorities ended up with "the account," a motivated and partial record of "available" spaces, frequently provided by residents themselves. The spirit of popular participation in the accounting of built space ran the gamut, from voluntary to opportunistic to despairing, but in the absence of positive rights to living space, there was no option to sit the project out.

The fourth chapter opens at what would become a turning point in the management of seized goods: the establishment in February 1920 of an institution called Gokhran to sort, appraise, and prepare those seized things deemed "valuable" for foreign sale. The chapter exposes what we might think of as lay theories of revolutionary valuation, developed by Gokhran's administrators and staff in the course of their work. These theories were informed not only by the inbuilt assumptions of neoclassical economics that had guided much of prerevolutionary economic life, but also by the influence of Bolshevik ideology, the mechanics of hyperinflation, and the politics of secrecy that shrouded market information in the nonmarket Republic. Gokhran failed spectacularly at its task of conjuring the market value of its wares, for which its staff paid a devastating price. But as this chapter argues, this failure resulted not so much from the venality of Gokhran's staff—as the criminal charges against them would allege—as from the tensions embedded in the ideas of value they tried to realize, tensions in the project that the Bolsheviks resolved with violence.

It is a conundrum for all revolutionaries—at least, all those who are successful: How should the revolution end? The end of dispossession began in April 1920, with the Sovnarkom's "Decree on Requisition and Confiscation," a measure intended to curb dispossession and whip local legalities into a central order. Over the next two years, as the final chapter shows, revolutionary authorities made a series of unsuccessful attempts to curtail dispossession using law, sometimes borrowing prerevolutionary and foreign legal concepts to do so. These directives shared a common aim: to erect a firewall between the earlier period of disorder and the present, which the central decrees established as the beginning of a new era. And while similar measures were employed with success following other cases of mass dispossession during and after the First World War, in the RSFSR they foundered on the difficulty of creating a legal framework for dispossession without, at the same time, creating one for possession. The only way to stop revolutionary dispossession, it turned out, was to demand it be forgotten.

Municipal Socialism

"IT IS A REAL REVOLUTION THIS TIME, comrades, and make no mistake about it. Come to such-and-such a place this evening; all the neighborhood will be there; we are going to redistribute the dwelling-houses." So wrote a renowned theorist of anti-capitalist revolution and scion of a noble Russian family, from his perch in a decades-long European exile. This theorist was not the future leader of the Bolshevik Party, Vladimir Lenin, but the revered anarchist Pyotr Kropotkin, who fled Russia in 1876 before gaining fame in Paris and London as the international voice of anarchist rebellion. His tract on the place of buildings in revolution appeared in 1892 as part of his French-language manual for revolutionary takeover, *The Conquest of Bread*. Before the Revolution, it was perhaps the most serious consideration of the topic of redistribution of private property in the built environment by any Russian revolutionary thinker, although it was written at a great distance from Russian urban conditions. Against the growing ranks of Russian Social Democrats, Kropotkin presciently insisted that private property could not be abolished in pieces. "On that day when we strike at private property, under any one of its forms, territorial or industrial, we shall be obliged to attack all its manifestations," he predicted, including objects of consumption, such as houses and personal property that his socialist rivals believed could "remain private."[1] The seizure of the part would catalyze the seizure of the whole. This, Kropotkin believed, was for the best. For it was only when the revolution turned at last to the "expropriation of houses" that "the exploited workers will have realized that new times have come, that this Revolution is a real fact, and not a theatrical make-believe, like so many others preceding it."[2]

Kropotkin lived to see the revolution made real, although it was the Bolsheviks who made it, not his anarchist followers. He returned to Russia an old man in 1917, just in time to experience the tumult and transformation of the expropriation of dwellings. Documents held in the files of the Administrative Directorate of the postrevolutionary Sovnarkom indicate that Kropotkin's was an archetypal, if privileged, experience. Assigned a two-room dwelling from the "requisitioned" stock in Moscow, Kropotkin nevertheless lived under the near-constant threat of displacement. On account of his advanced age, someone filed a petition on his behalf with the Sovnarkom in late 1919 demanding that the neighborhood soviet abandon its efforts to "requisition" his apartment and leave the old man in peace.[3] Like so many Muscovites, Kropotkin was thrust into a revolutionary whirlwind that, much as he had predicted, did not stop with the expropriation of the "instruments of production," reaching deeper into the intimate spheres of material life. As he had not predicted, however, it turned out that one seizure was not enough—that already-"requisitioned" apartments could be seized again and again, including from figures such as Kropotkin and even from institutions of the state.

The redistribution of the built environment—"living space," in later Soviet parlance—became the calling card of the Russian Revolution, elevated to this status by the Bolsheviks as well as their literary foils, writers such as Mikhail Zoshchenko, Mikhail Bulgakov, and Boris Pasternak.[4] Its consolidation as a supposedly natural and inevitable element of Soviet socialism occurred with astonishing speed, such that already by 1920, when the staff of the Moscow Soviet (Mossoviet) set out to commemorate their institution's achievements over the previous three years, they were genuinely surprised to discover that the seizure of the built environment had not been a special part of the socialist program before the October Revolution at all. "Neither in prerevolutionary programs of the socialist parties nor in the political platforms or socialist press of the period up to October," they explained in *Krasnaya Moskva* (*Red Moscow*), the compendium of revolutionary history they produced, could one find the barest "mention of the municipalization of building ownership." Paging through stacks of socialist pamphlets, the authors were unable to find support even for the municipalization of urban land, which they recognized to be a "long-standing demand of bourgeois reformers" at the time.[5] Indeed, the only reference to Bolshevik perspectives on the status of urban buildings before the October Revolution they came across was a "pair of articles by I. I. Skvortsov-Stepanov" published in the Moscow *Izvestia* during the summer of 1917, "in which the author, with the utmost delicacy, almost timidly suggests that perhaps it would be possible, without great trouble, to get by without landlords."[6]

Had they searched slightly further afield, the Mossoviet authors would have discovered that, although the Bolsheviks did not incorporate the seizure of urban real estate into their platforms that summer, their rivals in the Socialist Revolutionary (SR) Party had. While known as the party of Russia's peasants, the SRs developed a platform for the "socialization" of the city in 1917, according to the SR-pamphleteer Vladimir Trutovsky, "not just because cities are alive and we must preserve and build out their legacy, but also because the bourgeoisie have municipal programs."[7] Indeed, it was the Left SR Trutovsky, and not a Bolshevik, who would be confirmed as the short-lived "people's commissar for local self-government" on the night of December 9, 1917, after the Sovnarkom signed an agreement permitting SRs to serve in the new state.[8] But by 1920, even this brief SR filiation with the seizure of living space—and the hint of a broad and urgent politics of housing and urban real estate in the summer of 1917 that it evinced—had been scrubbed from the books.

In later decades, several narratives about the origins of expropriation and redistribution crystallized among historians of the Revolution in the Soviet Union and the West. These approaches to revolutionary dispossession varied widely in their analytical aims and political instincts.[9] But they shared an underlying attention to dispossession within the frame introduced by the Bolsheviks themselves, and a corresponding inattention to the politics of urban property in Russia in the era of war and revolution, and more particularly, to Russia's experience of what was, in fact, a period of global turmoil in the construction and allocation of built space, the fate of the industrial city, and the role of states and markets in shaping it. Sewing Russia's experience into this wartime story illuminates an alternative genealogy of the dispossession that came after it, situating Russian debates about how to build a more functional, rational, and just city on the eve of the Great War within the transnational policy agendas and research networks to which practitioners and politicians in Petersburg and Moscow were attuned. The main event of this book—the multiple seizures of the built environment after 1917, which included the legal abolition of private property rights in buildings and the physical appropriation of built space—will not appear until the next chapter, and some readers may wish to skip ahead. But the ground covered here enriches the story of revolutionary seizure in the city by exposing some of its component parts: prewar obstacles to regulating private property and the attendant allure of "municipalization"; the wartime emergence of housing as a site of political upheaval no less than material deficit; the rise of "building committees" and the decline of landlords. At the same time, it highlights how these component parts, before October 1917, did not add up to the seizure of built space.

Revisiting the origins of revolutionary expropriation involves addressing some master narratives in the history of property in Russia. Especially influential has been the account advanced by Richard Pipes, which linked Russia's susceptibility to Bolshevism to the inadequate development and defense of private property as an institutional form and cultural value before 1917. As Ekaterina Pravilova has observed, many later historians have argued against Pipes's essentializing interpretation of Russia's trajectory, while nevertheless continuing to work within the "'private property' paradigm" he proposed, connecting the "limited development of property rights" to the "absence of freedom," before and after the Revolutions of 1917.[10] In recent years, several works have challenged this framework, most notably that of Pravilova herself, whose analysis of the idea of public goods in the nineteenth century inverts Russia's problem of property, revealing that imperial Russia suffered from a surfeit of private property defenses, rather than a deficit of them. Fearful that "encroachment on private property would destroy the social foundation of the monarchy," Pravilova finds, tsarist bureaucrats blocked significant efforts to limit and regulate private property, as well as renovations to the state needed to advance what a rising class of experts viewed as the rational use of Russia's resources.[11]

Pravilova's argument reframes the question of property in the history of the Revolutions of 1917 as well. Rather than appearing as the radicalization of a society already suffering from anemic protections to private property, on this evidence the October Revolution marks a reversal—from a tsarist state that refused to circumscribe the rights of private owners to one that eliminated those rights wholesale. This, too, is a tale of radicalization and reorientation, but of a different kind. The continual impediments to renovating the tsarist property order in a way that would recognize the emerging category of public goods over private interests amplified a sense among prerevolutionary experts and intellectuals that "the reform of property rights [was] the ultimate solution for nearly all of Russia's problems."[12] The result was a "reversal of values" attached to public goods and private property in the early twentieth century in Russia as compared to the Western European scenario: Russian liberal experts embraced statist intervention, while the autocratic government and its supporters positioned themselves as defenders of private property rights and the "freedom" of owners. This reversal provides an essential backdrop to the works by Peter Holquist and Eric Lohr that illuminate the radicalizing pressures of the First World War on Russia's political class, in search of statist solutions to the tsarist state's infuriating inadequacies. Such solutions were frequently confiscatory and violent, and as Holquist and Lohr each show in their respective studies of the seizure of grain and of enemy alien property, they emerged before October and beyond the Bolshevik milieu.[13]

The story of urban property presented here builds on the reconfiguration of Russia's property problem offered by these works. It first explores the interplay between different circles of thinkers about city problems from Russia, Great Britain, and continental Europe, and between different sets of tools developed to identify and fix those problems. The toolkit of European urban reform deployed in the early twentieth century was a poor fit for Russian cities in two ways: first, because Russian city governments, unlike Europe's industrial capitals, already owned significant quantities of land and other urban resources, and second, because the regulatory measures that were the first line of intervention in Europe were, in Russia, out of reach. The tsarist government's refusal to regulate private urban property led to an explosive conflict over housing during the First World War, when the regulation of housing shifted in status from an ordinary question of policy to a consuming preoccupation in public life. As the problem of housing spread, so too did the range of voices involved in it. In the months before the February Revolution, housing emerged as a locus of revolutionary politics, with apartment buildings reimagined as vehicles of democratic politics, the lowest building block in a new order of "democracy."[14]

Thus, rather than being introduced by the Bolsheviks after the October Revolution or materializing spontaneously amid its wild upheaval, the turn toward "municipalization" in the built environment began during the First World War.[15] Insofar as owning buildings meant wielding a bundle of powers and duties, their "municipalization" likewise represented a complex of changes, involving the rearrangement of financial, legal, and administrative powers.[16] And yet, for all that, the first concrete plans to seize built space in 1917 did not emerge out of municipalization or the dire housing politics produced by the war. Instead, they appeared as part of the Provisional Government's proposed evacuation from Petrograd. Ultimately, the Provisional Government failed to implement its proposed seizure of built space—not for lack of desire, but rather, for lack of imagination. Provisional Government officials foundered on the task of imagining built spaces available for seizure, a point of stark contrast with their successors, who led their own evacuation from Petrograd to Moscow not six months later, and who had more than enough imagination to go around.

Moscow's Missing Crisis

The city of Moscow grew in concentric rings, out from ancient fortified walls that first enclosed the glittering domes of its Kremlin, and then the neighborhoods of merchants nestled up alongside.[17] By the turn of the twentieth century, the "Garden Ring" contained much of the city's original center, and almost all of its wealth. Its leafy western quarters were studded with the historic stone and stucco villas (*osobnyaks*) of the gentry. The bustling Tverskaya thoroughfare cut across the rings like a spoke on a wheel, its mix of shops and grand government buildings draining out at the base onto the Kremlin. Newer quarters of multistory apartment houses rose up on either side, adorned with the elaborate sculptures and mosaics that were the signature of the late-nineteenth century "Moscow moderne" architectural style.[18] The eclectic mansions and hotels of the city's burgeoning business class—merchants and bankers, the owners of textile concerns and food producers—clustered to the Kremlin's north and east, while the quadrants farther east and to the south bore a more industrial feel.[19] The Zamoskvorechye district, across the Moskva River from the Kremlin, was home to half of all Moscow's large factories, as well as the dormitories, churches, and squat apartment buildings that served their workers, managers, and clerks.

Moscow's growth diverged from the patterns established in industrializing European capitals in several respects. Timber in Muscovy was plentiful and stone was scarce. Moscow was an unusually low-slung city for a place of its size, its warrens of wooden structures earning it a reputation as Russia's largest "village."[20] In 1912, a building census revealed that half of the city's structures were of one story and another 40 percent of two; the first five-story buildings appeared in the 1880s, and six-story buildings in 1902.[21] The tallest buildings were made of brick or stone, and were home to the city's wealthiest residents inside the Garden Ring, who made up a quarter of the city's two million people in 1917. In contrast to many European capitals, where the poorest people lived in the densest quarters, Moscow's most dense neighborhoods were also its most elite.[22]

Moscow was also set apart from western European capitals before the Great War by the fact that the city owned much of its important infrastructure.

Muscovites relied on a network of electric trams owned and operated by the municipality.[23] They drew water from the city-owned waterworks; their streets were lit by gas lamps built through foreign concession and purchased by the city in 1905; the sewers were city-owned from the start.[24] Russian cities owned and operated a number of other types of enterprises, sometimes in partnership with local philanthropic councils (*popechitel'stvo*), and sometimes as private owners. Most of all, Russian cities owned land: before the war, one estimate held that more than half of all cities owned one thousand *desyatinas* of land or more.[25] This remarkable breadth of municipal ownership was not matched, however, by a correspondingly robust scale of service. Electricity in Moscow barely extended outside the Garden Ring, while the sewage system served just 27 percent of the city's buildings by 1916.[26] Russia's largest "village" earned the epithet of Europe's "unhealthiest big city," suffering repeated bouts of cholera, typhus, and smallpox before and after 1873, when the city formed its first public health commission. Its mortality rate of 26.9 per 10,000 in 1910 topped that of Paris (at 16.7), Vienna (at 15.8), and Berlin (at 14.7).[27] Perhaps unsurprisingly, given these figures, Moscow also had to fund public health and other initiatives on the cheap, having the lowest per capita spending of any European city of its size.[28]

Fin-de-siècle cities were awash in statistics like these, charting a city's progress as compared to its counterparts abroad and to itself in the past. The figures were the handiwork of experts in the new field of public health, who came of age in tandem with the industrial city and the distinctive set of social ills it produced. Whatever their native setting, these metrics seemed to reveal a basic insight: that the remedies required to secure the public health in the industrial city simply could not be "made to pay," as the historian Daniel Rodgers put it, according to the "private calculus" of capital.[29] Private owners only stood to lose money by improving their properties to the level required for the public health. Reform would demand new powers of state compulsion, from regulation to expropriation. And so, as the industrial city gave birth to new forms of expertise, so too did it come to rely on a new domain of administrative power—the municipality—to govern its social and technical complexity. Across the Atlantic world, existing municipal administrations undertook structural reforms designed to tighten the bonds between a city's population, territory, and government.[30] The powers and duties gained by cities differed from place to place, but, notably, the advent of municipal governance was not confined to the liberal states of the West. In the Russian Empire, the municipal reforms of 1870 bestowed property rights over land holdings to city governments, while also creating an elected municipal legislature, or *duma*, served by an executive board, the *uprava*.[31]

In Russia, a growing cadre of public health specialists, jurists, and economists closely followed the studies on urban governance produced in European capitals by progressive reformers known as "municipal socialists."[32] But the precepts of municipal socialism were an awkward fit for the Russian urban environment, as became clear in studies of the industrial city's signal danger: "congestion." Like other dimensions of the public health, the idea of congestion crystallized in measurements that were tested and exchanged across national borders. The most influential metrics came from Germany, where exhaustive statistical surveys performed in the 1880s fixed a "normal" level of density in built space at two people per room.[33] The quantification of density in Berlin revealed not only that the city's poor were inhabiting too little space per person, but also that they were paying too much for it. Statistical surveys comparing the cost of a cubic meter of air in an apartment in a poor district with its cost in a middle-class or wealthy district found that the poorer households paid significantly more for air that was undeniably more sickly than that in better quarters.[34] Surveys performed in Paris and other cities replicated the German findings.[35]

Everywhere, it seemed, high rents and high density fed each other in a vicious circle: in order to meet the monthly burden, households took in room-renters and doubled up with other families. But the culprit was not the landlord, reformers emphasized. It was the speculative urban land market. Tackling congestion meant tamping down the value of urban land, a task to which reformers brought three main tools. The first approach, which was considered the least interventionist, targeted density through sanitary codes.[36] The second preempted the market for buildings by regulating land use itself.[37] The third tool—and the one considered the most aggressive—was municipal construction and ownership, adopted before the war only in London, where the city built housing intended for workers on land seized through slum clearance.[38]

Russian reformers likewise sought to apply the norms for congestion developed in European studies to the local urban environment.[39] But their effort backfired, revealing instead key differences between the political economy of Moscow and that of Paris or Vienna, thereby calling into question the applicability in Russia of some basic tenets of European urban reform. In 1899, the municipal socialist I. A. Verner set out to perform the first large-scale census of Moscow's housing stock. Verner measured volumes of air and their costs in the grim warrens of Moscow's red-light district, Khitrovka, and in the "well-built" apartment houses of the neighboring Myasnitsky district. As anticipated, the study revealed appalling deficits in the volume of air available to residents in Khitrovka. With a "normal" quantity of air fixed at 1.5 cubic *sazhen*s per person and a "minimum" of 1.0 cubic sazhen', the study found that 66 percent of the flophouse quarters fell short of the "minimum," and 98.5 percent fell short of the "normal" quantity. But when it came to costs, Verner's study could not replicate the European findings for the inflated prices of poor people's bad air. The archetypal case study, performed in Vienna, held that air in the wealthier quarters unjustly cost much less than it did in the slums—2 florins 85 kreuzers per meter in a central Viennese district against 3 florins 24 kreuzers per meter in the impoverished outskirts. But in Moscow, air in the well-built apartments of the Myasnitsky neighborhood cost 1 ruble 60 kopecks per cubic sazhen', against 1 ruble 61 kopecks in the neighboring Khitrovka flophouses, a difference of just one kopeck. Meanwhile, air in the nearby rooming houses (so-called corner-cot apartments) came in at 1 ruble 41 kopecks, nearly 20 kopecks less than in the wealthy Myasnitsky.[40]

Moscow therefore had the tragedy of overcrowding, but not the scandal of the speculative markets, a fact that Russian municipal socialists did their best to obscure. The municipal socialist M. D. Zagriatskov, future chair of the Moscow Duma's Commission on Housing Questions under the Provisional Government, published a tract demanding "external intervention" to relieve congestion in *Moscow* with reference to the injustice of *Vienna's* prices for air, avoiding mention of Moscow's prices altogether. Meanwhile, Verner, the author of the 1899 survey, having gone to the trouble of measuring quantities of air, stressed instead their putrid quality in his published report.[41] The surveys, Verner wrote, were "a call to action," leading to the "unavoidable conclusion that improving the living conditions . . . can be done only by means of external intervention. The question is in what form, and from whose side should this intervention come."[42]

Not only did Moscow have different problems than the cities of Europe; it also had different tools at hand for intervention. The conventions of municipal socialism held that the regulation of private property was the least invasive mode of intervention, followed by zoning, and then by the most aggressive option, the municipal ownership (which, in Europe, often followed expropriation) of urban infrastructure. In the Russian Empire, however, this valence was roughly inverted: cities already owned comparatively large slices of the urban infrastructure, while the power to regulate private property was inaccessible. Paradoxically, this inversion in the politics of property was part of municipal socialism's appeal for Moscow economists, urbanists, and administrators, who anticipated that Russian cities might have a head start on the path to development, precisely *because* they differed from the European ones in their basic structures of ownership. The Ministry of Internal Affairs itself encouraged this approach as early as 1896, endorsing municipal ownership of "enterprises that serve city needs and have a commercial significance" and "services that should not serve as the source of profit," such that the one could fund the other.[43]

But the faith placed by the precepts of municipal socialism in the power of city ownership as a solution to complex problems turned out, in Moscow, to be misleading. Much as Pravilova has shown of forests, waterways, and art, the management of municipal resources required the imposition of limits on private property rights—regulations of precisely the sort that the tsarist state refused to undertake.[44] The problem was therefore not that Russian cities did not own enough to shape markets or operate state enterprises, as municipal socialists said of the European capitals. Rather, it was that in Russia, the municipal ownership of individual pieces of infrastructure turned out to matter less than the Atlantic example had suggested, a truth one could clearly see—or rather, smell—in the example of Moscow's sewers.

As early as 1874, the Moscow Uprava resolved that sewers, about to be built, should be installed exclusively as a "municipal enterprise," "as only the latter would allow for the sincerest interests of the population to be fulfilled, allowing no basis for private capital to profit."[45] But the willingness of city authorities to preempt the private market did not translate into a robust sewer system, because, no matter who owned it, the construction and expansion of urban infrastructure required powers of compulsion over *all* private property that Russian cities did not possess.[46] The absence of such powers was felt in the sewers from the very start. The tracts of land needed to install the lines—small pieces along thoroughfares—could not be alienated from private owners according to existing laws. Instead, it was expensively purchased from them, at a cost consuming much of the project's budget and delaying construction by a number of years.[47] When the first line opened in 1895, it operated at a huge loss because, although "planned for the use of all properties within the Sadovoye Ring," large numbers of building owners refused to pay for connection— and the city could not compel them to do so.[48] Moscow petitioned the central government for the right to force connection repeatedly until the tsar's order at last granted it in 1912.[49] But the years of deficits left their mark: by 1916, sewers served just 27 percent of the city's buildings.[50]

For Russian cities, the regulatory tools that formed the basis of European decongestion efforts were likewise out of reach.[51] In 1903, the Moscow Duma petitioned the central government for the right to regulate the Khitrovka flophouses and surrounding environs. But after four years of deliberation, the Ministry of Internal Affairs informed the city that the authorization of powers of municipal regulation must await the comprehensive revision of the City Statute.[52] The Moscow Duma formed its own "Commission on Housing Questions" during the revolutions of 1905, but after five years of consideration, it, too, came to the conclusion that "issuing regulations [on housing matters] was premature," as it would lead to the "closure of existing buildings" and the scattering of residents onto the streets.[53] In the interim, the city passed a police ordinance requiring 0.75 cubic sazhens of air per person in living quarters, which reformers complained was rarely enforced. There were no regulations on building height, the footprint of a building on its lot, or the mandatory supply of clean water.[54] Instead, the City Duma jumped straight to the most radical approach in the toolkit, embarking upon "positive efforts to provide housing" of its own accord. In 1912, it approved a quixotic project to build a vast settlement of inexpensive rooming houses with shared kitchens and cheap finishes on the city's periphery. But construction hinged on the city's ability to get cheap enough loans, which it could not.[55] Two years later, Prince A. P. Oldenburgsky darkly warned his cousin, Nicholas II, that Moscow's poor, "crammed into dirty and unhealthful apartments, rooms, and corners . . . had nothing to lose," before brightly offering an entrepreneurial solution: would the imperial family care to invest in a speculative venture to build garden cities in Russia? The Ministry of Finance rejected the offer on the tsar's behalf, but was inspired by Oldenburgsky's initiative to develop a program offering government-backed credit for new construction. It unveiled its long-awaited loan plan in June 1914, just weeks before the outbreak of war.[56]

On the eve of the war, then, Moscow had the "dirty and unhealthful apartments" familiar to urban reformers everywhere. But it lacked the conventional markers of housing crisis on which European and Atlantic reform programs were premised. To be sure, as Soviet-era accounts would emphasize, rents grew rapidly in the decade before the war.[57] Even so, the city held steady on a variety of markers of housing crisis (and drivers of high rents), most notably that of supply. The crowds at the Khitrovka flophouses had not abated. But across the city as a whole, Moscow was just barely keeping up with the pace of population growth.[58] According to the building census of 1912, Muscovites enjoyed an average of 1.7 cubic sazhens of air each—above both the "normal" 1.5 cubic sazhens and the "minimum" 1.0 sazhens.[59] Most significantly, the overall number of structures in the city was up 8.2 percent over the previous decade, while the number of apartments had risen by 19 percent, against a population increase of 20 percent. The outbreak of war initially relieved Moscow's housing stock even of this strain, "summoning a huge flow of people to the front," a Moscow jurist later recalled, and "freeing many apartments, especially in the big centers," that had been occupied "by the drafted and their families. The apartment question at this moment was normal. There was nothing to indicate the nightmarish problems to come."[60] When the nightmarish housing problems finally did arrive, one year into the war, it would therefore be a political deficit—the state's inability to regulate the built environment—and not a physical deficit of built space that would bring the city to its knees.

The Politics of a Housing Crisis

After decades of living in France, the anarchist Kropotkin optimistically conjectured in 1892 that "workers are coming gradually to the conclusion that dwelling-houses are in no sense the property of those whom the State recognizes as their owners," and that the value of a house had nothing to do with the owner's labor and everything to do with the surrounding "town which the work of twenty or thirty generations has made habitable, healthy and beautiful."[61] Even among the French, however, it was undeniable that this realization was coming on only very "gradually." Kropotkin never lost hope that "when the New Revolution comes," the seizure of houses "will be the first question with which the poor will concern themselves." Still, he worried that workers would need convincing that "in refusing to pay rent to a landlord or owner, he is not simply profiting by the disorganization of authority." He therefore anticipated a need for "earnest revolutionaries" to "work side by side with the masses . . . to prepare the ground and encourage ideas to grow in this direction." He especially insisted on the need for outreach to the "middle-class socialists": success would be assured only when even middle classes were prepared to seize buildings.[62] As with his prediction of the totalizing momentum that revolutionary expropriation would assume, here, too, Kropotkin proved prescient. What Kropotkin got wrong was the mechanism by which this lesson would be taught. As it happened, no earnest revolutionaries would be necessary. The war taught people entirely on its own that it was possible to "get by without landlords," as the Bolshevik Skvortsov-Stepanov suggested in the summer of 1917. By then, this was hardly a distinctively Bolshevik sentiment.

Housing became a site of social conflict in many cities during the war. What set Russia's housing crisis apart from those in other places was that by the winter of 1916–17, it had broken free from its native clime—the large industrial city—and could be found all across the Empire, an "apartment bacchanalia, currently in full fire," even in small towns.[63] The first signs of trouble appeared in the spring of 1915. Unlike other combatants, the tsarist government refused to issue a ban on eviction for the duration of the war, out of deference to the property rights of landlords. This refusal set Russia apart: in France, where memories of seized property during the Paris Commune lingered, the central government evacuated soldiers' families from the capital within days of the mobilization, preventatively suppressing demand for space. It then suspended rent payments for more than 70 percent of the population for the duration of the war, over the objections of the Parisian city council. Evictions were forbidden across the board.[64] The British government waited longer to act, but when it did, it enacted the sweeping Rent Control Act, returning rents to their levels of August 3, 1914, and forbidding evictions.[65] German measures more closely resembled those adopted in Russia, protecting tenants in piecemeal fashion, and covering landlords' costs with state funds, delaying the onset of the crisis there only until the end of 1916.[66]

On top of these other differences, Russian cities had to contend with an influx of several million refugees during the war, fleeing east to escape the front.[67] Many cities lost apartments to hospital conversions at the same time as they tried to absorb these new residents; Moscow alone took on more than 400,000 people in 1915.[68] Rents began to rise "not by the day but by the hour," according to the jurist V. N. Gursky. "With each new train, new crowds drove everything up . . . and a crisis exploded on an elemental scale."[69] "There appeared a true bazaar," Gursky recounted, a "bacchanalia of prices." Landlords orchestrated public auctions for units, with "dozens of prospective tenants" ready to bid. Apartment bureaus were "jammed with the hungry and thirsty" people, "who had to wait on the streets in long lines."[70] The Ministry of Internal Affairs waded into the chaos only in the waning days of 1915, issuing a "Required Order on Limiting Prices for the Rental of Living Space" that directed regional governors to consider "living spaces" as "goods of first necessity," like grain, suffering an "unusual rise in prices" due to "landlords and various middlemen making use of the present difficult circumstances for personal goals of their own." The order recast landlords as middlemen rather than owners, and sought to limit their profits on this basis. But it resolutely protected their right to evict, as a constituent part of their enjoyment of their private property. Perversely, this arrangement incentivized eviction: rents were fixed for existing tenants, but not for new ones. Given the large numbers of displaced people, new tenants were easy to find. The number of evictions therefore skyrocketed at the end of 1915, when the rent-fixing measures went into effect.[71] And so while Parisians recalled the unusual quiet on the streets on rent days during the war, so different from the flurry of moving carts seen in times of peace, Muscovites watched as their city began to churn.[72] By the spring of 1916, the newspaper *Rech'* declared the "housing crisis" to be the most serious deficit pressing on households in cities across the Empire, a greater source of worry than the shortages in either food or fuel.[73]

The effects on both urban daily life and governance were profound. The Ministry of Justice unveiled an empire-wide "Apartment Law of August 27, 1916," which "establishe[d] the apartment question as a general problem of state in the view of the law-giver." Much like the British Rent Control Act, the law retroactively fixed rents at their "normal" levels from 1915 for all apartments under a certain rent limit. But unlike the British one, the Russian law already had to contend with severe inflation, which was rising so quickly that the number of apartments subject to the law fell between its promulgation and enforcement.[74] The speculative market thus continued to reign over much of the city, as only the cheapest apartments, housing the poorest residents, fell subject to the new rules, as a result of which these properties often became loss-bearing. According to D. Kuzovkov, one of the first employees of the postrevolutionary Moscow Soviet's housing administration, this was the critical moment: now operating at a loss, landlords in this situation began to let their buildings fall into disrepair, in some cases abandoning them completely.[75] "Instead of trying to do battle with this crisis," Kuzovkov sniped, "building owners gave them [the buildings] over to the care of the city and the state, which began more and more to service Moscow real estate." As early as 1916, according to Kuzovkov, the majority of property owners "abandoned their duty to provide heating fuel for their properties" (by longstanding convention, the provision of heating fuel was a landlord's responsibility). Some landlords also stopped paying for refuse removal, triggering the effective "municipalization of sanitation."[76] Between their dereliction of care, the subsidies offered by the city, "and the nascent municipalization of various adjacent enterprises," Kuzovkov observed, significant moves toward "the municipalization of housing" had already begun, brought to Moscow not by the Bolsheviks, but by the war.

Everyone in the Accounts of their Neighbor:
The February Revolution in City Governance

Looking back from 1920, it was clear to Kuzovkov not only that landlords began stepping back from their properties before anything had been legally taken from them, but also that the city government had stepped in to fill the breach. But the city government was not the only pretender to the role. For more a year, from the end of 1916 to the beginning of 1918, urban real estate stood in a kind of no-man's land. To be sure, for much of this time, it remained the legal property of private owners. But after the February Revolution, which brought about the end of the Romanov dynasty and put in its place a fractious regime of "dual power," confidence in the solidity of urban real estate began to dim. Amid a rising tide of spontaneous land seizure in the countryside, the urban real estate market grew more speculative, and property owners cashed out at eye-watering prices.[77] Meanwhile, an array of new city and civic institutions sought to capture the powers and duties over buildings that were peeling off private owners walking away from their buildings, in pieces or whole. In Moscow, the municipal socialist M. D. Zagriatskov took up a seat in the city uprava's Housing Commission, as did other leading housing reformers. They set to work revising the tsarist Apartment Law in concert with the Provisional Government's Ministry of Justice, work that culminated in the new "Apartment Law of August 5, 1917." The new law abruptly shifted nearly the entire burden of the war's havoc onto landlords. It stripped landlords of their power to evict and suppressed their practice of auctioning off rentals, requiring them to register spaces for rent with their prices at city-run "registration bureaus" open to all. Even more dramatically, it turned back the clock on the rents themselves: where the Law of August 27 had pegged rents at their levels of January 1, 1915, the Law of August 5 pushed them back all the way to July 19, 1914.[78]

The significance of these policies was diluted by the fact that the Revolution did not rest at the level of policy. Its target was the institutional bedrock, as people who had not previously recognized themselves as a political constituency suddenly did so, and sought to fashion institutions for their own representation. Many of these were fleeting. "The first days of the Revolution," recalled the Moscow police official A. N. Voznesensky, were "days of rose-colored hopes"—including for the city's thieves, for example, who gathered at the Nikitin Circus in March to convene a meetings of thieves "trying to find a place for themselves among the free citizens of a new Russia." On the day of the meeting, the circus "overflowed" with "almost one hundred percent thieves." Similar gatherings were held by prostitutes and building caretakers (*dvorniks*).[79] Institutions of governance also proliferated in this same period. Moscow's Duma survived the February Revolution, and was joined not only by the Moscow Soviet but also by "neighborhood dumas," newly formed at the district level and answering to neither the citywide Duma nor the Soviet. Over the course of the summer, as the Bolsheviks picked up seats in the neighborhood dumas and the Moscow Soviet, another body appeared to coordinate their activity, the so-called Council of Neighborhood Dumas. The multiplication of governing authorities meant a net diminution of governing capacity. And as the search for stable institutions intensified, its locus grew smaller: from citywide organs created in early spring, to neighborhood organs created in early summer, to the emergence of the smallest territorial unit possible—the address of a single apartment building.

"Building committees" appeared first in Petrograd, for provisioning buildings with things that landlords had stopped providing, and also as a forum for resolving grievances between landlords and residents. Building security was a serious preoccupation: the opening of the city's prisons during the February upheaval, combined with trainfuls of "self-demobilized" soldiers, led to a shocking rise in crime, precisely as the police forces disbanded.[80] Building committees organized residents in shifts for nightly patrols and organized the purchase of fuel and other necessities.[81] Building committees also offered appealing new possibilities for governance; in the eyes of their boosters, they promised to resolve both the deficits in goods that residents endured, and also the deficits in authority and trust growing so pronounced in revolutionary urban society. These prospects, pamphlets encouraging the formation of the committees explained, were rooted in the loose but intimate kind of knowledge of neighbors they had the potential to harness. "Comrades!" read a leaflet sponsored by the SR fraction in the Moscow Duma in the fall, "the cold time has arrived! Standing in lines will become tortuous and dangerous to one's health. In neighborhoods where building committees have been organized," the pamphlet touted, "lines for bread have completely disappeared." This was because, thanks to building committees, it was now possible to identify forged ration cards, cutting down on fraud and time. People knew their neighbors, and therefore which cards were fake. The beauty of the committees, the SR pamphlet reflected—much as the Bolsheviks would realize when they took power—was that "everyone is in the accounts of their neighbors."[82]

Building committees enjoyed wide support in the summer of 1917. Notably, this was because they seemed to offer a bulwark against the deepening "partification" of political life, as a "new civic basis for control over all institutions working for the city, bringing to life the idea of the peoples' power [from a] supraparty position," according to the "Union of Citizens' Committees" in Petrograd.[83] Their legal status was nebulous: in September, the Moscow Uprava ordered all "apartment and room-renters to form a building committee."[84] But the committees lacked legal rights as an organ of municipal government, leading one supporter to characterize them simply as a "union of human strength and resources."[85]

In this form, they spread to other cities, including Kyiv, Tiflis, and Rostov.[86] They spread even to places that had no housing shortage, but which nevertheless absorbed the moment's distinctive imbrication of the built environment with revolutionary politics. By the summer of 1917, this was nearly everywhere: the politics of the housing crisis spread seemingly independent of material deficits and to places that were not industrial cities—places like luxury resort towns that made up the "Caucasian Mineral Waters Association." The four towns of the Association—Pyatigorsk, Kislovodsk, Yessentuki, and the titular Mineral Waters—had weathered the wartime housing crisis with comparative ease. As deputies to the Pyatigorsk City Soviet recounted in 1917, the summer season of 1916 was "normal." But the market began a sharp ascent around the February Revolution, in preparation for the season of 1917. Suddenly, vacation apartments in Pyatigorsk and Kislovodsk were going for triple or quadruple their rents of the previous summer.[87] No one was sure how to explain the swift change. An official in Pyatigorsk cited the "influence of the deficit of space" as a leading cause, while another official attributed the explosion to an "increase in demand."[88] But the overall number of units available had not changed, and there was no evidence of an increase in the number of vacationers seeking accommodation. Another line of reasoning more plausibly focused on inflation. The Kislovodsk landlords' union attributed the surge to the "ever-rising general expense associated with the rapidly growing quantity of money in the country." A different official rejected the effort at explanation entirely, characterizing it as a "case of prices rising in connection with absolutely nothing," which was how inflation must often have felt.[89]

The wealthy clientele of the resorts preferred overpaying to enduring upheaval at home. But they could not outrun the housing crisis. In Pyatigorsk, the soviet created a "Housing Commission" that, on its own authority, canceled the empire-wide Apartment Law of August 27, 1916. With the towns of Yessentuki and Mineral Waters, it replaced the law with fast-acting housing courts that could calculate fixed rents and resolve disputes "in emergency order." The courts had to act fast, local officials explained, because the tenants—the area's wealthy vacationers—almost always simply paid the extortionate rents for summer quarters, "prefer[ring] to overpay 100–500 rubles over entering into a lawsuit that could take a year or more."[90] The soviet in neighboring Kislovodsk, to the contrary, sided with the landlords. It begged officials in Petrograd to appreciate that these were places "where mostly wealthy classes travel," not out of need but "for their amusement." There was no risk of people "being stuck under the open sky," as the deputies in Pyatigorsk put it; if the vacationers did not like the terms, they could stay home![91] But the Pyatigorsk Housing Commission insisted that it was necessary to have "a totally correct understanding of living spaces as a good of first necessity, like food, fuel, and so forth."[92] Housing entered into the center of political life, not just for the poor but for the whole of society, in capital cities with deficits in space and in resort towns with none, without "earnest revolutionaries" having to lift a finger.

From a Housing Crisis to Seizure for the Revolutionary State

"The expropriation of dwellings contains the germ of the whole social revolution," Kropotkin declared, his final prophecy on the topic in his 1892 handbook. After the October Revolution, this sentiment became commonplace: the Bolsheviks would struggle for decades to mobilize what they believed were the special, consciousness-raising powers of housing in general and domestic interiors in specific toward the transformation of individual residents.[93] But this was not what Kropotkin had in mind. Rather, Kropotkin believed that the expropriation of people's homes was the "germ of the whole social revolution" because it would generate a new kind of administrative power. He intuited that in order to seize space, one had first to see it—"the number of flats and houses which are empty and of those which are overcrowded, the unwholesome slums, and the houses which are too spacious for their occupants and might well be used to house those who are stifled in swarming tenements." The process of expropriation would generate its own capacity: groups of "volunteers" would "spring up in every district, street, and block of houses, and undertake to inquire into [spaces] healthy and unhealthy, small and large, fetid dens and homes of luxury. Freely communicating with each other, these volunteers would soon have their statistics complete."[94] As the following chapters elaborate, this was correct: the biggest hurdle to seizing space, and the thing that would make it transformative, was the problem of creating new tools for parsing homes and their occupants in order to identify what to seize and from whom.

The First World War dramatically expanded the possibilities for state seizure, both on legal terms and on the margins of the law. Shortly after mobilization, the tsarist government unveiled orders on "requisition" and "confiscation," establishing the principles by which military and select civilian authorities could alienate private property for the war effort. "Requisition" denoted the state's compulsory and compensated alienation of an object or resource formally identified—and approved as such by a special commission—as essential to the war effort. "Confiscation," by contrast, was the compulsory, uncompensated, and permanent alienation of a thing as punishment of its owner.[95] In fact, confiscatory measures intended for application against enemy aliens during the war, as Eric Lohr observes, were used by local authorities to seize the property of Jewish subjects of the tsar and those with German-sounding last names. Indeed, animus against the latter group ran so high that in 1915, after a three-day riot resulting in four deaths and great loss of property, a city official sought permission to resettle Muscovites of German origin on the outskirts of the city. The scheme was not realized, but it bore striking similarities to campaigns targeting ethnic populations at the front.[96]

Acts of seizure after the February Revolution drew upon this legal vocabulary, even as they unfolded outside the boundaries of the law. The first seizures of space after the February Revolution were spontaneous and popular. Crowds targeted buildings associated with the old regime, especially the political police, and the imperial family. In Petrograd, they threw open the prisons and set fire to the offices of the political police. They broke into the sumptuous mansion of Matylda Krzesinska, an aging ballerina and former mistress of Nicholas II, who fled. The house sat vacant for a short time before being taken over by the Bolshevik Party for its new headquarters. Krzesinska appealed for help recovering her property to the Menshevik Nikolai Sukhanov, who was sympathetic to her plight. "I fought against the private seizures of houses and businesses as much as I could," Sukhanov recalled from exile, "but I did not have much success." These acts of seizure were commonly referred to as "requisitions"—emphasizing that they were necessary, like those officially undertaken in the service of the war effort, with the difference now they were undertaken on the Revolution's authority, and in its service.[97] Sukhanov remembered himself as one of the few revolutionaries who did not believe that property could be "requisitioned by right of revolution." As he emphasized, this belief was not rooted in party platforms, but in what everyone around the Tauride Palace understood as the extraordinary condition of revolutionary power. The defense of private property as a "principle collided with the crying needs of the new organizations that had sprung up, which had a right to exist."[98]

To a striking extent, revolutionary institutions conceived of their "right to exist" as a right to built space. The police official Voznesensky was not a revolutionary, but he, too, observed that "it was tight for revolutionary institutions," especially for the Moscow Soviet, "horrifically cramped in the former building of the governor-general on Skobelevskaya Square."[99] In the early summer, the Mossoviet therefore sought authorization from its own executive committee, or *ispolkom*, to perform what it called a "requisition" of a neighboring building of furnished rooms, the Hotel Dresden, which it planned to turn into offices. "Months before October," Voznesensky recalled, the Mossoviet's requisition of the Dresden was "the mother of all the evictions of the days to come."[100] When the Dresden's residents filed suit against the Mossoviet, a district court ordered the Ispolkom to suspend the eviction pending review of the residents' case. The Mossoviet hired lawyers to defend its case in court and respected the court's temporary suspension. It offered compensation to the Dresden's residents, as mandated by law for requisition in war, and laid no claim to ownership of the building. But when the court ruled against it, the Mossoviet moved to evict the residents on its own authority, issuing an order to that effect. Nothing happened, Voznesensky explained, raising the question "of how this eviction of residents should occur." According to Voznesensky, the police eventually agreed to carry out the eviction, but only after receiving a series of threatening visits from two Bolshevik deputies.[101]

Over the course of the summer of 1917, tensions between the legal order of seizure for the war and its upstart usage in the service of revolution flared repeatedly, often over built space. But as a general rule, it was not the local soviets leading the charge; it was the Provisional Government, which determined to evacuate itself from Petrograd in order to escape the revolutionary tinderbox the city had become. The Provisional Government began planning its evacuation in June. Evacuation was a known phenomenon by this point in the war, following a similar pattern wherever it became necessary, with a handful of staff from evacuated institutions sent to the capital and the remainder dispersed to regional offices of their choosing. In evacuating from Petrograd, the Provisional Government decided, only the "central organs of each ministry" would go to Moscow, while other offices could choose their destination, a task they considered with regard to two factors: food supply and the availability of built space. In September, the government formed a "Plenipotentiary for Evacuation" to assist them, which sent "specialists to various cities for inspection and the search for free spaces." The Plenipotentiary instructed the ministries to calculate a "general sum" of "floor space" needed to house their staffs at work and at home, according to a new norm of two square sazhens per employee at work and three square sazhens at home, with a family limit of nine square sazhens.[102] At this stage, requisition was not discussed.

But the calculations revealed a stark reality. The evacuation would require huge quantities of "free space." The Ministry of Finance reported that it had identified 6,600 square sazhens for itself, spread in cities across Russia. But it needed more than 30,000.[103] One department in the Ministry proposed that it would search "in the direction of the southeast, as a region safe from the enemy," but its scout reported that "in this locality nearly all the emptied-out [*pustovavshiye*] spaces are already occupied by military organizations, hospitals, and refugees."[104] The director of another office had, "for [his] part, identified the Vladimir and Nizhny Novgorod regions" as likely destinations, before being told by his Vladimir counterpart that "there were nowhere near enough apartments for workers." His Nizhny Novgorod counterpart "rejected the possibility of evacuating the institutions I control to the Nizhny region for the same reason as everywhere, the apartment crisis."[105]

Officials took two lessons from these excursions to the provinces. First, if there was an apartment crisis "everywhere," and not just in the capitals, then they might as well go to Moscow. And second, if "there is in fact an apartment crisis at the present time across all Russia," there was really only one way out: "in order to supply the evacuated institutions and their workers with their families it will be necessary to turn to the requisition of buildings—civic, educational, and otherwise."[106] A second finance official hit upon precisely the same conclusion, at precisely the same moment: "in the absence of free space [*svobodnye pomeshchneniya*] there remains one path, the requisition of space."[107]

On October 11, exactly two weeks before the Bolsheviks seized power, the Provisional Government authorized the "temporary occupation of space" by commercial, state, and civic institutions connected to the evacuation, for accommodation in "their new places of residence."[108] Like requisition, the "temporary occupation of space" would be compensated, but it came with few other directions. Days after the new rules appeared, the Ministry of Finance tried to put them to use, submitting a request to the Plenipotentiary for a "requisition" of built space in the city of Yeysk. It provided the Plenipotentiary with the information about the number of people evacuating, assuming the Plenipotentiary would find the needed space on the basis of the norm. But the Plenipotentiary declared that it could not "perform the requisition of space in Yeysk without being told exactly which spaces are needed." The Plenipotentiary was prepared to seize, but it needed to be led to the front door.[109]

Local authorities met news of the evacuation with anxiety, nowhere more palpably than in Moscow. At the end of September, with the city overrun by envoys from Petrograd searching for space, the uprava formed a Commission for the Supply of Space to State and Civic Institutions.[110] At the same time, it directed its standing Commission on Municipal Housing Politics, "in view of the rumors about the evacuation of government institutions from Petrograd and the wave of refugees into Moscow," to study the "question of the form by which the mass demand for residences will be satisfied." It was to consider two options: "whether it is possible to make use of existing housing and which namely, or whether it will be necessary to turn to the construction of barracks and where namely."[111]

This question had both technical and legal components. As a technical matter, the Commission studied empty dachas, trading spaces, and, most radically, "large apartments," with the intention of settling them more densely, a practice that would shortly come into use under the term "concentration" (uplotneniye). Its chairman, the municipal socialist Zagriatskov, and its other members did not shrink from the seizure of built space on principle. But they saw no way to settle the newcomers within the existing built environment. The city's building stock was simply too fragile—especially its toilets. It was the revenge of sewers past: the city's long-standing failure to develop the sewage system meant that even large, spacious apartments could not be "concentrated," for fear that the toilets could not take the strain. The construction of barracks, by contrast, was judged "necessary, timely, and to be commenced without delay."[112] As a legal matter, requisition also failed. Put before the Duma's Housing Commission on October 11, a draft decree empowered the neighborhood dumas to requisition residential space on a temporary, compensated basis, a power that would lapse one year after demobilization. The vote would be the Housing Commission's last, and the requisition of buildings failed, eight votes to four.[113]

————

The more Russian cities could be made to look like European ones before the Revolution, the stronger the Bolsheviks' later claim to have found universal solutions to the industrial city's problems after it. Contrary to these claims, however, Moscow had different problems than its counterparts in western Europe, as well as a different set of tools at its disposal to intervene in urban life. The inverted politics of property in the Russian city favored municipal ownership of key resources, including housing, while at the same time preventing the robust regulation of private property. During the First World War, the failure to regulate housing markets proved catastrophic. This widely shared experience of disaster thrust housing problems to the foreground of debate over the just allocation of the war's burdens. At the same time, and no less significant for the transformations to come, both the contours of ownership and the political status of apartment buildings began to change in the months just before February 1917, and rapidly accelerated after it. The number of landlords who overtly abandoned properties was likely small. Still, the degradation in services provided by owners and the rising hostility between tenants and landlords fueled the rise of building committees in cities from Petrograd to Tiflis. Their ascent was likewise powered by political dynamics independent of housing politics, as a path to participation in the Revolution outside the increasingly "partified" political landscape.

Against this unsettled backdrop, two different kinds of seizure emerged in the built environment. The first, typified by the Mossoviet's takeover of the Dresden, was the "requisition by right of revolution." The second was the legal order for the requisition of buildings created by the Provisional Government, which went unrealized. In the days after the October Revolution, these two powers to seize—in the name of the Revolution, and for the needs of the state—would merge, and dispossession of factories, land, buildings, coats, and cookware would become an overarching mission for all bodies of the revolutionary state and claimants to revolutionary power. The all-consuming force of this mission opened up new horizons of possibility, not only for how the allocation and possession of material things should operate in revolutionary society, but even for imagining what these things could do, and what kinds of strain they could bear. One of the hallmarks of Bolshevik management from Magnitogorsk to Chernobyl was its commitment to pushing machinery and laborers past their breaking point. But in the days before the October Revolution, fears for the integrity of the equipment—the sewer lines—weighed heavily on official minds. Moscow's municipal officials could not quiet their concern for city toilets. And whatever their loyalties, they could not bring themselves to settle even a fraction of the central government inside the city's Garden Ring. "It was definitively declared to me that settling all the institutions of the Ministry in the center of Moscow will be completely impossible," an envoy lamented to his boss on October 21.[114] Settling this Ministry, and all ministries, in the center of Moscow would be among the first of the Bolsheviks' many completely impossible feats.

1

Making Space for Revolution

SORTING PEOPLE AND SPACES IN THE REVOLUTIONARY CITY

IN THE SUMMER of 1918, the city of Novouzensk, two hundred kilometers to the southeast of Saratov, found itself in a quandary. Nearly a year after the Bolshevik seizure of power, with civil war raging and lines of communication broken down, Novouzensk was running out of money. In the previous months, the city had suffered the same fate as a number of other towns in the region: "bands of Cossacks" had whipped through and emptied the vaults of the state bank branch during their stay. Unlike its neighbors though, Novouzensk's soviet complained, "there were no landowners" in the immediate area who might serve as a source of revenue. "The only resource left to the population was grain," and this in insufficient quantity for profit or sustenance. What was more, "until the most recent time," the soviet wrote in November, "the city was cut off from the center, surrounded by the Cossack bands. The *sovdep* [an abbreviation of *soviet deputatov*, or council of deputies] did not receive decrees." Novouzensk was on its own. If it was going to identify the resources it needed to survive, it would have to find them within itself.

The chairman of the city soviet, a Bolshevik identified as Comrade Kotkin, saw only one path forward: for the city "to nationalize rapidly." Nationalization, in Novouzensk, initially meant holding a fire sale of "all goods that had been abandoned by the bourgeoisie who fled with the counterrevolutionary Cossacks." These goods were "confiscated, appraised, and . . . sold to the local population." The soviet next branched out into "trade." It created a "department of local economy" to perform "an account of all agricultural inventory," set fuel prices, arrange purchases "all across the country," and initiate "logical distribution." The city expanded soap production and opened bakeries and sausage-makers, which turned a profit. Finally, the deputies of Novouzensk turned their nationalizing sights to a new horizon—to the substance of the city itself, its buildings. They created "an apartment subdepartment" responsible for "nationalizing all spaces which were rented out by landlords, and also those buildings of the bourgeoisie and the kulaks who ran off with the counterrevolutionaries."

The nationalization of buildings was performed "without compensation" for their previous owners. A report from the soviet to officials in Moscow described how seized apartment buildings were "used now for the benefit of the soviet, settled by the poorest population."[1] One of them housed a home for the elderly, as the deputies were concerned with "doing [their] duty before the aging population" and sought to ensure them "the best conditions for the sunset of their lives."[2] Although the topic of the report was local finance, Novouzensk's soviet boasted to Moscow that its confiscation of the buildings had enabled striking interventions in the city's social and political life, quite unrelated to its financial situation. As of November, the soviet was "battling with the kulak peace-eaters and all those who left with the counterrevolutionaries, and are now returning to the city." These people were being "registered with the Extraordinary Commission [Cheka] which conducts surveillance of them, and with the city police." They were "getting nothing to eat, and they have to pay the soviet for the use of their houses." These two projects unfolded in unison: the "buildings of the bourgeoisie and the kulaks who ran off with the counterrevolutionaries" were seized without compensation, while the bourgeoisie and the kulaks themselves—identified as such through their places of residence—were "registered with the Extraordinary Commission."[3]

While patently composed to tout the city's successes and sing Comrade Kotkin's praises, the triumphalist tale of the "nationalization" of Novouzensk illuminates several key features of the great wave of state seizure that burst across Russia in the wake of the October Revolution, sweeping everything from land to bakeries to apartment houses into the nominal holding of the Soviet state in under two years. Novouzensk's municipal campaign to "nationalize" started with the comparatively low-hanging and familiar fruit of local enterprises, city ownership of which was not uncommon before the Revolution, before progressing to more novel assets like apartments. The program combined carryovers from prerevolutionary notions of municipalization as a form of commerce generating profits for the city with new elements of autarchy, local discovery, and territorial self-reliance, infused with a radical ambition to build a socialist city that was affiliated but hardly monopolized by the

Bolsheviks. Once in city hands, however, Novouzensk's buildings empowered the city soviet to intervene in residents' lives far more deeply than bathhouses or bakeries could have ever allowed, and unsettled the existing property order at the root, in the things people held closest, in their homes.

———

Although state ownership of all major industries, the land and its products, banks and services, transport and real estate, theaters, hospitals, schools, apartments, sofas, and bed linens came to be understood as a core feature of Soviet socialism and the logical extension of the Bolsheviks' stated ambition to abolish private property, it was, in fact, a surprise. As Silvana Malle and other scholars have demonstrated, prior to October the Bolsheviks "had not formulated any concrete alternatives to the existing economic institutions," and while talk of nationalizing industry grew louder over the summer of 1917, in his seminal pamphlet "Can the Bolsheviks Retain State Power?" Lenin firmly rejected "countrywide expropriation," famously declaring that, in the short term, "confiscation leads nowhere."[4] But just one day after the Bolsheviks seized power, they aligned their revolution with the vast confiscatory project that was already underway—the seizure of land from estate owners, in which peasants and soldiers had been engaged for the past several months. The "Decree on Land" formalized the release of land surfaces and their underground riches from the strictures of private property "forever," forbade their private sale, transferred the land to the "all-people," and the underground riches to the "state."[5] In the months that followed, the new executive organ, the Sovnarkom, issued decrees nationalizing banks, specific factories, and entire branches of industry.[6] These orders could not hope to address themselves to each and every industry, factory, and market; inevitably, the decrees left many kinds of things untouched. But they signaled quite clearly that the state no longer defended private property rights, sparking confiscatory campaigns on a gargantuan scale, as revolutionary institutions raced to locate and subsume resources connected to their mission or necessary to their staffs.

Among state institutions, whether local or central, "nationalization" was an intensely competitive affair. In both February and April 1918, the Sovnarkom found it necessary to defend its monopoly on the "confiscation of enterprises" against other institutions, issuing repeated warnings that it alone possessed the power to nationalize (a power later extended to the VSNKh).[7] But the snowballing quality of nationalization proved impossible to contain. Local governments were active and, indeed, autonomous participants in the seizure of all sorts of resources on their territories. As officials at the People's Commissariat of Finance (Narkomfin) wrote in a brief internal history of the nationalization of private enterprise in 1922, neither the orders of the Sovnarkom nor those of any other central institution could be said to have directed statization, the seizure of property to the nominal benefit of the revolutionary state. "Industry began to enter into the control and administration of the state by happenstance [*sluchaino*], without any preparatory work." The local authorization of "nationalization," the officials complained, was endemic.[8] As of June 1, 1918, by their estimate, "513 enterprises were nationalized," but only one-fifth of these had "entered into the property [*sobstvennost'*] of the Republic by orders of the central powers." The seizure of the remaining four-fifths "was accomplished almost exclusively by the localities, without any participation by central institutions and outside of considerations of economic expediency." Four years after the fact, the Narkomfin officials remained uncertain of how to conceive of this process, and what to call it: the first draft of their report referred to it as a "process of state possession" (*obladanie*), indistinct and agentless, a term someone later overwrote by hand (replacing the *b* with a *v*, and the second *a* with an *e*) with the more definitive "state seizure" (*ovladenie*).[9]

Property systems are commonly understood to consist of a bundle of duties, rights, or powers over things, through which the individual or collective subjects of rights negotiate their access to things and their relationships to one another.[10] In an effort to discern how the Soviet system of property differed both from the imperial system that came before, as well as from property systems in the West, scholars have most often compared and contrasted the rights and duties awarded to particular parties over particular things. In this vein, the statization of private property during the Russian Revolution appears as the transfer of this bundle of rights and duties from one group, the private owners, to another, more or less equivalent owner, the Soviet state. Through the story of the takeover of the built environment, this chapter confirms the portrayal of statization, offered by Malle and others, as a messy and improvised process, one filtered through Bolshevik ideology rather than rigorously charted by it.[11] But it delves deeper into the category that sits at the end of statization, "state property." This chapter shows that in the course of transfer from private owners to the state, the bundle of powers and duties that had been wrapped up in owning city buildings, already under strain before the October Revolution, came apart.

In eliminating private property in general and dispossessing "bourgeois" owners in particular, the Bolsheviks conceived of the statization of buildings as a blow against those private owners, the nonlaboring element, and in favor of their opposites, the laboring element. But, as this chapter argues, the abolition of private property in buildings and the transfer of rights to the state did not cease action at the borders of the "bourgeoisie" or any of the other population categories that, as a weapon in the class war, it was meant to target. It ricocheted through Russian society, its effects reaching deep down the social ladder, into the working class, and up to the pinnacle of the state itself. In the years after the Revolution, it was therefore not just the bourgeoisie who lost the right to own the things in their possession—everyone did, including those newly endowed with stuff thanks to their status as workers, as well as the state institutions nominally charged with managing the people's bounty. All Soviet subjects were thrust into this new arena of propertylessness.

The chapter conducts its analysis of propertylessness through the story of the takeover of Moscow's built environment in 1918 and 1919. This story is split into two acts, which unfolded in parallel and were merged early on into a single administrative process: the conquest of Moscow by the central government evacuating itself from Petrograd beginning in March 1918, and the redistribution of built space according to principles of social justice, with the aid of nonmarket allocative tools, which began in the spring of 1918 and continued more or less unabated for the next two years. I use the language here of takeover and conquest, and not solely of statization and property, as this process involved transformations in governance as well as ownership. As this chapter contends, as the bundle of powers and duties that had characterized the ownership of buildings began to dissolve under the pressure of state seizure, the concept of ownership did not merely shed some of these powers and elevate other, already existing ones. In fact, the revolutionary state generated and assumed new powers over things in the takeover, mixing attributes of ownership with the core processes of revolutionary governance: social transformation in general, and the search for "bourgeois," "parasitic," and "nonlaboring" elements in particular. The term for this fused takeover of the built environment was "municipalization," which came to denote, as in Novouzensk, not merely the transfer of a building's ownership from private owners to the state (in the form of municipal government), but a merger of this possession with revolutionary governance.

Apartment buildings emerged from this process as one of the chief instruments of social revolution, not because they were successfully made into transparent quantities of abstract built space, as some plans for nonmarket allocation had intended, but rather, because they functioned as an index of the population for local authorities eager to sort and categorize in pursuit of anti-bourgeois class war. The great labor of the Revolution, the continual subdivision of the population into status categories from "laborer" to "parasite," was brought to life through the places where people lived. By the same token, thanks to its imbrication in class war, the possession of space became extraordinarily fragile for everybody. In the years after the October Revolution, it came to seem as if buildings, immovable though they were, had been doused in oil. No one could keep hold of them or the spaces they contained—not even the state institutions to which their possession had been nominally awarded. This chapter therefore unearths the imperfect strategies developed for holding onto built space in the freefall of propertylessness.

Municipalization: The Tasks of Postcapitalist Governance

On the day after the Bolshevik seizure of power, the Second Congress of the Soviets approved the "Decree on Land," ruling on the fate of minerals deposited below the earth, trees that grew out of it, and the rights to its cultivation.[12] But in keeping with the inattention to the problems of urban governance characteristic of Russian leftist politics, the decree did not address itself to land in cities and towns, or to the buildings which sat upon it. Lenin spoke publicly about the fate of buildings for the first time since seizing power on November 8, giving his blessing to the "requisition of apartments of the rich for the needs of the poor."[13] Several weeks after that, he drafted "Theses for a Law on the Confiscation of Buildings Rented to Tenants" by hand, specifying that "all (urban) buildings systematically rented out are confiscated to become the property of the people," thus making such buildings roughly equivalent in status to agricultural land.[14] The Sovnarkom took up his theses for discussion, considering a number of possibilities for intervention in the built environment. The Bolshevik Yuri Larin later recalled a proposal to grant organs of municipal government the right to "sequester emptied out [pustuyushchiye] spaces suitable for housing so as to settle them with people needing housing," a project he anticipated would play an important "agitational-instructional role." Another proposal called for the "requisition" of one month's worth of rents as a temporary measure, until the arrival of a formal decree. In order to prepare the necessary decree, a specially organized commission worked feverishly for roughly a week, producing the "Draft Decree on the Nationalization of Urban Real Estate and the Requisition of Rent," as it was registered in the Sovnarkom's docket on November 23. This draft was discussed and approved for submission to the Central Executive Committee (TsIK); a version entitled "Draft Decree on the Abolition of Private Property Rights in Urban Real Estate" was published in the *Newspaper of the Temporary Worker and Peasant Government* and *Pravda*. But just then, around November 26, the measure was abruptly and somewhat mysteriously abandoned. Several weeks later, the Sovnarkom approved an order forbidding the sale of urban land and buildings. But it did not return to the regulation of real estate for nearly a year, until August 1918, when it issued a virtually unchanged version of its draft from December 1917 as its "Decree on Municipalization."[15]

The Sovnarkom's decision to publicize but not promulgate its order abolishing private property rights in urban real estate created fractious dynamics over the following year, not only within cities, but also between municipal governments and the central organs. Within just a few weeks of dropping the "Draft Decree on the Abolition of Property Rights" from its docket, the Sovnarkom was forced to confront the question of the "nationalization of real estate" once more. But this time, the discussion focused narrowly on Petrograd, where the Bolshevik City Head, M. I. Kalinin, sought the Sovnarkom's approval for a binding agreement, to be signed by all the people's commissars, affirming that it was "not desirable to excessively rush the decision of the question of the nationalization of real estate in Petrograd." In the early months of 1918, as discussed in the following section, neighborhood soviets in Petrograd embarked on new projects to settle "emptied out," "abandoned," and other "available" spaces with Petrograders needing housing—projects the Sovnarkom now sought to slow. But Petrograd was by this point hardly alone; a number of cities began experimenting with local initiatives of "municipalization," "nationalization," and resettlement, even without a central order directing them. As the Soviet historian V. V. Zhuravlyov later concluded, "the practical activities of local Soviets in this period testify to the fact that the delay in the publication of a law on the nationalization of real estate in cities in general did not negatively influence the process of [municipalization and resettlement]."[16]

The reasoning behind the Sovnarkom's turn away from the regulation of real estate remains opaque. The following year, in a rare public acknowledgement of the draft decree being waylaid, Larin blamed the situation on Kalinin. The historian Zhuravlyov suggested that, just as the Sovnarkom took up its draft decree, it entered into a new, more detail-oriented and "careful" phase of rule, holding the project back in order to attend to the many complications of canceling property rights in real estate. But this does not bear up against the barrage of nationalization orders that followed on other equally complex matters. Moreover, between the time of the draft decree's introduction and its eventual promulgation, it hardly changed: as in the draft, the "Decree on Municipalization" empowered cities to seize all buildings whose owners collected rents worth above a certain figure. The only difference was that the draft decree proposed concrete sums of 10,000 or 25,000 rubles for this value limit, while the actual "Decree on Municipalization" specified that the limit should be fixed locally. Another possibility for the "delay" was said to be the Sovnarkom's purported desire to allow municipalities to continue to collect real estate taxes, knowing these formed a major basis of local budgets. But this also seems unlikely, given that so many municipalities went on to eschew tax collection entirely in favor of seizing the buildings outright.[17]

Once it finally promulgated the decree in August 1918, the People's Commissariat of Internal Affairs (NKVD) belatedly formed a Department on Municipalization. As its first order of business, this department sent a communiqué to various municipalities, asking what each had done to implement the decree and, more broadly, to characterize the city's municipalizing agenda. The request garnered many replies from cities across the republic. The replies overwhelmingly made clear that in many places, by the time the Sovnarkom got around to issuing its "Decree on Municipalization," municipalization had already occurred. What is more, it had taken a shape that far outstripped the imagination of the Sovnarkom's decree, which was after all still rooted in the weeks just after the October Revolution. To be sure, many replies reflected efforts to enact the decree more or less as it was printed. The town of Tsarskoe Selo, home of the Romanov dynasty's palace retreat as well as the ancient piles of many noble families, described a project to rank buildings into five categories—from "palaces, manor houses, theaters and trading spaces set apart from the usual," down to "nonresidential basements and sheds"—on the basis of "location, conveniences, and finishes."[18] Pereslavl, outside Moscow, reported that for its part, municipalization meant that rents were now brought to the soviet, unchanged in amount; Bogorodsk, outside Nizhny Novgorod, recalculated rents and took them as revenue.[19] But in a number of places, municipalization had arrived months before the decree, and in a more audacious format.[20] One submission, from the city of Belyi, not far from Tver, included notes from a meeting of the local soviet held back in May 1918. Three months before the Sovnarkom's decree, Comrade Pyotr Selitsky proposed pursuing the "nationalization of apartments in the city of Belyi" in order to mitigate the "unequal distribution of housing conveniences in the population" and to bring about "the construction of better conditions for life of the City poor." To that end, he proposed "counting up the housing of the city of Belyi," and "distribut[ing] it" such that "residents of the city of Bely should have enough space for a comfortable family life."[21]

Belyi's newly created housing commission remained focused on buildings, which it sorted into three categories, based on the "conveniences" afforded by different ranks of built space. Elsewhere, however, the responses to the NKVD indicate that by the time of the decree's arrival, municipalization had accrued meaning much beyond the built environment. Indeed, it had become connected to a process of resource mobilization that, rather than focusing on any one category of material thing, be it buildings or land or shops, instead led cities and even neighborhoods to search out whatever they might claim and defend against other takers on what they were becoming increasingly aware to be their territory. At a congress devoted to questions of "municipal administration" held in the latter part of 1918, the delegate from Petrograd observed that, embedded within the decrees ordering the statization of different things, were serious questions about the organization and hierarchy of the state itself. "If there is some factory in a city," the delegate theorized, "then this factory is the national wealth of the whole state, and as such it should be controlled by the SNKh [sovnarkhoz]," that is, by the regional branch office of the VSNKh. "The city economy," by contrast, "is differentiated by its smaller scale," suggesting that "smaller" things redounded to it. The city economy "has great meaning for the existence of the city," but ultimately, he allowed, the jury was still out on what exactly it was: "we must precisely fix what remains in the limits of the city economy."[22] That same uncertainty about territory and scale meant that desirable resources might end up bouncing back and forth between center and locality, though in practice, a delegate from Samara complained, their movement typically flowed only in one direction. "I will show this with an example from the Communal Department of Samara," he explained. Early on, the city seized a soap factory that made 3,000 *poods* of soap each month. "We wanted to boost this, we gave it some steam engines. Now the factory makes 20,000 poods a month, enough for the entire region and to send some to the center. But now the SNKh says that the factory serves general state needs, meaning it is part of VSNKh and Tsentrozhir." Samara lost the soap factory, together with the steam engines and its investment.[23]

As the seizure of resources came to be embedded in revolutionary governance, debates arose as to its purpose: what was the transfer of resources into state hands supposed to do? In this, it rekindled debates familiar from the era of municipal socialism prior to the Revolution; the same delegate from Petrograd to the NKVD Congress on municipal administration asserted that the aim of municipal administration, and the local seizure of resources, was to "raise the level of the person, to increase consumption such that all live in comfortable conditions, so that this is not an affair of the few. I do not understand how it is possible to argue about this." Toward that end, he proposed, it should be oriented toward "the lighting of the city . . . a special department will concern itself with ensuring that old houses are put in good order, building new ones in the new type, to settle [people] more or less correctly, and the like. The upkeep of the streets also relates to this." ("So this will resemble the *zemstvo*," he added. "Let it!")[24] Other cities envisioned a more dramatic upheaval, as in the forward-thinking city of Yelets, which unveiled a comprehensive plan for municipalizing "trade enterprises," dividing them into three categories in conjunction with the unveiling of a new city plan that made use of German principles of zoning. Seizure would be carried out by members of a joint party-state commission, each of whom would be granted wide-ranging powers to bring these enterprises "under his control." With regard to the actual substance of municipalization, it was specified only that each member of the party-state commission would be "supplied with a stamp."[25]

As the example of the soap factory in Samara made clear, localities did not seize merely as lower-order branches of a national institution, but as competitors against those national institutions. It thus made sense for them to attempt seizures of resources that were not simply located within the boundaries of their territory but could also be construed, one way or another, as subject to their authority qua municipal institution. Soap factories, even those inside city limits, would come and go; what was left to the city was the city itself—its buildings, its streets, whatever it had that no other institution might plausibly claim. In this aspect, seizure operated not merely as a transfer of possession over existing things but as a form of conquest and creation. It was up to municipal governments to squeeze water from the rocks, finding or creating things that other branches of the state could not see.

So autarkic a notion of statization produced an unusual calculus for assessing what, precisely, bore value in the process of takeover. More specifically, it encouraged the conviction—which flourished in the ranks of the central government as well—that *everything* necessary to sustain the population could be found within the limits of the territory, if only one looked in the right places. In October 1918, in Moscow, the Khamovniki sovdep argued for the

"organization of a neighborhood museum." The significance of the neighborhood museum was genuinely universal. It "should be created in such a way as
to give an idea of the cultural and historical stages . . . a mirror of the culture
of the working class, the history of its development, the culture of humankind
in general, the history of the person." The execution, however, would be purely
local. As the rapporteur explained: "The task of museums is to pry those valuables that today are hidden in boxes and storerooms of various residents out
of their paws, to systematize them and open them to the wide masses. I propose entering immediately into the organization of the extraction of these
valuables from among the various bourgeois nooks and crannies, and after the
careful cleansing of them from the gray residue of the old world, gathering them
in a systematic order in our neighborhood museum." As "fate had allowed," the
neighborhood was already possessed of the perfect space in which to house the
proposed departments of fine art, history, and the proletariat: a local mansion,
the rooms of which "an insane millionaire got it into his head to decorate in various [historical] styles," and which now, "with wise usage of this good thing
under our noses," would allow the neighborhood to capture the march of the
"centuries" in one neighborhood house. The rapporteur was "confiden[t] that in
our neighborhood, we will find a great deal of valuable material."[26]

The competitive dynamics of state seizure merged an ethos of local self-
sufficiency with revolutionary expropriation, compelling localities to identify
and extract key resources in their midst, preferably resources they had a prospect of retaining. The task of all neighborhoods was to identify the materially
or culturally valuable resources around them. Some localities had soap factories, others had the culture of humankind. But what if, after looking, a city
came up empty-handed? What if the city could find no such things, or central
institutions moved too fast, vacuuming up all the good resources before the
municipality had a chance to seize them itself? This was the fate of Novouzensk, described in the introduction to this chapter, which found itself
bereft of gold and short on grain—until it discovered a new resource to mine.
The resource was itself: its businesses, to be sure, but also its buildings, and
most critically, their residents. The roots of Novouzensk's transformation lay
in its identification of its buildings and their "bourgeois" and "kulak" populations as repositories of wealth and more than that, as resources of power. Novouzensk narrated its experience with unusual acuity—its account, too, was
produced for the NKVD's query on municipalization—but its realization was
not unique. In the city of Podolsk, for instance, local authorities reported that,
yes, they too had seized buildings and fixed rents according to the presence of

central heating and other metrics. But by its own measure, Podolsk had "not yet succeeded in accomplishing the full municipalization of real estate and movable property." This referred not to the statization of buildings as property or the seizure of their revenue streams, but rather to the disposal of the spaces and the registration of the people within. In pursuit of what they called "full municipalization," the Podolsk officials had in mind that "all spaces belonging to private people in the city of Podolsk, gradually and stubbornly will be taken onto strict account"—not necessarily owned, that is, but known—"and carefully-carefully all these apartments and rooms will be distributed ex- tremely justly, and in the first instance will be given for living space to the very poorest worker-peasant population." The department had "already satisfied the sharpest need of the poor with large families" in this regard.[27]

Thus, in many places municipalization became synonymous with the power to dispose of built space, independent of the questions of a building's legal ownership and the collection of rents that were the focus of the Sovnar- kom's decree. It represented a type of power wielded by the cities as much as a format for possession. As such, municipalization encompassed an account- ing not just of the structures themselves but also of their inhabitants, such that the enterprise of "taking the bourgeoisie onto account" became no less a part of "municipalization" than the expropriation of property. For this reason, a number of localities, in their correspondence with the NKVD as to whether "municipalization" in the region had been carried out, did not mention the status of building ownership at all. Where Soviet power had been "established," as in the small city of Buinsk outside of Simbirsk, an inspector from the NKVD re- ported in October, "the bourgeoisie of the city and the district have been taken onto account."[28] Where "the old bourgeois laws" of property continued to be implemented, "the bourgeoisie was not taken onto account," and, what was the same, "the system of categories and ration cards [by category] was completely absent." How was this accounting of the bourgeoisie, and the classification of the population on which it depended, to be brought to life? As in Novouzensk, it would be done through the seizure of the buildings where they lived.

"Petrograd in Moscow"

Socialism in the city, like socialism in all places, was a revealed truth. The Bol- sheviks studied the history of their own upheaval for clues to the future and signs that they were on the right path. As the seat of the revolutionary govern- ment and the beating heart of Russia's working class, Petrograd's revolution became the archetypal version of the October Revolution in the city, a status that would be secured for decades by the powerful Bolshevik memorialization apparatus.[29] But in the event, on the question of how to make socialist revolution in the urban environment, the dominant contemporary model was not Petrograd, but Moscow.

Moscow's elevation to the status of model city became inevitable after its rebirth as the capital of Soviet power in March 1918, thanks not only to the prestige of this role but also to the questions and experiences the city faced in the course of becoming the capital, which made the scale of property transfer and resettlement more rapid and extensive than virtually anywhere else. Moscow's experience held particular sway in the arena of building seizure and management, which happened also to be questions on which the central government refused to rule for its first year in power. Even after the Sovnarkom issued the "Decree on Municipalization" in August 1918, it remained silent on a number of other questions connected to the most basic aspects of urban life, involving who could use things of all kinds and who got to decide. As the Legal Consultation Department of the People's Commissariat of Government Control (Goskon) observed in December 1918, "the requisition of living space in the current strategic situation of the Soviet Republic has acquired extremely important meaning" in daily life and governance. Questions and files flowed into the office "from the different ends of the Republic," as cities across the country seized buildings and embarked on programs of redistribution that had not been foreseen by the Sovnarkom's "Decree on Municipalization." "In the absence of a general decree on housing matters, one that would be obligatory for the entire space of the Soviet Republic," the Legal Consultation Department reported that both its office and the localities searching for suitable rules had been "forced to be governed by the orders [of the Moscow Soviet]." Moscow's local decrees, that is, had been adopted as the prime source material for making revolution in the built environment in the country at large, despite having "legal force only for the city of Moscow."[30]

The seizure of built space in Moscow differed from Petrograd's archetypal story in its process and also in what it sought to accomplish. In Petrograd, as had been the case in February, the October Revolution occasioned spontaneous popular attacks on rich buildings and "searches" inside people's homes. As Hubertus Jahn observes, for nearly a year, Petrograders endured and participated in the "uncontrolled" redistribution of residential space, with Red Guards and self-appointed representatives of the working classes going door-to-door, demanding entry into rich apartments, seizing personal property, and causing inhabitants to flee.[31] These also occurred in Moscow, particularly in the northern and western quadrants of the inner ring, where anarchist bands took up residence in villas and mansions, using them as bases for their street "raids" and stripping them for luxury goods they could sell.[32] But in Petrograd, expeditions into private homes were integrated early on into the practice of neighborhood soviets (which were formed in the winter of 1917 in Petrograd, but which did not become active in Moscow until the spring and summer of 1918). The first official "confiscation" of an apartment, from a landlord who owned three, was performed by the Second City Neighborhood Soviet in January 1918. Not long after, the Petrograd Soviet (Petrosoviet) formed a commission to explore the "forced occupation of space," culminating in a project adopted on March 1 for the "settlement of workers and their families in the apartments of the bourgeoisie."[33] This report established the existence of a "norm" for the consumption of "living space," to be measured not in square sazhens, as a sanitary minimum, but in rooms—one room per adult household member and half a room for each child younger than ten.[34] Ten days later, with the class-based resettlement of apartments just getting underway in Petrograd, the Administrative Director of the Sovnarkom, Vladimir Bonch-Bruevich, packed Lenin and the rest of the institution onto a train under the cover of night and set out for a new life in Moscow.

In Moscow, a very different kind of seizure of buildings had already occurred, one focused not on who lived in buildings, but on who owned them. On December 12, 1917, three months before the Sovnarkom arrived, and alone among the republic's major cities, the Moscow Soviet authorized the "municipalization" of the city's largest residential buildings. The Mossoviet modeled its order on the Sovnarkom's draft decree, but unlike the Sovnarkom, the Mossoviet passed and implemented it. The Mossoviet's measure brought all buildings where total rents exceeded 750 rubles per month into city possession, amounting to roughly one-fifth of the city's 20,000 buildings in total and housing nearly half its residents, an estimated 800,000 people. Where Petrograd's seizure of space was trained from the start on class-based resettlement, in Moscow the city targeted property rights. Neighborhood soviets in Petrograd harassed landlords, extracting "extraordinary contributions" on their properties.[35] They also harassed the original, "bourgeois" tenants of apartments after they were resettled with workers, with the former residents remaining responsible for the rent, while newcomers lived rent-free. The Petrosoviet found ways to accomplish all of this without touching the legal status of buildings. In this sense, Moscow's "Order on Municipalization of

December 12, 1917," was actually rather quaint; the Mossoviet had not yet come to appreciate possibilities of revolutionary power that the Petrosoviet had already grasped.[36]

For implementation, Moscow's municipalization relied upon the new institution of the building committee. With landlords out of the picture, building committees became responsible for collecting rent, bringing it to the Council of Neighborhood Dumas, the interim municipal administration, while also performing all the other unremunerated duties they had taken on. Four days after the Mossoviet's municipalization decree, neighborhood-level unions of building committees representing all twenty-five of the city's administrative districts at the time voted to form a superunion, called Tsentrodom. Tsentrodom, as its first order of business, rejected the municipalization until the "question [of municipalization] had been decided on an all-Russian scale," encouraging its 23,000-member building committees to continue to bring rents "as before." While Tsentrodom was later remembered in the Mossoviet's *Krasnaya Moskva* as a jealous guardian of the "old [property] order," a contemporary account announcing Tsentrodom's formation reported excitedly that it was prepared to "grapple with the major juridical and economic questions" of "building organization," and that it sought not a return to the old order but rather to foment the creation of "one grand shared cooperative," in which Muscovites and residents of all cities would be members. In short, it is likely that in the months between the municipalization order and the Petrograd Bolsheviks' arrival in Moscow, building committees collected rent and kept it for themselves, using the funds for upkeep and supply.[37]

As one of its first acts upon arriving to Moscow, the Sovnarkom called new elections to building committees, simultaneously formalizing their role in municipal government and crushing their potential as independent nodes of political or social organization. Only those deemed eligible to vote in elections to the soviets—those employed in "socially useful labor," over the age of eighteen, and registered as residents in the building—could participate in the new building committee elections. Where no residents in a building cleared this bar, neighborhood dumas, by now also firmly in Bolshevik hands, were empowered to install "commandants" from outside the building. Buildings where residents still refused to bring rent to the Council of Neighborhood Dumas saw their committees disbanded, with control over the building awarded "to a janitor delegated by the Union of Janitors."[38]

The arrival of the central government in March 1918 transformed the landscape of power in the built environment in other ways, too. In the five months since the October Revolution, Moscow had been living through its own version of the revolution going on in Petrograd. As Diane Koenker notes, this version was not a "time-lagged variant of the Petrograd model," but a distinctive "revolutionary process."[39] The story of the central government's evacuation to Moscow in 1918 amplifies this claim, exposing the jolt delivered to the city by the arrival of the Petrograders, their "model" of revolution, and the institutions that already went along with it. Like Petrograd, Moscow had anarchists who seized mansions and lived dissolutely off their fat. But unlike Petrograd, it had no Cheka to take the anarchists and their mansions in hand. Moscow had only "Rogov's Commission", a pale imitation of Dzerzhinsky's Commission, as the Cheka was known in Petrograd, where it was one of several organs of internal security created in December 1917 to combat what the Bolsheviks labeled "counterrevolution."[40] Rogov's Commission tried and failed to evict the anarchists from the city's lush art-deco mansions three times in the early part of the year, before the Cheka arrived in April and immediately shelled them out, one mansion after another, sometimes battling for hours against the heavily armed bands holed up inside. Rogov's Commission died out not long after, no match for the superior discipline and brutality of the Cheka. The arrival of the Petrograd Sovnarkom also prompted the formation of a Moscow Sovnarkom, the Moscow Regional Sovnarkom, formed in early March by V. P. Nogin, who led the seizure of power in October, and the Bolshevik historian M. N. Pokrovsky. They sought for months to establish it as a counterweight to the (Petrograd) Sovnarkom by issuing competing decrees, accepting popular petitions and complaints, and countermanding the orders of the Mossoviet. But it, too, withered in the shadow of the Petrograders, who ladled party members and powers onto the Mossoviet when they arrived, building it up into the authoritative body of municipal government in the city.[41]

Among the most important of these powers in the early days after the Sovnarkom's arrival was the power to dispose of built space. Envoys from Petrograd began to appear on Moscow's streets again in February, as rumors of an imminent German invasion rose to a fever pitch.[42] Train stations in Petrograd were overrun by people wanting to flee; before he left, Joseph Stalin gamely volunteered to "provide security and machine guns" in the waiting halls.[43] But barely a week later, with the ink still fresh on the Treaty of Brest-Litovsk between Germany and the Soviet Republic, the popular exodus from Petrograd came to a sudden halt. The coaches reserved for the population were "not only not packed, but not even full up to the norm."[44] And yet, the pace of the central government's evacuation did not slow. To the contrary, it accelerated, shifting in character over the course of a few weeks from a temporary accommodation to a permanent abandonment of the Russian state's purpose-built home. This development mystified some onlookers. "With the peace with Germany signed and military activities ceased," a directorate in the People's Commissariat of Finance wrote, "the directorate sees no purpose or need for either a general or partial evacuation," least of all one undertaken in a hurry. A hurried evacuation, the official accurately predicted, "would call forth, to say nothing of the huge expense, total disorganization" in work and life.[45] But within several months, it had become clear to all that *not* evacuating to Moscow—or evacuating to a place other than Moscow—was the functional equivalent of an institutional pink slip, reserved for departments (such as the Mint, ordered to Siberia) whose fate in the new system was "not clear."[46]

Soon, Moscow newspapers introduced a new section to report on the new arrivals: they called it "Petrograd in Moscow."[47] To receive these newcomers, the Mossoviet created a Central Requisitioning Committee. There was no mention of barracks or fear for the integrity of toilets this time around. By this point, revolutionary administrators had already "requisitioned" food and train cars. Red guards (and their many criminal imitators) requisitioned people's winter coats and wallets. Buildings, too, would be requisitioned, like these other things essential to the revolution. There were no legal orders specifying how this would happen, or what it meant for owners, tenants, or the institutions themselves. In their first weeks in Moscow, most envoys from Petrograd trod gently. Lenin and other members of the Central Committee and Sovnarkom took up residence in the National Hotel before eventually decamping to the Kremlin, once damage from the fighting in October had been repaired; the National Hotel became the First House of the Soviets, where high-ranking officials jockeyed for rooms.[48] Meanwhile, institutional envoys sought to renew the arrangements made the previous September, for the villas, academies, and other large buildings.

The "requisition" of these buildings did not generally involve displacing their existing residents, and if it did, this occurred by agreement. The private sale of real estate was forbidden in the fall of 1917, but in certain respects, these early requisitions closely resembled sales.[49] Individual commissariats sometimes paid money to building owners or building committees upon reaching an agreement to "requisition" a building in whole or in part. It is not clear whether this money functioned as rent or as a bounty, securing the building for the institution against offers from different institutions. One building owner asked for something like a closing document after agreeing to turn her villa over to Narkomfin, listing all its features and their condition at the moment of handover.[50] The Mossoviet's Central Requisitioning Committee existed, in theory, to register and confirm the requisition of a particular building by a particular institution, which it marked by assigning a "requisition slip" for the building to the institution. The competition for space and the uncertainty around tenure, however, were such that the mere possession of a "requisition slip" for a building did not secure its final disposition—not least because there was no systematic register of requisitioned buildings, such that it would have been possible to know if one building or another was already assigned. The Central Requisitioning Committee could fill out a blank slip with a building's address for one institution, and could easily do so for another. Securing the approval of the building's owner or the building committee, through money or papers or some other favor, was therefore part of the strategy necessary to maintain a hold over a space in the tenuous period between receiving the official requisition slip and taking physical occupancy.[51]

Norms also reappeared early on in the evacuation, as a means of documenting need for space and giving shape to the search for it. But they proved almost impossible to act upon, due to what would become a perennial dilemma of socialist allocation in the built environment—how to align the abstract quantities of built space they conjured with the real volumes of actual buildings. The commissariats used the norms inherited from the Provisional Government's planning documents, rather than those instituted in the first week of March by the Petrosoviet; measurements, that is, were in square sazhens rather than rooms and half-rooms per person. The commissariats also composed tables displaying each office's consumption of built space in Petrograd against the quantities they would require according to the norm in Moscow; Narkomfin, for instance, consumed 14,263 square sazhens of office space in Petrograd against the 9,939 square sahzens proposed for Moscow.[52] The planning documents crafted by the commissariats instructed their Moscow envoys to "order space for 1,000 people, and rooms and apartments for 300–400," as if space was something one could order like food off a menu, from local authorities implicitly presumed to possess a large fund of available sazhens of built space.[53] But just as before October, no such fund of space existed; it would have to be made.

In this, the Mossoviet's Central Requisitioning Committee, although in charge of securing space for the central government, was of little help. In response to requests for "space for 1,000 people," the Central Requisitioning

Committee offered to furnish envoys with a "search permit," empowering them to enter houses and apartments at will.[54] For perhaps two months, from March to about May 1918, the searchers sought out "free apartments" and, more controversially, "free rooms." Free apartments meant uninhabited apartments, this was clear; but the meaning of free rooms was, like the concept of requisition, laced with uncertainty and the threat of direct interpersonal conflict. "Free rooms" were not necessarily uninhabited rooms; rather, they were rooms that, in the view of a space-seeker, could or should be made free by an apartment's existing residents in order to be filled up by new residents. The designation of one room as "free" necessarily involved an assessment of the utility and density of occupation of the other rooms in the apartment.

Without formally announcing it, that is, the turn to "free rooms," in fact, marked the turn to already-inhabited space, with the aim of its "concentration." Insofar as there were at least two metrics for this assessment of density in circulation at the time—the evacuation norm of two square sazhens per person and the Petrograd norm of one room per person—this was an undertaking ripe with potential for dispute. Complaints from residents describe hostile encounters over apartment thresholds between the envoys demanding entry and the apartment's inhabitants. Some institutions hired "Muscovites, knowing the city well" to facilitate their search; "knowing the city well" could presumably mean many things, including knowing neighborhoods, apartment buildings, and even individual apartments likely to contain "free rooms."[55] Other institutions gave up on inspecting particular spaces entirely, sending out dozens of notices to entire apartment buildings announcing their imminent "requisition," and informing residents they would be "concentrated according to a norm fixed by the Presidium of the Moscow Sovdep, in a manner agreed by the building committee," then seeing who fell for it.[56]

Trainloads of officials arrived every day, whether they had a place to live or not. Narkomfin secured the Capital Hotel for its first employees arriving to Moscow in March, where they would stay during the "search for permanent living space." Once they found it, the hotel was "meant to be presented to the second group," and so forth, until all employees had been housed. This plan broke down right away; "permanent living space" for the first group had not been found when, several weeks later, the second group arrived from Petrograd, jamming themselves into the Capital Hotel alongside their colleagues.[57] A Moscow newspaper reported in astonishment that officials from the Commissariat of Labor, having failed to secure space before leaving Petrograd, appeared to be living and working out of the train car in which they had arrived, and which was still parked at the railway station.[58] In May, a few weeks after reaching Moscow, the Customs Department reported back to Narkomfin that it lacked both office and living space, that the latter had emerged as "an extremely dire question at present," that employees "lived in the most impossible conditions," which were "exceptionally difficult for families," and which "powerful searches for living space" had been unable to resolve. No matter; by the end of the month, Narkomfin alone had transported 3,533 workers, 4,762 family members, and more than 230,000 poods of cargo to Moscow.[59]

It did not take long for the tens of thousands of people needing places to live and places to work, knocking on doors to find "free rooms" in inhabited apartments, to become embroiled in conflicts with the Muscovites they had started to displace. In early April, the Mossoviet created a new, more permanent department to take over from the Central Requisitioning Committee, called the Central Housing-Land Department (TsZhZO), which it charged with finding space for the new arrivals and displaced Muscovites alike. Chaired by M. F. Vladimirsky, the future Commissar of Internal Affairs, the TsZhZO would remain Moscow's authoritative center of building politics and allocation for the next five years. Its administrative structure reflected the incredible diversity of buildings and ownership structures in the city, and the profound confusion about their present legal status. The TsZhZO opened a Subdepartment of "Municipal" Buildings, responsible for buildings that had been city property before 1917, and a Subdepartment for "Soviet" Buildings, responsible for buildings that, in the end, would be no less municipal than those administered by the Subdepartment for Municipal Buildings, but which had not been city property before 1917.[60] It opened a Subdepartment of Accounting and Distribution of Living Spaces as well as a Subdepartment of Accounting and Distribution of Nonliving Spaces (even as this division was erased in real life by the occupation of apartments by state offices). The assignment of space to central institutions was concentrated in the TsZhZO's Collegium, as the main interface between Moscow and the central government; the assignment of residential space for both government employees and displaced Muscovites was henceforth handled by the Subdepartment of Accounting and Distribution of Living Spaces.

The advent of the TsZhZO unleashed a radical new chapter in the conquest of Moscow's built environment and its residents. In its first six weeks of existence, the TsZhZO asserted two sweeping powers over people and space. First, in an effort to concretize its power over the allocation of buildings, the TsZhZO informed the central commissariats (although not the city's residents) that it now claimed the right "to requisition space and perform evictions" *everywhere* on the territory of Moscow, even in buildings that "belonged to other institutions and societies," or to "private owners, on the basis of the principle that all real estate in Moscow is at the disposal of the Mossoviet."[61] Authorities in Moscow thereby arrived at the realization their Petrograd counterparts had had months earlier, that the soviet could control the disposal of buildings whether or not it owned them. And second, the TsZhZO issued an order on the "concentration" of apartments according to the "norm" of built space. But where the Petrograd envoys had treated the norm as a measurement of space against a number of bodies, the TsZhZO's "instruction on concentration" paid close attention to the bodies themselves—to the residents, and more particularly, to whether they constituted "bourgeois or nonproletarian elements." Here was the key that would unlock space for the needs of the state and the people: finding particular addresses would be accomplished through finding bourgeois people.

Sorting People, Sorting Space

The project to manipulate and "concentrate" built space by applying norms and searching out class enemies reflected an underlying vision of the material world as more pliable than it had previously been adjudged, and of society as an "artifact," to be cultivated, molded, and "cleansed"—a term put into use almost immediately in planning for evacuation and resettlement—of pernicious "elements." In Bolshevik ideology, the technique of effective management was aimed at the long-term production of homogeneity.[62] But its execution, especially in the transformative era of revolution, required the short-term elaboration of difference through detailed practices of individuation and sorting. In practice, sorting the population through the built environment proved to be arbitrary, sloppy, and deeply inefficient as a method of promoting either the rational use of built space or its just allocation—the two stated goals of the project. Where it succeeded, however, was in mobilizing city residents to involve themselves not only in the surveillance of built space but in the assessment of their neighbors.

Just as in preparing for the evacuation of Petrograd the Sovnarkom had sought to ensure that "criminal elements" would get out of the city "in last place," so, too, did it prepare for its arrival to Moscow with an order banishing Muscovites not engaged in "productive labor"—namely, "prostitutes, speculators, brokers, middlemen, and those occupied in street trade."[63] The idea that it should be possible to cleanse the city of socially or politically undesirable populations in order to make room for Bolsheviks and the central state apparatus was therefore already in play when the TsZhZO announced its "Order on Concentration" on April 1. The principle of concentrating the density of inhabitation of space was also already in play, having been introduced into practice in earlier weeks by the envoys from Petrograd wielding search permits, seeking out spaces that were not occupied up to the new "normal" level. The innovation of the TsZhZO's "Order on Concentration" was to merge these two guiding principles by applying the norm of space specifically to the socially and politically undesirable households of the "bourgeois and nonproletarian elements." In this framework, the norm functioned not as a universal entitlement, but as a tool for the uncertain work of identifying the "bourgeois and nonproletarian elements." There were plenty of people in Moscow who did not enjoy an ample quantity of space according to the norm; the norm was not for them. In contrast to the prerevolutionary norms of sown area in land or cubic volume in healthy air, the norm of built space was conceived as an upper limit on consumption rather than as a subsistence minimum.[64] Consumption of space in a quantity above the norm itself indicated "bourgeois" status, filling the category with content by bringing individual households into focus as bourgeois on the basis of their consumption of space.

For this reason, a common defensive strategy against the Mossoviet's "Order on Concentration" was to pack one's apartment with friends and acquaintances preemptively, a tactic known as "self-concentration" (*samouplotneniye*). By the time the plight of the genteel Manuilova sisters came to the attention of their Sovnarkom acquaintance Bonch-Bruevich, in the summer of 1918, they had managed to accumulate eight people living in their three-room apartment. Their neighborhood soviet likely saw the elderly sisters as a soft target, and so went after them craftily, on the grounds of "overconcentration," that is, living *more* densely than the norm allowed. But Bonch-Bruevich himself intervened to block their eviction, scolding the soviet for its misguided application of the norm where it did not belong. First of all, he lectured, the norm had no place in the Manuilova household because the sisters, while of noble origins, had inspiring prerevolutionary biographies, having aided the revolutionary movement in their younger days. But equally, he explained, "overconcentration" was simply not how the norm worked. It was a ceiling on consumption, not a floor. The sisters and their cohabitants must be allowed to stay, he informed the neighborhood, as "there is nothing in the law saying that people cannot live more densely than stipulated" by the norm of built space.[65]

The selection of households as "bourgeois" and in need of concentration fell to the TsZhZO's Subdepartment on the Concentration and Distribution of Space. The Subdepartment, in turn, tasked the initial round of both identification and implementation to the envoys and even individual officials of the central state seeking out housing for their staffs or themselves. The people who needed a place to live, that is, were put in charge of concentrating Moscow's apartments. The TsZhZO printed up "permissions" to concentrate, which were to be carried by the prospective new resident, in his or her own name, and presented to the building committee at the specified address.

PERMISSION

[date]

The Subdepartment on the Concentration and Distribution of Space of the Housing-Land Department of the Moscow Soviet of Workers' and Red Army Deputies permits comrade _____ to occupy in the course of concentration one room in apartment No. ____ in building ____, on _____ street.

Signed.[66]

The permission did not specify how building committees or the residents of individual apartments were to rearrange themselves to make way for newcomers; the details were left to residents themselves. One building committee requested intervention from Bonch-Bruevich when it received a concentration order for an apartment presently occupied by "its owner, A. M. Obukhov," and his six-person household. The order had been presented to the committee by its intended beneficiary, an employee of the "Commissariat for the Affairs of Caucasian Nationalities," newly arrived to town. Insofar as the apartment was, in the building committee's view, already full, it tactfully suggested that "the information of the Housing Soviet [sic] does not correspond to actual fact." Bonch-Bruevich took the trouble of clarifying matters with the TsZhZO before reporting back that there had been no mistake. The housing officials "knew the apartment under discussion was not empty, but in view of the lack of space, it was presented [to the bearer of the permission] as a measure of concentration."[67]

The search for the bourgeoisie operated as a cultural enterprise rather than a juridical or statistical one. "Antibourgeois" sentiment suffused revolutionary culture and had wide political purchase; even before the Bolsheviks seized power, moderate political forces as well as radical ones accepted the existence of bourgeois plots against the Revolution and the necessity of discrimination against the bourgeoisie.[68] Much like the later searches for kulaks, *bais*, and other so-called class enemies, the bureaucratization of antibourgeois sentiment produced categories that were "ambiguous, shifting, and frequently contested."[69] Ambiguity enabled the creative application of cultural models already in place to the task at hand. As a form of invective, "bourgeois" filtered outward from a socioeconomic context into other spheres of cultural production and social life, deployed among soldiers to impugn officers, among peasants to inveigh against the spread of city clothes, and among city folk against those who were not merely wealthy but excessively self-regarding.[70] Outward appearances mattered greatly in these appraisals, as attested by a dormitory manager in Moscow named V. I. Orlov, who learned in early June 1918 that he was in danger of losing his apartment, due to his "bourgeois appearance."[71] To counter this impression, Orlov compiled a hefty dossier about himself, entitled "INFORMATION ABOUT V. I. ORLOV," with all the necessary records to prove his true, nonbourgeois status: party history, employment history, and the progressive politics of his parents. But as he noted, it was his "appearance" that had turned the wheel of fate over the previous year: having been forced off a local council for "suspicion of Bolshevism" after the February Revolution, in April 1918 he was informed "through private channels" that he was under investigation by the neighborhood soviet for his "bourgeois appearance," in connection with which, it turned out, the soviet's chairman sought to occupy Orlov's apartment himself.

In the early summer, the Sovnarkom directed the TsZhZO to escalate efforts to clear the city by searching out a new population category, "parasitic elements," also identified as "nonlaboring elements," who were also to be forbidden from living in capital.[72] A month later, the campaign against undesirable social and political "elements" intensified again, with the Mossoviet issuing its first formal schema to guide the identification of "parasites" and more broadly, to sort the city's entire population into fixed categories depending on their occupation and source of income. These two initiatives unfolded in conjunction with the start of the "Red Terror," the campaign of political repression and mass violence unleashed by the Cheka in September 1918, which resulted in the execution, according to officially published data, of 5,381 people that year, 3,470 of whom were killed in the month of September alone.[73]

Alongside the extermination of the Bolsheviks' political and class enemies being mounted by the Cheka, the Mossoviet released a four-part rubric to accomplish the division of the city's entire population into four categories, according to which their access to both housing and movable property would be regulated. The first category was composed of "workers," who were entitled "to stay in the apartments they currently occupied" and "could not be evicted without their consent." They retained "all furniture" in their possession and additionally gained "the right to receive objects of domestic furnishing from among those entering into the accounts of the neighborhood sovdeps." The second category comprised "low level and middling employees" of private and government institutions and enterprises, as well as clerks, teachers, and doctors employed by the state, actors in Soviet theaters, "and the like." They too retained all "furniture and domestic objects" in their possession; they gained nothing. As to housing, they could either remain in their present apartments or be resettled in the neighborhood where they worked, if this was deemed necessary by their local housing department. "Senior employees of industrial, trade, and civic institutions and enterprises, owners of trading and other establishments" constituted category three. They were "deprived of excess domestic furnishings, with the exception of those objects needed for the practice of their specialty." They could also be deprived of their housing, if located in a building "intended for workers," although, like the second category, they were entitled to replacement housing nearby in this event. Finally, there was the fourth and last category, "people living on nonlabor income: industrialists, landlords, and other representatives of the major bourgeoisie." They were "deprived of all furnishings and domestic things to the limit of the most essential." When it came to housing, the order simply went silent.[74] Evidently, they were entitled to nothing.[75]

Unlike the discriminatory campaigns at schools or workplaces, the Mossoviet's rubric was designed to catch up the whole population, and to do so right where people lived. The sorting of all residents by category was operationalized through building committees. They were to present lists of "nonlaboring elements" as well as "parasites" to the TsZhZO, which handed them over for publication to the major daily newspaper *Izvestia* in order to ensure that individuals and households classified in the fourth, worst category in one neighborhood were not able to secure new housing in a different one.[76] Even those at the very pinnacle of Bolshevik power seem to have been caught off guard by the capacious radicalism of the order. Bonch-Bruevich received a frantic letter from a staffer on the Supreme Military Council, V. V. Orlov, whose wife and mother, both of whom were his dependents, had recently been ordered to leave the city within three days "on the basis of the decree of the Sovnarkom

FIGURE 1.1. Vladimir Bonch-Bruevich and Vladimir Lenin explore the
Kremlin, 1918. Image courtesy of Alamy.

on the clearing [*razgruzka*] of nonlaboring elements from the city of Moscow."
Bonch-Bruevich held off on replying directly to Orlov, forwarding his letter
instead to Narkomiust with a pointedly neutral note at the top: "are they required to leave? They are his wife and mother. Bonch-Bruevich." Only after
hearing back from Narkomiust that "people located in direct lines of descent

from heads of household, as well as wives, are considered to be one family, and are not subject to eviction," did Bonch-Bruevich pen an indignant missive to the housing authorities declaring it "obvious that the Sovnarkom decree on clearing the nonlaboring element from Moscow was not under any circumstances meant to destroy families"—although not so obvious that Bonch-Bruevich himself had not needed to ask.[77]

The actual mechanics of identifying a household or certain members within it as parasitic or bourgeois remained vexingly opaque. Again, this was true among the Bolsheviks no less than among the general population. Like other residential complexes in the city, the Kremlin had a building committee. Upon learning of the Mossoviet's order on sorting the population into categories, the Kremlin's own building committee—unpaid and in a hurry like all building committees—"pasted announcements" around the complex asking residents to "inform it who is registered to what category." "This is extremely disorderly," fumed Kremlin resident Bonch-Bruevich. "The building committee should have precise information about who belongs to which category" and should "not ask citizens, 'inform us, please, to which category you belong.'"[78]

But from where, if not from self-identification, was this information supposed to come? Building committees received no guidance beyond the information contained in the initial order, characterizing each category by occupation. How were the building committees to determine who was a senior employee and who was in the middle? Outside the Kremlin walls, methods of identification varied significantly. Based on complaints made to Bonch-Bruevich alleging improper categorization, it is clear that building committees, and especially building commandants, took a number of impressions of their fellow residents into account when making their determinations. These included a person's job, of course, but they also included whether the household had servants—one consequence of this unofficial metric was that a number of female household servants overnight became "relatives" of their former employers, and identifying a female household member as a "relative" raised the question whether that person was, in fact, a servant. An apartment's furnishings and their class significance was another source of friction, as was a resident's general demeanor.

All of these status indicators gave off conflicting signals to the building committees, commandants, and neighbors charged with reading them, which meant that categorization unavoidably became a site of conflict and negotiation between residents and those charged with sorting them, a process with room for threats, escalation, and extraction built in. As a female clerk at the

Sovnarkom named Charykova complained to Bonch-Bruevich, her building commandant initially dubbed her a member of the "laboring intelligentsia." This category did not exist in the rubric invented by the TsZhZO; perhaps Charykova's building commandant invented it himself, or perhaps he borrowed it from unofficial circulation. At any rate, Charykova and her commandant seem to have agreed that it put her roughly in category two, allowing her to remain in the apartment where she lived with her elderly father and, suspiciously, a "female relative," neither gaining nor losing in movable things. Some weeks later, however, the commandant evidently changed his mind. He informed Charykova that she would have to relinquish one room in her apartment, "concentrating" with her father and "relative" into the one remaining room and the foyer, effectively shifting her into category three. Charykova protested his decision on the spot, declaring that she was a "soviet worker," employed by the Sovnarkom, to which point the commandant "mockingly replied that he knew 'soviets' like me, and began to take an inventory" of her furnishings, "adding as a taunt that soviet employees were not supposed to have so much furniture." Things escalated to the point that he threatened twice to have Charykova arrested, stomping his feet and "permitting himself to shout" in her presence.[79]

Tales of aggressive building committee chairmen and commandants filled Bonch-Bruevich's mailbag. Occasionally, he wrote them threatening letters; he, too, threatened arrest if the chairman and commandants did not change their ways.[80] On the whole, however, there was greater concern that building committees would use their power to protect undeserving residents than that they would unjustly, as Bonch-Bruevich wrote of one commandant, "terrorize entire buildings."[81] For this reason, the TsZhZO issued follow-up instructions to its sorting rubric specifying that information developed by the committees was to be verified and supplemented by the neighborhood-level housing departments, which would then "determine the buildings from which parasitic elements should be evicted" and compose a list.[82] In a further step of officialization, neighborhood housing departments hired "controllers" to go from building to building, checking these lists of bourgeois and parasitic elements against reality. This was how the household of Ekaterina Peshkova was outed as "parasitic." Peshkova's apartment, she explained to Bonch-Bruevich, had five rooms and five windows. She lived with her son, her mother, and two other couples; her husband stayed with them "when he [was] in town." Much like the Manuilova sisters, Peshkova seems to have preemptively self-concentrated. "As you see," she confidently explained to Bonch-Bruevich, "we are already above the specified number" (*sverkh komplekta*). But the controllers were un-interested in her apartment's level of concentration. Instead, they demanded proof of employment, which neither she nor one of the men in the group could provide. The man was a "scientist at the Bliumenthal lab," who had un-luckily left his papers at work. Peshkova—though the inspectors did not real-ize it—was the legal wife of the writer Maxim Gorky (né Aleksei Maximovich Peshkov) and immersed in volunteering with the Political Red Cross, a group that aided political prisoners.[83] She too was "deemed a parasitic element and evicted," a "truly offensive" decision, she complained, as she could "not recall a single day that was not jammed with work."[84] Bonch-Bruevich fired off a warning to the NKVD, the housing authorities, the Mossoviet and the Goro-dskoi neighborhood soviet, drawing attention to the fact that "the author of this letter is the wife of Gorky. . . . It is extremely necessary to cancel the evic-tion and requisition of property in express order." [85]

By early September 1918, the pace of redistribution in built space had ac-celerated so rapidly that, according to the Muscovite merchant and diarist Nikita Okunev, "it is only in the rare building that eviction and resettlement has not occurred. At first it was unsystematic," he noted in his diary. But with the introduction of the category system, resettlement had become "practically an art form."[86] Already in May, the TsZhZO discovered in its first (and only) building census that it had overseen the requisition or concentration of 27,723 rooms, resettling 43,247 people in just two months.[87] By early November, the "Central Evacuation Commission," which had been involved in facilitating the government's departure from Petrograd and was now located in Moscow, re-ported to Bonch-Bruevich that "the eviction from apartments being under-taken by neighborhood soviets now bears a mass character." It knew this not because of the great success it had enjoyed in resettling other offices of the state in Moscow, but rather because thirty of its *own* employees had recently been evicted from their new living spaces by order of neighborhood soviets, while one hundred more had received warnings to expect the same.[88] In late November, *Izvestia* published an article entitled "The Bacchanalia of Eviction," decrying the "incomprehensible and unnecessary bacchanalia of eviction that is costing the working people masses of strength and energy and awakens in the masses nothing but ill will." The article resonated so strongly with readers that one, an employee at the People's Commissariat of Transport, sent a clip-ping of it to Bonch-Bruevich, with key passages underlined.[89] The pace of eviction fell somewhat in 1919 from this peak, but it remained brisk, with the *Evening News of the Moscow Soviet* reporting that "housing was allotted to

25,858 people" in the second half of 1919, and to another 27,000 people in the second half of 1920.[90] This data, generally replicated in secondary studies on the topic, presents resettlement as a one-sided process, as if the recipients of housing were the only ones affected by the move. But redistribution was, numerically speaking, a two-way street: it affected those coming in and those going out or being concentrated, suggesting that these figures should be treated as low estimates of total allocation.

Insecurity of tenure over living space was the dominant feature of living in the city, including for those who had only recently been awarded it, even if they were workers or otherwise belonged to the privileged categories. As the transport employee explained to Bonch-Bruevich in a letter included along with the newspaper clipping, he did not object to being ordered to move from one apartment into another one, as he recently had done. This non-objection was, incidentally, a relatively common feature of petitions asking authorities to block a proposed eviction, which typically went on to explain why, in this instance only, eviction was not merited. The stories people told to defend their claim to a space rigorously avoided the slightest whiff of "property" as a legal principle.[91] Instead, they drew attention to elements of their biography or circumstance that merited secure tenure over living space, such as social class, life history, and, quite often, illness: an aunt too infirm to move, a wife persistently sick after giving birth, a bank worker rendering valuable service to revolutionary accounting while also suffering from a neurodegenerative disease.[92] The transport employee, too, had a sick wife, but, atypically, his letter to Bonch-Bruevich emphasized instead the administrative irrationality of his eviction: the neighborhood soviet had ordered him to move from a three-room apartment suited to his household size (presumably based on the norm) into a five room apartment that would "certainly be subject to concentration all over again." He had already weathered a first round of "filling up" in his building some months earlier, during which "people with no particular occupation" had been evicted, while he and other "soviet employees" had been permitted to stay. The distinction between himself and those with no particular occupation made sense enough to the railway employee. But now, he saw a future in which he, too, would be evicted, "and whom are they evicting—a worker just like themselves."[93] It was a future in which, as the old police chief Voznesensky described it, "Moscow citizens were consigned to roam from place to place," in perpetuity.[94]

The speed of evictions was a special source of aggrievement. In November, Bonch-Bruevich received a telegram recounting how earlier that same night, the director of the "housing committee" in a town near Tula "arrived at the house of the secretary of the local party committee (*mestkom*) and demanded that the latter clear out of the apartment he occupied this instant." Failure to comply, the housing official threatened, would result in the tossing of the party secretary's belongings out the window, which is indeed what came to pass. At no point was the party secretary informed as to why he was being evicted, causing the telegram's author special umbrage as it was "in violation of the Sovnarkom's decree from July 27 [1918] No. 158/422," requiring specification of cause. The Sovnarkom had not, at that moment, ruled on the categorization of the population and its application to the disposal of housing. That a decree on the speed of eviction had become necessary, of course, indicates that in many instances, eviction occurred without cause—which is to say that by July 27, measures ostensibly targeting class enemies had proliferated to such an extent that eviction for no reason at all had become commonplace.[95] A subsequent decree required that evictees receive seventy-two hours' notice of their eviction, although a number of testimonies make clear that even this little waiting period was frequently violated. This was possible only because, in tandem with the explosion of eviction, building commandants and the local police who attended evictions increasingly blocked evictees from bringing their possessions with them (see chapter 3). There was no need to give people time to pack.

Many qualities increased a household's risk of being targeted for eviction by its building committee, local housing department controllers, or, indeed, its neighbors: class background and profession, as well as other forms of social vulnerability, such as age and gender (see chapter 4). But with rare exception, no one was fully insulated from the instability created by the effort to redistribute living space according, at different moments, to norms or inverted social hierarchies or both. Regular culls of residents occurred even in the "Houses of the Soviets," buildings that served as official dormitories for senior employees of the Sovnarkom, VTsIK, and other leading institutions in the new party-state.[96] The life history of an apartment's residents mattered a great deal. Interestingly, so, too, did the life history of the apartment itself.[97] Time and again, Bonch-Bruevich and others heard stories of apartments, once occupied by class-enemy residents, having rubbed off on new inhabitants, greasing them with indeterminate counterrevolutionary suspicions that were hard to wash away. In one case, a pair of illiterate young women and their male flatmate, a veterinary nurse who tended to horses for the Red Army, found themselves targeted by the Khamovniki neighborhood police chief; the police chief wanted their apartment. The trio had moved into the apartment in stages over the previous year, but recently a rumor began to circulate that they had ties to the apartment's former owner, "Gvatuv, who ran off with the Whites." Gvatuv was alleged variously to be a distant relative of one of the young women, and to have given them copious amounts of luxurious furniture, charges the trio vehemently denied. As the veterinary nurse, Danilov, explained in his petition for help against the allegations, it was his "personal opinion that all these testimonies [against the group] are ANANYMOUS [sic] as at the 13th police precinct someone came up to me and asked me a question?: 'who got so mad at you and has denounced you?' and I answered him, if you know this person, please, tell me, so I can complain of him, but he did not answer me." Danilov was correct. The Goskon official who investigated his complaint secured a copy of a letter written by the 13th precinct chief himself, Miachkov, denouncing the group as furniture speculators tied to a counter-revolutionary relative who had lived in the apartment before them. Miachkov helpfully offered to take over the apartment and keep an eye on its furnishings while the case was sorted out.[98]

The taint of previous residents likewise figured in the case of a new resident of the Sokol neighborhood, a former military officer injured during the First World War who, in the summer of 1918, moved into the apartment of a man rumored to have "fled to the Czechoslovakian front"—that is, to the Whites fighting in Siberia. The officer's son served in the Red Army and his wife worked as a "soviet employee," both of which should have protected the household against eviction; the brain injury sustained by the officer in German detention left him in constant need of rest.[99] His new building committee chairman nevertheless harassed him with persistent rumors predicting the officer's imminent arrest—not as the officer he actually was, but, improbably, as an "accomplice to the flight of the former owner the apartment in which I now live." Like the veterinary nurse, the former officer suspected a connection between the rumors and a desire to grab his new space: "*this was obviously done by someone's denunciations so as to free up my apartment*," he wrote urgently to Bonch-Bruevich, a family friend. "As you well know, I returned from captivity only on June 14 and the owner of this apartment ran off back in March." Still, he was haunted by the ghosts of the apartment's recent past.[100]

These ghostly associations soon calcified into the administrative practice of neighborhood housing departments. Only with an adequate stock of people or buildings that could be ranked as bourgeois were the neighborhood soviets able to execute their basic mission, which was the continual reconfiguration of society through the built environment. In order to fulfill this mission, neighborhoods had to have at their disposal the necessary raw material. As became clear in an administrative scuffle over neighborhood redistricting in Moscow, which played out in the summer of 1919, built space was this raw material— more specifically, "bourgeois" buildings, a characterization that depended not on the building's material qualities so much as its life history, its association with the bourgeoisie before the Revolution, no matter who occupied the building after it. In an effort to streamline the municipal administration, the Mossoviet proposed altering the administrative borders in the northern part of the city, shifting the First and Third Meshchansky neighborhoods out of the larger Sokol district's jurisdiction. As the Sokol district soviet complained, the change would siphon off "more than half of the municipal economy of the neighborhood." In specific, Sokol stood to lose eleven of its thirty-one tea houses, eight of its twenty cafeterias, more than half of its schools, the two larger of its four libraries, three of its four bathhouses, and 205 of its 298 municipalized buildings. Most important, "the departure of the first and third Meshchansky commissariats from [the Sokol neighborhood] would deprive the latter of any hope of reducing the housing need of workers, as the most suitable buildings are in those commissariats." The buildings that would remain in the neighborhood, by contrast, "have nothing. It is not possible to concentrate them and there is no bourgeoisie there [to serve] as an object of eviction."[101] If the first and third Meshchansky commissariats were shifted out of Sokol, it would be left holding the bag on "sad flophouses" and the people stuck in them—workers.

Given the waves of redistribution that had occurred over the previous year, it was unlikely that the buildings in Sokol that had once contained "bourgeoisie as an object of eviction" still did so at the time of the dispute. As early as October 1918, officials at Narkomfin concluded that the makeup of revolutionary society had changed so dramatically in the previous year that it rendered prerevolutionary sources of information about wealth unusable for the purposes of contemporary extraction—that is to say, there was no point in using prerevolutionary tax records as a guide to material wealth now. "Many representatives of the former bourgeoisie either left the territory of the republic or lost their wealth and sources of income; from the other side of things, new speculators and kulaks were born," reported officials in Moscow. By the end of 1919, no less an authority than the eminent economist I. Kh. Ozerov expressed confidence that the bourgeoisie as a class "was dying out" and could no longer be considered as a meaningful source for taxation.[102] Still, the Sokol neighborhood sought to preserve what it viewed as its share of bourgeois buildings, whoever lived in them, because such buildings, no less than bath-houses and schools, were essential resources of governance in the revolutionary city. Paradoxically, the prospect of governing an all-worker neighborhood was a disaster for the Sokol neighborhood, as it prevented the soviet from performing its constant duty of transformation.

Property Stories for Socialism?

Among other functions, property concepts enable legibility of tenure, making clear what belongs to whom, such that owners need not keep constant guard over their things.[103] According to the legal theorist Carol Rose, the attribute of legibility is the essence of any property system, and what separates owning something from the "territorial," animalistic state of merely possessing it; only owners need not keep constant guard over their things.[104] In revolutionary society, the abolition of private property disaggregated the rights and duties bundled up in belonging, but even more than that, it disrupted the system of signals that broadcast belonging, and the standards by which belonging was adjudged. What happened when revolutionary authorities released the state from its traditional role as the defender of private property rights was thus not simply that actual, existing private property owners lost their rights to things; it was rather that all real and prospective holders of things did, including institutions of the state. The proliferation of competing entities that claimed the authority to appropriate and occupy property intensified the instability of tenure. Principles and proclamations of state ownership to the side, state institutions no less than individuals therefore had to keep constant watch over buildings, in order to ensure they were not poached by another contender at a moment of inattention. This vigilance appeared in how they searched for space as well as in the tactics they devised to retain their grip on slippery buildings, which accelerated and expanded the trajectory of statization itself.

Tactics for keeping hold of space were built into the search process. They involved selecting spaces to which one could make a strong claim. Sometimes strength could be martialed through the process of staking the claim itself, by securing requisition orders from all and sundry or by seeking cooperation from a building's existing owners or inhabitants.[105] Initially, as already noted, it appeared that norms would be useful in staking claims to space. Institutions highlighted an alignment between the floor space of a building and their own needs for space.[106] But it became clear that, while norms might demonstrate that an existing occupant was *not* suited to their space, they did little to secure a hold on a space once it was empty. This was because norms made spaces appear more, not less, interchangeable—more, not less slippery. As a result, although norms appeared frequently in declarations of need for space, they almost never appeared in petitions defending space from seizure by another institution. Paradoxically, claimants to a space typically sought to make it appear less fungible in their appeals. This meant making it appear more particular or unique, which, in turn, meant that in addition to relying upon the formal rules for acquiring space, institutions also sought out spaces over which they could wield a special or unique claim, independent of allocation procedures.

State institutions therefore took to crafting narratives demonstrating the unique alignment between themselves and a desired space, telling stories about their claims to space even in the absence of actual property rights. Efforts to repel requisition unfolded in a similar register, in which competing institutions laid claim to space as the particular stewards of its proper use. Rival claims to property commonly elicit arguments about proper use, which in the legal structures of liberal markets is typically conceived as use that favors the maximization of economic value.[107] But the logic of revolutionary statization turned this argument on its head, as can be seen from the takeover of a large industrial complex in Varvarskaya Square called "Delovoi dvor" ("Business complex"). Delovoi dvor was occupied by numerous "producers of metal, machine-building, dyeing, cloth, paper, cement, and other forms of industry," who kept their "warehouses and offices, that is, their spaces of wholesale trade and administration" there. These were outfitted with "essential specificities that distinguish Delovoi dvor from other requisitioned spaces." The space was fitted to its occupants like a glove to their productive hand, powering industry across Russia. As its occupants explained to Bonch-Bruevich, "Delovoi dvor is the pulsating center of all the living productive forces of the Central trade-industrial region, and at the present moment it can be said—of all of European Russia." At least, this is what Delovoi dvor had been until several weeks earlier, when the two "Main directorates," or *glavki*, responsible for overseeing these very same industries appeared and "announced their pretensions to the space" in entryways four and five, bringing all work at the complex to a standstill.

At no point did the tenants of Delovoi dvor claim a right to space on the basis of lease or legal ownership. Industrial concerns, like individuals, did not tell "property stories" in the idiom of legal property. Instead, the occupants of Delovoi dvor implausibly suggested that the glavki—textile producers Tsentrotkan' and Tsentrotekstil'—were going after their space by mistake, in violation of the basic precepts of economic use. According to the value-maximizing logic of proper economic use, they trenchantly explained, Tsentrotekstil' and Tsentrotkan' "should assist rather than imperil the flow of labor organized here over the course of many years." "Tsentrotekstil' and Tsentrotkan' are the very institutions called upon to distribute the labor products associated with the forms of industry" located at Delovoi dvor. Seizing the space would bring about the "forcible cessation of the work" that the glavki were meant to sustain.[108] This fact was, of course, almost certainly what had brought Tsentrotekstil' and Tsentrotkan' to Delovoi dvor in the first place—it offered up a perfect storm of particular features over which the fabric glavki could lay unique claim. For Tsentrotkan' and Tsentrotekstil', the takeover of the buildings at Delovoi dvor pulled double duty, giving Tsentrotkan' and Tsentrotekstil' a roof over their heads while also driving out of business their private-sector equivalents and bringing the leftover physical plant directly under their control.

In a bid to make spaces less interchangeable, and thus easier to grasp, revolutionary institutions freely mixed claims on the specificities of buildings with claims on the business of the existing tenants. Appeals to the unique qualities of spaces that happened also to house similar or competing organizations became commonplace, so much so that they were aped in confrontations over buildings where no such specificities could truly exist. When Yevsektsiya, the Communist Party's Jewish Section, attempted to take over a nine-room Moscow apartment where a rabbi and his family offered night courses in Hebrew for adults, it argued that "the apartment is necessary 1. Because it is close to the typography on Lyalin Lane" where Yevsektsiya planned to open a journal, and "2. Because"—in a stunning coincidence—"the editorial board [of the journal] requires precisely 9 rooms," the same number contained in the Hebrew school's apartment. "On top of this," the purported night school was really "a zionist religious school [*kheder*] for children," but this fact was included as if to sweeten the deal, which focused purely on the qualities of the space.[109] Because this was merely an apartment and not a manufacturing complex for the textile industry, these qualities were difficult to render with precision. Why did Yevsektsiya need precisely nine rooms? Because "we in Moscow do not have any communist Jews (*yevreev-kommunistov*) who could work at our publication," and precisely nine such people had been plucked "from Kiev, Kharkov, Odessa, and Vitebsk. We must supply them with apartments." Why did the Jewish editors require living space close to the typography? Because the Jewish editors, like all editors, had to "work at night."[110] The family who ran the Hebrew school countered that there were many apartments closer to the proposed typography than its own—and also that their school was not a Zionist kheder. The first claim was definitely true, and the second claim was true enough, at least in the eyes of the Mossoviet's own Department of Enlightenment, which petitioned against Yevsektsiya on the school's behalf.[111] But only the Lyalin Lane apartment offered Yevsektsiya the opportunity to lay claim to a space already housing Jews and being used in the service of (undesirable) Jewish cultural production—the opportunity to consolidate its authority over its functional brief, Jewishness, with its grip on a piece of real estate.

The imperative to find space with narrative resonance ran in both directions: it became possible to go after institutional rivals through their buildings and to go after space through the qualities of inhabitants. Who could say whether Yevsektsiya was more interested in occupying the apartment or disbanding the Hebrew school? In the event, it did not have to choose—it got to do both at once. This was how the statization of the built environment transpired, with institutions coming to Moscow and running their erstwhile private counterparts down, knocking on their doors, and making themselves at home. The qualities of buildings and the takeover of the buildings; the qualities of building occupants and the conversion or displacement of those occupants: these became inseparable plot points in the narratives of possession that the new institutions told one another. Their stories about spaces did not all succeed. They *could* not all succeed. Moscow, like all cities, contained a finite number of spaces; there were good matches and better matches between old and new; there were personal deals, cash deals, and rule-following that intervened. But it was rare that stories like these were not told.

These narratives seamlessly blended the material and the ideal, stressing not just practical utility but social transformation: in seizing space, even from one another, institutions cast themselves as realizing the promise of the Revolution. In its request for Bonch-Bruevich's help in uprooting the existing occupants of what had once been the Orphanage of Metropolitan Sergei, the Commissariat of Enlightenment (Narkompros) incorporated not one but three different stories about its tenure over the building. The first was a procedural claim, citing an order from Bonch-Bruevich's own office ruling in its favor from several weeks earlier. The second was a spatial-utility claim that drew on the building's life history: that in its prerevolutionary life, the building was an orphanage, but its occupants now were not orphans. They were not even children. And the third was a revolutionary claim: that not only was a children's orphanage inhabited by adults, but those adults were invalids, and those invalids were crooks, "involved in speculation on a large scale, accused of such activities as the forgery of documents and an attack on an Ispolkom member while he was attempting to fulfill his duties." Meanwhile Narkompros proposed using the space as "a home for defective children," a project the speculator-invalids had already "delayed by more than two months.[112]

———

More than a transfer of existing property rights over material things from individual owners to the state, municipalization combined attributes of possession with new powers of revolutionary governance. Under its auspices, institutions of the newly formed state (as well as individuals purporting to act in its interest) seized control of material resources and, at the same time, of other people's lives in the service of class war and the consolidation of Soviet power. Apartment buildings served as a central locus of class war in the revolutionary city, not simply as its vehicle but as an embodied guide to sorting the urban population.

Yet, the effects of the municipalization and redistribution of buildings could not be limited to those portions of revolutionary society directly targeted by the Bolshevik ideology of class war and the fight against counterrevolution. The degradation of property concepts made it difficult even for the new owner of buildings, the state, to keep hold of its things. Partly this was a problem of indeterminacy in the rights of possession, that is, of knowing the rules by which things could be held. But it was also a problem of indeterminacy in the subject of property rights. Who was the state, and on what basis were its many instances and employees to possess buildings or built space? By 1920, a large proportion of the population of Moscow could claim employment by a state institution. A professional census conducted in August 1920 found that 231,140 of the city's residents claimed to be "state employees." This represented a fifth of Moscow's total population, and an even greater proportion of its working population; the census did not ask about the size of the respondents' households, making it difficult to judge the number of households with the affiliation. Astonishingly, the Mossoviet alone employed nearly a third of these people.[113] In the absence of positive rights to possession specified formally or informally by revolutionary authorities, state institutions became the clearinghouses for contests and conflicts over space—not just in the housing departments but also, as in the battle for the apartment on Lyalin Lane, in those devoted to all other matters. Allocation and occupancy continued to clog the gears of state, and buildings continued to change hands in an ongoing cycle of requisition.

2

Movable People,
Immovable Things

THE DISPOSSESSION, DESTRUCTION, AND
REDISTRIBUTION OF HOUSEHOLD GOODS

ON SEPTEMBER 17, 1918, a building committee chairman at the edge of Moscow's Baumansky neighborhood awoke to find that his building, No. 3 Sadovaya-Chernogryazskaya Street, had been "fortified" overnight by an unbidden contingent of "security."[1] When asked, the security agents informed the chairman that later in the day, No. 3 Sadovaya-Chernogryazskaya, a gracious if not especially notable apartment building located on the city's busiest thoroughfare, would be "requisitioned" by the so-called "Commission on the Requisition of Building No. 3 Sadovaya-Chernogryazskaya Street." For the next several hours, the residents were plunged into an agonizing wait. Nothing happened. The taciturn security agents milled about. At last, at midday, the members of the alleged Commission appeared; they were later identified as "Maria (Masha) Chernyak, Mazhokhin, and Gorbunov." They ceremoniously presented the building committee chairman with a piece of paper authorizing the building's "requisition" and bearing the stamp of the Railway Neighborhood Party Committee (partkom). The Railway Neighborhood, unlike the Baumansky neighborhood where the building stood, was not a geographical location. It was an occupational association for railway workers. Earlier in the Revolution, the railway workers had formed their own soviet, which was later put on the same footing as a "neighborhood soviet," claiming ambiguous jurisdiction over railway workers citywide. On the same grounds, they operated a Railway Neighborhood Party Committee. After presenting the building committee chairman with the paper stamped by this partkom, the members of the

"Commission on the Requisition of Building No. 3 Sadovaya-Chernogryazskaya Street" announced that, effective immediately, the building's existing committee was dispersed, the building committee chairman relieved of his duties, and a new commandant installed. Conveniently, they brought a candidate for the position with them, a railway worker like themselves by the name of Agafonov. The building committee chairman objected that legally, "the building could be requisitioned only by an order from the [Mossoviet's] Central Housing-Land Department (TsZhZO)," and not by a slip of paper stamped by an "extraterritorial" neighborhood partkom. Agafonov shrugged and suggested that the proper orders would be presented soon enough. In the meantime, the commission members "broke up into several groups" and began the work of "requisitioning" the apartment building, that is, "inventorying both the residents and the property (*imushchestvo*)," demanding the house book (*domovaya kniga*) for the task, and recording all those present, both the Commission members and the apartment-renters or owners of things.

Four days earlier, on September 13, an "Order on the Defense of the city of Moscow" from "parasites" had appeared in the pages of *Izvestia VTsIK*. Per this Order, issued by the Mossoviet, the identification and removal of "parasites" was to be handled by neighborhood commissions formed especially for that purpose by local soviets. The Commission on the Requisition of Building No. 3 Sadovaya-Chernogryazskaya Street was not one of these commissions. It had not been formed as an arm of its neighborhood soviet for the general removal of parasites on neighborhood territory; it set its sights solely on the parasites in No. 3 Sadovaya-Chernogryazskaya. Standing a stone's throw from Moscow's major intercity railway stations, this was a building that the railway workers might have walked past on their way to work, a building they presumably knew. At any rate, inspired but not commanded by the Mossoviet's order, authorized by their party committee but not a territorial soviet, "Maria Chernyak, Mazhokhin, and Gorbunov" appeared at No. 3 Sadovaya-Chernogryazskaya at lunchtime, installed Agafonov as the new building commandant, seized the house book, and set to the task of finding the parasites. By the end of the day, at least three residents of the building—identified occupationally, this being a question of parasites, as "the midwife Elizaveta Ginzburg," the "legal defender Boris Monfor," and the "Lithuanian citizen Ivan Rekets"—had been evicted from their apartments, and in the process also dispossessed of their movable belongings.

It would have been fairly easy, given its quasi-official instigation and the uncredentialed Commission that carried it out, for the requisition of No. 3

Sadovaya-Chernogryazskaya to have escaped notice in official paperwork. That it did not is thanks to a process of review conducted by a former lawyer named Vasily Grigorievich Belsky, among the first employees in the newly opened Central Bureau of Complaint. A department of the People's Commissariat of Government Control, the Central Bureau of Complaint reviewed complaints about the actions of state institutions or personnel submitted by members of the public, after which it made non-binding recommendations to the institutions involved. Its most consequential formal powers were of petition and referral: the power to petition to higher instances in the government, and the power to refer individuals to People's Courts for prosecution or to Chekas for further investigation.[2]

While, administratively, the Central Bureau of Complaint belonged to Goskon, physically it was housed at the Lubyanka, in the offices of the Cheka. This unusual arrangement came about in the hopes of saving shoe leather for the Bureau's staff, insofar as a great number of the complaints received by the Bureau concerned Chekists—in correspondence, the Bureau was sometimes identified as the "Bureau of Complaints about the Ch.K.."[3] Belsky hoped that housing the Bureau inside the Cheka would allow controllers to integrate their work more seamlessly into the Cheka's rhythms, approaching agents only when they were not too "busy" for questions.[4] But the collaboration was short-lived; the following year, the Bureau was evicted from the Lubyanka, under mounting attack not so much from the Chekists, who seem to have tolerated its small staff well enough, as from the new People's Commissar of Government Control, Stalin. (As part of an effort to undermine the Bureau, Stalin alleged at a meeting of Goskon's collegium in September 1919 that the Bureau did very little work, as "the number of complaints it received had fallen to two per day." In reality, Belsky furiously corrected him, the Bureau received 1,264 complaints in July 1919, and 1,328 complaints in August.)[5]

The events of September 17 were among the first reviewed by Belsky, in whose hands they became a "case" put before Goskon and the Mossoviet, eventually reaching the pages of *Izvestia*. These repeated passes at the building's story reflected the profound ambiguity lodged in the events of that day, rooted in the different facets of revolutionary law and lawlessness it embodied: widespread knowledge of official orders combined with their open violation; the claims of individuals to represent the Revolution and wield its authority independent of the revolutionary state; institutional fecundity that blurred the lines between state and nonstate, official and unofficial. The effort to parse the meaning of ambiguous real life events was institutionalized in the Bureau of Complaint, but it occurred widely in revolutionary society. It has a particularly important role to play in writing the history of revolutionary dispossession of movable things, especially things found inside the home.

As one of its few historians, the Belarusian scholar Konstantin Kharchenko, has remarked, "the process of seizing domestic objects has been the least studied [of all forms of seizure during the Revolution]," a fact Kharchenko attributes to "the minimal social sanction for the alienation of this form of property" both before and after the fall of the Soviet Union.[6] This relative inattention is not unique in the annals of twentieth-century episodes of mass seizure. Before the collapse of Soviet power, other major instances of dispossession had gone similarly unexamined, including the aryanization of Jewish property during the Holocaust, for reasons also at play in the Soviet case: a sense that property crimes paled before the extermination of human life with which they were connected; an unwillingness, particularly among those who were involved, to attest or document the seizures, due to the severity of the violations of social mores they had entailed; and, at the same time, a sense among some scholars that drawing attention to property losses would somehow reinforce the hegemony of the liberal property order.[7]

In Europe, the collapse of Soviet power triggered a surge of interest in questions of financial restitution for the crimes of the Second World War and the postwar settlement. This, in turn, spurred new historical research into the wartime and postwar dispossession of property by national governments, political parties, and individuals under the auspices of Nazi aryanization programs, military occupation, and, in the East, Soviet-sponsored state-building.[8] But this wave did not reach the study of revolution in Russia, where, among other differences, the forcible seizure of property, if not celebrated during the Soviet period or after it, was also not categorically understood as theft, retaining instead its connection to the needs and essence of socialist revolution.[9] Kharchenko's own study of the revolutionary "property cataclysm" remains one of the few to examine revolutionary seizure as such, across multiple objects, including movable things.

The challenges to writing a history of revolutionary dispossession of movable things—what would later be known as "personal property"—are both conceptual and practical. Like the seizure of apartments, the seizure of the movable property inside them was only weakly inscribed in prerevolutionary ideology. After the Revolution, vague exhortations to "steal what was stolen" were paired with concrete campaigns to abuse those identified as the "bourgeoisie," including by ransacking their homes and pasting yellow "bourgeois tickets" on their walls.[10] But the restoration of the category of "personal property" in Soviet legal codes in the 1920s meant that, inside the Soviet Union, there was little incentive to valorize or preserve what turned out to be an ideological hiccup.[11] For historians outside the Soviet Union, most notably Richard Pipes, the scarcity of attention to the seizure of movable goods in Bolshevik ideology combined with its ubiquity in practice indicated that seizure was instrumental to the primary goal of political domination, a view premised on the assumption that private property really does serve as the essential repository of the self. In this telling, the Bolsheviks accurately intuited that purposefully stripping away movable property was a form of debasement and degradation that would lead to political demobilization.[12]

More recently, scholars have shown how revolutionary upheaval intersected with the uncontrolled spread of violent crime. Neither the Provisional Government nor, initially, the Bolsheviks, as Tsuyoshi Hasegawa demonstrates, succeeded in containing the explosive increase in the numbers of people who engaged in murder, robbery, and other crimes. Hasegawa associates this explosion with the phenomenon of state collapse and widespread social "anomie" in the year between the February Revolution and the government's move to Moscow in March 1918, during which time, as the police force melted away and soldiers embarked on unsanctioned demobilization from the front, the Provisional Government lost the monopoly on violence required to meet a Weberian ideal of state integrity, as well as its capacity to defend private property.[13] Eric Lohr and Joshua Sanborn likewise emphasize the significance of "state collapse," employing a normative ideal of the state, and highlighting rising levels of violence and insecurity as one key to the "structural demobilization" of urban society that paved the way for the Bolshevik takeover.[14]

The prevalence of theft during the Revolution can be interpreted in several ways, not least because the meanings of theft, alongside those of property and law, were not stable across this period. In addition to reflecting the weakness of the revolutionary state, the skyrocketing incidence of theft in the years after the February Revolution heralded the definitive lapse of the regular order, marking the start of a caesura during which the legitimacy of social and political action sprang not from a legal order but from the exceptional, self-reflexive authority vested in the idea of the revolution itself.[15] This caesura, writes the historian Dan Edelstein, is constitutive of the modern phenomenon of revolution. Indeed, as Edelstein argues, the authority of the revolutionary idea in France in 1789 was explicitly premised on the violation of law, from the overthrow of the monarch to subsequent acts of disorder in the Revolution's name, acts that might be recognized as unlawful and legitimate at once. Much like the staff of the Bureau of Complaint, French revolutionaries sought to parse this disorder, to separate the revolutionary from the criminal, the legitimate from the illegitimate, generating to that end a "secondary normative framework, which had the power of reversing standard moral charges." And much as in Russia, this process stretched out months or sometimes years after initial events.[16]

Revolutionary property disorder also has clear connections to the post-revolutionary order, that is, to features of Soviet governance that endured. A decade after revolutionary dispossession ended, collectivization brought not only renewed efforts to sort the population but also regular depredations against their movable goods—thefts, incorrect seizures, abuses of power, depending on what was seized, by and for whom.[17] The Soviet conquest in Poland in 1939, as the historian Jan Gross argues, opened with a general period of lawlessness and a particular toleration of theft, as though to offer a willfully thuggish introduction to the Soviet manner of rule.[18] Even beyond these episodes of upheaval, the category of theft remained freighted in Soviet society and governance. Theft has often been interpreted as a form of social deviance, including in the Soviet Union, but as the historian Juliette Cadiot shows, it also stood at the center of the Soviet project to create non-private forms of possession, not so much an antisocial aberration as embedded within routine practices of governance and daily life. In part, this status derived from the difficulty of defining and defending state property. With all land owned by the state, for instance, the acceptable practice of fishing hinged on whether a fish was alive or dead when it came into a person's control; catching a live fish constituted acceptable use of a public asset, while obtaining an already-dead fish outside of sanctioned channels represented the theft of state property. Property violations had to be dealt with harshly, precisely because the rubrics of who owned what remained so unclear. And yet, as Cadiot shows, the economic and practical knowledge developed at the intersection of socialist property and theft was also recognized as an important asset by the party-state, and was even prized in hiring for certain professions in the Soviet establishment.[19]

Any reckoning with the vast upheaval in material life of this period therefore has to contend with both the phenomenon of pervasive crime, including theft and official malfeasance, and also with the instability of the idea of property amid a socialist revolution aimed explicitly at upending it. To be sure, tsarist-era laws on theft remained in force after the Bolsheviks seized power.

But, critically, laws on property did not. If in many instances it remained possible to identify thieves of one thing or another, it was often not at all clear who actually owned what—one individual or another, or a new, broadly available third party, the revolutionary state. That is, the revolutionary state after the October Revolution did not simply lose the capacity to protect the private property of its subjects, as a state collapse model would suggest—it also declined to serve in that role, even when it came to movable things that would, after the new legal codes of 1922, gain recognition as the legitimate "personal property" of individuals.[20] The result was that, as officials in Narkomiust observed in 1920, "citizens of the RSFSR are not so much owners of their movable property, that is, their apartment furnishings and things of this sort, as they are its accidental holders, and they can be deprived of even this at any moment by order of the local sovdep."[21]

This extraordinary evisceration of basic forms of legal possession in daily life was accompanied by near-total silence from the central government on the legal contours of revolutionary dispossession, a feature that affected both how it occurred and the way records about it were kept. Prior to April 1920, the Sovnarkom declined to provide formal legal definition for either "requisition" or "confiscation."[22] This silence kept it ontologically adjacent to theft, with which it mixed liberally in practice: as cover for established bandits, who demanded entry to people's houses on terms indistinguishable from those of the Cheka; as cover for officials, who stole for their own benefit in the very same act as they seized on behalf of the Revolution; and as cover for those who, like the self-appointed members of the Requisition Commission at No. 3 Sadovaya-Chernogryazskaya, viewed seizure for their own benefit as identical to seizure on behalf of the Revolution. The proximity of requisition and confiscation to theft, in turn, meant that in many instances (as was sometimes true of aryanization during the Holocaust as well, but not always, because the Third Reich kept the broad legal infrastructure of private property intact) those involved in revolutionary dispossession sought to destroy official records of their activity, or, better yet, to ensure no records were made in the first place.[23]

In the absence of authorizing documents, laws, and prescriptive texts, the chief records of dispossession are the copious documents of complaint—like the ones generated at No. 3 Sadovaya-Chernogryazskaya. These grew to be so numerous that revolutionary officials found it necessary to create several different bodies, including the Central Bureau of Complaint, to reconstruct, formalize, and make meaning out of these revolutionary events and experiences, such as the experience of dispossession. These documents, which are the primary source material for this chapter, offer a window not only onto the experience of dispossession but also onto its aftermath, as those who had been involved in various acts of requisition and confiscation sought to make sense of it all. Paradoxically, and for all the contemporary complaints of dispossession as a "bacchanalia," the revolutionary state kept careful records of the chaos, and of its own failures of documentation and control.

This chapter tells the story not only of how people lost movable things, but also of the revolutionary state's attempt to make such things into state property through practices of physical control, allocation, and accounting, a process that was neither automatic nor ultimately successful. If Bolshevik conquest meant familiarizing the population with depredations against property rights of all kinds, it also posed a new problem of property. The extent to which the socialist state could or would bear property rights for itself or as a stand-in for a collective subject over large and productive objects was a topic of sustained debate in fields ranging from industrial and agricultural management to cultural production.[24] But nowhere were the challenges of sustaining the state as owner greater than in the seizure and disposal of things that belonged in the home. This chapter outlines the key pathways by which the dispossession of movable things, comprising significant domestic objects such as furniture as well as personal items such as clothing or books, occurred in the revolutionary period: first, at the hands of the Cheka, and second, in the course of the redistribution of built space. Following movable things through the official pathways of accounting, storage, and redistribution after their seizure, the chapter finds that the Revolution did not so much transfer property rights to such things from one class of people to another, nor even from one class of people to the state, as it dissipated such rights entirely. Much as was the case in buildings, the transfers of movable goods brought about by this whirlwind of dispossession were unstable and insecure for the institutions of the revolutionary state, no less than for the individuals who had been made into their "accidental holders."

Requisition and Confiscation

The terms "requisition" and "confiscation" were, by 1917, well-established in the Russian lexicon of governance, having been propounded in wartime decrees granting to military authorities the rights of compensated (requisition) and uncompensated (confiscation) seizure. But the practice of requisition and confiscation in the Revolution was something new. For one thing, the salient difference between the two in wartime usage—compensation—had largely disappeared. The wartime regulations established "requisition" as the compensated state seizure of material things deemed "necessary to the war effort." "Confiscation," by contrast, related to the status of the owner; the confiscation of movable property was carried out against enemy or Imperial subjects guilty of treason, and it was uncompensated because it was a punishment.[25] But as seizure grew more widespread after the October Revolution, this distinction began to fade. Both terms continued to be used, even as their respective meanings blurred. One official, upon inspecting the treasury of the Cheka, insisted in a memorandum that it was "necessary for the Cheka to precisely define which objects are subject to requisition confiscation—that is, are not subject to return, and which things sooner or later could be given back to their former owners."[26] As an auditor at the Commissariat of Government Control complained to the People's Commissar Karl Lander in January 1919, "there is no sharply drawn border between confiscation and requisition: what is factually performed is confiscation, which is incorrectly called requisition, as in actual fact the property is taken during requisitions of apartments without any compensation to the owners for its value."[27] Indeed, it became increasingly common for the two to appear as a compound word, as in one Muscovite's demand for the cancellation of the "measures of requisition-confiscation" being applied to his apartment.[28]

The "requisition-confiscation" of movable goods mapped onto neither prerevolutionary requisition nor confiscation. It encompassed some tasks of traditional statecraft, such as revenue extraction, and some tasks peculiar to the revolutionary era, such as social leveling and terrorization. This form of dispossession entered official use through several pathways at once. One of these was carved by the First World War, when Russia, like other combatants, responded to the pressures of total warfare by extending the state's power to mobilize privately owned resources deemed urgently necessary to the war effort. As the war dragged on, official appetites for requisition and confiscation rose sharply across the Imperial state.[29] After the February Revolution, the quality of requisition and confiscation grew more violent, as the state turned to forcible extraction of grain in order to overpower disordered private markets.[30] Meanwhile, regular revenue streams faltered: in the spring and summer of 1917, the collection of taxes plummeted in regions across the country. In some places, people simply stopped paying in anticipation of political change. "Among the peasants of the Tavricheskaya gubernia," or province, officials reported in April 1917, "there has appeared the view that the changed political order of

Russia has removed the old tax system and with it, the state income tax."[31] In other places, officials reported that tax collection had become too dangerous. According to officials in Volhynia, the "half-anarchic conditions sharply increased the risk that the tax collectors will be robbed, which of course makes for great difficulties in composing a staff for this institution."[32]

These two developments—the rise in crime, and the shortfalls in taxation—shared a root cause, which was the dissolution of the police force after the February Revolution. Before the Revolution, police were responsible for maintaining the public order and extensive administrative functions, including the collection of some taxes.[33] After it, not only did the tsarist police force break up, replaced by ineffective city militias, but the eastward stream of tens of thousands of soldiers from the front to their homes in cities and villages, carrying no food or money for the journey, precipitated a shocking surge in crime, especially along the rails and in the capitals.[34] As Hasegawa explains, the causes behind this surge were multiple: they involved not only the breakdown of the basic state function of keeping order and protecting property, but also an actual "expan[sion]" of the "criminal population" beyond the circles of the "professional criminals" who had long worked Russian cities and streets, and who went free in large numbers after prisons were thrown open during the February Revolution.[35] New members of the "criminal population" often came from the ranks of soldiers sweeping back from the front. The literary critic Shklovsky recalled witnessing this change in the men serving with him as they made their way back home, passing through Petrograd and Moscow. Upon encountering one of his former students from the military driving school where he taught that year, Shklovsky asked:

"What are you doing now?"
"Robbing houses, sir. If you'll indicate apartments for us to rob, we'll give you 10 percent."
Strictly a business proposition.
He was eventually shot.

Shklovsky then observed in his student's defense, "[h]ardly anyone was above a little thing like . . . petty thievery of various kinds. The laws had been repealed and everything was being revised."[36] That is, according to Shklovsky, it was not just soldiers who developed a new tolerance for "petty thievery," but friends and acquaintances from his own social circle, who both found themselves in unusual circumstances born of the upheaval, and, at the same time, sensed a shift in the ethical underpinnings of private property as well as the laws. Another episode related by Shklovsky was told to him by a friend, a writer like himself, who one day received a visit from some acquaintances passing through his neighborhood. After a bit of conversation, the acquaintances unceremoniously asked whether Shklovsky's friend had a crowbar. When questioned, they explained they needed the crowbar for cracking a safe; the friend asked no further questions. These people were not thieves, in Shklovsky's telling. They were living through the Revolution, which had opened up new choices and new horizons of possibility. He relayed these episodes not simply to observe that cracking safes had become something ordinary people might find themselves needing to do, but also to emphasize that they displayed no compunction about it—no fear that their acquaintance might ask why they needed to open the safe, whose it was, whether they were stealing the contents or had lost their key. Needing a crowbar to crack a safe had, in the circumstances of the time, become regular.

This is not to say that people did not try to protect themselves against such depredations and were not dismayed by them—they did and they were. "In Moscow," reported the merchant and diarist Nikita Okunev, "and, I think, across all Russia now have been adopted the very strongest bolts, iron and wooden shutters, and, as in the olden days, especially at night, everything is so locked up, so closed, so bolted, peopleless, dark . . ." Even so, "there has been such a mass of armed attacks that one cannot even count them."[37] The problem was that locks did not offer protection against thieves to whom you opened the door, thieves who entered apartments under the guise of performing what emerged after the October Revolution as a new, quintessentially revolutionary act—a "search." After October, the city police collapsed all over again, the flood of self-demobilizing soldiers continued unabated, and economic conditions further deteriorated. "They are robbing endlessly and promiscuously: palaces, sacristies, townhouses, clubs, from the rich, from the poor," Okunev lamented in the winter of 1918. "In the past few days my mother, my brother, and his daughter have been robbed." Thieves came at night and took everything in the family's closets: "overcoats, clothing, dresses and shoes—all that 'bourgeois' accumulation."[38] But perhaps the biggest reason crime surged after October was that thieves could now ride the back of the search.

Even searches with official sanction from revolutionary organs commonly occurred at night. Their stated purpose was to uncover criminal and counterrevolutionary activity, both which could be identified by the same indicator— the possession of weapons. Over the previous months, large numbers of people had acquired firearms. These included self-demobilized soldiers, garrison soldiers, erstwhile members of defunct city militias, affiliates of revolutionary parties and institutions, as well as many people who picked them up by chance, as they were distributed from stockpiles broken open after the February Revolution. Searches therefore began as searches for weapons. In the first few weeks after the October Revolution, they were conducted by the Red Guards; in early December, searching migrated over to the new "extraordinary" commissions—in Petrograd, these were Vladimir Bonch-Bruevich's Extraordinary Commission against "pogroms," and Felix Dzerzhinsky's Extraordinary Commission against Counterrevolution and Sabotage, the Cheka; in Moscow, Rogov's Commission and the assorted, loose military units attached to the Mossoviet. On February 21, 1918, shortly before the Sovnarkom left for Moscow, local authorities put the city on a war footing. "Criminals" were given 24 hours to leave town or "cease their activity," after which anyone caught engaging in "pogroms against private houses, institutions, or administrative buildings," or acts of robbery would be shot by firing squad. All "organizations" without express permission "to be armed" were ordered to turn in their firearms and ammunition. Carrying a weapon without permission was made grounds for arrest.[39]

The search would become a ubiquitous tool of revolutionary statecraft for the next four years. It was, at the same time, very easy for people who did not have revolutionary credentials to imitate, whether "professional thieves" or soldiers returning from the front, who may have already participated in the looting of houses in the course of their retreat.[40] People like Okunev had little hope of discerning whether the pounding on their front doors signaled the start of a violent encounter that would end in their arrest, the start of a violent encounter that would end in the burglarizing of their home, or some combination of the two. Another resident of Moscow that winter, a former officer named Vasily Klementyev, later recalled:

> There was not one night when searches were not conducted in Moscow. Who and by what right forced themselves into rich apartments, stole all kinds of things, beat people up, murdered the inhabitants, was not clear. 'Lawful organs of power' did this, 'bands of anarchists' did this, and the most ordinary bandits did this. . . . They limited themselves to the declaration that they were searching for counterrevolutionaries. They searched for counterrevolutionaries, and took the valuables.[41]

Thieving and searching made up the two sides of this sharp degradation of security, not simply in public spaces, but in homes during the Revolution.

Domestic space became highly permeable, what with the space-seekers, parasite-finders, and inspectors demanding entry during the day, and the Chekists and their mimics barging in at night. In an effort to aid apartment dwellers, revolutionary authorities early on instituted a permitting procedure for searches. Local soviets printed small slips of paper, with space to write in a name and date, granting the bearer the right to "search" any space, valid for a day, week, or month. Permits were to be signed and stamped by neighborhood authorities. One neighborhood Cheka encouraged residents, improbably, to verify the signatures of local officials before allowing entry to their homes. Forged search permits and false papers were common. One night on Plyushchikha Street in Moscow, a group of young men serving in the Moscow Military Commissariat (*voenkom*) forced their way into the apartment of a janitor by brandishing their identity papers before his illiterate wife, claiming they were search permits. The young men were neither professional thieves nor wholly-authorized searchers, but something in between: as one later testified, "the voenkom gave us the same instructions as always," to go "where we knew there were weapons." This was their usual mission, which led them on this night to the building on Plyushchikha. One of them had worked there as a plumber before joining the voenkom and recalled that the building committee chairman had a pistol left behind by the building's previous owner. But the building committee chairman was not at home the night of their search, and so they held the janitor's wife until her husband and some other men living in the building returned. The men from the voenkom were arrested for allegedly demanding a bribe to go away. The police commissar subsequently released them on the condition that they be fired from the voenkom. But several days later, the men were back on Plyushchikha street. "They appeared again the building," the police commissar complained, "in this way clarifying that they were not cast out of service. I repeat, they are out again plying their craft." The "craft" they were plying was the search.

As the story from Plyushchikha Street makes clear, within the first few months of Bolshevik power, a number of institutions made recourse to the search as a tool of governance. These included the revolutionary security organs, such as the Chekas, voenkoms, and police, but they also included institutions inherited from the old regime, regular departments of local soviets, municipal administrative organs, especially their finance departments. Cut off from the center and in need of money, municipalities concocted an array of novel taxes to fund local government and pursued new methods of collection. In early 1918, before policies had been set in Moscow, the city of Kazan announced a plan to recapture "unjust profits" earned by merchants during the war by establishing rigorous surveillance of commercial activity. The surveillance included railroad checkpoints and reports prepared by proprietors of furnished rooms, detailing the activities of their guests.[42] Other municipalities turned their attention to domestic movable property. The city of Vyatka, among others, instituted a "one-time property tax" on all citizens and juridical people in early April 1918, applied to buildings and their movable contents. In some places, the one-time property tax was meant to distinguish between property serving commerce and property serving the "personal needs" of the household. Thus, in the Shenkursky region, which also instituted a local "one-time property tax" that spring, the provisions explained that "small machines such as sewing machines and the like that do not serve for production but for the needs of one's own family are not subject to assessment," while sewing machines that did serve in production were taxed, as well as all things "intended not for the personal needs of their owner or his family but for sale." But in Vyatka, the city soviet decided to levy the tax from *all* objects within the home, including those serving exclusively personal needs. The soviet noted explicitly that "furniture and domestic fixtures" should be assessed, as should "all objects of luxury, watches, gold and silver, domestic livestock, carriages, paper money and other paper instruments of value." The only things freed from assessment were items narrowly connected to the spiritual or physical upkeep of the person: "icons, other objects of the cult, books, dishes, samovars, utensils, clothing, shoes, and linens." [43] The punishment for nonpayment was "confiscation" of all property, a term unfamiliar enough in early April 1918 that local officials explained: "when a payer refuses to pay the tax, the soviet confiscates /seizes/ his property."[44]

How would such taxes be assessed? How could local soviets possibly come to know the contours of a household's property in the intimate detail such a tax would require? Through the rough instrument of the search. Irregular assessments in the spring and summer gave way in the fall of 1918 to a countrywide "Extraordinary Revolutionary Tax," also known as "The 10-Billion Extraordinary Tax on Kulaks, Speculators, and People Living off Unearned Income and the Like."[45] The tax was assessed according to the old-fashioned system of apportionment (*razvyorstka*), calculated on the basis of prerevolutionary tax revenues by region; regional governments then assigned sums to lower organs, all the way down to the district or neighborhood soviet. Some finance officials lamented the return to assessment by apportionment, which had been triumphantly superseded before the Revolution in planning for the first (and last) collection of the Empire's income tax in early 1917.[46] At a regional congress of finance commissars held in Penza over the summer of 1918, several delegates declared their intention to mount a "progressive income tax against speculators" using more sophisticated income declarations, but were curtly informed by the plenipotentiary from Moscow that "we do not have the ability to [implement such a tax] right now."[47] Instead, local soviets charged "extraordinary tax commissions," which had been formed on the same principle (and often with the same personnel) as the Committees of the Poor, with the job of assigning and collecting tax bills from individual residents.[48]

Beyond the sum due, localities received little instruction as to the methods of collection or enforcement. In Moscow, city finance officials boasted of employing a combination of personal "declarations," extreme penalties (death) for lying on declarations, and robust surveillance by "extraordinary district commissions" to sniff out people hiding wealth.[49] Domestic property formed a major basis for assessment of the tax, and also for punishment in the event of nonpayment. After an alleged timber speculator, Mendel Podnos, fled the city of Arzamas to evade his tax bill, not only was his wife Khava arrested by local police, but their household was confiscated save for "those things necessary for the tax non-payer and his family" to live. Agents of the Cheka as well as the local Communist Party cell approved the sale of the family's "items of excess and luxury."[50] Near the city of Tver, a tax commission levied a 1,000-ruble tax on the citizen Zhurkin, who happened to have stepped away from home when the commission arrived to collect. Zhurkin was sent for and "truly arrived within the hour," a complaint explained, but the commission had already "broken in through the window in all haste and performed a confiscation of things." The commission seized household goods valued at 2,726 rubles, which were subsequently resold at public auction for 3,242 rubles. After Zhurkin arrived, the commission members "permitted themselves to threaten him with a revolver, demean him with crude language, and blame Zhurkin for inciting their behavior." Before leaving, they set an act about the "confiscation" of Zhurkin's tax bill, but not about the fact that the confiscation occurred "in kind" rather than in money, nor—ominously—"about what happened with the piglet," the fate of which remained "unclear, but was such that once they themselves became convinced they should return it this was no longer possible."[51]

By the fall of 1918, the Commissariat of Government Control judged searching, requisition, and confiscation endemic across revolutionary institutions. "In Moscow as in other populated places of Soviet Russia, the requisition of the movable property [*dvizhimoe imushchestvo*] of citizens is occurring by the orders of various powers," Goskon reported. Such property was being seized "by all kinds of orders, by separate groups, by the directive of individual people, their right to do so founded on the simple fact of their having been sent [to the place of requisition] with several armed people." Objects as diverse as "foodstuffs, being held by their owners in quantities excluding even the suspicion of speculation, . . . clothing, domestic objects, valuables, money, artistic objects, books, and objects bearing a scientific importance" were being requisitioned, absent any common method or standard for seizure. The People's Commissariat of Enlightenment issued orders concerning the registration of art and historical monuments; other governmental bodies on the "accounting and distribution of furniture," still others on permissible quantities of food, warm coats, gold, and the seizure of quantities above those norms. "None of these are united," the department observed, "nor do they agree with one another, nor do they cover all forms of requisition or set out foundations for it."[52] The Commissariat of Enlightenment searched for works of art, setting its own definition for what constituted a work of art; the Commissariat of War sought out military equipment, which turned out to include domestic collections of historic uniforms, firearms, and knives, and large quantities of items brought back from the Eastern Front by demobilized soldiers. Objects like these, Goskon observed, had been "alienat[ed] for the benefit of the government." But it was not clear what this meant, or which institution represented "the government" in receiving, accounting, and utilizing seized goods. Summing up the legal uncertainty surrounding the practice, the department posed these questions, none of which would receive an answer from the Sovnarkom for almost two years: "To whom, through which body, where, and for which goals are requisitions of personal possessions permitted, and what kinds of possessions exactly? On what basis, equalizing or otherwise, and by which norms should requisition be conducted? How are the requisitioned goods to be understood—with whose permission, in what order, and by which norms should they be distributed, and on whom lies the responsibility for all of these goods from the moment of their alienation for the benefit of the government to their release from a storage space, either to individual people or institutions?"[53]

Searching and seizing, as Goskon's memorandum complained, had become the revolutionary industry par excellence; many institutions competed to wield the power to requisition and confiscate movable property in the home. But only one institution had the sense that searching and seizing belonged to it and no other: this was the Cheka. The Cheka claimed this right gradually, using several tools to further its monopoly, including the opening of investigations into other state institutions it perceived to be stepping on its toes. In the spring of 1919, a "Railway Cheka" centered on the Petrograd-Warsaw Line opened a case against members of a local soviet in Pulkovo, just south of Petrograd. The Railway Cheka accused the Pulkovo Soviet and the Pulkovo Committee of the Poor of systematically mounting sham searches in order to seize, among other things, bicycles. This appears to have been true, and is at the very least extremely plausible: at one household, residents later testified that when they asked to see the Pulkovo Soviet employee's search permit, they were told to "quit chitchatting and hand over the bicycle."[54] Searching and seizing in this manner was also precisely what the Chekas themselves did, as will be seen in greater detail below.[55] The problem with the Pulkovo Soviet's behavior then was not that it was searching with the express purpose of extracting bicycles, as the Railway Cheka would allege, but rather that the Pulkovo Soviet was doing so without the mediation of the Railway Cheka or in competition with it. The Railway Cheka presented its findings to the Petrograd Ispolkom for further investigation, with a suggestive note that the "mood in the region, for analogous reasons, is as known to you."[56] In claiming its monopoly on seizure, the Cheka also claimed a monopoly on the power to establish which seizures were legitimate—to answer a question that had been dogging revolutionary society since October. Requisition, confiscation, crime on the job, or theft? It was the job of the Cheka to find out.

A State within a State

If searching and seizing in the Revolution had become a "craft," as the police commissar on Plyushchikha Street attested, then the Cheka was its master practitioner. In his first statement to the people of Moscow, Dzerzhinsky announced that he viewed the primary task of the Cheka as "the battle for the total security and inviolability of all persons and property from arbitrariness (*proizvol*) and violent aggressors and bandits."[57] There were, however, no guarantees on the security of persons and property against nonarbitrary nonbandits; searching and seizing, that is, was not the problem, just its misapplication. In the short term, the arrival of the Cheka deepened Moscow's crime wave, offering the city's bandits yet another identity to assume as they went marauding about town. As Dzerzhinsky acknowledged when he announced especially severe penalties for those "presenting themselves as Red Guards and members of different revolutionary organizations," agent of the Cheka quickly became one more identity for the city's professional thieves to assume as they went about their business.[58]

For this borrowed identity to bear weight, however, it had to have support in reality; that is, the behaviors of the bandits and the Chekists had to more or less coincide. Allegations that Chekists profited personally from requisitions dogged the commission from its founding. On March 24, 1918, just two weeks after the Cheka arrived in Moscow, the newspaper *Novoe Slovo* published an article entitled "The Secrets of the Investigative Commission," alleging that agents of the Cheka had engaged in acts of "theft during the search," "ransoming in return for freedom," and the arrest of people positioned to expose those crimes. Dzerzhinsky angrily rebutted the charges in public circulars, as did his deputy Ya. Peters, who bore primary responsibility at that time for the Cheka's finances.[59] The latter published a broadside against the Cheka's "opponents" who, "under the influence of heated polemics have even declared those who enter the extraordinary commissions are people 'prepared to take up banditry.'"[60] The next month, however, Peters gave an interview acknowledging "the extraordinary abundance of crime on the job" among Chekists themselves, especially "at the beginning," due to "the fact that during the period of the February and October Revolutions, the criminal elements pillaged the courts," destroying their files and making it impossible to verify the criminal histories of the Cheka's new hires.[61]

Claims that the Chekists did not simply behave as criminals but were themselves card-carrying members of the Russian Empire's criminal underground nevertheless persisted long past the Cheka's "beginning."[62] Imprisoned members of the Socialist Revolutionary Party bitterly recalled witnessing agents at the Lubyanka and other places of detention entering "the cells of murderers and thieves, and joyfully call[ing] out their names, and they would kiss each other and the criminals would be free. And then they would often join [the Cheka]."[63] Exiled Socialist Revolutionaries remembering their time in Soviet prisons obviously had any number of scores to settle with the Bolsheviks, but other observers, watching other moments of Soviet institution-building, made a similar point—of the Soviet occupation of Western Belorussia and Western Ukraine in 1939, Jan Gross observes that Soviet security services had a reputation for absorbing people known to their communities as criminals.[64] Hiring direct from prison cells also had a history in the prerevolutionary political police, the Okhrana, mainly in the recruitment of informants.[65] After the Revolution it persisted, despite the strong official preference for staffing

Chekas with Communist Party members.[66] Indeed, even Communist Party members were made vulnerable by service in the Cheka, a fact sagely observed in 1919 by one of Dzerzhinsky's own deputies, M. Ya. Latsis. According to Latsis, the Cheka had not so much hired thieves as made them: "no matter how honest a person was," Latsis wrote, "or what a crystal-clear heart he possessed, the work of the *Chrezkom* [alternate abbreviation of Cheka] comes with virtually limitless rights and unfolds in conditions that act powerfully on the nervous system."[67]

The Cheka's first forays into the seizure of personal possessions and household goods occurred within days of its founding. Initially, the Cheka conducted searches as auxiliaries to arrest. On December 9, 1917, three days after its creation, the Cheka conducted a search of the apartments of five men accused of "blackmail."[68] As the mission of the Cheka expanded to include counterrevolution, speculation, and other forms of malfeasance, however, searches were increasingly conducted for their own sake.[69] The first major searches of commercial enterprises were performed in Petrograd in late December.[70] By January 14, 1918, the commission had accumulated a sufficient quantity of "things taken during the course of arrest," as it called them, to order a newly appointed member and Left Socialist-Revolutionary Pyotr Sidorov to open a storeroom for requisitioned goods.[71] Minutes from the meetings of the Cheka indicate that by February, it was in possession of quantities of gold and silver, "confiscated for the profit of the Soviet Republic." It had seized cigarette cases, watches, and wallets, as well as a Ford, a Mercedes-Benz, a "Bezho" (likely Peugeot), and numerous trucks. Like other agencies of the new government, the Cheka termed these seizures "requisitions" and "confiscations."[72] Around this time, evidence also began to appear that the Cheka was making use of the objects it seized. A "requisitioned" batch of shoes was distributed directly to employees, at a rate of one pair per person.[73] A few days later, the commission ordered that "confiscated weapons can be given out only to members of the VChK, its soldiers, and its intelligence officers."[74]

The Cheka seized both goods and money, the latter in the form of "fines" and "ransoms." The assessment of fines and ransoms was sometimes precisely targeted, as in the extraction of 35,000 Finnish marks from a businessman, A. D. Grinberg, just moments after he secured special permission from the Commissar of Finance to withdraw it.[75] At other times it arose by happenstance, as when agents went looking for a man they had already shot and arrested his brother, who lived next door, by mistake. When the family realized there had been a mix-up, the agent on the case—with whom they had made direct contact—agreed to free the brother, but only in exchange for a ransom of several hundred thousand rubles.[76] Judging from a sample of intelligence reports prepared by the Moscow Cheka (MCheka) in the summer of 1919, it was reasonably common for a search not to produce an arrest; only twenty-five of the sixty-seven searches conducted by the MCheka's Special Department from July 4 to July 28 yielded arrest. By contrast, forty of the sixty-seven searches yielded material objects "found," "discovered," "confiscated," or "seized." Just twelve searches yielded no objects (the remaining fifteen had no report). Searches commonly expanded from their original targets to include neighbors, friends, and passers-by, caught up in a rising whirl of requisition and confiscation. Particularly after the neighborhoods formed their own Chekas, searches were often conducted on a building-wide basis. A report from early September 1918 announced that a recently created neighborhood Cheka had performed an overnight "search at building No. 36 (the former Beliaev) Dolgorukovskaya Street in the Sushchevsko-Mariinsky neighborhood. The search was conducted from midnight until six in the morning. Fifty-three apartments were searched."[77] Neighbors also experienced each other's searches through the practice of the "ambush" (zasada), in which agents staked out the apartments of people they had arrested, waiting in the vestibule or just behind the door for several days in order to arrest anyone who came by to check on friends.[78] One former prisoner, having spent a year in Moscow's Butyrka prison, claimed that people arrested in ambushes or otherwise by "chance" made up a majority of the prison's population.[79]

If, after investigation, the arrested party was cleared of suspicion or released without charge, the goods seized in the course of the search were sometimes returned and sometimes not. Many people freed from the Cheka sought the return of their seized possessions in the belief that being cleared of charges nullified the grounds for the seizure. In the case of the Muscovite Voyevodsky, suspected of speculation in tea and metal, a search of his apartment revealed no tea or metal, but it did turn up two hundred *funt*s of caramel. This was seized upon Voyevodsky's arrest, and it was not returned upon his release, despite the fact that it had belonged, he claimed, not to him alone but to all the residents of his "concentrated apartment," and was stored in a shared cabinet.[80] The apartment of Yevdokia Yuryeva, an employee of the Rumyantsev Museum, was searched the day after her arrest. Missing after the search were her typewriter and camera—objects in great demand within state offices—as well as a gold brooch, an American fountain pen, a stamp with her initials, and a black leather portfolio, which she never got back.[81] Both Voyevodsky and

Yuryeva were cleared of charges and released; the seizure of their goods functioned something like a tax for having passed through the Lubyanka and availed themselves of the Cheka's services.

Complaints against the Cheka, and requests for intercession with its agents, appeared immediately. Many people addressed themselves to the Cheka directly, which opened a bureau to field the large numbers of queries it received concerning the whereabouts of loved ones who had disappeared into the bowels of the Lubyanka.[82] This bureau refused to answer questions about the disposition of seized goods, however, leaving most of these inquiries to the Sovnarkom, the soviets, and once it was formed, the Central Bureau of Complaint. The complainants were not just individuals who had been searched and arrested at home; as the Cheka irately informed Bonch-Bruevich in late April 1918, the attitude toward its agents within the people's commissariats, among high-ranking employees of the revolutionary state, left much to be desired when it came to searching and seizing.[83] "We inform you," a group of Cheka department heads wrote to Bonch-Bruevich, "that we are constantly meeting with obstacles in the commissariats, and also with the city police, as we go about the discharge of the duties laid upon us. When we arrive at a Commissariat and present our permit to search and arrest, so that it can be registered with the commissar, the latter addresses us with indignation, what are you here for, why is this necessary, what kind of order do you have that gives you the right to a search, and then seven to ten people show up and gather around, and then we end up losing one to two hours on something that should have happened quickly in one second."[84]

It was against this backdrop that Bonch-Bruevich began a regular practice of circulating complaints he received about the Cheka's activity to the Mossoviet, Sovnarkom, and other institutions. He also commonly forwarded the complaints to Dzerzhinsky himself. On May 23, 1918, Bonch-Bruevich sent Dzerzhinsky a note authored by an engineer named Kirpichnikov, in which, as Bonch-Bruevich explained, "the author notes what you too would undoubtedly recognize as irregularities [nepravil'nosti], for which reason would you not consider it expedient to form a special commission from representatives of the Commission for the Battle [i.e., the Cheka], the Commissariat of Justice, and the Commissariat of Internal Affairs to work up some changes in the activity of the commission with the aim of alienating these kinds of irregularities that you yourself recognize." The following day, Bonch-Bruevich sent Dzerzhinsky two more petitions he received, one inquiring about an arrest, which Bonch-Bruevich characterized as "obviously criminal," and the other about a citizen

Shpanov's 240 rubles, his wallet, and "other things, copied here," taken in the course of his arrest and not returned upon his release from the Lubyanka.[85]

Bonch-Bruevich's needling went on for several more weeks, until in early June 1918, the Sovnarkom at last "discussed the question of making use of confiscated resources and property located at Dzerzhinsky's commission," and resolved that "all confiscated resources and property enters into the use of the [State] Treasury and is distributed to the suitable commissariats."[86] In this manner, the property entering the Cheka would become the property of the revolutionary state as a whole, represented by the State Treasury and the commissariats, which the Sovnarkom charged with putting seized things to use. (The Mossoviet sought to override this order, demanding that all goods seized by the VChK on the territory of the city—municipalization at work—be brought immediately to the Mossoviet.)[87] To be sure, the Sovnarkom was already putting seized things to use, as were a number of other state institutions, which called upon the Cheka to supply them with things they needed from its store of seized goods. Bonch-Bruevich himself, on the very day that the Sovnarkom passed its resolution mandating the transfer of money to the Treasury and things for use by the commissariats, asked whether the Cheka's Economic Department might provide the Sovnarkom a selection of men's and women's shoes, fabric, preferably black, light gray, and light brown, one women's jacket, and several pairs of children's sandals.[88] Over the course of 1918, the Sovnarkom asked the Cheka to issue it hard-to-find perishables such as sugar and port; thirty revolvers for its couriers; and typewriters. The Cheka was generally willing to provide what was asked, when it had the stock—sometimes even agreeing to seize objects on request, such as typewriters, if the requesting agency could provide an address where such might be found—so long as it was not leather suits, the Cheka's sartorial calling card. Bonch-Bruevich requested twenty-nine such suits, twice: "jackets, pants, caps, and gloves," for "agents serving the Sovnarkom's Administrative Directorate." Alas, the Cheka demurred, there were enough only "for the essential needs of employees of the commission."[89]

The Sovnarkom's resolution in June 1918 represented a formalization of the central state's claims on the Cheka's bounty. In this, the measure failed. There is no evidence that the Cheka began turning over either goods or money after June, although the heightened attention on its finances did prompt the hiring of its first bookkeeper, Shepelinsky, in early August. Around the same time, as E. H. Carr and others have recounted, the first in a series of attempts to trim the Cheka's sails got underway, culminating in its reorganization in

FIGURE 2.1. The Lubyanka Headquarters of the Cheka as it appeared
before the Revolutions of 1917, prior to which the building housed the
All-Russia Insurance Company, an assortment of smaller insurance firms,
assorted workshops, and a restaurant. The insurance companies were
evicted from the premises to make way for the Cheka in 1918. Source:
(https://commons.wikimedia.org/w/index.php?curid=8709009)

December 1918 and the abolition of the death penalty—temporarily, as it
turned out—in January 1919. As Carr observed, the Cheka evaded these efforts, thanks in part to its support at the pinnacle of power, and in part to its
prodigious ability to shapeshift, giving the impression of change without
changing or while actually growing stronger.[90] An enabling feature of the
Cheka's autonomy was its financial independence. For the first several years
of its existence, both the VChK in Moscow and its branch organs lived almost
entirely off their seizings. Indeed, as an agent sent by Goskon was about to find
out, up until August 1918, the Cheka seemed to have almost no financial relationship with the central state—this, at least, was how things seemed. It was
difficult to ascertain, because, in fact, the Cheka had no account books whatsoever from before August 1, and neither before nor after that date did it consent to maintain a budget.

These and other shocking discoveries were made in the fall of 1918, when in
a concession to the pressures of reform, Dzerzhinsky allowed Yu. A. Ozerevsky,
a representative from Goskon who was also a Communist Party member (and
trained in double-entry bookkeeping to boot), to make at least two visits to

the Lubyanka headquarters and review the Cheka's account books, such as they were. As was typical of a visit from a Goskon controller, Ozerevsky's visit involved acts of physical review, an audit of the account books, and most important, extensive interviews with the staff of the institution under review—in this case, the chekists.

What Ozerevsky found inside the Lubyanka was so extraordinary that he deemed it "necessary to offer the general impression made upon me during my visit," so as to give his readers—who would have included members of the Sovnarkom—a sense of the fantastical space. He started with the Storage Department, on the ground floor:

> A former wine cellar [the space had previously housed a restaurant, the famous *Billo*], damp, packed with everything imaginable, poorly guarded, with broken glass windows through which a man of average corpulence could fit. The storeroom has a tendency to expand, that is, to become more and more stuffed. Goods, such as cotton and other materials, are rotting, shoe leather is growing moldy. . . . There are things stored in boxes, suitcases, and other packing materials there, sealed up. What is stored inside of them is unknown to the proprietors of the storeroom, and I would wager that no one else knows either.[91]

Of the Lubyanka's treasury, Ozerevsky likewise thought it "necessary to give a few of my impressions as to the nature of the chaos that reigned prior to our appearance at the VChK," he began, "and to say a few words about the very space."

> The treasury of the VChK is located on the first floor, with unsecured Venetian windows opening onto the courtyard of the commission. It is divided from the main corridor of the commission by a light glass door, and from the general space of the Storage Department by thin glass barriers that do not reach the ceiling. Any employee of the VChK can enter, as there are no special passes required and no special security guards in place.
>
> The interior: a small space [15 × 15], packed with random objects that have nothing to do with the treasury—three large, warped canvas boxes that had come in, according to the administration, from the Storage Department; rolling around on the floor were bags of silver coins and boxes full of money.[92]

Perhaps the most astonishing feature of these spaces, however, was how little their minders seemed to know of them. Discovering badly kept account books was a routine occurrence for a government controller like Ozerevsky. The surprise was discovering no account books at all. When Ozerevsky arrived at the Lubyanka, he was introduced to its treasurer, Rutenberg, and the new accountant, Shepelinsky. Ozerevsky judged both men competent; Shepelinsky was also versed in double-entry bookkeeping.[93] But neither could tell Ozerevsky what or how much the Cheka had in its depositories. Rutenberg was unwilling even to hazard a guess at how much was in the cashbox he controlled at the present moment.

At first, Ozerevsky recounted, the "ignorance on the part of the people charged with directing the treasury of how much was stored in it" struck him as "strange"; but "upon further acquaintance with the work of the treasury, this occurrence turned out to be completely explicable: in fits and starts, hundreds of thousands of rubles pass through the treasury, and neither Rutenberg nor (his assistant) Bits nor the other assistants manage to count all these sums up and record them in an account book."[94] Rutenberg finally ventured a guess of "something more than two million rubles" in the treasury, but when Ozerevsky set to a thorough count he found more than two million rubles in just the first safe. Four "emergency cash transports" to the People's Bank followed in quick succession, and by the end of his visit, Ozerevsky had found more than five million rubles in cash, plus 6,930 gold rubles, 13,559 silver rubles, 38 funts (36 pounds) of silver bars, and 29 poods 30 funts (1,074 pounds) of copper coins.[95] "I will be so bold as to say that only our arrival forced the commission to free its treasury of the excess cash," Ozerevsky dryly noted. When he returned on November 4, it was as if his previous visit had never happened. "As is obvious from the act attached here, the turnover of the VChK's cashbox is enormous." In the month that had elapsed, the treasury had accumulated nearly three and a half million more rubles, not including the holdings of the Storage Department. By November 20, it was up to "7,518,675 r. 93 k. The current account grows daily due to ransoms and fines."[96]

In the months that followed, local agents of Goskon branches appeared at local Chekas to perform similar inspections. Their findings mirrored those at the Lubyanka. Upon entering the treasury in Astrakhan, for instance, inspectors were met by a solitary clerk sitting before a table piled high with gold, silver, and copper coins. "In response to my question, what is all this money," the inspector reported, "the treasurer Motin answered that these were the sums that had been coming in for the past few days but had not yet been entered into the books."[97] When the auditors asked to review the "account book of valuables," they were presented with "a book that resembled not the account of an institution but rather a simple scrap-paper notebook in which were recorded, aside from valuables and money, all imaginable domestic things seized from citizens, clothing, and also shoes."[98] In Perm, local Goskon inspectors were escorted into nearly identical spaces: sheds storing actual sacks of gold and silver shoved up against "bins of rags and various trash"; boxes of "broken" jewelry mixed in with simple metal utensils.[99]

The Cheka's inattention to its burgeoning wealth made it ripe for the kinds of predation prophesied by Latsis; many chekists turned out to have other than crystal-clear hearts. Efforts to rein in the pursuit of personal interest during the performance of official duties appeared almost immediately, with the introduction first of "search permits" in the spring, followed by "search protocols" in the summer of 1918. Protocols of seized objects were to be composed in the presence of the resident and the building committee chairman, the latter having been required to attend all searches performed by the Cheka in his building; both the resident being searched and the chairman had to sign the protocol, copies of which were deposited with all parties. The protocol was meant to constrain the party being searched no less than the search agent: only objects recorded on the protocol could be complained about as missing after the fact. This stipulation, as one complainant observed, required some mental gymnastics. "In accordance with the text of the protocol," he noted, "I have the ability to demand the return of the goods taken from me by the commission [Cheka], excluding those that are not described on the protocol. Consequently, I do not have the right to demand any kind of compensation in the case of the loss of some object or another during the search. This concerns me a bit," he explained, "as I had 8,000 rubles in cash at home" that was now missing. "I cannot establish the loss as a legal fact," he concluded, "as in order to do that it would have been necessary to have had, prior to the search, a verified inventory list, which, of course, not a single private person possesses, nor do I."[100]

The introduction of the protocol thus did not confer genuine protection against sticky-fingered search agents. But it did shape the encounter between the search party and the party being searched, primarily by cementing the practice of negotiation around how much would be seized and how much recorded. An unusually complete account of these practices survives from the city of Vyatka, where a chance intervention from Dzerzhinsky prompted a thorough investigation of the local Cheka. The investigation began in mid-December 1918, after someone discovered a severed finger lodged in a snowbank in the courtyard of the building that housed the Cheka, apparently open to passers-by. Empowered, perhaps, by the recent spate of efforts on the part of outside institutions to exert control over the Cheka, as well as Dzerzhinsky's wish to discipline local Chekas to Moscow's orders, an investigator from Narkomiust was sent to review the Vyatka Cheka following public outcry over the severed finger, tangible evidence of what was rumored to have been a horrifically violent and horribly unjust mass execution conducted in the courtyard on the night of December 10. But even with the power of Moscow at his back, the Narkomiust investigator found local officials unwilling to talk to him; the chair of the ispolkom explicitly forbade him from attempting to speak with members of the Cheka. Ordinarily, things would have stalled out there, but in this instance, just as the investigator was preparing to abandon his investigation, a train carrying Dzerzhinsky (and Stalin) arrived in the city, on its way to Perm, where the two leaders had been sent to stiffen Soviet defenses against the Whites. The investigator secured an audience with Dzerzhinsky, who personally ordered the local chekists to speak with him.

The investigator's point of departure was the severed finger, which came from the right hand of an older adult man "of fairly developed intellect," an examining doctor concluded, as the skin and nails were so clean. The doctor could not tell whether the finger had been severed before or after the man's death, but a witness to the clean-up after the execution of the twelve prisoners attested that the finger was cut off after its bearer had died. After shooting the men, the chekists "ransacked their pockets, and one, noticing a ring on the hand of one of the shot men, with a strike of his sword sliced the finger off him which was found the next day. . . . They divided up the property of the executed men among themselves right there on the spot" before carrying the bodies on a sleigh to the river for disposal. Eventually, the investigator narrowed his attentions onto a circle of chekists around an agent named Gutkovsky, who had already been fired by at least one other Cheka in the region before arriving in Vyatka; his previous boss, a steely old Bolshevik from Petrograd, claimed to have sentenced Gutkovsky to death for malfeasance. But Gutkovsky fled before the sentence was carried out, then got himself hired at the Vyatka Cheka.

The investigator produced a detailed account of Gutkovsky's activity in the days leading up to the execution, which included an account of his searches, composed through interviews with the people Gutkovsky and a group of chekists around him had searched. These testimonies indicate that negotiations as to how much got seized and recorded occurred throughout the search: in one, a grocer's apartment, Gutkovsky and another chekist seized "the meat, all of it, and the pork." Only when the grocer "asked very hard did they give back half of that, about 30 funts." Upstairs, in an apartment the grocer rented out, the encounter was between two women, the other chekist's wife—who was not an agent, but evidently participated—and the tenant's wife, who was home alone. The agent's wife pocketed the family's silver coins "without counting," at which point the tenant's wife "literally began to beg her to return the silver money." She complied. "[A]gain without counting, this woman pulled a few coins out of her pocket and gave them back to my wife," the tenant testified, "but it turned out this was just 75 kopecks." Before the search, the family had "12 rubles 65 kopecks total," meaning the woman took 11 silver rubles and 95 kopecks. The search protocol, by contrast, recorded a seizure of 8 rubles 0 kopecks, and the tenant's wife signed it: this meant that 75 kopecks went back to the tenant's wife, 3 rubles 95 kopecks went to the agent's wife, and 8 rubles went to the Vyatka Cheka. The negotiations were repeated, with the same outcome, over the family's 15 funts of meat.[101]

While Gutkovsky was identified by his fellow chekists as an outlier in the violence and baldness of his misdeeds on the job, other testimony makes clear that his conduct conformed to broader patterns at the Vyatka Cheka. Interviews with prisoners hinted at the agency's "systematic terrorization of the citizens of Vyatka, in the literal sense of this word." One peasant imprisoned at the Cheka headquarters reported witnessing the beating of another, brought in from a nearby village, "to a level where he coughed blood, and then on the second or third day after that, agents took the peasant out to his village, and seized from him fifty-five chickens, a cow, and half a pig, loaded it up onto three horses and brought it back to the Cheka. We the imprisoned watched as they unloaded." Afterward, according to a chekist who corroborated the story, the Cheka's cafeteria served chicken at every meal for two days straight.[102] Gutkovsky appears to have embraced the impunity offered up by his position to an unusual degree, even when attempting to follow the rules: early on in his first Cheka position, Gutkovsky was caught by his previous boss in possession of a silver reticule he allegedly took during a search. When pressed, Gutkovsky insisted the reticule belonged to his wife. Subsequently, he saw a young woman wearing a gold watch, and—evidently hoping to do things above board this time—he turned to his boss, the steely old Bolshevik from Petrograd, asking his permission to purchase the watch from the young woman. His boss, mystified, replied that "this was his own private affair, in which I had no desire to involve myself, but that if he was thinking of buying the watch from her, I would advise him to get her signature attesting to the fact that the sale of the watch was from her perspective voluntary." Soon after, the boss received a statement from the very same watch owner, alleging that Gutkovsky had come to her apartment in her absence, "given her small children ONE HUNDRED rubles, and taken the gold watch." To the woman's shock, and that of his boss at the Cheka, he then left a slip of paper with the small children bearing his own signature, not the woman's, stating that he had bought her watch (making no mention of the precious metal) for the paltry sum of one hundred rubles.[103]

Whatever Gutkovsky's idiosyncrasies, however, his practices were broadly integrated into the accounting system at the Vyatka Cheka, where, according to a junior agent working in the treasury, chekists routinely handed in sums that *exceeded* what they had recorded on their search protocols: "I will even say the number, 6,000 rubles, but in the protocol he wrote 5,000"—and the treasury employee knew this because Gutkovsky had turned over the excess 1,000 rubles along with the 5,000 on the protocol. Perhaps Gutkovsky was sloppy, or perhaps the done thing was to spread the haul around.[104] Either way, it turned out that the practice was common, and could be found at the Lubyanka, too. To Ozerevsky's astonishment, despite the fact that the Lubyanka treasury's doors were made of glass and its walls did not reach the ceiling; despite the fact that "any employee of the VChK can enter" and there were "no special security guards in place"; despite the ease with which chekists could have walked off with a portion of their haul, every audit Ozerevsky performed revealed not a deficit, but a surplus of cash as compared to what the accounts suggested. It was the opposite of what one might expect in the case of corruption or cooked books: in one Cheka inspection after another, there was always more money than what was written down.[105]

The Cheka could live off its seizings, as Ozerevsky discovered, both because it seized so much and also because it had no budget integrating its funds into those of the central state. This lack of full financial integration was not so unusual within the Soviet structures of governance: it was a status the Cheka shared, most notably, with the Communist Party in this period. Indeed, according to the party member and Narkomfin official who served as a personal conduit between the party's Central Committee and Narkomfin between 1918 and 1922, Arkady Osipovich Alsky, Goskon and its successor Rabkrin did not even have the right to review the financial transactions connecting the party to the government. (When the Rabkrin agent whom Alsky had blocked from performing such a review complained that it was "not acceptable that one or another order of the CC of the party should be mandatory for someone outside the party, even more for an institution of the state," Alsky proposed involving the Cheka in the question, invoking a threat of arrest.)[106] In the case of the Cheka, its financial independence speaks not so much of the incapacity of the Sovnarkom to assert itself vis-à-vis the Cheka, as it does to the Cheka's durable and tolerated role in Soviet governance, as what contemporaries had already begun to call a "state within the state."[107] Ozerevsky sought to remedy the Cheka's irregular bookkeeping by proposing that it compose budgets for submission to the State Bank or Narkomfin, of the sort that other institutions made, showing not only what the Cheka earned and spent but also what it gave and took from state coffers. But the Cheka's collegium declined. The matryoshka-doll quality to its finances, in which not just resources but information about them nestled inside individual administrative units, held true all the way down—Ozerevsky observed it not only in the dynamics between the Cheka and the central government, but inside the subunits of the Cheka, too. The accountant of the Economic Department, responsible for funding the Cheka's operations and paying its wages, told Ozerevsky that he had once tried to "separate" his department's accounts "from the general accounts of the entire VChK," thus establishing a distinction between what the Cheka spent on itself and the wealth it accrued through its nighttime labors, "but these efforts," Ozerevsky reported, "are not met with sympathy by the administration of the VChK."[108]

When the Cheka did agree to open itself materially to other institutions within the state, it was principally as an entrepreneur. This too was fairly common among institutions that claimed the power to seize, as evinced in the numerous public auctions of seized goods held by local soviets.[109] As already noted, the Lubyanka supplied the Sovnarkom with material goods upon request. At least one institutional client, Bonch-Bruevich at the Sovnarkom, appears to have been mildly taken aback at being subsequently presented with a bill for the items so distributed, although he saw it was paid. As always, it was a similar story in the localities, where the Chekas drove hard bargains with other branches of the state. The Povenetsky Cheka, outside Arkhangelsk, developed a habit of "confiscat[ing] goods from residents, and then giv[ing] them to the district provisioning committee, at which point it demanded payment for these goods, to one specific person, which was fulfilled by the provisioning committee. For what reason payment was required for confiscated goods, and why to that person in particular, rather than the treasury, was not clear," an inspector reported.[110] The Cheka also sold seized things to its own employees. Its Economic Department operated a shop in Moscow's historic commercial district where it sold requisitioned goods "to employees at prices lower than production costs [!]," Ozerevsky complained, leaving open the question of how the production costs of seized things might be calculated (see chapter 4). "And second," he continued, "the money earned from the sale of this property is not entered into the income of the republic, but rather remains with the Economic Department, and the latter, apparently considering it its own, spends it as it sees fit." On August 20, 1918 (the only day for which Ozerevsky could find records), the stores turned a profit of around 33,000 rubles.[111]

Having witnessed not only the Cheka's petty entrepreneurial activity but also the incredible waste within its storerooms, Ozerevsky was flummoxed by the Cheka's unrelenting urge to seize. "The VChK is first and foremost an investigative instance, and all claims on the right to utilize the property and sums once wielded by the arrested should be alien to it," he inveighed. "The VChK is a weapon of Soviet power for the battle against counterrevolution and its manifestations, it is not a commercial enterprise, the motto of which is: assess as many fines and perform as many confiscations as possible." Through greater accountability and intelligent management, the Cheka might contribute not only to the material well-being of the socialist republic, but to the creation of a new type of economy, in which even petty possessions were elevated by being endowed with social value. Instead of simply amassing bags of money and piles of objects like any other "Commercial enterprise," the Cheka's collected resources could be put to use: "fabrics go to Tsentrotekstil," Ozerevsky imagined, "and medicines to hospitals, and so forth. . . ." Instead, the Cheka served "simply as a warehouse of goods," where things either rotted or were sold to the chekists.

Why then did the Cheka seize so much? As the Cheka's role in the Soviet institutional firmament expanded, so, too, did the role of its dispossession, undertaken not only as punishment of counterrevolutionaries real and imagined, but also in the service of the Cheka's own material needs and those of other institutions. Yet the indifference toward its accumulating wealth that so shocked the inspector Ozerevsky casts doubt on claims that the Cheka seized with the express aim of enrichment.[112] Instead, the Cheka seized as much as it did precisely because it was singularly unfocused on enrichment, or any other use or disposal of seized things. This disinterested quality to the seizure of movable goods is easy to miss, because the scale of the seizure was so monumental; surely, one would think, the seized things were as important to the Cheka as they had been to their owners. But the scale of seizure was, in fact, a symptom of the disinterest in the objects themselves, a disinterest so widespread that it produced what Kharchenko has aptly dubbed a "crisis of overseizure," as revolutionary authorities seized things they did not detect a need for, on a scale far greater than they could hope to use.[113] The monumental scale of seizure testified rather to the scale of change the revolutionaries sought and the size of the project of social leveling on which they had embarked, in service of which the seizure of movable goods was performed.

Accidental Holders and Official Owners

Besides the Cheka, the chief pathway by which people lost their things during the Revolution was through the resettlement of living space, superintended by local soviets. And as was the case with the Cheka, the increased permeability of domestic space occasioned by the barrage of postrevolutionary searches and inspections amplified both formal and informal variants of resettlement-related dispossession. For the first few months after the Bolsheviks arrived in Moscow, the extraordinary surge in the requisition and resettlement of built space overall was not accompanied by a corresponding set of rules or laws specifying how this should occur, a deficit felt with special force in the arena of movable property. When Moscow and Petrograd did turn to the regulation of movable property, they arrived at strikingly different sets of rules, reflecting two distinct visions for the underlying legal and ideological status of furniture, personal possessions, and other things found within the home. But in both cities, local orders on the seizure and redistribution of movable things, once they appeared in the spring and summer of 1918, came into immediate and heavy use, called upon by local authorities as well as residents to govern the confusing new landscape of possession and dispossession.

Predictably, these regulations failed to address themselves to the profusion of novel situations created by resettlement. Moreover, in seeking to sway the outcome of one situation or another, those involved made recourse to a number of other principles, besides the legal or regulatory ones, including the imperatives of Bolshevik ideology, the defense of the Revolution, all-purpose "expediency," and broad notions of social justice. Even in cases where the regulations were not observed, however, they were constantly invoked by officials and residents alike. The legal and illegal, formal and informal, official and unofficial dimensions of dispossession were inextricably enmeshed, often in one and the same dispossessive encounter. What made dispossession so bewildering to the many who witnessed or participated in it was that it was both lawless and lawful at once.

The pairing of legal and illegal acts of dispossession within a single dispossessive encounter animated the investigation of events at No. 3 Sadovaya-Chernogryazskaya (where this chapter began). The midwife Elizaveta Ginzburg, the lawyer Boris Monfor, and the nobleman and Lithuanian citizen Ivan Rekets complained of the doubled quality of the "searches" of their apartments, during which, in one and the same visit, some of their possessions were "requisitioned," some "confiscated," and still others "stolen." In part, of course, this perception reflected the ambiguity around the terms themselves. Boris Monfor complained, of his winter coats and dressing gowns, that the "commission for *requisition*," in fact, "*confiscated*" his things, evincing a familiarity with the wartime distinction between requisition as compensated seizure and confiscation as uncompensated seizure, which was no longer consistently in force. Rekets protested that since he was "a Lithuanian citizen under the protection of Germany," his property should not "be subject to confiscation" at all; furthermore, he alleged that "a burglary was committed"—that is, in the course of the search resulting in the illegal confiscation of his property, additional pieces of property, in this case a watch, had been stolen. The distinction hinged on which objects had made it onto the "inventory" of his possessions. Rekets was no better or worse off from having some of his things recorded on an inventory list and others, such as the watch, left off it. He invoked the distinction instead to convince his readers that what happened to him was criminal.

Who was the victim of this crime? Was it Rekets, the watch owner, or was it the state, deprived of its due by dishonest agents? This was the question posed directly to Bonch-Bruevich by an old acquaintance from the city of Tula, a woman named Materina. Materina lost both her apartment and her possessions in stages, over the course of several months. Starting in the spring of 1918, people began coming through her apartment, on inspections, bearing mandates, and soon enough, to take up residence in it themselves. The first to arrive were the Tokarevs, a husband and wife. They were followed by another couple, the Bufetovs. Next came the Zapevalovs with the wife's old mother; then the Kolokolov brothers and their two wives; and then a single woman, Maria Lauktina. Each new arrival occasioned a new inspection, and each inspection was accompanied by spontaneous requisitions of "various household goods, as well as two ethnographic collections." Over the months, Materina noticed little things missing here and there. By the time they "finally evicted me, Materina" on September 10, the newcomers had "seized all the furnishings." As Materina observed, the absence of "decrees on the topic" left her unable to judge "by which principles" they "took all of my household goods into their private ownership (*chastnaya sobstvennost'*)." She denounced her former neighbors as "rogues of revolution," or "criminals of revolution," or people who "presented themselves as revolutionaries" but in reality were "living off the revolution like the most inveterate kulaks."[114] Bonch-Bruevich agreed, demanding the Commissar of Internal Affairs "investigate this matter immediately and once and for all put an end to this arbitrariness, when people having no right to it tear into houses, throw out the owners, and seize other people's property. These sorts of events are completely unacceptable in socialist Russia."[115]

But as Materina's case makes clear, dispossession was inseparable from eviction. To some degree, this was by design: the seizure of movable things occurred punitively, as a further layer of material damage imposed on people losing their place to live. In September, the Mossoviet formalized this principle in its order on the allocation of built space, dividing the population of the city as a whole into four categories, with the first category, laborers, to be offered new housing; the second, petty employees, protected from eviction; and the third and fourth categories subject to concentration and eviction. (See chapter 1.) The order further provided for the disposal of movable goods inside the apartments of people being resettled: it explicitly forbade the "sale and transfer of the movable property serving a space" as a general rule, a provision intended to impose further material losses on the third and fourth population categories, subject to eviction from their homes. The following month, in October, the Mossoviet issued a more detailed order on the disposal of movable property and furniture, roughly reproducing the provisions for eviction in the realm of movable things: to wit, households in the first category were entitled to receive necessary household goods; those in the second category were merely protected from requisition and confiscation of their things, neither gaining nor losing. Those in the third category were to be "deprived of excess household goods with the exception of those necessary for the practice of their profession," while households ranked in the fourth category, living on "nonlabor income," lost even those; they were to be "deprived of all household goods down to the most essential."[116]

Other residents of an apartment or a building, no less than local authorities, commonly enforced this rule upon those who were being concentrated or made to leave. In many cases, they had a vested interest in doing so, as it was the other residents, particularly if they were newcomers, who were most likely to benefit from the immobilization of an evicted person's movable things. This was especially true in cases of concentration. In one such case, a man complained upon realizing that his new neighbor, the apartment's original inhabitant, had moved all of the furniture out of the rooms slated for concentration; according to the new resident, the man had plenty of furniture for himself, meaning his action was clearly due to spite. Several weeks later, the new resident wrote back to the authorities, before anyone had a chance to intervene, reporting that the two men had settled the matter satisfactorily on their own.[117]

Given how common resettlement was becoming, however, the Mossoviet's provision forbidding the sale or transfer of furniture increasingly meant that dispossession also simply followed from eviction, or any kind of displacement—not as a measure of targeted punishment, but merely as a by-product of being made to move house, or choosing to do so. The curious phrasing of the Mossoviet's order, explicitly forbidding the "sale and transfer of the movable property serving a space," evinced a rising sense that movable things "served the space" rather than the people who lived in it. In this new reality, the things would stay put, while the people living among them were consigned to perpetual movement. Three employees of the Turkestan Irrigation Administration who had arrived to Moscow in the fall of 1918, for instance, were given twenty-two hours by the neighborhood housing department to leave their apartment, a timeframe that was possible only because they were forbidden from bringing anything with them except their "linens and dishes."[118] Their eviction was precipitated by no judgment against them or inspection of their class status; the neighborhood housing department simply wished to remove them from the space and install other people in it, furnishings and all. A few days after that, a man preparing to move in with his parents was expressly forbidden by his neighborhood housing soviet from taking any furniture with him, despite the fact that he was neither being evicted nor judged a parasite, but merely sought to move house.[119]

What was left out of the Mossoviet's orders on furnishings was a positive sense of which entitlements people might expect, and on what terms, according to their population category or otherwise. Only through the imposition of limits on *seizure* did the Mossoviet offer any concrete specifications as to what individual households could possess. In November 1918, the Mossoviet issued a stand-alone order "On the requisition, accounting, and distribution of furniture." The purpose of this order was to limit the exercise of requisition and confiscation against households in the third category, from whom, it was now declared, only "beds with mattresses, sofas, divans, chairs, armchairs, desks, kitchen tables, dining tables, buffets, wardrobes, commodes for linens, wash-basins, and shelves" could be seized. "No other objects of domestic furnishing are subject either to account or inventory, and following that, to requisition." Moreover, if a household possessed multiples of the objects on the list, its members could select from among their possessions which of their beds or desks, for example, they preferred to keep for themselves. This limit on seizure functioned as a kind of shadow norm—not a positive entitlement, but a brake on dispossession. According to the order, a household could possess—that is, it had to be allowed to keep—one dining table, desk, buffet, and wash basin per household, and one bed and one sofa per person. Single people could choose one armchair and two regular chairs; families could choose two armchairs as well as a commode, a wardrobe, and an additional sofa.[120] This was the closest thing to an official norm of household possession in Moscow before 1920, when the city's own Central Housing and Land Department (TsZhZO) complained about the absence of a "norm for the distribution of furniture among the laboring population," to which it attributed "the lack of system and chaos that reigns in the organs controlling the supply of workers with furniture."[121]

Petrograd offered a counterpoint to Moscow's system, although as it turned out, the existence of positive norms did not eliminate the "lack of system and chaos" of which the Muscovites complained. In contrast to Moscow, the Petrograd Soviet's orders on requisition and confiscation identified "norms" of consumption with a directly equalizing aim. According to the Petrosoviet, they were designed to ensure "the identical usage of furniture by all citizens living in Petrograd" regardless of social status. In an effort to provide "fully equipped and comfortable apartments" to all, the city outlined a "normal usage of furniture" for a room of six by nine square arshins occupied by one person, including dining table, sofa, wardrobe, bed, a side table, a mirror, two armchairs, and four regular chairs. Items like rugs and kitchen utensils above the norm would be provided exceptionally—in demonstrated cases of, say, "cold floors"—and "in a measure not exceeding natural demand," which was nowhere fixed. Any furniture not explicitly listed as part of the "normal usage," including "desks, buffets . . . and cabinets of all possible constructions" was characterized "as not being essential," but could be distributed "if available" and for "general use on a communal basis." Some apartments, the order allowed, might have "rooms bearing special names." The order presented these rooms as alien and unfamiliar to the new environment, requiring definition:

"'dining rooms,'" the order explained, might occur in apartments "of six or more rooms, inhabited by ten or more people"; "rooms bearing the name 'office' can have a place in the apartments of people occupied with intellectual labor"; "rooms bearing the name 'nursery'" might be found in apartments housing three or more children between the ages of three and 15, by agreement of all residents. Reflecting the rapid disappearance of such spaces in real life, as whole families took up residence in the dining rooms and offices of yore, the order specified that an apartment's own inhabitants would not be the ones to identify a given room as a dining room. This would be done, instead, "according to an investigation performed on the spot in each separate case."[122]

Finally, besides the question of how much people got, there was the question of what their tenure over movable things meant. Did those who received seized things now own them? Few questions cut deeper when it came to the meaning of the Revolution itself, what it was supposed to accomplish, and what the society that came out on the other side of it was supposed to look like. The differing programs of Petrograd and Moscow encapsulated two distinct answers to these questions. Moscow's orders divided the population into unequal categories, suggesting that their goal was not equalization of revolutionary society but punitive reversal of the social order. The Mossoviet's orders governed dispossession, but not possession; they dealt in what could be taken but not what could be kept, and on what terms. The Petrosoviet embraced the goal of equalization. Petrograd also addressed, albeit incompletely, the question of possession of seized goods. In the winter of 1919, it released a table specifying the "normal usage of furniture" for all inhabitants and what would-be consumers should be charged to acquire this normal quantity of things from city-held stocks. To be sure, not everyone had the right to acquire things at the city stores; official allocation was limited to those classified as "workers," "employees," or the "unemployed" registered on the labor exchange. The families of Red Army soldiers and sailors were to receive necessary objects for free, while everyone else paid normed prices, which were to be garnished incrementally from their paychecks. No one, not even workers, could acquire whatever they wanted; requests were supposed to be approved by building committees.[123] Prior to full payment, furnishings were not considered the "full property (sobstvennost')" of their possessor: they could not be removed from Petrograd under any circumstances, and could be moved within Petrograd only with permission from a "store agent attesting to the necessity of the move." Once the objects had been fully paid for by their new possessors, the furnishings were characterized as the "full property (sobstvennost') of the owner

TABLE 2.1. "Normal usage of furniture" and acquisition cost in rubles (Petrograd, Winter 1919)

Number of People	Table	Sofa	Armchair	Chair	Cabinet	Commode	Mirror	Bed	Buffet	Up to Rub.
1–2	up to 3	up to 1	up to 2	up to 4	up to 1	up to 1	blank	Acc to number of people	1	2000
3–4	3	2	4	8					1	4000
5–6	4	3	6	12		3 objects			1	5500
7–8	5	4	8	15	2	3 objects			1	7000
9–10	5	5	10	18		2			1	8500
						5 objects				

Source: TsGASP f. 1000, op. 2, d. 136, l. 15.

(*vladelets*)."[124] As Larissa Zakharova has shown, many people who acquired seized goods, through city stores or otherwise, came to think of these objects as their own.[125] But there were significant obstacles to acting on that belief. Insofar as private sale was still forbidden, and permission was still required to remove the object from city limits, the designation of objects as the "full property of the owner" primarily meant that "owners" did not have to compensate the soviet in the event of an object's damage or loss.[126] The privileges on offer were those of usufruct-plus—the right to use a thing and to ruin it.

Throughout the revolutionary period, turnover in space and furnishings remained brisk, such that progressively fewer households could be assumed the prerevolutionary owners of things. Even as their tethers to prerevolutionary owners faded, however, movable goods remained things weakly held—as difficult to grasp for the soviets that laid claim to them as they were for the people in whose possession they now stood. Toward the end of 1920, searching for new sources of revenue, and at a moment when the Sovnarkom turned to the task of endowing movable property with legal status, Narkomfin decided to renew a category of tax it had not made much use of over the previous three years—a property tax. Its proposed property tax would be levied on "movable property exceeding the consumption needs of its possessor," invoking the many indirect taxes on luxury objects that had been levied by localities over the previous years, as well as the consumption norms gestured at in Moscow, Petrograd, and many other cities. But upon review, Narkomiust declared that such a tax was impossible. Not only was the tax "unlikely to give any financial result," due to the complexity of assessing the value of "household goods, clothing, linen, dishes," things that were in the possession of "each citizen"; not only would it "call up the need to create an enormous technical and control apparatus, which would be given the right to tear into the intimate life of each citizen, calling up the need for extensive correspondence, many complaints, and attract malfeasance"—the biggest problem with the tax, according to Narkomiust, was that its legal basis was moot due to the fact that "citizens of the RSFSR" could still be "deprived" of their movable property "at any moment by the local sovdep." Narkomfin had no right to tax people on their temporary, insecure possession of movable things, over which they stood not as owners but as "accidental holders."[127] But if the citizens of the RSFSR were not the owners of movable property, who was?

In its first year in power, the Soviet state declared itself to be master of all kinds of material and immaterial things, in its own name and on behalf of the people. These orders were piecemeal and came in stages. But when it came to

personal possessions and movable goods inside of buildings, such orders simply did not appear. No decrees specified for whom such things had been alienated and, in particular, as the Goskon inspector complained in 1918, which
state institution bore "responsibility for all of these goods from the moment
of their alienation for the benefit of the government to their release from a
storage space, either to individual people or institutions."[128] As a legal matter,
then, the nature of the state's tenure of movable goods therefore remained
quite unclear. Practically speaking, however, state institutions claimed the authority to wield and control these objects in a number of ways; state possession of movable goods emerged as a backdrop to their seizure, even if it was
never trumpeted as a special goal.

The earliest orders on the seizure of movable property envisioned their
entry into state control as a physical passage. The alienation of movable things
and their transfer to the state, it was hoped, would be marked by the state taking physical possession of requisitioned household goods and furniture, removing them from homes and transferring them to warehouses before releasing them back into circulation. In Petrograd two institutions emerged to
perform this task—one called "Gorprodukt," a distribution agency that also
handled regular (nonseized) consumer goods, and the Petrograd Commune,
a consumer cooperative. Some months later, the management of seized goods
was assigned to a separate body, the so-called Inter-institutional Commission,
comprised of staff from the other two. In Moscow, the management of seized
movable things remained at the level of the neighborhood soviets, in "Furniture" or "Requisition" subdepartments within the neighborhood housing department. But in both cities, physical possession proved extraordinarily difficult to accomplish. Goskon inspectors observed early on in Moscow that the
objective to move seized furniture and housewares into warehouses was le-
thally "hard to fulfill," as there were never any trucks.[129] By late November, the
Mossoviet had already changed tack, declaring in its order "On the requisition,
accounting, and distribution of furniture" that the seizure of furniture would
be marked only on paper, in the form of an inventory, while the objects themselves could instead "remain in the apartment with the new residents under
their personal responsibility."[130] Petrograd, facing similar difficulties, held
tighter to the notion of physical transfer as the chief attribute of state possession. To that end, Petrograd availed itself of a tool borrowed from the police,
used in criminal investigations: sealing entire apartments with strips of paper
and wax, until such time as their contents could be inventoried and moved.
Sealed spaces were not unheard of in Moscow, but because of the premium on

space in the new capital, it was more common there for authorities to seal only rooms rather than entire apartments. This made for many anxious, unpleasant living arrangements, as new tenants feared being held responsible for the contents of neighboring rooms, shivered because of open windows in sealed rooms, and tiptoed around sealed doors.[131] By the end of 1920, more than nine thousand apartments seized from the bourgeoisie had been sealed in Petrograd for inventory by the Inter-institutional Commission, while the commission, which had only two staff members, had managed to inventory just three hundred.[132]

The project of inventorying the contents of sealed and seized spaces ran up against all the usual administrative hurdles of the revolutionary era: first there were no blanks on which to record the inventories; then there were blanks, but the inventory-takers grew confused about the task. They filled the forms in variably, sometimes writing "requisition" or "confiscation" in the space meant to denote what was happening to a given property, and sometimes writing instead what kind of property was being seized—"movable," "furniture," or something of their own design. A large number of transfers, of course, had taken place before the requirements to document them were in place. In November, the Mossoviet's Economic Department demanded that the neighborhoods provide it with "weekly information about the furniture released to all institutions and private people, so as to have a precise tally of all furniture given out according to demands and for what sum."[133] This request recast the seizure of movable property. Suddenly, it appeared that transfers that had occurred between households, new residents and old, as an expression of the class war were meant to be understood as redistributions out of *state* coffers, and seizures of *state* property, requiring accounting and payment to the state (not the original owners) for the property so gained. The order prompted panic in the Sokol neighborhood, where officials urged the Requisition Department to secure backdated "acts from people who have [in their possession] requisitioned furniture in the shortest time possible, to investigate these acts with owners of the property, to open a personal account on behalf of all those who have taken furniture, and to perform an appraisal of the furniture."[134] Some time later, however, Sokol's Requisition Department was forced to conclude that "things, furniture, and other objects of household goods were distributed and given out for temporary use and for free, to communes, schools, employees of the soviet, as well as sold for cash to needy workers."[135] In short, "there was no organized distribution," and they could not reconstruct paperwork for what had occurred.[136]

Perhaps the most powerful impediment to record-keeping were the record-keepers themselves, not merely because they were short-staffed and ill-trained, but because they too were fearful and uncertain of what had happened and their role in it. There is evidence that inventories of seized apartments were made, perhaps in large numbers, some of which survive in archives of neighborhood soviets. Even more, however, there is evidence that large numbers of inventories were destroyed. Some of this destruction was likely the product of an ephemeral sort of record-keeping, for which Housing Departments and a great many other institutions were frequently criticized. A subsequent inspection of the Baumansky neighborhood Furniture Section found that its staff "kept no books whatsoever in 1918 and 1919," by which it was meant that they recorded inventories and distributions in flimsy notebooks rather than proper account books. Because the books were so flimsy, "acts that were registered in notebooks are now lost."[137]

Equally, however, many records were purposefully destroyed, often in anticipation of an inspection. In the spring of 1920, the Commissariat of Government Control—recently reconfigured as the Worker-Peasant Inspectorate or "Rabkrin"—launched its widest inspection to date of the Moscow Central and neighborhood Housing-Land Departments and their subunits. The inspection revealed that the Gorodskoi neighborhood Requisition Department, upon learning an audit was imminent, knowingly destroyed its records of requisitions and redistributions. Insofar as the Gorodskoi neighborhood was home to the vast majority of the city's grand apartment houses and villas, its Furniture Section would have been responsible for controlling Moscow's most significant trove of bourgeois furniture and housewares. As the inspection revealed, records of these transfers had been made and kept up to this point. Evidently the staff of the Furniture Section deemed it more prudent to destroy them than to turn them over for inspection. "Whether the acts from the destroyed books were transferred to the new registration book is unknown and cannot be clarified," the Rabkrin inspector reported. The timing of the destruction was seen to indicate malfeasance, as were "the explanations of comrades Rudko (a clerk in the Requisition Department) and Tarasov (her boss) about . . . the destruction of the old registry of descriptions," which were judged "unsatisfactory and contradictory."[138]

Any number of things could have prompted the destruction of account books tracing the movement of seized things. It was undeniable that large quantities of such things had fallen to "theft." After uncovering a handful of surviving records in the Gorodskoi neighborhood, inspectors traced the fate of some of the domestic objects recorded therein, establishing what they

classified as "the theft of a portion of the property" in every case on the list.[139]
Tarasov himself confirmed as much in an interview with the Rabkrin inspectors, in which he stated that during the redistribution of built space, "the apartments of wealthy people had been inventoried." In these spaces, "there had
been clothing, fur coats, leather shoes, expensive dishes, paintings, clocks, gold
objects, silver, money." He estimated that "30 percent or more of this valuable
property disappeared from the apartments, a portion of it stolen by residents
of the building, and a portion of it sliced off [*vyrezana*] by employees of the
Gorodskoi housing section," its fate "completely unclear."[140] In the Baumansky
neighborhood, inspectors acquired an inventory made at the end of 1918 of
No. 10 Novo-Basmannaya Street, apartment #3, ostensibly a complete record
of its contents upon the eviction of its residents. They sought to verify the
record with the secretary of the building committee, who testified that in this
case, as in others, the movable properties in requisitioned spaces met mixed
fates: some went to the building's continuing residents, some to the Requisition Department staffs, and some to the Requisition Department as an official
entity. As at the Cheka, this was the whirlwind of dispossession in a nutshell,
in which popular acts of dispossession commingled with official requisitions
of furnishings and unofficial acts of theft. As the building committee chairman
at No. 10 Novo-Basmannaya apartment #3 testified in an interview with inspectors, a portion of the contents of the apartment, listed on the inventory
as "requisitioned," had indeed been "taken away by order of the economic
section," the officially sanctioned fate for requisitioned furniture. But during
the interview "it became clear that a portion of the furniture" was still "located
inside the building." In fact, it was located in the possession of "current residents of building." When the inspectors asked to verify the location of this
furniture, the secretary of the building committee threw up his hands, declaring that such verification "would not be possible, as it was spread about the
entire building," among all its residents, "and he could not show where one
object or another was located."[141]

Instances of more conventional malfeasance also appear in the surviving
records from Requisition Departments, which depict scenes that would become common in Soviet distribution networks for decades to come. Enormous local power accrued to the warehouse directors and the department
heads, who controlled the release of goods to the public. An internal audit of
the Furniture Department's warehouse in the Sokol neighborhood in May 1919
indicated that in the previous year, it had released items to 402 people. Most
of these people—268—were employees of the Sokol soviet. The remaining

134 recipients were "private people," unaffiliated with the Sokol soviet. Comrade Krauze, the department head, handled all requests, save for those he made for himself; his deputies Denisov and Filippov approved those. Of all recipients, Comrade Krauze dealt himself the highest value of goods—1,172 rubles' worth—"all of it very necessary." His deputies Filippov and Denisov received the next highest allocations, worth 529 rubles and 461 rubles respectively. In all, the warehouse had issued 48,000 rubles' worth of goods to the employees of the soviet plus the private people, for an average of 124 rubles' worth of things per person. But the seventeen members of the Sokol soviet's Ispolkom received more than double that average, or furniture worth about 352 rubles per person.[142]

The purposeful destruction of records combined with other documentary shortcomings made it very difficult to know what was inside the warehouses of seized goods, foiling even the best intentions for their expedient disposal. Because the staffs of furniture departments found it so difficult to keep track of the holdings, they generally approved requests from the public for items on a provisional basis—permission granted, if such a thing was found to exist in the warehouse. A review of the Sokol neighborhood's ad hoc Commission to Distribute Seized Property, formed in the spring of 1920, indicated that although the commission approved roughly 50 percent of requests, a far lower proportion of these was actually satisfied due to ignorance of what the warehouse contained.[143] In Petrograd, an inspector at the warehouse of the Interinstitutional Commission advised that "it would be better to call the Distribution Department the Department of Giving Out Orders, as to actually distribute something you would have to know whether it exists."[144] The process of acquiring a necessary thing from city stocks became so random that a number of building committees in Petrograd reportedly made it into an actual lottery, the inspector hissed, with chance operating where social justice was meant to be.[145]

Wave upon wave of inspections, firings, and reorganizations ensued, but nothing seemed to help. On the heels of a Rabkrin investigation in Moscow, the Gorodskoi neighborhood's Furniture Department was disbanded, its holdings brought under the control of its Workers' Housing Section. Three months later, there was the Workers' Housing Section, begging the TsZhZO for help in its effort to compel "all institutions that have a Worker's Building, as well as those that do not have such a building, to send two representatives in a week's time for temporary work . . . inventorying furniture in warehouses."

In the Sokol neighborhood, a new director was brought in to the Economic Department warehouse. He complained that the staff were sabotaging him because, "unlike the previous director, I do not allow them to blow into the warehouse however they want," opening the doors at 10 a.m., drinking tea until 11 a.m., "then a break for lunch, then after lunch they drink tea, and this goes on until two, as after the lunch break there remains the washing up to do." After two hours of work, they began "sorting themselves out" for departure, he reported. "I am going out of my mind."[146]

For documents meant to convey quantitative loss and gain, the audits and inventories of seized things produced during the Revolution are unexpectedly emotional, artifacts of the extraordinary passions that went into the project of social transformation through the redistribution of things. Many of them express a distinctive admixture of awe at the sheer scale of dislocation represented in the warehouses of seized things, combined with fury and despair at the seeming impossibility of realizing this vast wealth, this infinity of treasures. In Petrograd, an inspector at the warehouses of the Inter-institutional Commission fumed that "these warehouses give off the impression of a total absence of even the slightest desire to use the essential objects located there, such as dishes, tables, linens, beds, furniture, mattresses, pillows, clocks, a huge quantity of parquet, rugs, and other objects. . . . All this has been lying already for a year in the warehouses in the most chaotic condition, it is rotting, getting covered in water and eaten by moles and mice, with extremely little ever released. It creates the impression that there are no consumers for these things, as if Piter wants for nothing," he exclaimed in despair, only too aware that precisely the opposite was true.[147]

The inspectors struggled to explain this seeming paralysis in the redistribution chain: was there nothing in the warehouses, so little the Distribution Department ought to be called the Department of Giving Out Orders? Was there abundance, left to rot in water and feed the moles? It seemed impossible to tell. The documentary losses brought on by the whirlwind had a knock-on effect. As one Rabkrin inspector concluded in 1920, the transfers of movable goods that had occurred during the previous two years were "covered in the fog of uncertainty" [pokryto mrakom neizvestnosti], lost now to the passage of time.[148] Some records had indeed been saved, but an overarching suspicion clung even to them: inspectors found, in one instance, that the while "contents of a dead citizen's apartment were recorded, there was no stamp indicating that they indeed had been given over to storage. No one knew how much furniture was there or was supposed to be there, and so, of course," they wearily concluded "widespread theft [*khishcheniye*] of furniture took place."[149]

Their suspicion extended not only to individuals but to the state itself. It was held widely by other state officials, too, whose lack of faith in the state's own distributive capacity routinely colored official decisions about the disposal of movable things, as in the winter of 1919, when the Sokol neighborhood's Requisition Section began hounding a citizen Zheltysheva to "appear before the Economic Department in order to provide an explanation for the typewriter you have." Evidently the Department found unconvincing the supposition that an object so carefully controlled by state institutions could have been allotted appropriately. Also, the Requisition Section may have desired the typewriter for itself.[150]

So little faith did city governments across the RSFSR have in the capacity of their own distributive organs to manage the wealth of movable things entering state hands that, increasingly, they sought to avoid taking possession of those things at all—to sidestep the warehouses and the inventories by attaching the things neither to individuals, in possessive rights, nor to the state, in warehouses or inventories, but rather, to the spaces in which they originally were found. They sought to immobilize movable goods. In the Baumansky neighborhood, employees at the Furniture Department made a first stab at containing the mobility of movable goods by branding them, as if sofas were cows liable to up and wander off.[151] More capacious efforts were launched by city soviets in both Moscow and Petrograd, as well as some smaller cities, which all issued orders preventing the movement of furniture outside city limits, thereby casting movable property, no less than immovable, as a piece of municipal infrastructure. Like sewers or electric wires, movable property was designated to "serve" the immovable properties fixed to the neighborhood, and so neighborhood soviets in turn issued the same orders to prevent furniture from leaving their jurisdiction. In Moscow, other restrictions placed on the "movement of furniture inside the city limits" included an outright ban on the transfer of furnishings from one's city apartment to one's summer dacha, a measure that would have almost exclusively affected the high-ranking revolutionary officials awarded dachas.[152] Having started out using immobilization as a tactic of seizure against the bourgeoisie, in order to prevent valuables from escaping with their former owners, city soviets now deployed immobilization against everybody, even against their own institutions, in an effort to nail movable things down, to defer the problem of possessing them altogether.

The Fog of Uncertainty

Revolutionary dispossession did not merely bestow old things on new people, endowing workers and the poor with privileges and objects that had once belonged to the rich; its operation was both more powerful than this and far less precise. Requisition and confiscation, while never fully or neatly under official control, had many official aims: to equalize the population; to invert prerevolutionary material hierarchy and thus social inequality; to punish counterrevolutionaries. Yet the practical effect of revolutionary dispossession exceeded even these grand ambitions. Requisition and confiscation swept away the rights of particular people to particular things, but more than this, it swept away the practices and assumptions that undergirded stable possession of any kind, drawing into question virtually anybody's right to virtually any kind of thing. In this, the state was strikingly unexceptional as compared to its subjects. Just as individuals found themselves losing and gaining, so, too, the state, nominal owner of all furniture or all seized things (depending on the city), proved unable to take possession of them: to secure physical control, informational authority, powers of disposal, confidence in its own capacities. The problem was not simply that movable things kept moving; it was that people kept changing—they *would* keep moving house, losing jobs, buying on the underground market, undermining the judgments on them that the Revolution had already made. But since it was easier to immobilize movable things than it was to fix people in amber, the solution cooked up by cities across the republic was the juridical equivalent of nailing things down to the floor. Not only did these cities outlaw the movement of furniture beyond city and neighborhood limits—even the movement of furniture within cities and neighborhoods was treated as suspicious or illegal.

Revolutionary dispossession, like the Revolution itself, was meant to take place just once. The division of the population into categories operated on an implicit premise of original transformation: the sorting of workers from parasites was a one-time procedure, delivering everybody over to the other side, where they would live indefinitely with the consequences—deprived down to the "most essential," or enriched up to a "human" level, as the case may be. But the whirlwind of dispossession thwarted this procedure by turning it back in on itself. As the "fog of uncertainty" descended upon Moscow, blanketing what had transpired, the whirlwind looped back, rendering the arrangements in movable things it had wrought perennially open to questioning and revisitation. This was the lesson of No. 3 Sadovaya-Chernogryazskaya, where the complaints about the "mistakes" that had occurred in this basic labor of the Revolution threatened to undermine progress entirely.

The Goskon inspector charged with reviewing the case of No. 3 Sadovaya-Chernogryazskaya was the former lawyer, Vasily Belsky. Shortly after this inspection, Belsky would be appointed to head a new institution formed at Bonch-Bruevich's behest—the Central Bureau of Complaint—where his first hire was the accountant and party member we met at the Lubyanka inspection, Ozerevsky. In this role, Belsky acted as a fierce, if frequently dispirited, advocate for all those who had been aggrieved by revolutionary authorities (Ozerevsky was unable to bear up, Belsky later testified, leading him to quit the Bureau during his first week on the job, returning to service in the regular Goskon administration).[153]

At No. 3 Sadovaya-Chernogryazskaya, Belsky's initial review revealed a number of basic facts. "From the formal side of things," he explained, the defense of the "comrade communists Maria Chernyak, Mazhokhin, and Gorbunov" did not look good. The three had violated a number of "orders of Soviet power," including the rules for forming a commission to evict parasites, the rules on securing permission from the Central Housing Department to requisition a building *before* the requisition took place, and the terms of the building's requisition, which, even if it had been approved in advance, would have authorized the group only to "occupy the entire building of No. 3 Sadovaya-Chernogryazskaya" and in no way to evict or dispossess its existing residents. And yet, Belsky argued—against the Mossoviet, which sought to punish the trio for usurping state power—that Masha Chernyak and her associates should get off with a brief "explanation" that their actions "departed from the existing Mossoviet orders." Ginzburg, Rekets, and Monfor, meanwhile, were entitled to a return of their things "only in that measure in which the workers settled into building No. 3 on Sadovaya-Chernogryazskaya can get by without them"—which was not at all. The building's new commandant Agafonov testified that "we are communists we say [*sic*] comrades, workers, why do they demand the return of furniture and things and propose that [we sit] within naked walls . . . the only thing that we can propose to them is to go back to our burrows and solitary underground rooms, among the mold and rot, the bedbugs and stench of the back courtyards." To return the seized things would be to undo the Revolution, which, at any rate, Agafonov noted, had already advanced. Now, as Red Terror raged, he learned daily of "measures against the bourgeoisie in comparison with which [his own] actions . . . were in the highest measure soft and humane."[154] "Mistakes in an affair unfamiliar to the workers are unavoidable," Mazhokhin calmly explained. "If the workers are to be judged for every mistake they allow, then there would be no revolution."[155]

Surprisingly, Belsky agreed. The problem with the case at No. 3 Sadovaya-Chernogryazskaya, he argued, was that the events that took place there were, in fact, "juridically subject to overturning, but, actually, cannot be overturned in real life." Whether out of pragmatism or sympathy to the building's new residents, Belsky declared that "it is not possible to drive workers out of new apartments where they had only just managed to get set up like people [*po-lyudski*], having quit their old buildings." He was wrong, of course, about whether it was possible to turn people out of apartments they had only just moved into—this kind of repetition was by now a matter of routine. But he was right about the nature of revolutionary redistribution and resettlement, which could only be "cancel[led] on paper, and which cannot be subject to cancellation in reality."[156]

3

Accounting for Socialism

INVENTORIES OF THE BUILT ENVIRONMENT

ONE DAY IN AUGUST 1918, the 236 residents of No. 29 Povarskaya Street, a graceful art deco apartment house on a leafy boulevard in Moscow's Arbat neighborhood, received a letter informing them they had three days to vacate their homes. The good news was that the eviction order, sent by the Moscow Soviet's TsZhZO, did not apply to everyone: the building committee was instructed to "free" just two of the building's five floors of residents. The bad news was that the order did not specify which two floors, thereby leaving the unsavory choice of who would stay and who would go to the residents themselves. They had three days to decide.

By August 1918, ten months since the October Revolution and five months since the Petrograd Bolsheviks had arrived in Moscow to make it their capital, the building committee of No. 29 Povarskaya Street had seen enough to know what to do next. Within days, the building committee had learned through "personal conversations with the Central Housing Commission" that their eviction had been ordered by the Cheka.[1] Moreover, the committee learned that the Cheka expressly sought the top two floors of the building, "for operational purposes." More meetings with more housing officials in the following days netted the committee a stunning success: the deputy head of the TsZhZO managing their case rescinded the eviction order, replacing it instead with a "concentration" order that would require the building's residents to yield individual rooms in their respective apartments to new inhabitants, but would allow them to remain in their homes, a fate the residents accepted. But the very next day, they received a new slip of paper, this one announcing the requisition of the entire building, and the eviction of all its residents. Again, the building committee waged a campaign at the offices of the TsZhZO, meeting with any official who would listen. But this time, no one at the TsZhZO could say who ordered the requisition or why.

Perplexed, if not yet panicked, the residents turned to Vladimir Bonch-Bruevich, head of the Administrative Directorate at the Sovnarkom and, for the first year of the Revolution, its leading patron of popular appeal. True to form, Bonch-Bruevich personally brought their case to the attention of Dzershinsky, director of the Cheka, author of the original requisition order. "Here," Bonch-Bruevich sympathetically explained to Dzerzhinsky, was a "truly tragic situation," in which soviet employees, "really, the laboring element," were being thrown out of their homes in violation of "firm directives of the Mossoviet and the Commissariat of Justice." Dzerzhinsky took the time not only to reply to Bonch-Bruevich, informing him that in this instance, the Cheka was not behind the new eviction order, but also to use the investigative apparatus of his institution to learn who *was* behind it. Dzerzhinsky informed Bonch-Bruevich that the building was now being claimed by Goskon.

Bonch-Bruevich advised the building committee to undertake a new round of personal meetings, aiding them with a handwritten "request" from the Sovnarkom, in which Bonch-Bruevich personally pleaded their case. With this, their heady journey through the receiving rooms of the new state continued. They secured a meeting at the People's Commissariat for Government Control, where, to their astonishment, they were ushered into the office of the Commissar for Government Control himself, the old Bolshevik Karl Lander. Lander listened politely to their tale, sympathetically assuring the building committee members that he "agreed with all [they said]." Still, he sighed, "he would insist upon the eviction of the building's residents, for the reason that he 'needed' the building"—or rather, as he clarified, he "needed" *a* building. For his part, Lander was more or less indifferent as to which building, precisely, he received. And so he offered the building committee a reprieve, or maybe it was more of a trade: "you show me some other suitable building," he gamely proposed to the residents of No. 29 Povarskaya, "and I will put a stop to the requisition of your building immediately."

The residents of No. 29 Povarskaya left Lander's office baffled: Find him another building? Where did one go to "find" whole apartment buildings? Were they really being asked to serve as real estate agents to a commissariat of the new Soviet state? Mystified, the residents ignored Lander's proposition and plunged back into the task of protecting their building from requisition through petitions and meetings at the TsZhZO, where their "daily torment was met everywhere with nothing but senseless opposition. . . . That was the end of the closed circle we fell into," they concluded in their final letter to Bonch-Bruevich. Trudging home from their last meeting, where they were told their case was not yet decided, the members of the building committee arrived to find a fresh eviction notice waiting for them at the door. Two weeks after that, when the Cheka again investigated the building's status at Bonch-Bruevich's behest, it reported back that No. 29 Povarskaya "was fully occupied by [the Commissariat of] Government Control." Its previous inhabitants were already gone.[2]

Understandably, given the events swirling around them, the residents of No. 29 Povarskaya Street interpreted their plight as a judgement on their class status, and in their petitions they fought their eviction largely in these terms. They had clearly already mastered the basics of revolutionary self-presentation, composing comprehensive social and occupational profiles of themselves, listing their names, ages, and workplaces, with which they made the case that they were not class enemies, and should not be punished as such with eviction. The handmade document, which they submitted to Bonch-Bruevich, reveals that around sixty of the building's 236 residents worked in "soviet and civic organizations," while another sixty identified themselves as practitioners of "mental and physical labor," including "servants, day laborers, teachers, and the like." Several of these homemade categories—workers in "civic organizations" and practitioners of "mental labor"—would have been recognizable to people at the time for what they were not: civic organizations were *not* state (soviet) organizations; mental labor was *not* physical labor. The remaining residents were either children, adult dependents, or practitioners of free professions (mostly doctors and dentists), of which the building had around ten. They wisely cast their prospective eviction not as a burden for themselves personally, and least of all as a matter of property rights or entitlement to their homes, but rather, invoking a favored formulation of the time, as a danger to their employers and the labor productivity of the Soviet Republic as a whole. As they were nearly all "in service at soviet (and civic) institutions," they argued, "our eviction threatens to bring about not only our own complete despair but also will inevitably negatively express itself on the normal work of these institutions."

What was unnerving to the residents of No. 29 Povarskaya Street was that none of this seemed to matter. Contrary to their expectations, they did not appear to be losing their homes because of who they were. Instead, as Lander officiously explained, they were losing their homes because Lander had become aware of their apartment building, as if their building—their address—was somehow the only building, among all the apartment houses on all the leafy streets of Moscow, that he could see. And it was not only Lander: before he had even got a hold of their address, No. 29 Povarskaya had also surfaced in the Cheka's line of sight, and that of the TsZhZO as well. There was something undeniably strange about this chain of events—the "closed loop we have fallen into," as the building committee blearily wrote—as if, having seen No. 29 Povarskaya Street, these authorities could not unsee it; or, from the residents' perspective, as if they were losing their homes not because they deserved to but rather because their building had been spotted. How else to explain the perverse momentum of their case? No sooner had they dodged one eviction notice, when another popped up—and another after that. And how else to explain Lander's offer to release their building from requisition if only they found him a different building—an offer they viewed as so outlandish they not only ignored it, despite the relief it offered them, but they reported it to Bonch-Bruevich in disbelief?

———

For nearly a decade after the First World War, the great cities of the Atlantic world were mired in a housing crisis, born of global shortages in building materials, fuel, and labor that suppressed new construction and, combined with widespread in inflation, sent rents skyrocketing.[3] The pervasive sense of disorder in interwar real estate markets led some cities to outlaw "illicit speculation" in rents, targeting rents that had risen beyond the "'natural' limits of supply and demand," but, as Alexia Yates observes of Paris, such measures were exceptionally difficult to enforce. In the French capital, as in many cities, the real estate market operated with many special encumbrances on free exchange, which meant there was no citywide "market for rents that would make supply and demand transparent." Some of these encumbrances were legal, purposefully designed to make real property harder to exchange than other kinds of things in the interest of preserving social order; others were connected to the nature of the thing itself—to the fact that buildings could not move, such that their locations rendered them highly specific and harder to equate with one another, even as the rise of mass construction techniques made the buildings themselves ever more alike. The result, writes Yates, was a social panic about housing in Paris, and indeed in many other cities, after the First World War. "Accusations of conspiracies in the housing market were abundant," social trust was low, as was faith in the existing institutions of real estate provision and distribution. Alongside popular upheaval against landlords and estate agents there arose demands for centralized rent bureaus and calls for the forced public advertisement of vacancies to make the real estate market more like other markets, all designed to overcome the global crisis by making built space easier to see locally—by prospective tenants, buyers, developers, and the state.[4]

In Moscow after the First World War, the speculative landlords were gone, but, as will be shown here, the problem of seeing space remained. In the lead-up to the October Revolution, one Muscovite housing official would later recall, it had been widely anticipated that the municipal administration of the built environment would be "far easier" than many other municipal tasks, such as "running trams, managing the water supply, electrical enterprises or railroads." Although this conclusion was derived from the writings of prerevolutionary "bourgeois economists, underlining the simplicity of municipal construction and building administration"—mostly municipal socialists—it resonated with the Bolsheviks' own attitudes toward the technologies of economic management that would become available to them after seizing power.[5] Lenin, too, had anticipated that the identification, capture, and exploitation of the necessary information about economic life would be fairly straightforward—that the capitalist world, once it had been broken open by the abolition of private property, could be bent to non-capitalist objectives using its own tools of inventory and accounting, revealing reserves of wealth in the process that had up to now been hidden by the pursuit of profit.

This chapter examines the practices of revolutionary accounting and inventorying through the allocation of built space, from its seizure in 1918 through to its partial "demunicipalization" in 1922, with the turn to the NEP. The creation of information about the built environment was envisioned as a cornerstone of rational, nonmarket management, one that would facilitate the generation of an abstract, fungible new resource known as "living space." The chapter shows how, in the process of use, this accounting utopia was turned on its head. The story of No. 29 Povarskaya is the story of how the revolutionary state took possession of the built environment and tried to turn it into an object of socialist management. Lander's offer to allow the building committee to serve as his commissariat's real estate agent—his bid on their ingenuity, desperation, and moral flexibility—illuminates a key insight into the Bolshevik accumulation of power through the accumulation of things: the revolutionaries would accomplish the monumental social and informational labor that the abolition of private property entailed by enjoining the population to participate in the process. In place of the transparent inventory of the built environment, revolutionary housing authorities ended up with "the account," a motivated and partial record of "available" spaces, frequently provided by residents themselves.

The fact of extensive popular involvement in the identification of "available" living space is significant not only for what it suggests about the early Soviet state and the voluntarism embedded in statization, but also for what it reveals about revolutionary methods for managing material resources without legal markets. The previous two chapters have contended that, in abolishing the private ownership of apartments and their contents, the revolutionary state did not succeed in taking possession of these objects in a recognizable fashion, giving rise to a condition of propertylessness that was endured by state institutions no less than individual subjects. This chapter addresses the other side of the possessive relationship: the objects of the possessive relationship, and their definition and integrity in the transition to nonmarket management. In the aftermath of the municipalization of the built environment, revolutionary officials sought to achieve an allocation of the built environment that was both more rational and more socially just than what the market had bequeathed. The imperative to create an account of "available living space" was at the center of this effort, a mechanism for translating brick-and-mortar buildings into registers of "available living space" for redistribution. But as with so much else about the operation of nonmarket management, the standards for identifying this new resource were indeterminate. Prerevolutionary registers of built space, produced by insurance and tax authorities and created for the operation and regulation of real estate markets, were of little help in this endeavor, as they failed to capture not only the relevant range and features of built spaces themselves, but perhaps more essentially, had nothing to say about the particular quality of a "living space" that, it turned out, went the furthest in determining its availability: its residents, both who they were and how they lived. The act of "taking the built environment onto account" demanded a critical and creative interpretation of people and space. The identification and, indeed, the definition of this object, "available living space," therefore lay in the hands of revolutionary officials, housing department "controllers," building committee chairmen, dvorniks, neighbors, and residents themselves.[6]

A Calling to Accounts

The prerevolutionary socialism of Lenin and the Bolsheviks was an ideology of material abundance, premised on the notion that if only a modern society (Russia in a pinch, necessarily followed by the advanced European world) would unlock its productive and possessive capacities from the strictures of private property, enough could be made and enjoyed by all. Material abundance and its scientific, planful management was the long-term aim of communism as envisioned by Karl Marx, of course, but it was also the foundation of Lenin's belief in 1917 that the time was ripe for his party's seizure of power. Under the mobilizational pressures of total war, Lenin argued, capitalism had reached its final stage, its enterprises calcified into monopolies that concentrated all productive capacity and capital within themselves, merged with bank capital to form a new financial oligarchy. Not only did this oligarchy threaten the world with the prospect of endless war, as the biggest capitalist powers sought the territorial division of the world among themselves, but it had also finally created, in the process of its consolidation, precisely the tools of economic management that would be necessary after its own dissolution.[7] In the months before October, Lenin hammered home the argument that capitalism had evolved the necessary mechanisms for economic control, such as a national structure of accounting, that would be required for the transition to socialism. What remained was to seize control over them, to transfer their operation to the hands of the workers and employees—in essence, to find new ways of seeing what was already all around.[8]

The problem of seeing material resources of all kinds—articulating what resources there were, generating information about them, and rendering that information visible to institutions of the new state—animated both the revolutionary theory of the Bolsheviks and the actual practice of postrevolutionary governance. Right up until the Bolsheviks seized power, and indeed for several months after, Lenin argued that issue of property regimes was a smokescreen, and that the first stages of socialism would involve not the socialization or state expropriation of property but the self-government of enterprises by their employees.[9] This hinged on the workers' ready access to the accounts and records hitherto locked down under the capitalist precepts of "commercial secrecy." Up to this moment, capitalists had ensured these books remained hidden from workers, protected behind the veil of bourgeois law, but after the revolution, Lenin predicted, congresses of bank employees and clerks in industrial concerns would gather to throw open account books to the public. The transfer of property rights paled in significance before this deeper transformation in management and the aims of production, which he predicted could be achieved in one stroke, with a few "simple decrees."[10] As Lenin explained in *State and Revolution*, his last major text before seizing power, "accounting and control, that is what is mainly needed for the smooth working, the proper

functioning of the first phase of communist society. All citizens are transformed into hired employees of the state, which consists of the armed
workers."[11]

These hopes, as we know, were dashed after October. The political failure
of the workers' control movement as a foundation for the "commune state"
was accompanied by the failure to convince bank employees to throw open
their account books, and by the realization that accounts were still complex—
far beyond the reach of the average worker, even one who was armed. Between
March and June 1918, the ideal of self-government gave way to a whirlwind of
dispossession.[12] Yet this change in orientation did not quell the revolutionary
impetus toward accounting for material life. Once widespread state seizure
was underway, new fuels fed the inventorying fire. Because this was a materialist revolution—that is, because the transfer of power was broadly understood
to inhere in the transfer of things—the transcription of this movement was
likewise elevated into a record and mirror of the progress of the Revolution
itself, even when the things themselves did not move or change. Indeed, the
act of drawing a new inventory of an enterprise or warehouse did not merely
mark the Revolution's coming: it was the Revolution's coming—it was how
the Revolution could be made real within the ordinary spaces of material life.
According to the staff of the "Central Warehouse for City Cafeterias" in Moscow, the warehouse "began a new life" on November 22, 1917, with the opening
of a new account book—the old one having been destroyed in an act of "sabotage" after October.[13] Then, in February 1918, a self-appointed commission of
delegates from Moscow's cafeterias gathered "to conduct an investigation into
the accounts of the C.W. [Central Warehouse] from that very day, when it
began to live again, that is, from 22 November 1917, and then day by day, according to the materials, to *follow the life* of the C.W. . . . *how it lived* before, *how
it exists* at the present time, and *how it should live*" in the future.[14] So important
was the revolutionary caesura in accounts and so profound was the desire to
"follow the life" of accounts from that rebirth that Narkomfin accountants
were made to ascertain Russia's national balance as of October 25, 1917, despite
the fact that, as they explained, the quarterly schedule of accounts would make
such a task virtually impossible.[15]

The Sovnarkom approved the creation of the first organs of revolutionary
account on December 5, 1917, the same day that it created the Cheka. The "collegium of government control," later elevated to status as a People's Commissariat, inherited the prerevolutionary apparatus of control—tasked before 1917
with reducing waste and corruption in official spending—but was charged

early on with a different mission. Revolutionary organs of accounting were meant to operate as mass organs in two respects: first, in their incorporation of regular workers, housewives, and students into the performance of accounts, and second, in the massive scale of objects and enterprises over which they wielded jurisdiction. "Not one product," Lenin wrote after the Revolution, "not one funt of bread should exist outside of the account, as socialism, before anything else, is accounting." Proper accounting would reveal the really existing abundance all around, hitherto hidden not only by the pursuit of profit but also by the hopeless smallness of the individual enterprise, by the absence of a united, comprehensive knowledge of material resources. The accounts of the Revolution would be "the all-people's, the most all-encompassing, the most ubiquitous, the most precise and conscientious" that the world had ever seen.[16]

If accounting was everywhere after the Revolution, it also took on certain specific features connected to postrevolutionary economic and political life. The most notable of these was its resemblance to what had hitherto been thought of not as accounting but as physical inventorying. Particularly in the double-entry format that was common in Russia, as in Europe, before the Revolution, the purpose of an account book was to trace the movement of an entity's resources over a certain period of time, converting those resources into a money value and following that value through growth or contraction, profit or loss.[17] But in the aftermath of the Revolution, and more particularly, in the aftermath of the whirlwind of dispossession, the chief task of the account book appeared transformed. The core task looming before all revolutionary institutions was an assessment of what, quite literally, they possessed. With the value of the ruble plummeting by the day, there appeared little sense in representing these holdings in money; representation would have to be according to the material things themselves, that is, as a form of physical inventory. The production of a physical inventory on a national scale was, in this same vein, among the very first tasks announced by the People's Commissariat of Government Control (Goskon) upon its formation. To that end, Goskon proposed the creation of a special "account-instructional department," the chief purpose of which was to instruct regional governments on the preparation of an "account of all property" held by the new state.[18]

In the world of prerevolutionary accounting, inventories occupied a low status, looked down upon as little more than preparatory documents necessary to the creation of the more technically complex and theoretically sophisticated double-entry accounts. But inventories of the scale and scope required by revolutionary institutions were anything but simple. This was a discovery made early on by the renowned prerevolutionary professor of accounting, A. M. Galagan, who was hired by Goskon in the spring of 1918 to develop the format of this new, "comprehensive account" of the revolutionary republic's holdings.[19] Initially, the "comprehensive account" was intended to embrace "property of all types," including cash. The catastrophic scale of inflation brought work on money holdings to a standstill, forcing Galagan to attempt what later would be characterized as a purely "natural-quantitative account," and "very negatively influencing all account work" as it had been previously conceived—that is, as the expression of things in money.[20]

Galagan's focus therefore shifted to the problem of developing a classificatory schema that could embrace material "property of all types." As he explained in his definitive accounting textbook, written before the Revolution and reissued several times after it, the purpose of inventories was to render complex things "visible," to expose "perfectly clear and accurate views of subjects, facts, and phenomena interesting to us" through a scientific "method of observation and description."[21] This was as true after the abolition of private property and the delegitimization of markets as before it; the question was rather which "subjects, facts, and phenomena" mattered enough to be made visible, and to whom. Galagan proposed parsing state property in two aspects. The first, drawing heavily on his European training, attended to the proprietary status and the life history of things, dividing all things into two categories borrowed from French and Italian nineteenth century practice: "properties of general use," on the one hand, or "patrimonial properties" on the other. Into the first category would fall those things to which the "government had a right as the highest power, such as canals, waterways, ports, streets, squares, monuments, and the like;" the second category comprised "those things wielded by the government in its rights as a private owner, such as factories and railroads." This division captured an important historical distinction between different types of state property—the things the state held in public trust, which did not have a market value and thus had to be appraised using nonmarket methods, and the things the state held as a private owner, no different from any other private owner, which could be appraised using market price. But after the Revolution, of course, this distinction lost its salience. There was no market for either streets or factories, such that there was little cause to hold the two types of things apart in a state inventory.[22] Categorizing property in this way also presented a significant technical challenge, Galagan recognized, in that it amounted to an inquiry into the process of nationalization itself. It required knowing how properties changed hands, who ceded them, who received them, and—optimistically—"according to which documents," information that often did not exist.

Galagan's second schema for the categorization of material things was likewise beset by complications. This method divided all things in the material world into three categories: "real estate," "stock," and "material." "Real estate" (immovable property) was treated as self-explanatory and received no definition; "stock" was defined as the fixtures attached to a built space. Galagan was confident that both categories of property could be inventoried with relative ease, thanks to the fact that they did not "move around very much."[23] The third category, "material property" was a different story. "Material property" comprised everything else, and its registration appeared to Galagan as far and away the most daunting, indeed a nearly impossible task. "Creating one general nomenclature in the center [of government] for all forms of material property, while desirable, is hardly feasible in view of the extreme variety in types of objects, on the one hand, belonging to different State institutions, which have a name only in that particular kind of institution, and also on the other because fixing this kind of general nomenclature would take a great deal of time," he explained. The only solution would be for each state institution to make up their own naming systems for the kinds of things in their possession. Galagan advised patience: "this will bring great variegation, which will have to be temporarily managed. Gradually the thing will be brought to life."[24]

It was obvious to Galagan that the creation of this new thing, a national "material account," would require an array of new rules and guidelines, "blanks and books," to say nothing of the "creation and instruction of a staff of accountants." Above all else, it would require the formation of a "central organ of state property," where the work of generating and maintaining this information would be concentrated.[25] In the event, however, this is not what came to pass; inventorying was not confined to a single central institution, either the state's ostensible accounting agency, Goskon, or any other. Instead, like the statization of private property itself, it was something all institutions did—or failed to do—in the course of their regular, basic labor of material appropriation and transformation.

This feature of the takeover of material life had several important consequences. First, as Goskon complained in the fall of 1918, it meant that often, inventories did not get made. "In Moscow as in other populated places of Soviet Russia," a Goskon official lamented in October, "the requisition of the movable property of citizens is occurring by the orders of various powers . . . by separate groups, by the directive of individual people" leaving no "account of all the things that have been requisitioned."[26] The irregularity of seizure produced a corresponding irregularity in the state's knowledge of its supposed holdings.

At the same time, revolutionary institutions also created inventories for the purpose not simply of registering things already in their possession, but also in order to lay claim to things they thought should enter into their possession, whether the objects had already done so or not. Inventorying, that is, was an activist practice, enabling a given institution to present the material world in the way it wished it to be seen. In the summer of 1918, for instance, the Khamovniki neighborhood in Moscow set out to perform a comprehensive "investigation of pubs, cafeterias, teahouses, cafes, and other places of consumption in the neighborhood," with an eye toward realizing its vision of mass public dining.[27] The neighborhood's public dining department had resolved that in the future, "the capacity of each cafeteria should be not lower than one thousand lunches." The inventory was therefore performed with this ideal in mind, indicating the size of the dining room and storage sheds, the number and strength of the stove burners, in support of the plan to operate only cafeterias with a capacity to serve one thousand lunches; spaces that did not serve this goal were not included in the general inventory of dining resources and were instead put on a separate list for "closure."[28] Meanwhile, Khamovniki's Garden Department, noting "the absence of any kind of inventory of the land in the Khamovniki-Dorogomilovsky neighborhood," resolved to perform such an inventory—not of land per se, but rather of land suitable to its aim of "beginning work on the organization of gardens."[29]

Revolutionary inventories were imaginative documents, conjuring not just land but gardens; not just cooking implements but component parts of a thousand-lunch cafeteria. Against the backdrop of the tremendous asset grab that was statization, and in an environment that seemed rich with possibility for transformation of and through material things, the composition of inventories therefore served as a method of bringing about this transformation—of bringing the Revolution to life. Underlying this usage was, again, the Bolsheviks' basic faith that with proper, non-capitalist accounting—unencumbered by commercial secrecy, without the calculation of profit as its aim—the real-life material abundance that was all around would at last be revealed. Even in a country as poor as Russia, the Bolsheviks suspected, capitalism had perversely shielded this basic sufficiency from view. The built environment was an ideal vehicle for the realization of the

Bolsheviks' faith in latent abundance. The first challenge, then, would be determining how much there was.

In the first three years of Bolshevik power, Russian cities experienced catastrophic depopulation. From 1915 to 1920, the population of Moscow fell by nearly half, with roughly 900,000 people abandoning the city. Petrograd's depopulation was even more severe, plummeting from two million people to 700,000 in the same period. The general fact of depopulation, of course, was readily apparent at the time, but its significance for the allocation of housing in the capitals was not. This was because the devastation wrought by the Revolution on Russia's capitals was comprehensive: not only did it send people back to villages, it also saw those who remained tearing up wooden buildings and furniture for firewood, allowing pipes to freeze and buildings to flood for lack of heating fuel, living alongside sealed rooms. So while the fact of depopulation was visible to all, so too was the degradation of the built environment, which, it was rightly feared, would soon lead to a significant loss in the overall quantity of housing stock available for redistribution.

Later on, after several years of recovery afforded by the introduction of the New Economic Policy (NEP), Moscow's housing authority—the Moscow Directorate of Real Estate or the MUNI, successor to the TsZhZO—prepared a study on the basis of data that was even then, as late as 1925, characterized as incomplete and "orientational." This data was compiled as part of MUNI's attempt to generate a "complete, general account of the housing stock of the city of Moscow," an effort that was still ongoing. (See table 3.1.) This data revealed that around August 1920, the balance between depopulation and the degradation of the built environment had reached its most favorable level. In the summer of 1920, Muscovites had more space—18.1 square arshins per person—than at any point in the five years before or since.

But Muscovites at the time did not know this. They did not know that the summer of 1920 was the most spacious of their postrevolutionary lives. To the contrary, Muscovites at the time understood themselves to be living through a period of extraordinary housing dearth. The Sovnarkom recognized the problem as severe enough in 1919 to merit the creation of a high-level Apartment Commission chaired by Yuri Larin and charged with "discuss[ing] from all sides all the possible paths for improving the living conditions of workers."[30]

In the long run, early Soviet housing administrators anticipated that an abundance of housing would be achieved through new construction. In early 1920, a senior official at the Mossoviet's TsZhZO delivered a report entitled "The Housing Crisis and the Improvement of Worker Everyday Life and the

TABLE 3.1. Per Capita Housing Stock in Moscow, 1915–1925

Year/month	Housing stock in arshins (millions)	Population (millions)	Average space per person
1915	27.360	1.9	14.4 square arshins
1920/August	18.630	1.027	18.1 square arshins
1922/January	18.890	1.3	14.5 square arshins
1923/March	19.030	1.542	12.3 square arshins
1924/July	19.340	1.754	11 square arshins
1925/July	19.670	1.855	10.6 square arshins/ 5.4 square meters

Source: TsAGM f. 2433, op. 1, d. 118, l. 21.

Activity of Housing-Factory Commissions" at a conference on the topic.[31] The official, A. L. Gelbras, stated plainly that "the housing crisis will be finally resolved only through intensified construction of healthy housing answering to the needs of the new Communist orientation of worker life."[32] But in the short run, said Gelbras, who had been intimately involved in the campaign to evict "parasitic elements" from Moscow in the summer of 1918, it was necessary to set aside utopian fantasies—construction fantasies in particular.[33] "In the absence of the capacity for widespread construction of buildings at the present moment," he continued, "there is enormous meaning in the improvement of worker everyday life through rational distribution."[34] In Petrograd, housing officials declared that "of course, the real, so to speak, communist housing politics cannot be contained in the narrow frames of the tasks of the present moment," a transitional period in which grand construction was impossible. "But so long as these demands of the transitional period go unsatisfied, or, to put it in other words, so long as the foundation is not laid down, it will be impossible to build and bring to life a healthy housing politics in the conditions of the socialist system."[35] The foundation of healthy housing politics in the conditions of the socialist system was not new construction, that is, it was the account or inventory of the built environment. "Without an account, a consequential and correct implementation of housing politics is impossible," the Petrograd officials continued, and for that reason, "special attention was directed toward its organization and all possible measures were adopted for its actual implementation."[36]

The ambition to build was not abandoned, exactly. But insofar as it was declared unrealizable, attention shifted to inventory and accounting, which now figured as the realist stepping-stone to the maximalist construction utopia. By January 1921, accounting had decisively triumphed on Moscow's housing scene. "Right now," observers investigating the work of the TsZhZO's "Department of Building Administration" reported, "housing politics is moving in two directions, toward which there is intense interest and attention: the accounting and the distribution of space, in the center as in the neighborhoods, there you have the goals toward which all strength is being applied."[37] The inspectors were skeptics: would not "the ever-decreasing amount of housing" make "distribution and account an unattainable goal"? Could inventories and accounts overcome fundamental shortage? They thought not:

> No matter how expedient the system of accounting and distribution of housing to be implemented by specialists, no [system], no matter how practical its implementation, would be in a condition to achieve its goals at the same time as the quantity of space falls arithmetically and even geometrically. But instead of dealing with this issue, [how to prevent] the reduction of living space in Moscow, two other questions are being resolved: accounts and distribution. Even when done well, these two questions, which have consumed so much time of late, cannot solve housing needs.[38]

Yet none of this dimmed the conviction that, as another group of Petrograd housing officials put it at the end of 1920, "without an account of living space and of households [*domovladenie*], no implementation of the housing politics of Soviet construction is possible. For that reason," they confirmed, "the necessity of rapidly organizing an apparatus for accounting is so essential and so obvious that it hardly demands any kind of explanation."[39] By and through the "housing politics" of the present—that is to say, by and through "the account"—the Revolution would be brought to life.

Objects of Account: From Apartments to Available Living Space

The account was the politics of the possible, a method for transforming the built environment according to principles of social justice that did not require new construction. The urgency of creating such a document was broadly agreed. But its precise object was not, an ambiguity that emerged in the very first initiatives to gather information about the built environment launched by the Mossoviet's TsZhZO in the spring of 1918. The TsZhZO's founding statute indicated that it would perform several different kinds of account; in specific, the TsZhZO was charged with performing an "account of apartments and spaces on the territory of the city" and an "account of lands and define their uses." It was further tasked with "performing account and distribution between the population and the institutions of the existing reserve of housing and other spaces, for which task it wields the right of requisition of space and eviction."[40] Despite the seeming identity between two of these tasks— performing an "account of apartments and spaces on the territory of the city" and "performing account and distribution ... of the existing reserve of housing and other spaces"—they were listed separately, suggesting a distinction in practice that the Statute failed to capture. The Statute also made clear that, while the TsZhZO assumed material responsibility only for "municipal" and "soviet" buildings, leaving a small pocket of single-family homes and small apartment buildings in private possession (with attendant restrictions on right to sell, bequeath, and so forth), it assumed informational authority over all buildings "on the territory of the city," without regard for their property status. Also notable is what the Statute did not identify as an explicit part of the TsZhZO's informational duties: the collection of information pertaining to the economic value of the buildings.[41] Upon taking control of buildings, the TsZhZO often standardized rents among units, eliminating distinctions related to building story, for instance, which would have affected the market value of the space before municipalization.[42] But these metrics were evidently not expected to be central to the operation of the account.

Overseeing this work would be one of the TsZhZO's early hires, D. Kuzovkov, a housing specialist. The Bolsheviks characterized him as a "bourgeois consultant," while Moscow's former city head, writing from exile, remembered him as a rabid proponent of class war.[43] Among the first tasks entrusted to Kuzovkov in June 1918 was the creation of the TsZhZO's inaugural "informational section," where he set out to concentrate work on accounts.[44] The following month, the Collegium of the TsZhZO approved the salary lines for a group of "statisticians, second class," although it is not clear if any were hired.[45] Kuzovkov himself well understood, as he wrote later in the Mossoviet's 1920 compendium *Krasnaya Moskva*, that "all housing politics depends on a precise account of the space and registration of its current usage."[46] He recognized, that is, two distinct objects of account—a "precise account of space," on the one hand, and a "registration of its current usage," on the other. As a first order of business, Kuzovkov therefore set about convincing the Mossoviet to hold a citywide "general census" of the population at breakneck speed, which he scheduled for late August. The census was to be conducted by building, such that it would provide basic information about "current usage" in the form of population density per building and the availability of housing stock.[47] But in practice, he complained, the census-takers had simply counted people without recording their names, spoiling the result by raising the risk of double-counting.[48] They also took no information about the buildings themselves, which Kuzovkov hoped to remedy the following year with a separate "building census"—the "precise account of space." This ambition was also foiled: planned for August 1919, Kuzovkov was forced to abandon the building census when it was just "80–85 percent complete" amid fears that the city was about to be invaded by the White Army and the associated "worker shortages."[49] A population census would be conducted only in August 1920, and a building census some years after that—as noted earlier, according to the officials at MUNI in 1925, a complete inventory of the city's built environment was still "not yet finished."[50]

Housing authorities in Moscow and Petrograd continued to discuss the preparation of a comprehensive inventory of built space throughout the revolutionary era. Every so often, a new round of plans would appear for the creation of "an exhaustive account of all spaces," as in November 1918, for instance, when an enterprising statistician hired by the Khamovniki soviet announced a project to perform "the accounting of spaces" in the neighborhood as her first order of business, on the heels of Kuzovkov's failure to do so for the city as a whole. The account would clarify "the number of stone and wooden buildings and their uses, the number of apartments and rooms, the density of apartments, and other questions connected with the accounting of space."[51] The statistician, S. A. Tishina, proposed using "the card system" for this account, creating one "accounting card" per habitable space, with a separate, perforated tab where information about the assignment or disposal of the space would be recorded and separated, if needed, from the permanent section of the card. Two years later, housing officials in Petrograd likewise declared an urgent need for such a card system, which they characterized as "an archive: a collection of all material used with regard to registration for each property. Each property will have its own folder, a rich material for the history of each property, beginning from a certain time." The folder would contain plans, a narrative description of the property and its location, and a "detailed description of each separate apartment." On top of the comprehensive "archive" of spaces, the Petrograd officials anticipated a need "to begin work on a registry of changes that have occurred in the contents of the real estate and its various parts," subtly reflecting the two objects of accounting invoked in the TsZhZO's founding document: the register of buildings, and the account of their present use. Although plans for a register of this sort had been circulating for two years already, the Petrograd officials resolved with sudden urgency that "this work must be started immediately, right now, as soon as the census of 28 August [1920] is concluded. Each day that goes by represents a certain loss."[52]

Yet attention to creation of the "comprehensive account"—with its primary focus on the buildings themselves, the material they were made from, their area and total number of rooms—remained only sporadic throughout this period. Insofar as the last prerevolutionary building census had been performed in 1912, and insofar as there had been no new building starts of any kind recorded since 1915, there would have been ample sources of prerevolutionary information on which to base the preparation of a comprehensive account of buildings, had this been the foremost concern of housing authorities. Indeed, in October 1918, when agents from the Commissariat of Government Control performed a review of the neighborhood ZhZOs, they recommended investigating the "archives of the former City Uprava" for relevant data, referring to the municipal building census of 1912, which recorded the building material, number of stories, and sewage capabilities of every building then standing, as well as the records of the city-wide Appraisal of Real Estate performed by the Kazennaya Palata in 1916 for the assessment of the state property tax.[53] That housing officials were at least aware of these sources of information is evident from the work of Yuri Larin's Apartment Commission in 1919, which made use of both the Moscow building census of 1912 and the 1916 appraisals. Indeed, Larin's Commission, which counted both Kuzovkov and the head of the TsZhZO, M. F. Vladimirsky, among its members, even created a chart using data from the 1912 building census (table 3.2) to suggest that the key plank of revolutionary housing policy—the resettlement of workers into "bourgeois" apartments—would not in itself to resolve the housing crisis, due to the fact that "the very quantity of these (bourgeois) buildings is, compared to the quantity of workers and petty employees, limited." Larin's Commission concluded that resettling the working masses inside the Sadovoye Ring would effectively demand wedging three-quarters of the city's population into one-quarter of its apartments, which it judged an "insurmountable obstacle" to the plan's realization.

Yet the observation that proper accounting would not, in fact, bring about sufficiency left no trace in the work of the local housing departments, which continued to eschew prerevolutionary sources of information about the built environment. Why did the local housing departments turn their noses at the

TABLE 3.2. Apartments and Population, Districts in Moscow, c. 1912
(Prepared 1919)

Section of the city of Moscow	Number of Apartments	Population
Inside the Blvd. Ring	16,518	148,542
Between the Blvd. and Sadovaia	28,012	217,770
Beyond Sadovaia Ring	116,594	1,024,044

Source: GARF f. R-130, op. 3, d. 122, l. 95.

prerevolutionary data? It was not because they were ignorant of these sources or because they were reluctant to contend with the hard truths such information might convey. Rather, it was because prerevolutionary information about the built environment did not tell local housing departments what they needed to know. In fact, neighborhood housing departments had little interest in the comprehensive inventory of buildings proposed by Kuzovkov and pursued by his "Information Section." What they sought out instead was a form of accounting tied expressly to their central task of distribution—so much so that the majority of neighborhood housing departments named the subdepartment where inventory and account was meant to take place the "Subdepartment for Accounting and Distribution," as if they were joined in a single administrative process.

The TsZhZO's founding statute, as noted above, acknowledged the existence of two distinct forms of account within the housing department: the "account of apartments and spaces on the territory of the city," and also, the act of "perform[ing] account and distribution . . . of the existing reserve of housing and other spaces, for which task it wields the right of requisition."[54] Whereas accounting in the first aspect, the inventorying of buildings themselves, seems to have been the exclusive purview of the TsZhZO's Informational Section, the latter function of "accounting and distribution" was the object of significant institutional competition.[55] Not long after releasing the TsZhZO's founding statute, the Sovnarkom found it necessary to issue a special "Decree on the Accounting and Distribution of Space," the purpose of which was to defend the TsZhZO's exclusive monopoly on the "account and distribution" of built space in the city against the Apartment Commissions that had sprung up among the commissariats attempting to do similar "accounting and distribution" work.[56] No defense was needed when it came to making a comprehensive account of the built environment; no other institutions showed special interest in elbowing in on that job. But "account and distribution" was a different matter.[57] Many institutions sought to perform the "account and distribution" of built space, although, as a Goskon investigation later clarified, there was no agreement as to what, precisely, "account and distribution" was. In an effort to standardize the activity of the neighborhood housing departments, in November 1918 the Mossoviet issued an "Order on the Accounting and Distribution of Living and Non-living Space in the City of Moscow." But the Order, a Goskon investigator snorted, gave no information about what "accounting" was or how it was to be performed, merely reiterating that requisitioned and confiscated properties, "as the people's property, are subject to the strictest account."

Despite the absence of a formal statement of technique or definition, however, it is possible to gain a sense of what "accounting and distribution" was and how housing departments performed it from the copious documentation prepared during repeated Goskon inspections of the TsZhZO and the neighborhood housing departments made between 1918 and 1921. These investigations unfailingly revealed a staggering morass of incompetence and disorganization, painstakingly reconstructed in minute detail on the basis of dozens of interviews with staff, on time spent shadowing staff while they worked, and of course, on a thorough review of all extant files and correspondence, which was frequently found lacking. Their results, that is, should not be taken as proof positive of the housing departments' unique incompetence, nor of a broader pattern of state collapse in the revolutionary era, but rather as testimony to the perennial paradox of Soviet administration, already in place in the revolutionary era: that it kept extraordinarily careful records of its own shortcomings, "making the gathering of evidence on administrative disorder remarkably easy."[58] When it came to the housing departments, the Goskon investigations are especially good at revealing the presences and absences of documentation, records made and destroyed, given away, or lost, hinting at the extent to which—as will be the focus of the next section—the inventory of built space served as an active site of revolutionary politics as opposed to mere record of state capacity.

The "accounting and distribution" of a neighborhood's "existing reserve of space" began with the building committees. As one of its first acts in the spring of 1918, the TsZhZO ordered the neighborhood soviets to gather lists from all building committees on their territories, specifying the number of apartments in each building and the rooms and inhabitants per apartment, thus illuminating in a general way the density of inhabitation of particular buildings and areas. When the campaign to expel "parasites" from the city began over the summer, it was the building committees that were again charged with providing lists of "parasites" to their neighborhood housing department. The housing department, in turn, was to submit the lists to a specially formed Central Housing Committee, charged with composing a final list of parasites slated for expulsion, to be published in *Izvestia*. Publication was ostensibly necessary in order to ensure that the neighborhood housing departments possessed a city-wide list of parasites "before them and in the event that someone from one of the lists addressed them, they were to refuse to give them space."[59] But, of course, if the objective was merely to apprise the neighborhood housing departments of "parasites," the Mossoviet could have ordered the departments to circulate the lists among themselves. That *Izvestia* published the lists underscores not only that the search for parasites was meant to deprive and shame those so identified, but also that members of the public could consider themselves involved in the process, making their own use of the lists if they wished.

Building committee chairmen, primarily responsible for identifying residents as parasites, faced sharp penalties for concealing information. Still, the housing authorities struggled to trust them, even after new elections elevated representatives of the "laboring people" to positions of authority. As a result, neighborhood housing offices frequently ignored the information they received from building committees, "since building committees," the TsZhZO explained to Bonch-Bruevich later that summer when one such instance was revealed, were known to "protect the interests of the residents, and are not inclined to cede those interests," no matter what their social composition.[60] The TsZhZO's information architect, Kuzovkov, therefore proposed subordinating the building committees to a new organ of municipal governance he called the "quarter economic unit" or "*kvartal'noe khozyaistvo,*" "*kvartkhoz*" for short. Kuzovkov's plan, which was implemented in the summer of 1919, called for each kvartkhoz to oversee 150–300 apartments and their building committees, which would produce 700 kvartkhozy in total.[61] The kvartkhoz was responsible for checking all information about vacancies and registrations submitted by the building committees and for promulgating orders from the Mossoviet.[62] It was to be composed of either Communist Party members or workers belonging to categories one or two of the bread ration, a safeguard against political unreliability—and also a way to cut costs, as it was assumed that Party members and workers would labor voluntarily, after their regular jobs, at the kvartkhoz, and would thus not need to be paid.

The final destination of the information created by building committees and kvartkhozy was the neighborhood housing department, namely its subdepartment for accounting and distribution. Like all early Soviet institutions, the housing departments felt themselves to be acutely understaffed. They arrived at this assessment through comparing their existing employees against their own hiring plans, a metric that makes their actual condition difficult to judge. What is clear is that the majority of neighborhood housing department employees worked as "controllers," and that virtually none of the employees of the housing departments were Party members, despite the intensity of the housing departments' role in prosecuting the class war: in the fall of 1918, the Sokol neighborhood housing department reported two Party "sympathizers" on its staff of thirteen (who worked as a janitor and a courier, respectively, not in substantive administration). At the start of 1920, the city's largest neighborhood, Gorodskoi, employed one Party member only—its director, A. N. Ignatov. By the end of the year, it had hired thirteen more, for a total of fourteen Party members on a staff of 102.[63]

As the staffs of housing departments grew in size, the increase occurred almost entirely in the ranks of controllers; sixty-two of the Gorodskoi neighborhood housing department's employees worked as controllers in 1920.[64] Survey forms they answered in 1918 indicate that controllers were generally young men, although in the Khamovniki neighborhood, a Goskon inspector learned that women occupied the job, too—to the detriment not merely of the housing department's productivity, the inspector concluded, but also of the quality of its data, the "accuracy" of which it was deemed "impossible to know, as [Khamovniki] has only six controllers, one of whom is sick and two of whom are women."[65] It is true that the job required serious physical endurance; according to one controller in the Sokol neighborhood in 1918, he "made the rounds of apartments" for as many as nine or ten hours each day, starting at ten o'clock in the morning and continuing until seven or eight o'clock at night, "depending on the needs of the inhabitants."[66]

This curious formulation—that his labor "depend[ed] on the needs of the inhabitants"—hinted at an essential feature of the controller's work, which is that it was responsive rather than systematic, ebbing and flowing in reaction to particular situations generated by the residents themselves. There were periodic efforts to change this aspect of information gathering and its "control" in the housing departments. Toward the end of 1920, the Khamovniki housing department held a day of unpaid, weekend labor—a "voskresnik," like the better known "subbotnik," but held on a Sunday rather than the usual Saturday— during which controllers were paired with other professionals from the neighborhood, such as engineers, in the performance of an intensive "accounting" of apartments.[67] It was more typical, however, for controllers to visit individual apartments or apartment buildings in response to information submitted by building committees, kvartkhozy, and residents themselves. The latter source, according to one of the Goskon inspections, was arguably the leading source of spaces "submitted to the account."[68]

Once inside an apartment, the task of the controller was to assess not only the apartment but also its inhabitants, and, more particularly, their usage of the space, according to a shifting and largely unwritten set of criteria. These included the "density of inhabitation" according to the norm of two square sazhens per person, although, as seen in chapter 1, the application of the norm depended substantially on other, social factors, including the employment status of the head of household, and the social status of the residents. Controllers recorded their findings on "protocols" or "account cards," the latter in the event that their inspection turned up space they believed was subject, for one reason or another, to redistribution. Account cards, that is, did not reflect information about the apartment independent of its perceived suitability for redistribution; they did not specify how many rooms an apartment had in total, only how many rooms it had available for new residents.

This distinction is where the real work of control was found. It was a controller's job to interpret not simply the space but the residents, the apartment, and the relation between them—and not just as a matter of density and social status, but also in a more mundane register. In one case, from the Khamovniki neighborhood, controllers were called to an apartment where a husband and wife occupying one room claimed to have divorced, which entitled them to two rooms. Unfortunately, their case does not indicate who lodged a complaint against the couple. But, among other things, the controller sent to investigate learned through interviews on site that the divorced husband and wife, in fact, continued to sleep in the same bad, such that the alleged "intimate motives (divorce)" for their claim on two of the apartment's six rooms "in reality exist[ed] only on paper."[69]

The act of accounting was thus inevitably also an act of interpretation. For this reason, it frequently required multiple visits from a controller to assess a space—a sore spot among controllers, who resented having their work second-guessed in this fashion. On the day of a voskresnik in the Khamovniki neighborhood, one controller "took onto the account a room being used as a dining room" in a three-room apartment on Myortvy Lane, occupied by a family of four. By chance, the controller later passed a colleague in the street, "and asked 'where are you headed,' he said to me to No. 11 Myortvy Lane, apt

1, where a room has been incorrectly taken onto the account." A dispute ensued right there in the street, with the first controller insisting "that it was correctly done, but evidently Com. Kramer-Ageev," a more senior neighborhood housing official, "was not satisfied with this, and sent the [other] controller a second time . . . without warning me."[70] In the end, the controllers could not come to agreement as to whether the room belonged on the account— that is, should be made available for redistribution—and the matter was turned over to a newly created body called the Conflict Commission, a three-person body of appeal for the resolution of housing disputes.

As this usage indicates, "the account" of built space was not conceived as a comprehensive inventory of buildings and rooms. It was not an account of purely physical spaces, but rather, a fluid record of particular living spaces deemed "available" for resettlement at the time. "Available" was not the same as unoccupied. Perhaps the most substantial labor involved in the account's creation was thus not the gathering of information about physical spaces per se, but the investigation and verification of the conjoined qualities that made up an available living space—an admixture of features of the space, features of the residents, features of the residents' use of the space, which the controllers had to interpret. The technology of the accounting cards, envisioned by the statistician Tishina and the consultant Kuzovkov as the latest word in administrative rationalization, instead enabled the operation of the account in this subjective manner, not least because, before April 1921, the cards were not uniquely numbered, and could be held by controllers "in unlimited quantities." This feature allowed controllers to "create several cards for the very same room," by accident or on purpose. By the same token, a controller might "take a room onto the account and then destroy the card," with no one the wiser—no unique numeration meant never having to explain when a card went missing.[71] But the account worked this way even in neighborhoods where accounting cards had not been adopted, as in Khamovniki, where according to Goskon investigators, the most sophisticated account books of all the city's local housing departments were kept: a registry of "free rooms and apartments," recorded by the date on which information about them was received; a log of these same spaces, ordered alphabetically by street name; and a "book of candidates" wishing to receive space.[72]

All of these challenges were well known to the Goskon inspectors, who reviewed the housing departments for the first time in the summer of 1918, and returned regularly thereafter: in October 1918, January 1919, and then nearly continuously between November 1920 and October 1921. They were reliably appalled by what they found. At one point, the relentless cycle of inspection and condemnation so aggravated the staff of the Gorodskoi neighborhood housing department that it declared a ten-day hiatus, because it, the neighborhood housing department, was too short of space to carry on. "No reorganization or improvement in work is possible," the department huffed, "the *zhilotdel* [abbreviation for "housing department"] has repeatedly asked the presidium for more rooms and better space and has not received it and so work has ground to a halt."[73] Around this time, the first criminal investigations of the staff of the housing department commenced, targeting, among others, the TsZhZO's early employee A. L. Gelbras. A complaint made against Gelbras from the end of 1920 called out his "tactless rude address, damaging the prestige of power [*vlast'*]" as well as his "inactivity in fulfilling the formal tasks of his position," which included attention to physical condition of neighborhood buildings. When these failings were raised with him, Gelbras promptly agreed that "he did not know about repairs, he was occupied exclusively with the accounting of housing." In a subsequent interview, Gelbras was said to have helplessly "claimed he was not capable of [making] the account, but he was, it was just his evil refusal" to do so that hampered the job.[74]

Goskon's investigations painted a stark picture of malfunctioning across the housing departments. The investigators reported on messy offices, with papers strewn about and files spilling off work tables. In one neighborhood, the pages of the account books were not numbered, making it impossible to retrieve information once it was registered.[75] In another, the books were found "in extremely careless shape, thus for example: there are notes in pencil everywhere," entries inexplicably "underlined and re-underlined, sheets torn, and parts of them are lost."[76] Staff work habits were judged lacking. In Khamovniki, where investigators spent time observing the staff at work, they determined that "account takes place by some coworker of Com. Tishchenko," who was in charge of the account, "yelling out from the neighboring room, 'Com. Tishchenko! Put the following space on the account!'"[77] In interviews, few housing employees could answer what the inspectors believed should be basic questions about their work. In Khamovniki, "neither the housing department nor the kvartkhozy" could state the "level of concentration of their neighborhood." The kvartkhozy were "in no condition to check" the information presented by the building committees, "as they have no workers, and those they do have work roughly two hours a day," after their regular jobs. "Thus the entire basis of the housing system is supposed to be the kvartkhozy, of which there are about 540 in Moscow, that are totally incapable of playing this role."[78] The

Sub-departments of Accounting and Distribution thus "do not know how much free space they have as the kvartkhozy and building committees do not tell them and they do not possess the apparatus to find out," due to the fact that the controllers—whatever it was they were doing in their ten-hour days of visiting apartments—had failed to perform the necessary "control."[79] The accountant Galagan, when preparing his plan for a registry of state property, had anticipated that real estate would be the easiest object to inventory, because it could not move—yet, somehow, buildings were escaping the housing departments, left and right.

There was also, to be sure, evidence of purposeful malfeasance. In his interview with the Goskon inspectors, none other than the "bourgeois consultant" Kuzovkov provided testimony that an underground market had emerged "at both the center and in the neighborhoods, a system of transactions and bribes, up to and including the ability to receive a room or apartment for a fixed tariff."[80] "Written evidence of bribes, due to the nature of housing paperwork," could not be established, but it was clear that the activity focused on the accounting cards as keys to space. The reliance on volunteer labor at the kvartkhozy facilitated backdoor dealings, but the housing officials were also at fault. "Housing power [zhilishchnaya vlast'] consists entirely of personal trust [personal'noe doveriye]," wrote the Goskon inspectors. "Thus far the choice of leaders for this department has been extremely unsuccessful," they concluded.[81]

By the metrics of comprehensive inventory laid out by Kuzovkov and embraced by Goskon's investigators, the housing departments had undoubtedly failed at the mission set out two and a half years earlier in the TsZhZO's Statute: to produce "an inventory of apartments and spaces on the territory of the city" and to clarify "the level of housing need among the population." From what the inspectors saw, "there is no account, in either cards or books, held by the center or by the neighborhoods."[82] They repeated this conclusion for each of the neighborhood offices they visited, sometimes drawing it straight from the mouths of ZhZO employees. In the Baumansky neighborhood, they were told, "a precise and correct account of rooms and apartments in the neighborhood does not exist, nor is there any account held at the kvartkhozy." There was also "no information about how many rooms or apartments had been given out" or "how much free space" remained to be distributed. The housing officials, that is, claimed to know neither what there was, nor what they themselves had done.[83] The director of the Gorodskoi neighborhood housing department declared that it had proven "impossible to achieve a precise account of living spaces. All kinds of methods of accounting have been attempted to keep track of spaces," the director declared, "but they all proved inadequate before the rapidly changing picture in the use of space." Finally, he claimed, "it was decided to conduct accounting in its simplest form, that is, to keep no account whatsoever."[84]

But here was the real mystery: despite these shortcomings, the housing offices serviced an extraordinary number of space-seekers. In the month of December 1918, the ten people working in the Khamovniki neighborhood housing office—a director, an accountant, two clerks, and six controllers—processed 237 requests for apartments and 604 for rooms, of which they satisfied 196 and 478 respectively.[85] By 1920, the office had "huge lines," composed mostly of new arrivals to Moscow, "looking for space, who end up having to spend the night at the train station. Sometimes they live there for weeks," the Goskon inspector observed. Still, over the course of the year, the Khamovniki housing office met 3,407 of 4,145 requests for apartments, and 6,681 of 7,611 requests for rooms.[86] It had records for all of this activity. Between 26 April and 15 December 1920, the Baumansky neighborhood office, with a staff of thirty-three—four directors, ten clerks, two instructors and twelve controllers—had satisfied 5,115 of 6,407 requests for rooms and 1,113 of 1,478 requests for apartments.[87]

To explain this high rate of satisfaction, an investigator spent the day of December 8, 1920, observing the work of the Gorodskoi neighborhood housing department. He estimated that 150 people came through the office that day, of whom "around 50 were satisfied." Yet only "an insignificant number" of the spaces they received, "perhaps seven over the course of two weeks," had been assigned in "the usual order, that is from cards registered in the logbooks of space."[88] The great majority of applicants, by contrast, somehow found space on their own.

> Such cases took place as follows: seeing that there was no free space on the registers, the applicant himself finds a free room and acquires the necessary accounting card at the kvartkhoz; the 'greater part' of citizens bringing such fortunately acquired cards to the department are given the order of occupation by the department for the space they found, although each such instance is 'examined separately.'"[89]

Instead of the housing department finding space for the citizens, then, citizens were finding space for the housing department—much as Lander had expected the residents of No. 29 Povarskaya to do for him. "Often, the department makes use of accidental [*sluchainye*] bits of information," inspectors wrote of the Khamovniki office. "Sometimes citizens bring information about free space with them in the hopes of receiving it for themselves and with a heap of papers, demonstrate their right to the space."[90] Sometimes the housing department bestowed the right to occupy the hard-won space on the petitioner who found it, but often it did not, and the space found by one person was given to another. Inevitably, the inspector mused, "the matter ends up with the conflict commission," the neighborhood-level committee composed of representatives from the local soviet, the housing department, and occasionally the party or the Cheka, charged with resolving disputes about space; "and in this way, only those spaces that somehow come across their desks get distributed."[91]

Back in early December 1918, at the height of the campaigns to evict parasites from Moscow, Bonch-Bruevich received an angry complaint from an employee at the Commissariat of Transportation being threatened with eviction, making a nearly identical observation about the rationality of management, or lack thereof, in housing allocation. Comparatively speaking, the circumstances of his eviction were not so bad: the TsZhZO had offered him space in a five-room apartment just up the street from his home. And yet the prospect of the move infuriated him. It was not just that he was being made to leave a three-room space that suited his small household for a five-room apartment that would, in turn, inevitably "become subject to concentration all over again," or that there was no one at home to manage the physical labor of the move. What infuriated him was its "aimlessness." "If my eviction was brought about by some positive necessity, for the needs of renewing the country, I would not wait even an hour to leave my apartment," he vowed to Bonch-Bruevich. But what positive need was there for moving him into an empty apartment a few houses down the street, and then moving different workers, just like himself, into his apartment?[92] "I really agree with the article that appeared in *Izvestia* on November 29 [1918], No. 261," he wrote to Bonch-Bruevich, "about how it is completely wrong for soviet employees to be moved around from one building to another, viewing in this only the influence of some evil will." In case Bonch-Bruevich had not seen the article in question, titled "A Bacchanalia of Eviction," the railway worker attached his own copy, with important passages underlined. "There is being created some kind of incomprehensible and useless bacchanalia of resettlement," the article trumpeted. Having started with a "healthy and understandable idea" of "giving the proletariat good apartments, the ability to leave the basements and cold hovels and move into more or less suitable conditions," the housing departments were instead "resettling and evicting and concentrating absolutely everyone, without any sorting." They had produced legions of "unhappy, unlucky sufferers, who are evicted and moved two, three or four times, and these are not even bourgeoisie, but petty soviet employees and workers." What united them was the irrationality of their movement, the consequence of one thing and one thing alone: that information about them and their living spaces had happened "one way or another to fall into the [housing authorities'] hands."[93] The through-line in all of these scenarios—from Lander's offer at No. 29 Povarskaya to the Goskon exposés to the "Bacchanalia of Eviction"—was the basic problem of accounting and visibility: housing departments could only distribute the spaces they could see.

Black Lists, Out of Line, and Off-Book: Nonmarket Accounts of Living Space

Although it looked and felt chaotic, even random, to the transportation worker and countless others in his position, which living spaces a housing department could see was not, in fact, a matter of chance. Which spaces a housing department could see—its list of "available spaces"—was an artifact of an accounting system that cast light on some spaces while putting others into shadow. As historians of double-entry bookkeeping and other forms of accounting have long argued, all accounting systems produce resources as much as they reflect them—through the categories of things they recognize, the audiences they assume, or the time scales they invoke.[94] But as Caroline Humphrey argues, the nonmarket accounting systems developed in the Soviet Union afforded distinctive opportunities for resource-creation, available not only to those in charge of the accounts, but also to others engaged in the productive process an account was meant to control. While focused on economic life in collective farms after the Second World War, Humphrey's argument illuminates several important dynamics of nonmarket accounting that were present in the work of the revolutionary housing departments as well.

The "intention of bookkeeping practice" in the postwar collective farm, as was the case for the comprehensive inventory of the built environment after the Revolution, was "to leave no possible gap for illicit operations, such that every single production unit is accounted for in a variety of overlapping documents."[95] In the absence of market indicators, Soviet economic planners developed an array of alternative measures designed to achieve blanket control, checking and cross-checking individual "production units" against half a dozen different metrics, each signed by multiple employees. These were both administratively burdensome and technically complex, as they required mastery of nonmarket pricing concepts such as "self-cost" (*sebestoimost'*) that were a struggle for economic experts, let alone farm managers, to define. As a result, Humphrey shows, "the bookkeeping system itself, entirely legitimately, create[d] the possibilities for the emergence out of nowhere" of "manipulable resources," or "products which are really surplus, or extra, to the state delivery plan."[96]

These so-called manipulable resources also emerged in the course of negotiations between the farm managers and state planners over the farm's annual production plan. Lower, more manageable production targets led directly and indirectly to a farm's acquisition of manipulable resources. On the one hand, lower targets allowed even a comparatively unproductive farm to exceed its production goal, leaving a surplus for farm managers and workers to exploit. On the other, as Humphrey shows, the existence of manipulable resources in itself smoothed the production process for farms that had them, providing much-needed material for a variety of aims—increasing feed reserves for livestock, improving the diets of workers in exchange for extra labor time, bartering with other entities for necessary machinery, arranging school entrances for farm children with local officials. Each of these could boost the farm's physical output, which led in a circular fashion to higher yields and plan surplus that could be used at the farm manager's future discretion. Indeed, the utility of manipulable resources was such that, when a farm failed to produce actual plan surplus, its managers saw little alternative but to skim the farm's regular produce in order to create some. In this case, surplus was produced through purposeful manipulation of accounts to hide the skimming. These possibilities meant that a politics of accounting suffused farm operations. What to put on the account and what to leave off it was a matter of strategy and debate, as was the question of to what end such resources should be put. To be sure, farm managers and laborers sometimes sold the surplus into the "shadow economy," but this was not uniformly the case. Manipulable resources were neither purely illegitimate nor purely legitimate. Rather, they could be created and disposed through both legitimate and illegitimate channels—transacted as goods between farms, between farm managers and laborers, and through other, nonmarket passages.

In the management of the built environment during the revolutionary era, of course, there was no production plan to which certain quantities of living

space could be "surplus." But there was an expectation—on the part of Kuzovkov, the Goskon investigators, and many others—that the informational
picture of the built environment generated through the account would be total
and comprehensive, precisely as the accounts of the collective farm were
meant to be. As a result, there was also, and in ways similar to the kolkhoz, the
potential for the emergence of housing-specific "manipulable resources," produced through the accounting system itself. The inventories produced in housing departments, as already observed, were not actually of buildings and
rooms, ceiling height and square meters—rather, they were of "available,"
"free," or "excess" living space.[97] And living space *was* a substance being made,
even if physical buildings were not: it was produced through the labor of the
controllers, and by others involved in taking the built environment onto account, as is evident from the exquisite documentation of the controllers' work
process and the daily operations of the housing departments prepared by the
Goskon investigators. As these reports make clear, the designation of a room
or apartment as available living space was unavoidably a matter of interpretation—of the space itself, of the people who lived in it, and of the relationship
between the two. Like manipulable resources on the collective farm, living
space was produced through the system of accounting itself.

In order to guide the interpretive labor of controllers, officials, and residents, rules about what constituted living space emerged precisely in this period. Like the accounting rules at the collective farm, these rules raised as
many questions as they answered. On top of the metric of the norm (the
room's size against number and age of residents), such rules addressed many
features of built space and the claims upon it. Rooms which functioned as
passageways to second rooms, where there was no other point of access to the
second room, could not be assigned as the sole living space of an individual or
a family; the same was true of rooms with windows looking out onto an interior space, called "dark" rooms. Both kinds of rooms, however, could be
counted as living space in certain other situations, for instance if a household
member required additional space for performing "responsible work" at home,
or if the window looking onto interior space was situated such that the room
was not, in fact, "dark," but "light." Similar rules, also requiring interpretation
on the part of controllers and others, emerged with regard to the household
members. Many such decisions focused on class status, but there was also
much to consider in a less ideologically charged register. Children were entitled to consume the adult norm of space only from age sixteen, but in cases
where families had two children, one an adolescent boy and the other an

adolescent girl, a housing department might agree that they were entitled to separate spaces before a sixteenth birthday.

Insofar as these rules inevitably left much to the discretion of controllers, it was entirely possible that two controllers visiting the same apartment could arrive at different conclusions as to the "availability" of a particular room as "living space," like the two controllers who crossed paths during the accounting voskresnik. Indeed, this seems to have been fairly common. According to a report prepared by the Gorodskoi ZhZO of its activities between April and September 1921, its forty-four controllers managed to perform a whopping 15,780 "regular inspections" of spaces during those months, which resulted in 870 rooms being taken onto account as "available living space." Of these, 766 rooms were subsequently "put out into distribution," meaning that 104 (13 percent) of the rooms initially taken onto the account were later removed from it. Removal from the account typically followed a second inspection, and maybe even a journey to the conflict commission, the neighborhood troika empowered to resolve conflicts over space that the housing department, for one reason or another, could not resolve on its own.[98] Conflict commissions typically had several "controllers" at their disposal. These controllers also performed site visits to reinvestigate spaces, verifying not only the information that had led to a room being taken onto the account, but also the allegations in subsequent complaints on the matter. In preparing submissions to the conflict commission, the interested parties, who included both residents and housing departments defending their interpretation of the space, often drew up floorplans of apartments by hand, showing doors, windows, and the layout of rooms. Conflict commission controllers would then draw floorplans of their own, and in 1921, reflecting the sense that this information was essential for the resolution of conflicts and the interpretation of a space, floorplan-drawing became a formal part of the inspection. New "protocol" cards printed for the use of the controller had a large empty box in which the controller was meant to draw the floorplan. Beneath it, the protocol contained a section for the "description of the rooms and the people living [in them]." (See figure 3.1.)

Living space was made and unmade in the course of these visits—by controllers, who inspected the spaces, and also by residents, neighbors, and other bystanders, who campaigned to have rooms placed on and taken off the account. Goskon inspectors upbraided housing departments that shed rooms from the account in this manner, suspecting malfeasance or incompetence. But it was also the case that spaces and people proved genuinely difficult to read, leading to conflicting interpretations of a space's availability according

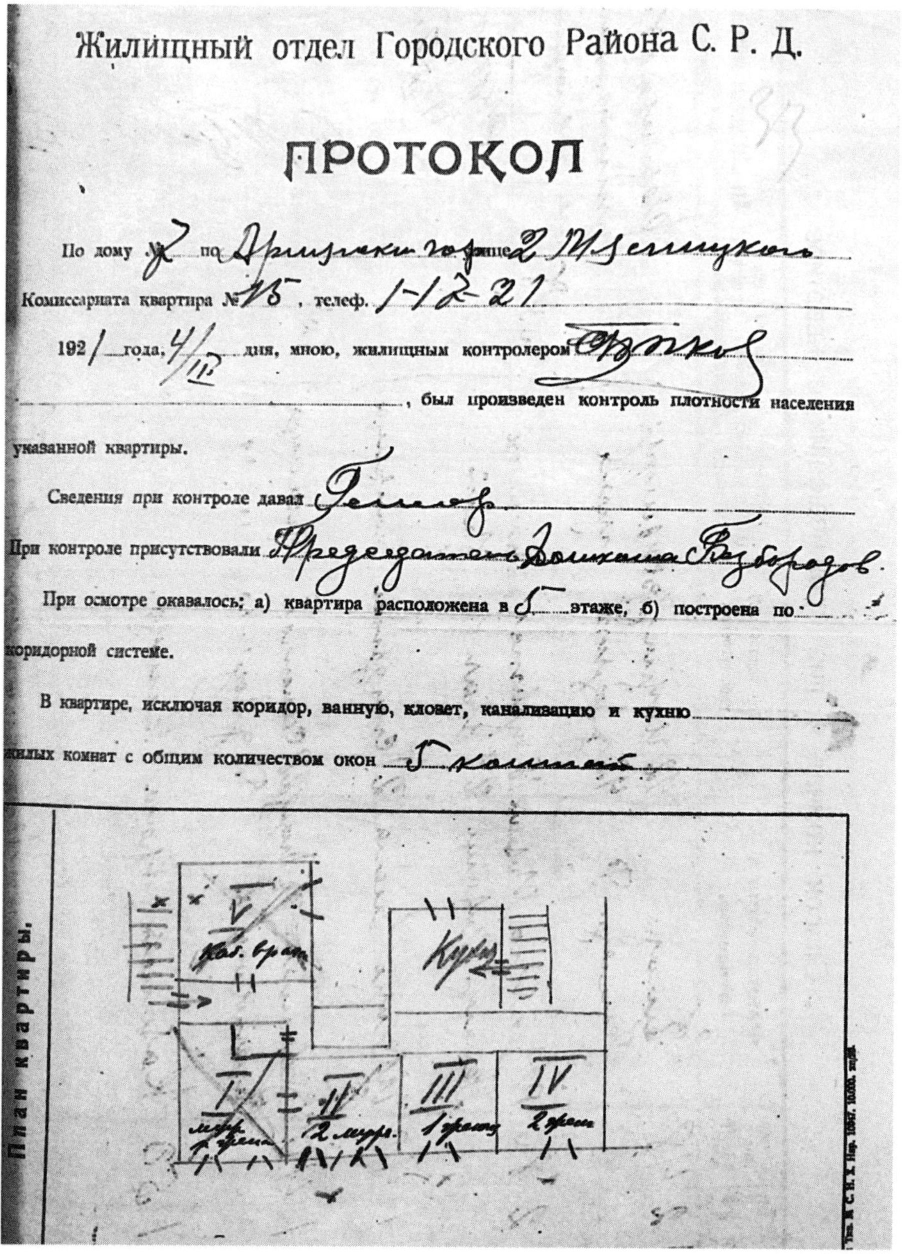

Жилищный отдел Городского Района С. Р. Д.

ПРОТОКОЛ

По дому № 7 по ... Комиссариата квартира № 15, телеф. 1-II-21

192**1** года 4/II дня, мною, жилищным контролером ..., был произведен контроль плотности населения указанной квартиры.

Сведения при контроле давал ...

При контроле присутствовали ...

При осмотре оказалось: а) квартира расположена в 5 этаже, б) построена по коридорной системе.

В квартире, исключая коридор, ванную, клозет, канализацию и кухню ... жилых комнат с общим количеством окон 5 комнат

План квартиры.

FIGURE 3.1. An inspection form from the Housing Department of the Gorodskoi Neighborhood c. early 1921, performed to "check the density" of inhabitation, with space for a hand-drawn floor plan reflecting current inhabitation. Credit: Courtesy of TsAGM, photographed with permission by the author, July 13, 2017. TsAGM f. 2434, op. 1, d. 29, l. 33.

to the rules. One case in the files of the Gorodskoi ZhZO relates to a room taken onto account from the four-room apartment occupied by Dr. Gustav Genrikhovich Geller and given to a metallurgist and "responsible worker" of the Central Committee of the Union of Metal Workers, Com. Smirnov. Geller succeeded in having the room removed from the account two days later, but this was only after the metallurgist Smirnov had been granted the right to occupy the room. Smirnov brought a complaint before the conflict commission, which ruled in favor of Geller. But Smirnov continued to pursue the room, submitting a file to the Presidium of the Gorodskoi soviet that included "records of the commandant of the dorm of the Central Committee of the VSRM [Metalworkers' Union], copies of decisions from the ZhZO," and even "protocols from the conflict commission." These included sketches of the apartment's floor plan—a hand-drawn sketch made by Geller, and another drawing made by the controller—as well as testimony from the building commandant, who insisted that it was "undoubtedly possible to situate" Geller's family of four in just three rooms, leaving one available for Smirnov, because, in fact, Geller claimed one of the four rooms as a reception for his patients—he was a doctor, and doctors were permitted a room for seeing patients. According to an inspection, "there [were] no signs that the doctor saw the ill at home, as in his room there stood just a piano and curtains, [the only trace of his profession] was a calling card."[99] The resolution of the case hinged on this question: did Geller's room bear evidence of use as a doctor's surgery or not?

Such judgements were difficult to make on the basis of inspection alone. Controllers and housing departments therefore relied heavily not only upon the building committees and kvartkhozy formally charged with passing information to them but also upon the receipt of "accidental information" or "indicated addresses." According to the Gorodskoi neighborhood report, while the 15,780 "regular inspections" made by controllers between April and September 1921 netted 766 rooms for the account, the neighborhood housing department received 578 rooms for the account "according to indicated addresses"— that is, according to addresses provided by the population. Over the course of the year, the neighborhood claimed, reliance on "indicated addresses" had decreased, but at the start of it, indicated addresses may well have exceeded rooms found through regular inspection.[100]

Reliance on invitations to inspect space was not unique to the housing departments of Moscow. A file of documents collected between April and December 1919 by the Petrograd Communal Economic Soviet, labeled "Acts of investigation of apartments and correspondence with the Central Housing

Department," contains numerous examples of what might be called targeted requests for space—requests, tips, and invitations from Petrograders, pertaining to spaces that the petitioners already knew about, and that they deemed, for one reason or another, available for redistribution. On 18 November, for example, the Housing Department of the Spassky neighborhood in Petrograd received the following statement:

> Citizen Vasily Sintsov would like to receive an apartment (occupied as housing) on 25th October Prospect in building No. 46, apt. 23, from which [the previous occupant] has left for his homeland and not returned, and [which] at present is occupied by nobody, the apartment consists of one room there is a stove in it.[101]

The Housing Department received similar declarations from people interested in occupying a one-room apartment on Karl Marx Street whose owner had "left for his homeland"; an apartment on Panteleimonovskaya Street, where an unregistered couple was squatting with their servant; two rooms with furniture in No. 5 Baburin Lane; a two-room unoccupied apartment in No. 29 Morskaya Street; and either apartment 5 or apartment 6 in No. 53 25th October Prospect, both purportedly empty.[102] "Indicated addresses" were also submitted by people who did not wish to claim the space for themselves, in order to alert housing authorities to real or perceived misuses of space, violations of the rules of occupation, or excesses of space according to the norm. Of course, tips were not always submitted on the basis of close observation. One tip led controllers to the apartment of a doctor and his family of three, who occupied six rooms (as discussed in chapter 1, the norm in Petrograd was conceived not in sazhens or arshins, as in Moscow, but in rooms—one per person—until the early 1920s). To someone who knew the residents only by sight or by reading the list of inhabitants posted at the building entry, this would appear excessive. But inspection revealed that it was "not possible to present a room in accordance with statement No. 3651," the original tip, "as the doctor occupies two rooms for receiving patients and four people live there," bringing him in line with the Petrograd norm.[103]

Independent of the spaces they occupied, certain kinds of people were more vulnerable than others to having their addresses "indicated" as suitable for redistribution. As one might expect, these included people with undesirable social histories—the wife of a man shot for speculation; an aged woman with servants—but it also involved other social and personal attributes.[104] Judging from the "indicated addresses" compiled between April and December 1919 in Petrograd, single women were disproportionately at risk of having their living space pointed out to housing authorities (a pattern observed at other key moments of revolutionary seizure as well).[105] In one case, the housing department ordered an elderly resident of No. 116 Maly Znamensky Lane, citizen Stulova, to vacate the room she shared with another old woman, Karaseva, shortly before New Year's Eve in 1920. The women were to be moved together into a large, freezing room in a different apartment, unoccupied because it was so hard to heat. The women were given just ten hours to move, a demand so egregious that the building committee refused to implement the order. But three days later, a Chekist named G. F. Sosnovsky appeared with a group of armed policemen, demanding Stulova's resettlement "within a period of four hours." A subsequent investigation conducted by Goskon's successor, Rabkrin, revealed not only that Sosnovsky had first begun eyeing Stulova's room back in November, but also that he sought eventual control of the entire four-room apartment. Among the papers gathered by Rabkrin was an order issued by the director of the Operational Department of the Cheka and boldly stamped as "Operational—TOP SECRET," containing important intelligence about the living circumstances of all the old women in apartment number one: the elderly Stulova who shared a room with her aged servant, Karaseva, and another old woman, Kabatova, who shared with a servant of her own. Various obstacles prevented Sosnovsky from evicting the women immediately, a situation he resolved by threatening to throw Stulova's belongings out of the room himself, "without vouchsafing their integrity," unless she left the room and "signed a document" testifying that her move was "voluntary."[106]

The Cheka's unique authority in revolutionary society gave it unusual sway with the housing authorities. But its access to information about people's domestic circumstances was arguably no less important in the success of its claims to space. Evictions like Stulova's conformed to a pattern of Chekists using their privileged access to information about people's living circumstances to secure housing, targeting socially vulnerable people to do so. Several months after Sosnovsky gathered information on Stulova through the VChK's Operational Department, another Chekist, Comrade Dymov, appeared at an apartment building on Kolokolnikov Lane with a police officer and a female friend. He gained access to the apartment of an actress named M. V. Dantsiger-Ponyatkovskaya by "presenting himself as an employee of the VChK." The three toured Dantsiger-Ponyatkovskaya's two rooms, one of which Dymov's female friend declared that she "liked very much." Dymov forbade Dantsiger-Ponyatkovskaya from returning to the room, even to retrieve her possessions, and threatened to break down a door unless Dantsiger-Ponyatkovskaya signed a document relinquishing her claim to the room "voluntarily." Rabkrin investigated the events at Dantsiger-Ponyatkovskaya's request, during which it learned that the neighborhood housing department's attention was first drawn to Dantsiger-Ponyatkovskaya's apartment by none other than Genrikh Yagoda, then director of the VChK's chancellery. This request triggered an inspection by a housing department controller, who "investigated [the apartment's] level of concentration" just a few days before Dymov arrived.[107]

For people without access to the Cheka's information-gathering apparatus, it was necessary to scavenge for tips in other ways. People in search of living space questioned friends, employers, and housing authorities for help. People walked the streets, inspecting apartment numbers and even poking around entryways. One of the most significant unofficial tasks of the building committee chairman or the local kvartkhoz commandant was to manage the many inquiries into spaces in the building, which could turn hostile. One kvartkhoz volunteer related in distress to the local soviet that he had unwittingly shown the room of a mother absent with her sick child to a stranger who inquired, seemingly by chance, only to learn that the stranger had, in fact, already secured permission to inhabit the space, purposefully threatening the mother and sick child with eviction.[108]

The motivations of those who indicated addresses to the housing departments ran the gamut. Some people submitted tips in search of justice. In the fall of 1920, a letter arrived for the Khamovniki ZhZO angrily and anonymously "tell[ing] the story of apartment 25," and urging the ZhZO to remember that Soviet laws were "meant to defend the proletarian interests and that soviet power is not meant to give rooms to the bourgeoisie as a gift."[109] Others submitted tips in search of direct or indirect personal benefit. In May 1921, the residents of No. 79 Sadovaya-Zemlyanka Street in Moscow learned that their building committee chairman, Batkov, had actively colluded with the factory committee of the nearby Ustinsky factory to designate their building a worker-commune under factory control.[110] In a general meeting, they confronted Batkov, seeking "an explanation about why he did not inform the residents in a timely fashion about the possibility of the building being transferred [to the factory] and why he did not take the necessary measures to protect the interests of the residents by requesting that the TsZhZO cancel its order."[111] In a similar case from Petrograd, one group of residents, all employed at a factory nearby, indicated their *own* building as "bourgeois" to the neighborhood housing department, triggering an order from the housing department that the building "be settled exclusively by workers at the factory," effectively evicting their unaffiliated neighbors. Here too, the residents confronted one another at a building-wide meeting attended by more than five hundred people. Here, too, they produced a transcript, which they submitted to the Central Bureau of Complaints. In the transcript, the building committee chairman recounted his efforts to convince the factory workers to abandon their campaign to seize the space, demonstrating that the unaffiliated residents could not be considered "bourgeois," and were, in fact, themselves also workers. Following his speech, however, one of the factory workers shocked the crowd with a malicious declaration that "we will nevertheless manage to occupy this building and evict you all," eliciting pleas that he "not introduce enmity between workers." It was too late; as subsequent petitions made clear, enmity was now felt all around.[112]

As the inspection of the Moscow neighborhood ZhZOs revealed, indicating an address to housing authorities was not a guarantee of receiving it oneself. No matter how they gained information about space, housing departments stocked addresses for immediate and future use, merging "indicated addresses" and "available living space" identified in the course of regular inspections into a common pot. From there, an address might proceed along one of four basic paths. The first of these was regular distribution in "the usual order, that is, from cards registered in the journals of space," to people registered on the regular list of space-seekers. The Rabkrin inspector claimed that in the Gorodskoi neighborhood, only an "insignificant number" of spaces were assigned in this way, numbering perhaps seven out of the fifty assignments made on the day of his visit. The majority of people were satisfied in some other fashion, either by bringing in addresses themselves, or "out of turn," with the help of something called a "black list."[113] Black lists were composed of "free spaces that," according to one inspector, "were not supposed to enter into the general account at all."[114]

Black list distribution represented the second possible avenue for the disposal of available living space, and it came in two variants. According to the housing staff, they kept such lists for emergencies: "for the settlement of workers evicted from worker-buildings and dormitories," and the loss of housing due to a fire. The black lists, that is, were composed of spaces that, like manipulable resources, housing department staff held off the account illicitly in order to meet legitimate institutional ends. Black lists were meant to be ephemeral, destroyed as soon as the spaces recorded on them had been distributed. But the Rabkrin inspectors managed to uncover one specimen, allowing them to investigate the status of the fourteen spaces listed on it. They found that two of the spaces on the list had indeed been used in the intended way, to resettle workers suddenly evicted from worker-buildings and dormitories. But the remainder had been distributed "according to official, as well as unofficial handwritten notes [*zapiski*] from, for example, a chair of a communal economic council, the director of the Central Housing Department, the director of the accounts, members of the presidium of the neighborhood soviet," and other important personages.[115]

This was known as "out of turn" distribution, and while this designation was meant to signal infrequency and irregularity, "out of turn" distribution, like the black list itself, was routine. According to Rabkrin inspectors, out of turn distribution was most common in the city's most elite neighborhood, Gorodskoi, and least common in the worker stronghold of Baumansky. Indeed, in the Gorodskoi neighborhood, it was distribution in the "regular" order that was deemed "unique and exceptional." Out of turn distribution occurred "in the majority of cases, at the request of Narkoms, central institutions, and even particular individuals." A representative request came from Lenin's Administrative Directorate at the Sovnarkom in 1918 to the TsZhZO, asking that one of its own staff, Stepan Yevseyevich Skripov, together with his uncle, receive "the right to an apartment out of turn, in apartment No. 42, building 11/13 Trekhprudny Lane."[116] Lenin's own interventions, also through the Administrative Directorate, chiefly concerned protecting spaces from requisition and concentration, as for his dentist, Vasily Samoilovich Yudelovich, who treated not only Lenin but also "extremely responsible workers from the Narkoms, including coms. Trotsky, Krasin, Chicherin, Tsyurupa, and others."[117]

There was no way for the housing departments to meet demands for out of turn satisfaction without keeping black lists of available living space held back from the general account. Even so, as evidenced by their treatment in the Rabkrin reports (and much like manipulable resources at the collective farm), black list distribution and out of turn distribution were both tinged with illegitimacy, even when put toward the legitimate ends of housing evicted workers or servicing the orders of the Administrative Directorate of the Sovnarkom. This is likely one reason the lists were destroyed after the spaces on them were distributed, in order to ensure there would not be record of the routine irregularity they represented. The destruction of information about the spaces on black lists, in turn, raised the particular ire of the Rabkrin inspectors, who viewed it as likely evidence of malfeasance. To be sure, the existence of black lists undoubtedly improved conditions for bribe-taking, opportunities for which would have abounded in the housing administration, from building committee chairman to controllers and beyond. The frequency of bribe taking in the administration of living space is difficult to judge, even from the Rabkrin inspections. Kuzovkov testified to inspectors that bribe taking was common enough to be standardized in "fixed tariffs." Yet it is equally notable that, amid the near-constant inspections by Rabkrin and the copious evidence they tossed out of the failings of the housing departments, allegations of criminal malfeasance appear only infrequently. In mechanics, the allocation of space for a bribe and the allocation of space out of turn would have been difficult to tell apart; the chief difference lay not the means, but in the ends.[118]

Needless to say, keeping track of all of this was an incredible amount of work. On-book registration, off-book registration; in turn distribution, out of turn distribution—the accounting system created by the housing departments may not have been comprehensive in the sense that Galagan, Kuzovkov, and other early visionaries of nonmarket accounting had imagined, but it absorbed enormous quantities of information. As anticipated, this information concerned buildings and their inhabitants, but it also concerned leaky windows and old mothers, doctors seeing patients in living rooms and divorced spouses who might really still be sleeping in the same bed. The housing departments had little choice but to make room for all these stories. They gathered these stories up and took testimonies, and when they could not decide what to do, they passed the files over to the conflict commissions. And then, when there was still not enough housing, Rabkrin inspectors arrived at the housing department offices and never left, checking and double-checking the account—both the stories and the addresses—over and over again. In 1919, as previously noted, Larin's Commission on the "housing crisis" determined that the city's supply of "bourgeois" housing was fundamentally insufficient for the task of housing all of Moscow's laboring households. The revolutionary vision to house workers in bourgeois spaces, to reveal the material abundance all around, would not be realized—not least because, now that the Bolsheviks had come to power, no more bourgeois housing could be made. Unlike milk or timber or the other things cities brought into themselves to sustain their populations, there was no way to produce more "bourgeois" housing: thanks to the Bolsheviks, bourgeois buildings had become a nonrenewable resource. And yet, despite this early realization, the persistent insufficiency of the built environment continued to figure as a mystery, to be solved with more investigations and better accounts.

This mystery played out not only as a saga in the lives of apartment dwellers everywhere, but as an administrative battle between the housing departments and Rabkrin. While hostile to Rabkrin and its findings, the housing departments were prepared to concede a great many failings on Rabkrin's list of charges: yes, the "controllers are often illiterate"; yes, the department of accounting and distribution exhibited "careless storage of books and papers"; yes, "files were released from the archive without being signed for."[119] All of this could be conceded because, as the head of the Gorodskoi neighborhood Subdepartment for Accounting and Distribution explained, the ZhZO's decision to act even "in the absence of a complete account, to give decisions without accounting cards," was, in fact, "not accidental, it was decided at a meeting of responsible workers," in light of the demands of "higher and central institutions, beginning with the CC [Central Committee] of the Party, to consider and right then and there decide these issues without any excess formalism . . . I repeat, the most attention was cast on the actual decision of the question." For the same reason, the Gorodskoi ZhZO had no trouble agreeing that it commonly allowed the "release of files from the archive without being signed for"—files that contained the complaints and petitions, inspection records and protocols that went into the "actual decision of the question" of who got to live where. The Gorodskoi ZhZO was only too happy to offload this archive of interpersonal relations, indicated addresses, and floorplans from its crowded office. "If some petition was missing . . . this was because when petitions [for space] were refused or a person wanted to see his file in his hands, he would present its number and it was returned to him fairly eagerly, as the Distribution Section was hardly setting for itself the goal of accumulating multitudes of demands for spaces," and other records, "which were fairly numerous in any case."[120] The housing departments lacked files, they cheerfully explained, because they routinely handed them out to the interested parties. Even the conflict commissions—where the thorniest questions were actually decided—were found, astonishingly, to keep no archives at all. (Records from the conflict commissions appear here only because some parties also submitted their files to Rabkrin, which kept them.)[121]

This was perhaps the most remarkable thing about the information gathered in order to allocate living space: how very little of it was saved. The housing departments and conflict commissions dug deep into people's lives. The quantity of information they produced about people and spaces was remarkable and voluminous—and they threw it all away, which was another way of ensuring that it was bound to happen all over again. The churn of people through space made virtue of a necessity: there was not enough living space in Moscow. There was not enough bourgeois housing to resettle the workers, as the Larin Commission learned already in 1919, and there was not enough housing, total, to accommodate the city's population at the norm, even as the norm fell. The churn kept ever-growing numbers of people moving through a diminishing resource. It turned a nonrenewable resource into a renewable one, constantly generating new spaces by opening and closing particular doors, limiting consumption by keeping people on the go. Each one of these confrontations presented an opportunity to assess the residents and their usage of the living space, and no two confrontations were exactly alike. Each resolution was therefore highly specific, which meant that ironically, for a system of allocation premised on a norm, there was almost no hope that the solutions discerned for one living space might be applied to another. No comprehensive account could keep track of these arrangements, which hinged not so much on the qualities of the built environment, but of the people who inhabited it. The doors of two apartments might open and close in the same way, their floor-plans might be identical, but what of their residents?

Soviet power was unable to achieve abundance through the construction of new buildings after the Revolution. Instead, it made "available living space," a physical resource produced out of the built environment, through the interpretive labor of accounting. While buildings and "available living space" obviously overlapped at many points, they were not the same thing. Measuring the physical dimensions of buildings, even recording detailed information about a building's qualities, its number of rooms, how many of these were light or dark, freely accessed or pass-through, still would not yield up a neat figure: square arshins of available living space. Available living space could not be discerned in the absence of information about inhabitants—existing, prospective, even past. This distinction underscores a basic feature of nonmarket management, which is that after the abolition of private property, it was not just the owners of things that changed—the things themselves changed as well. New resources requiring care and cultivation appeared—resources such as available living space—which neither replicated nor could be reduced to the physical or notational objects of ownership and management in prerevolutionary economic life. It was precisely these objects of socialist management that had to be unmade when, in the early 1990s, the Soviet project came to an end. As Michael Heller has observed, during its lifetime the Soviet party-state "defined the boundaries of objects of socialist property in unfamiliar ways," often failing to delineate either ordinary physical or legal boundaries between two properties. In the course of the post-Soviet privatization, it therefore became common to see clumps of officials pacing about in the space between two buildings, trying to determine where one plot ended and another began.[122] The objects of property relations did not remain stable amid the transformation of property systems. The story of available living space, then, is the story of a new system at its genesis.

4

The Wealth of the Whole Nation

SEARCHING FOR VALUE AT GOKHRAN

"The brightest symbol of that sharp boundary between the old and new worlds, telling us that what was before the wealth of a few individuals and served as an object of their enjoyment or a means of accumulation has now become the wealth of the whole nation, concentrated in the hands of the proletarian state power for the use and good of all."

—REPORT ON "GOKHRAN"[1]

"In the first period, expropriate what was expropriated was wholly correct. In the second—the device should become: count up the expropriated and do not let it be held onto, and if it is held onto directly or indirectly, those violators of discipline should be shot."

—VLADIMIR LENIN[2]

A LITTLE AFTER TEN O'CLOCK on the night of October 31, 1921, following four days of hearings, a court in Moscow handed down its judgment in case No. 10069. Though charged with a variety of crimes, ranging from improper storage of an amethyst ring to harboring their husbands from the law to offering bribes of more than forty million rubles, the fifty-nine defendants in the case had been grouped together by the court in recognition of their common tie to an institution called Gokhran, the State Depository of Valuables. Gokhran's job was to collect everything valuable from every corner of the Republic in the coffers of the former municipal pawn bank on Moscow's Nastasinsky Lane. The rules governing what, precisely, constituted a valuable remained nebulous. The long answer was a regularly changing list of objects that included anything made of gold, silver, platinum, or precious stones, no matter how useful or useless—teaspoons, asparagus forks, candelabra, crucifixes, watch chains, watches—as well as objects made of other sumptuous materials, such as silk and fur. The short answer was, if it had been seized at some point in the previous four years, and it seemed fancy, it should probably go to Gokhran. There, it would be sorted, appraised, "depersonalized," and then stored, until such time as it could be put to use, most likely through "foreign trade, to get things from the capitalist countries of Europe that are necessary for the development of Soviet Russia's economy—silver for industry, nickel silver for rest homes," and the like.[3]

But that was not what had happened at Gokhran. According to testimonies presented at trial, the silver had not been spent on industry, and proceeds from the foreign sale of nickel silver had not been devoted to the development of rest homes. Instead, relentless "investigations" into Gokhran conducted by every major control institution of the Soviet state and Communist Party concluded that work at Gokhran had been ruined by a staff that turned out to be both exceptionally venal and exceptionally incompetent, in nearly equal measure. And that was why they, the wives who sheltered them from arrest, and the fathers who offered bribes of forty million rubles to shield them from capital charges, now found themselves on the docket of case No. 10069. Hours after the guilty verdicts were read, the nineteen-year-old son in whose name the bribe had been offered was shot, as was the official who accepted the bribe. The father was sent to a labor camp. The daughter who refused to reveal her father's address to the Cheka received a sentence of six months' imprisonment; her father was shot. The wife who sheltered her husband and her father from arrest was imprisoned for a year; her husband and her father were shot. In all, on the night of October 31, 1921, nineteen people were executed in the case. Another thirty-five were sentenced to imprisonment in jails and labor camps for periods ranging from six months to thirteen years. Five were cleared of charges.[4]

Case No. 10069 ended. But the problems at Gokhran did not. The most common charge against Gokhran's staff had been not theft or bribe-taking but "criminal negligence." Criminal negligence is what brought down Gokhran's appraisers, controllers, and its erstwhile director, Eduard Levitsky, a former nobleman and longtime head of Moscow's municipal pawn bank before the Revolution, who was sentenced to five years of forced labor on account of his "criminally negligent relationship to his work."[5] At Gokhran, criminal negligence appeared in two aspects: first and most obviously, in the physical insecurity of Gokhran's holdings, which had allowed for theft on a massive scale. Such insecurity was not unique to Gokhran; Ozerevsky's investigation of the Lubyanka had revealed similar, unusually basic defects at its storerooms—things like unlocked doors, unattended spaces, and open windows. The fact that some among Gokhran's staff had taken advantage of this insecurity was not so difficult to explain. But how did Gokhran's valuables, its diamonds and its gold coin, cross pendants and wedding rings, become so vulnerable in the first place? How had the experienced jewelers hired to handle the gems failed so abysmally to protect them—failed not only to implement their specialized knowledge of proper storage and accounting, but also to adhere to elementary precepts of common sense, like locking doors and sealing packages? These shortcomings bled into the other dimension of criminal negligence at Gokhran, just as damaging if less clearly malicious, which was its objective failure in the performance of its chief task: valuation. Gokhran bungled each of its major shipments of precious objects abroad, preparing a package of diamonds worth fifteen million gold French francs for transfer to Poland when the agreed-upon sum was supposed to be just five million; failing to get a ten-million-franc shipment to Riga entirely; succeeding, after the personal intervention of Lev Trotsky, at getting a shipment to Riga, only to see it sit in a warehouse for months, unsold.[6]

Consensus within the Cheka, which spearheaded the criminal investigation into Gokhran's failure, settled on the idea that both of these problems stemmed from the same root cause: Gokhran's rotten employees, who, when they were not cheating and stealing, utterly refused "to employ their many years of knowledge and experience" in their work.[7] The inspectors from the Worker-Peasant Inspectorate (Rabkrin), meant to oversee Gokhran's appraisers, earned the similar charge of "failing to warrant the trust placed in them," as well as their fair share of "systematic theft."[8] A major shortcoming of this explanation for Gokhran's failure, however, lay in the fact that none of these employees had given any indication of their tendencies prior to working at Gokhran; on the contrary, most had been hired expressly for their platinum-level "honesty." At a meeting hosted jointly by Leonid Krasin, the Commissar of Foreign Trade, and Sergei Chutskaev, Deputy Commissar of Finance, back when Gokhran was being formed in February 1920, all had agreed that in the matter of staffing, everything came down to "elementary honesty, so that stuff does not disappear," as Krasin put it. He proposed "searching out" the "Jews [he] knew, specially occupied with this" matter, because they worked "disinterestedly."[9] This had been done; the Jews had been searched out and hired.

Krasin personally recommended hiring "an extremely experienced" jeweler who had been entrusted for work "at the Moscow Chrezvychaika, it would seem, by the name of Aleksandrov." Aleksandrov was hired. Chutskaev suggested tracking down "Comrade Pozhamchi, he is experienced," and was known to the group. Pozhamchi, too, was added to the ranks.[10]

But whatever it was that allegedly happened at Gokhran—a transformation of some kind, or a taint—overtook them there. The Jews were subsequently arrested; Varlam Avanesov, deputy commissar of Rabkrin and member of the Cheka, received desperate letters from their wives, pleading for their lives.[11] Moreover, the explanation that Gokhran's workers were corrupt, or that work at Gokhran corrupted its workers, did not address the second major dimension of its failure: the difficulty it had in executing its basic function—namely, assessing the worth of "valuables." While Gokhran's employees might have profited personally from stealing valuable objects in Moscow, there was no percentage for them in sending fifteen million francs' worth of diamonds abroad when they were only supposed to send five; no benefit in pricing a shipment too high or too low so that it would languish unsold in Riga, of all places.

———

This chapter asserts that Gokhran beached on the rocks of valuation—on the problem of determining what kinds of things were valuable and what value was in a socialist polity. The story of Gokhran continues my analysis of the politicization of economic life in the previous chapter, a process that incorporated not only the politics of ownership and decisions as to the proper aims of economic activity, but also the practices of creating knowledge about what there was and, as will be examined here, what it was worth. Defining the nature of economic value, measuring it, and establishing its relation to other sorts of "values"—in part through determining prices—these were both ideological and practical challenges in the revolutionary era. Both at the time and in later Soviet mythmaking—Gokhran was the subject of an Estonian feature film, "Diamonds for the Dictatorship of the Proletariat" (1975), with a score by Arvo Pärt—the emphasis on Gokhran as a site of malfeasance obscured the more profound dilemma it presented: how to identify nonmarket value, and the relationship of this value to price. Gokhran's disorder was the product not merely of sabotage and institutional inefficiency, but of the multiple, conflicting theories of value operating simultaneously there, which routinely unsettled the flow of work.

While today they generally appear as synonyms, in classical economic thought—and in Russia at the turn of the twentieth century—"value" and "price" referred to distinct concepts. Both represented the attempt to discern the ratio of one good to another.[12] But price and value were also understood to express one another: prices were conceived as the concrete manifestation of an abstract value, and theories of value in turn were called upon to explain empirical prices.[13] These classical theories of value might be grounded in logic, history, or ethics, but, as Philip Mirowski has argued, they all treated value as a "metaphorical substance poured into a commodity, whence it might flow into another commodity produced from the first."[14] Debate revolved around the nature of this metaphorical substance, and around how to relate it to prices, and one of the most stubborn questions had to do with how to resolve an evident contradiction: to the extent that the metaphorical substance of value existed, it had to be absolute. Classical theories of value, whatever their animating principles, only made sense on the condition that the value embedded in commodities through labor or otherwise, once put there, could not subsequently change.[15] And yet, empirical market prices did vary, a fact that theorists from Smith to Marx struggled mightily to accommodate.

On the eve of the First World War, writes David Woodruff, "the classical approach to value was collapsing under its contradictions," and, more specifically, under pressure from "marginalists," continental economists who shifted the focus of the discipline onto the determinants of price, and who led the charge in what would become the abandonment of value, except as price's synonym.[16] Russian economists followed these debates closely, and although up to the war they generally remained loyal to the classical view, aspects of marginalist theory filtered into the work of a number of prominent economists, most notably that of the political economist and Kadet Pyotr Struve.[17] After the war, the "trend in the discipline of economics [toward] discarding value as an organizing concept" accelerated in Europe, while in Russia, with the Bolshevik accession to power, something like the opposite happened. What changed in Russia after the Revolution was not merely that a classical view of value as distinct from price triumphed, forcibly, in economic thought. It was rather that the question of value and its relation to prices migrated into a new register, what Caroline Humphrey has called a new "level, which hardly exists in many societies. . . . This is the level of the theoretical model," brought to life in statutes, instructions, explanations of instructions, textbooks and the categories of account, all meant to express and impart the operation of the model's "laws."[18]

The theoretical model changed over time, a process typically described as the "rectification of earlier mistakes." Through all the changes, its "laws" were commonly adduced to, although often not "clearly attributable to Marx." And while in the West, economic theorists increasingly sought to relate supply, demand, and other phenomena to the vicissitudes of subjective preferences and human intervention, the Soviet theoretical model of economic life resolutely insisted on its own "objectivity"—that is, the idea that it was "not subject to purposive human intervention."[19] The challenge was that, like other elements of the project, or as Yuri Slezkine has evocatively put it, the "prophecy," the objective laws were not known ahead of time.[20] They lived in the realm between theory and practice—the new "level." They were objective but they also had to be discerned. This necessity caught their would-be interpreters in a quandary that was both technical and existential, expressed with particular clarity in the problem of value and price, and thus, at Gokhran. "Since prices in the Soviet system are not determined by market forces," Humphrey wrote, "a *decision* has to be taken as to their level."[21] But in the absence of a market, on what basis was this decision to be made? This question of nonmarket valuation, which would dog Soviet theorists and planners for the next seventy years, appeared almost immediately, at the project's inception.[22]

This chapter illuminates how technical, seemingly mundane processes such as appraisal were infused with political content after the Revolution, and how difficult it was to undo this infusion, even when this was desired. As the first part of the chapter shows, experiments in nonmarket valuation flourished in a variety of settings after October. While often rudimentary and chaotic, these experiments drew on a shared set of strategies, animated by a redistributive and statist ethos.[23] Unlike ordinary attempts at price-fixing, the acts of political valuation performed by local soviets and central commissariats were generally not crafted with a primarily economic orientation or aim. The most important distinction in the assignment of an object's worth was its classification as "valuable" or "nonvaluable": according to principles developed across early Soviet institutions, nonvaluables were paradoxically the most useful objects, such as foodstuffs, clothing, and other essential goods. Valuables, whether useful or not, were seen to have some other quality superseding their utility, perhaps because they were made of a precious substance, or, less commonly, made in a special way, possibly constituting art. Nonvaluables would remain within the RSFSR, and as an expression of their utility and of the revolutionary state's social justice commitments, were meant to circulate without a market price. Removed even from the signification of the market, their redistribution was accomplished either by entitlement or at a fixed price, arrived at by one of several common tactics: assigning different prices for the same object depending upon its recipient; assigning the same price to objects of differing qualities within a general class (i.e., "tables" or "typewriters"); and empowering particular social groups (i.e., "the poor," "laboring people") to appraise objects according to principles of social justice or as they saw fit.

For nearly three years, the fate of the mountains of seized "valuables" in this new material landscape was not clear, nor was it even much discussed. But in early 1920, with the end of the civil war in sight and the stubborn failure of revolution abroad bearing down, the Sovnarkom created Gokhran with the hope of turning imperial Russia's useless valuables into real goods for socialism—that is to say, into objects of foreign trade. Gokhran thus belongs to a recognizable and enduring genre of institution in the Soviet firmament. Like Torgsin in the 1930s and others in the years beyond, Gokhran ferried between the socialist economy and the capitalist one on the other side of Soviet borders; its cargo was precious metals and other things suitable for foreign currency exchange.[24] These institutions have sometimes appeared as oases of market practice inside the Soviet Union, employing principles of arbitrage and profitability for the benefit of the state that would have appeared unforgivably speculative elsewhere inside the Republic.[25] But as will be seen, Gokhran was no market oasis. Looking not only at policy but at the practices of accounting and valuation employed at Gokhran, this chapter contends that, despite its market-facing orientation, Gokhran's leaders imagined it as a "factory" for the production of special kinds of nonmarket value, which they characterized variously as true, just, or objective—and which could not be captured in postrevolutionary market prices at home or abroad. As this chapter documents, Gokhran's search for value without market price led it to experiment with an array of alternatives in its methods of appraisal, including domestic and foreign historical prices, assessments of utility, embedded labor, and raw materials. All the while, its administrators conducted this search in a vocabulary borrowed from capitalism and its Marxist critique, a continuity in terminology that, as Humphrey argues, for long obscured the novelty of socialist economic phenomena. Gokhran's trials and tribulations open a window onto how this important phenomenon came to pass, connecting the exploration of a new concept of self-cost (sebestoimost') to what would become a perennial search for objective values distinct from empirical costs, for prices not as they were but as they should have been.[26]

In its search for true value, Gokhran embodied the paradox of the revolutionary project: that in distancing itself from foreign capitalist markets, the Soviet Republic at the same time grew more reliant on them. Gokhran sought to discern the worth of objects with the noise of the market stripped away. Its leaders understood market valuation as both technically inadequate and politically threatening to Bolshevik authority. Yet, insofar as the eradication of the market was neither automatic nor comprehensive, information about market prices at home and abroad continued to circulate through official and unofficial channels, posing the question of whether and how to listen to it. By tracing this circulation inside Gokhran and adjacent institutions, the chapter exposes the politics of secrecy that clung to market information in the non-market Soviet Republic, even as the legal toleration of some market institutions and practices increased.[27]

Sites of Valuation

As Soviet accountants loved to remind themselves, the father of Soviet accounting was Lenin. "It was Lenin who developed the pure Russian idea of subordinating absolutely everything to the will of the state," wrote one theorist of accounts, "of the primacy of vertical connections [among enterprises] over the horizontal, of people, not things themselves, as the object of the account." Most importantly, it was Lenin who understood the essential role to be played by accounting in bringing about the transition to socialism by "ripping off the masks," abolishing commercial secrecy, and thus "exposing productive relations in their pure form."[28] The account books of capitalism would pave the road to socialism by illuminating the true costs of production, including the cost of capital itself, conceived not just in the sense of interest on cash or equipment, but as the portion of the productive process that was spent on profit, illegitimately tacked on along the way. In time, with the return of market activity under the New Economic Policy of the 1920s, the revolutionaries would be forced to confront the "price forming variables" in sharper detail, in the course of which, Mark Harrison has pointedly observed, "the concept of markups on costs proved intractable for non-specialist discussion."[29] But in the revolutionary moment, the notion that economic life had previously been padded with markups that could now be repurposed as the start-up fund for the new society animated the revolutionaries' management of the Imperial inheritance. Throwing open the account books would allow revolutionaries, at last, to see the truth behind the numbers; it would allow them to embark upon the revaluation of economic life.

What made this ambition especially difficult to realize—leaving aside the mechanics, the "almost total degradation of accounts" during the Revolution, the "hundreds of millions, even billions that have disappeared in this absence of order, or more accurately, this disorder"—was the fact that it ran headlong into another of Lenin's own ambitions: class warfare, and the rise of politicized valuation undertaken in its service.[30] In revolutionary usage, the value of things was to be determined not by market forces but by political decision. The search for a truer, more just mechanism for determining value suffused revolutionary society, from economic theorists at the top to local soviets, tax inspectors, and Committees of the Poor engaged in the dispossession of individuals through "property-leveling." Reflecting on the state of the RSFSR's "general financial politics" in 1921, it appeared to the young Bolshevik and Deputy Finance Commissar A. O. Alsky that together with the broad "deterioration" of the financial infrastructure and "absence of naturally occurring economic relationships," the most critical development of the previous four years had been the "property-leveling effected by the revolution on the population."[31] Of the myriad ways "property-leveling" occurred, the most widespread was the seizure of personal assets at home or on the street. Paradoxically, the papers and bureaucratic instruments generated to contain seizure, a practice that worked intentionally and otherwise to scramble the conventions of market-based private property regimes, also depended on concepts of value and valuation that were borrowed from these same market-based regimes. Seizure documents are thus among the richest repositories of information about revolutionary practices of pricing and valuation, which figured prominently at two moments in the seizure process: first, in the determination of what should be seized, and second, as at Gokhran, in efforts to determine what had been taken and what was thus now held by state institutions.

The earliest efforts to establish standards for the prosecution of the class war involved the establishment of limits on personal possession. These limits were of two types: one fixed the material parameters of a household according to its size in space and people, and the nature of the labor they performed. The other fixed a value limit expressed in rubles on a household's total property, independent of the objects themselves, who its members were, and what they did. Value limits first appeared in the winter of 1917–18, in the imposition of "extraordinary" taxes on households or firms deemed capable and deserving of paying.[32] Neither the Sovnarkom nor any other institution of the central government appears to have issued a comprehensive statement on such limits at the time, but through a smattering of local decrees and circulars on related topics, the figure of 10,000 rubles emerged as the upper limit on permissible holdings—a value limit, affixed to both money and things.[33] The 10,000-ruble limit assumed a status as the legally recognized value ceiling even in circumstances when none had been proclaimed.[34] Its solidity was convincing enough that in January 1921, despite never having been formally established, it was formally repealed, with new possession regulations fixed at "twenty times the minimum salary" per family, to reflect the devastating pace of inflation.[35]

The 10,000-ruble value limit was attended by many exceptions, hinging sometimes on the status of the owner and sometimes on the presumed origins of the things."[36] While basically arbitrary, such exceptions authenticated the notion that the prices assigned to individual objects were real prices, representing the real value of the objects. Yet, in individual acts of appraisal being performed in places across the Republic, hints of a rising unreality in prices, a decoupling between assigned price and some real value, had begun to creep in. This disjuncture between price and value had two sources: one was the inflation, which was sincere, alarming, and unstoppable; the other was a purposeful manipulation of valuation, which the inflation undoubtedly facilitated, but which was distinct.

The purposeful manipulation of prices, or political valuation, worked in several ways. To implement the value limits, some localities introduced appraisal commissions, composed of residents, similar on the face of it to the commissions proposed during preparations for the Empire-wide income tax in 1915 and 1916. But the revolutionary commissions had little in common with these predecessors. As Yanni Kotsonis observes, revolutionary assessment commissions represented an institutional expression of social upheaval rather than expert technocracy. Their composition varied from place to place, but in nearly all cases centered on the participation of the local poor. In the city of Vyatka, the city soviet appointed a commissar charged with "justly assessing the income of all those subject to the tax and defining their tax burden," to be aided by a "commission from the poor (neimushchiye or have-not) classes of the population."[37] The task of such commissions was not merely to verify income declarations but to appraise objects of property "justly," from the viewpoint of the "have-not classes," at a moment when the economy was coming unraveled and the ruble was in freefall.

Already in decline when the Bolsheviks seized power, the value of the ruble dropped precipitously during the Revolution and civil war, with especially steep falls beginning in 1919, when the Soviet government abolished legal limits on emissions; between 1914 and 1923, the ruble depreciated roughly fifty million times.[38] The instructions provided by the Shenkursky district finance department to its appraisal commissions in the spring of 1918 commented directly on the unreal quality of prices at the time as the dual product of inflation and the legacy of market capitalism, which had falsified value and had now to be overcome. The local assessment commissions were therefore instructed to base their appraisals "on two evaluations, namely: the appraisal before the war and the appraisal according to current cost [*stoimost'*]," as if the "current cost" could not, in itself, adequately represent the object's true value. "Say that a building was assessed before the war at seven hundred rubles," the instructions clarified. "Now it costs not less than seven thousand rubles. We put these two sums together and take the average cost from them—7,700, we divide in half = 3,850." This district had a 5,000-ruble threshold for the assessment of its extraordinary property tax, beneath which this imaginary building crept in. This was where the social judgment of the commission entered into play. "If the appraisers/assessment commission finds it necessary to assess this property," it could do so by assigning the property a different value—the base rate of 5,000 rubles. [39]

The purpose of the prices assigned in this fashion was not to signal scarcities or balance supply and demand or any of the other aims to which prices are commonly put in a market economy.[40] Rather, prices were envisioned as an instrument of class warfare. As with the seizure of movable and immovable property, to the extent that prices served an economic purpose alongside this political one, it was to redistribute resources in a way that equalized possession or reversed the scales in favor of preferred groups such as Red Army soldiers, workers, and party members. Sometimes this meant pricing things too high, as in the assessment of the real estate in Shenkursky district. Sometimes this meant pricing things too low, as in the appraisal of household things owned by a citizen Zhurkin, prepared in the course of their seizure to cover his outstanding "Extraordinary Tax" bill. Although Zhurkin owed just 1,000 rubles, when members of the *volost'* soviet in his district near Moscow appeared to collect the tax, they seized goods worth 2,726 r. 50 k. "at a very low estimate," which later sold at public auction for 3,242 rubles, all in Zhurkin's presence.[41]

Zhurkin suspected the agents had purposefully lowballed his things, which was almost certainly correct. Yet in the absence of a legal market—housewares could still be sold in certain circumstances, but trade in furniture was forbidden—and amid spiraling inflation on the illegal market, on what basis should prices, whatever their purpose, be assigned?[42] Conceptual uncertainty crept even into acts of appraisal that betrayed no effort to misrepresent the value of things. In the summer of 1918, the Central Statistical Administration sought to compose what had been, before the Revolution, a mainstay of administrative practice: a set of statistics on "market prices." Immediately it encountered "two characteristic features that greatly differentiate[d] the current period from the previous one": first, the "unstoppable and extreme growth in prices, as a result of the devaluation of money, the insufficiency of all goods, the difficulties in trading"; and second, the pronounced divergence of "so-called market prices," which were found to be "different at one and the same time, for one and the same goods," not just in different places but "even at one and the same market."[43]

The process of political valuation continued after goods had been seized, with their entry into official pathways of account and distribution. But its practice here took a different shape, oriented first and foremost around a basic judgment as to whether the object in question was "valuable" or "nonvaluable." Valuables, paradoxically, were those objects officially deemed worthless inside the domestic economy of the Soviet Republic; as an expression of their worthlessness, they were permitted to circulate at something approximating market prices, whether at home, insofar as this was legal, or abroad. Nonvaluables, by contrast, were the most essential things, some of which fell into the wartime category of "goods of first necessity." These objects were to remain inside the Soviet Republic, and as an expression of their significance and the triumph of the proletarian dictatorship, they were either to be distributed without a price, or to be released at a price fixed by local authorities. A third category of thing, art, straddled the two: essential at home, albeit not in the sense of utility that applied to "goods of first necessity," while remaining available for sale abroad to raise foreign currency.[44]

The categorization of things generally fell to the requisition or furniture departments of local soviets. In Petrograd, the city created the Inter-institutional Commission for sorting things inside "bourgeois" apartments, which worked in parallel to neighborhood housing departments tasked with collecting and redistributing objects seized from households.[45] The objects they handled varied considerably in quantity and quality from one neighborhood to the next. In Petrograd's Vyborgsky neighborhood, it was said, "the neighborhood is poor, and the valuables are few," so most work consisted of traipsing through abandoned apartments, sorting their contents, and directly "distributing [them] among citizens in need," more or less on the spot.[46] In the Smolninsky neighborhood, by contrast, workers came upon quantities of porcelain, bronze, silver, and copperware, which in their view merited transfer to the center as valuables. Reports on the municipal distribution agency, Gorprodukt, indicate that its workers stripped the spaces they inventoried down to the bones: the director of a Petrograd neighborhood warehouse was castigated for failing to record the size of carpets and pieces of flooring ripped out of apartments and brought to his storeroom.[47] Periodically, Gorprodukt announced a "*razvyorstka*," or forced levy on the neighborhood warehouses for necessary goods, such as fabric, shoes, and needles; otherwise, neighborhoods often distributed nonvaluables directly from requisitioned apartments.[48]

The sorting of seized things continued at warehouses, where staff faced the decision of how to characterize objects—as valuable, nonvaluable, or, less commonly, as art. Goods of first necessity coming out of "bourgeois" apartments were meant to be "distributed by the [inter-institutional] commission itself." Valuables were destined for "Narbank [the People's Bank], gold and precious things, the portion for museums and the Commission for the defense of artistic monuments, [and] for the expert commission of *sotsobespecheniye* [state welfare organ]." Quite often, however, the contents of apartments identified as "bourgeois" were automatically classified as valuables, no matter how useful they might be. As a result, it happened that many "essential objects . . . such as dishware, tables, linens, furniture, beds, mattresses, pillows, clocks, a huge quantity of porter, carpets, and other goods" taken from "bourgeois" apartments ended up "rotting" in warehouses, rather than being redistributed.[49] No firm directives existed to guide the separation of valuables from nonvaluables, even in the case of "goods of first necessity," seemingly the more straightforward of the options. Nearly all definitions of the category included basic clothing, some essential household goods, and a fixed subset of furniture. Other items rotated in and out of standing. But a great deal of friction built up along the borders separating valuable from essential, as can be seen in the treatment of silver tea spoons. Silver cutlery generally entered the circuit of "valuables"; its precious metal content was seen to outweigh its utility, and once Gokhran came into existence, neighborhood soviets sent silver cutlery there as metal, to be melted down. But at Gokhran, it was later revealed that silver tea spoons had unaccountably not been melted down, with staff evidently stymied as to where they belonged; they were being stored in a pile, seen as too precious for domestic redistribution, too useful to be melted down, too quotidian to be sent abroad as a luxury good.[50]

Staff likewise stumbled over the demarcation of valuables from art, with sensibilities shifting dramatically from one year to the next. No matter what their artistic merit, objects crafted from precious metals were considered first as metal. But other kinds of things, such as tapestries, decorative crafts, and "collections" proved much harder to parse. Out in the apartments, where the first round of sorting occurred, fine objects, particularly collections, were initially interpreted as "art" rather than as "valuable" or "luxury"; this was the conclusion drawn from a review performed by the Museum Directorate, *Glavmuzei*, responsible for inventorying all works of art in Moscow, of its own accounts in April 1922. Upon review, Glavmuzei recategorized 7,000 of some 9,000 objects that had been seized as "artistic productions" during "the beginning period of the revolution, in mass order," but which, according to notions of art in 1922, constituted instead "objects of luxury, hardly belonging to [the sphere of] artistic production."[51] A special review of the objects seized as part of collections determined that only five or six of the groupings merited the name.[52]

For objects categorized as nonvaluable, the final stage in the sorting process was preparation for redistribution, which involved the decision to assign a price. Like the categorization of the objects, their translation into a money price was volatile. Inspectors in Petrograd found that the redistribution of seized goods occurred both "for payment and for free."[53] The assignment of a price to a seized object, even a fixed price, generally marked it as less "essential" than the "goods of first necessity." Instructions regarding redistribution from 1919 indicated that the least essential seized objects could be sold to those who desired them for "cash payment," while the most essential were to be considered part of the consumption "norm," issued for no payment.[54] This treatment reinforced a claim staked out in other dimensions of economic life: that in the wake of the socialist revolution, the things most essential to life were those provided to the population at no cost. As the economist Pavel Genzel (Paul Haensel) observed in July 1921 in a memorandum for Narkomfin's research department, the Institute for Economic Research (IEI), the view that the most essential things should be free—the principle of *bezplatnost'*—animated thinking in a number of spheres, as witnessed in the provision of urban utilities. The city of Moscow now provided running water, baths, laundries, and tram rides at no cost to the general population. But "in economics," Genzel insisted, "nothing comes for 'free,' and if someone is able to use for free some kind of economic good, then in each economy it is necessary that there be someone else, who will by their own labor cover the economic benefit of another." Now characterized by Soviet authorities as essential, Genzel argued, running water in Moscow was, in fact, a luxury—half the population lived in buildings without access to it—and should be paid for as such.[55]

The principle of bezplatnost' peaked in the winter of 1920–21, as spiking inflation fed interest in "material accounting" and dependence on distribution in kind.[56] But it was short-lived: money taxes, cancelled in February 1921, were reinstated in July.[57] Payments for rails, post and telegraph, housing, and health care, progressively abolished in the second half of 1920 and the first quarter of 1921, were restored by October. Even at the peak of bezplatnost', the distribution of seized goods commonly occurred for payment. One method of assigning prices pegged price to the type and qualities of the thing. Here, the central point of debate was whether prices should vary according to those qualities or whether all objects of the same type should have the same price. Inspectors at a Petrograd warehouse, for instance, chastised its managers for their failure to fix "hard prices for typewriters"; those set by staff "fluctuate between 5,400 rubles and 13,000 rubles for one," interpreted as evidence of the warehouse managers' ignorance of appropriate practice.[58] The report does not specify whether the typewriters were of the same brand, or whether one was newer than the other.[59] At the same time, the director of a warehouse of seized things in the Sokol neighborhood of Moscow followed precisely this principle—assigning the same price to all objects of the same type—and was castigated for it. The warehouse director had fixed prices such that "for the same objects, the prices for all buyers were the same." Inspectors at the Moscow warehouse deemed this unfair because it failed to take into account the objects' "level of wear and tear."[60] Evidently, both approaches to pricing on the basis of things appeared equally plausible: the one in Petrograd that ignored the qualities of particular objects; the other, in Moscow, that was attuned to those qualities.[61]

There was at the same time a second principle of pricing at work in the warehouses of seized things, which entailed assigning prices not on the basis of the thing at all, but rather according to the status of the object's prospective "buyer." In this version of pricing, discounts from the fixed price were awarded to people identified as needy, party members, or on some other grounds. In the Sokol neighborhood, the soviet prepared two copies of the inventory of possessions seized from a citizen Glike, in advance of their transfer "for cash payment" to a "Military-Engineering Club." The first recorded Glike's "broken" grand piano, at 8,000 rubles, and other things, for a total of 10,970 rubles' worth of furniture. The second served as a receipt for the club's cash payment for the goods, showing heavy discounting—the piano was marked down from 8,000 rubles to 750 rubles.[62] Discounts of this sort were standard practice, called into question only when the discounted price deviated too sharply from fixed prices.[63] Yet the impulse to assign prices based on the status of the buyer remained powerful in spite of these concerns. As one finance official put it, after the socialist revolution, "a Rothschild and an old woman [should] no longer pay the same price for the same thing." To that end, he proposed standardizing discounts by issuing every citizen a colored card, for display at point of purchase, each color representing a certain discount. Economists of the IEI mocked the proposal not only for its implicit assumption that society would remain unequal, but also for being "a party plan rather than a state idea," by which they seem to have meant it was unrealistic: "there is not enough ink in the world to divide everybody up."[64]

—————

But what, in all of this, of the valuables? What of the riches, the gold, the diamonds so plentiful there was a room named for them in the Winter Palace? What of the diamonds that had no room named for them, the modest diamonds, hanging from less elevated ears and sparkling on less grand fingers? What of the gold, methodically sucked up from bedstands and safes, brought to Chekas near and far? What of all that had been violently, urgently seized from former owners, hauled to the warehouses of the new state, only to sit mutely, assuming it had not already been stolen?

Well into its third year, the Revolution seemed to have no use for these objects. Its leaders seemed even to have no interest in them, save for ensuring their total removal from the possession of their original owners. Every so often, a kind of fit would come over the revolutionaries, a wave of remembering the material treasures gathering in state hands. The fear of pilfering was the focal point in these waves of concern. One such wave splashed across the Moscow's inner ring in October 1918. It hit the Lubyanka, where the government controller Ozerevsky discovered Venetian windows broken and treasury doors unlocked.[65] It hit the eminent curator Igor Grabar, tasked with running a special commission to locate and secure the jewels evacuated to Moscow from the Diamond Room of the Winter Palace in July 1917, together with their inventory paperwork, both of which had been misplaced. Briefly, it appeared to Grabar that not all the Crown Jewels detailed in the most recent appraisal (itself from 1884), had made the trip to Moscow. It was learned that there was "a certain doubt as to the number of [safe deposit boxes] evacuated together with the things of the former Tsar's family" surrendered at Tsarskoe Selo on August 17, 1917, without a proper inventory, such that it was impossible to say what had gone.[66] Grabar's commission next studied valuables belonging to the Commissariat of Foreign Affairs [NKID], eighty-seven boxes of which were discovered by surprise at the Kremlin, having been shipped from Petrograd in September 1917, forgotten about, and, more than a year later, uncovered in the Grand Palace. When asked how it wished to dispose of the valuables, the Commissariat had no answer, and as "a consequence of its indecision—which things would NKID keep for itself, and for which needs, which should be given to the Department of Museums, such as dishes which do not have artistic or historic value, what would happen to the remaining things[—]an inventory was not undertaken, and the room in which the boxes were stored was sealed."[67] By March 1919, after several months of regular "checking of the locks" on the sealed rooms, this wave of interest subsided.

In Petrograd, too, valuables had been piling up. For more than two years, they accrued at the Cheka headquarters and in the disused building of the British Embassy, where, in the fall of 1919, they at last attracted the attention of an Expert Commission, affiliated with the NKVT and newly formed with the purpose of mounting an exhibition of bourgeois "artistic and historical objects and so forth," the prize exponents of which would be displayed to the public in their native habitat, the British Embassy building.[68] Plans for the exhibit petered out, but the British Embassy remained "stuffed" with valuables, according to the Commissar of Foreign Trade Leonid Krasin, "partly household objects, partly materials for museums and such," none of which had been sorted.[69]

What changed, in the winter of 1920, to convince Lenin, Krasin, and the others that the jewels and housewares that had been piling up in official storage units for nearly three years now merited their attention? What led them to the sudden realization that, in fact, they were sitting on a veritable gold mine? Or indeed, better than a gold mine, as Yakov Yurovsky, executioner of the royal family and future plenipotentiary at Gokhran, reported to the Sovnarkom in 1921: "one can say without exaggeration that, even after two years of systematic theft," there was more metal awaiting discovery in official storerooms "than our gold and platinum mines will give in the next five-ten years."[70]

Gokhran's founding documents made little effort to explain why it came into being when it did. "When, in the process of liquidating the capitalist system and socializing the weapons of production," began an early draft of Gokhran's origin story, prepared for review by Alsky, the Deputy Commissar

FIGURE 4.1. Previously home to the municipal pawn bank, No. 3
Nastasinsky Lane became home to Gokhran from 1920.
Source: (https://tsarnicholas.org/category/russian-crown-jewels/)

of Finance, "the time came for Soviet power to liquidate private enterprise and
credit as part of the capitalist world, then into the hands of Soviet power there
gradually accumulated a large amount of valuables of a material character,
pieces made of precious metals, gold, silver, platinum, and precious stones."
On the one hand, Alsky explained, "the storage of these valuables in various
spaces posed a great danger in the sense of retaining them"—that is, protecting
them from theft—"and a great inconvenience in the sense of making an account of them. In light of this, there arose a great need to create a united apparatus for accounting and storage of these valuables."[71] On the other hand,

no one was so worried about the valuables in the years before Gokhran's formation, during which instances of theft and especially smuggling abroad had periodically risen to the attention of senior administrators at Narkomfin and Goskon.[72] The fact of theft, that is, cannot explain Gokhran's creation, any more than it can explain Gokhran's problems—not least because evidence suggests that storerooms of valuable things suffered from problems roughly equivalent to those holding less valuable things. These included theft, of course, but in far greater measure, they included the scourge of basic ignorance as to what such facilities indeed contained, such that, when careful counts were made, amounts invariably turned out to be much higher than expected.

Rather, to the extent that theft played a role in the creation of Gokhran, it was as a symptom of a broader shift in the appreciation of valuables that was already underway. "Two years ago," wrote Yurovsky, looking back from 1921, "we looked at all of this as something that did not merit attention, that, oh the revolution of the west will arrive tomorrow, and all these kinds of things, like diamonds, precious stones, and the like, they are not necessary to us." But sometime in 1920, Yurovsky recalled, and "certainly by the end of that year, it became necessary to take a different approach to things."[73] The site of this new approach, to the things and to the balance of forces between Russia and the outside world, would be Gokhran.

The Production Costs of Seized Things

Gokhran emerged amid what Lenin, Krasin, and other Bolshevik leaders were coming to understand to be a gap between a socialist Russia and a capitalist West, polities separated by geographical borders and an unexpected chronological lag. As Yurovsky's analysis from 1921 makes clear, the intensified attention on precious things that made Gokhran appear necessary was intimately connected to the growing consensus among the Bolsheviks that revolution in the West would not "arrive tomorrow." Surviving in the interim required a new attitude toward Russia's artistic heritage and luxurious inheritance. Expectations continued to run high that revolution abroad was, if not imminent, then still on the near horizon. It was therefore essential to gather up all of Russia's precious valuables, worthless at home, while they still bore maximum value in the eyes of the foreign bourgeoisie. "If the revolution abroad begins, everything will be lost. We have to move [these things] immediately onto steamships," Krasin exhorted those gathered at Gokhran's first organizational meeting in February 1920.[74] Gokhran began not as a concession to the durability of capitalism but as an extension of the bet on its demise.

Gokhran was one of several initiatives at the end of the civil war created to take stock of the Russian Empire's vestigial wealth. Around the same time, a Special Commission on the Destruction of Archives, which had been charged by the Sovnarkom with the "urgent destruction of all bonds [*protsentnye bumagi*] in all storage places in Moscow and the provinces," discovered that among these archives were many foreign bonds, stocks, and other credit instruments, the destruction of which "could be wholly unprofitable (*nevygodno*) for the interests of the Republic." Belatedly, representatives from Narkomfin joined the commission in order to "separate out those papers in foreign currency, which might bear a relation to new trade-industrial enterprises in newly formed political territories such as Poland, Lithuania, Georgia, and the like," rescuing nearly thirty billion rubles' worth of the now-foreign credit papers for future use.[75] In part, such efforts were prompted by the European treaties settling the First World War, to which the Soviets carefully attended. Inspired by the Treaty of Versailles, signed one month before Gokhran's founding, Narkomfin's research institute launched a broad study of the principles of indebtedness and reparations employed in the settlement, looking for concepts that could be of use to Soviet Russia in the new geopolitical environment—making careful study, for instance, of the methods proposed for the valuation of German railroads that might aid in the appraisal of railroads being ceded by the RSFSR to independent Poland.[76]

On top of these external developments, inside the RSFSR there was a growing sense among revolutionary officials in different spheres of economic life that Soviet Russia had exhausted the cushion of excess profit bequeathed to it by capitalism—the cushion of profit that was to form the start-up fund for socialism. In the winter of 1919–20, for instance, the Sovnarkom opened a special commission on apartments, chaired by Yuri Larin.[77] It found that "the winter of this year, as it happens, was the very moment when the [postrevolutionary] reduction of the most essential spending on the upkeep of housing reached its limit." Through an analysis of pre-war rents, the commission determined that up to 1913, most landlords earmarked thirty percent of the rents they collected for maintenance and amortization, while sixty-seven percent amounted to "pure profit" for the owner. Since 1917, even as inflation ate away the value of money, municipal authorities had either held rents flat or cancelled them entirely, in the belief that they were eating not into the capital asset (buildings), but only into the exploitative "pure profits" enjoyed by the dispossessed landlords.[78] But now, the commission concluded, existing rent payments precisely equaled the sum spent on upkeep; the cushion of "pure profit" had been wiped out, and the bills on maintenance—in the form of crumbling roofs, burst pipes, ruined wires—were about to come due.

While partly a question about the utility of rents in the new economy, as debate unfolded, Larin's analysis became connected to a deeper, recurring encounter between the new authorities and a material inheritance it seemed the Soviet Republic could ill-afford. As economists like Pavel Genzel informed Narkomfin at the same time, in Russia's present circumstances, "the economic and normal conditions of the urban population in general do not allow the luxury of water, sewage, electricity and well-built stone buildings and the like"—all of which Soviet cities had inherited but could not any longer sustain.[79] Genzel's vision of Russia as an heir who could not cover the death taxes on the family estate was not unique to the ranks of "bourgeois" economists (such as Genzel) firing memos off to the revolutionary apparat. Poverty talk of this sort, a sense that Soviet Russia was living off the fumes of its capitalist past, pervaded debate about the discovery and disposal of a great many assets, from the magnificent built environment of Russia's capitals to the gaudy jewels of its bourgeoisie. Some of these assets were easy, intellectually, to slough off. "Oh well," sighed Krasin during a discussion about selling off a handful of English investments, "we'll let them go." But what of the "metallurgical valuables," Deputy Commissar of Finance Chutskaev objected, "we could never let those go." "Why ever not?" Krasin dryly replied. "Why stand on ceremony? There is a real balance of forces at play here." Later on, Krasin played the other side of the issue, declaring that not everything would be sold off: "we're not so poor that the Russian people won't have a notable hat left to look at."[80]

The search for valuables for export hinged on two variables, both relatively unknown, but one more recognizably unknown than the other. The recognizably unknown variable was the future of socialism: what would it be, and what kind of things would it require? "The entire future of Russian art is held in these museums," wrote Natalya Trotskaya (Sedova), wife of Lev Trotsky and an official at Glavmuzei, in a report arguing against the sale of art and cultural monuments.[81] "Is the Republic really in so hopeless a position that is has become necessary to sacrifice its future? The situation is apparently not so bad as to require the liquidation of other things, which will be useful sometime in the future though it is unclear how or when, such as [things relating to] the study of magnetic anomalies, electrification, plant nurseries, the preparation of new rail lines and canals." And yet it was art, and not magnetic anomaly instruments, being put up for sale now, she complained. "Why should museums suffer?"[82]

Why indeed? The answer had as much to do with revolutionary ideas about capitalism as it did with expectations for the future of socialism. The present and future state of the foreign capitalist market was hardly better known than the socialist future, particularly when it came to the kinds of objects now proposed for sale abroad. The foreign sale of museum valuables, for instance, was meant to concern explicitly "high value pieces," although, as Sedova complained, no one involved possessed the current "knowledge, taste, and special talent" required to operate in the notoriously fickle international art markets. The Soviet Republic would "earn farthings" from the sale; "selling off museum goods to save the budget is like running out to water the fields with a teapot."[83] Sedova herself was not much better informed, and made her case largely on the history of other revolutions, in which "such sales have not been profitable."[84]

These debates confirm the "absolute centrality of the international economy as a concern for Bolshevik policymakers" of the period.[85] But this economy was not something that Bolshevik policymakers perceived directly, neutrally, or transparently. Foreign markets were, in fact, extraordinarily difficult for revolutionary policymakers to perceive, not simply because of post-war economic volatility, but because of how volatility intersected with Soviet officials' own assumptions about market (mal-)function, their criminalization of exchange, and their suspiciousness of market prices, all of which led them to treat not just material objects but even information about foreign exchange and prices as contraband. Decisions about foreign exchange therefore had to be made in an echo chamber, premised on the Bolsheviks' own notions of what capitalism valued. The economist Genzel, in a short memorandum for the IEI on gold and paper money from 1921, cautioned against what he viewed as the undue preference for gold emerging "in government spheres" over the past year. In part, he believed, this preference stemmed from a misguided but popular idea that inflation would harm only the bourgeoisie and not all people using money. He further suspected that the allure of gold derived from unfounded assumptions about its intrinsic value as compared to other commodities. As he insisted to his official readers:

From the point of view of commercial or speculative accounts . . . gold, grain, skimmed fat, and so forth are one just as profitable as the other. They are all valuable in the same way on the foreign market. The question is whether they are valuable in the same way on the foreign market as opposed to the domestic market.

As Genzel emphasized, contrary to the precepts of valuation at Gokhran, this accounting was "not possible to demonstrate in advance. This is a matter of prices on foreign markets . . . not having in my possession the courses of bourgeois prices and deprived of the ability to do the necessary arbitrage calculations, I must decline definite proofs on this issue."[86]

In fact, Genzel's arbitrage calculations assumed a preference for profit-maximization that was far from ubiquitous among Bolshevik policy-makers and remained unsettled at Gokhran. Whether foreign trade should be profitable, or whether its aim could be merely the acquisition of needed substances—foreign currency, expertise, some other concrete good—was a matter of serious political debate.[87] There is little evidence that revolutionary authorities engaged in arbitrage calculations in deciding which assets to keep and sell. "We were ripping out diamonds and precious stones during the [civil] war, that is all understood," Yurovsky reflected of 1920, Gokhran's first year of operation. "It was the war, it was conspiratorial work, we needed currency, there was no time to judge."[88] It would have been hard even had they wanted to judge, due to the suppression of markets at home and the insistence on conspiracy in regard to market information from abroad. Genzel speculated that the absence of a legal market in gold had driven its price on the illegal domestic markets higher, which in turn burnished its appeal in official circles. "It is undoubtedly true that gold and especially gold coins are valued abnormally highly among us. This is explained, of course, by our paper money inflation," Genzel noted, but also by "the laws of Soviet power, which threaten the accumulation of material goods with high fines and confiscations, artificially creating a premium for gold and gold coins."[89]

Despite Genzel's exhortations, foreign prices were not known, and indeed were not sought out prior to the decision to sell off Russia's valuables abroad. When Krasin, Chutskaev, and other specialists gathered to hash out Gokhran's future operations at their planning meeting in February 1920, they sketched out a vision of a foreign market populated by caricatures of bourgeois life, with Swiss princesses who could be "hired to serve as go-betweens, maybe they would agree to distribute" photographs of Russia's precious wares among their friends. "It would be good to present catalogs in America, saying we have these or those spoons, other objects," Krasin proposed. Debate flared over whether "Germany was a market" for precious things, with Krasin and Chutskaev sour on Berlin, against the enthusiastic precious metals expert and newly appointed head of Glavzoloto (Chief Directorate for the Gold and Platinum Industry), A. M. Bruk. "Berlin was never a market," Chutskaev grumbled. "They're only thinking of how to get a bite," surmised a different official, Solomon, before Bruk stepped in, confidently asserting that, in fact, Berlin was a great market, thanks to "all the petty and major bourgeoisie trying to buy as many diamonds as possible." The others then assimilated this information, turning on a dime: of course Berliners wanted diamonds, "to protect themselves from the falling course," Solomon now concluded.[90] Bruk likely had the most authoritative knowledge about foreign prices, having trained in Berlin, but in the course of discussion it emerged that the prices he possessed—for platinum—were from the previous summer, a lifetime ago in the volatile postwar market.[91] Nevertheless, these appear to have been the only prices available. They formed the basis for Gokhran's work for much of the coming year.[92]

Officials had similarly scanty information about the RSFSR's own holdings. No one doubted that, after more than two years of Soviet power, Russia's bourgeoisie had yielded up a fortune. No one doubted that in storerooms across the Republic, there sat a trove of riches awaiting discovery. But on the eve of Gokhran's founding, no one knew what was in that trove, either. At the planning meeting, Krasin and Chutskaev traded mental accountings of what different cities and regions might hold. "We should set a list of which institutions are working on the gathering up of valuables right now," Krasin began, "as we do not have one, meanwhile a whole series of institutions store such valuables. We know the Moscow Chrezvychaika has jewelers and we do not know what is going on in Petrograd, whether there are storerooms [at the Cheka] on Gorokhovaya or not."[93] Some 1,643 boxes of valuables were thought to be in Nizhny Novgorod, "probably a lot in Siberia," and "just from Petrograd, more than 28 railway cars [of valuables] had been brought" to Moscow, and now awaited processing at the People's Bank.[94] The contents of these boxes and train wagons, filled with objects deemed "valuable" at some point in the process of their dispossession, was unknown. Krasin surmised that "there will be some domestic goods, some materials for museums and the like. . . . The English embassy is stuffed full [of goods for the exhibition of "bourgeois" wares], many buildings are, but precious valuables [*dragotsennosti*] in the true sense of the word will be comparatively few."[95] Indeed, there was little clarity as to what these valuables truly were. "What Gokhran in reality represents, that is something that remains to this moment known to nobody," Yurovsky later reported. "After the October Revolution, the valuables of major factories and stores were requisitioned and confiscated, further there is what was requisitioned and confiscated by the extraordinary commissions and all kinds of other organizations across all the Republic. This latter is something unbelievable, starting with diamonds and ending with trousers. . . . Everything counted all up, it is enormous, possibly billions [of rubles]."[96]

And yet, Gokhran's founders did not need to know the specifics of the foreign markets, or even exactly what they had, because they knew that all the objects in question shared one quality: they had been seized. An awareness of the life history of these goods loomed large in the debate about their disposal.[97] "We have many watches," Chutskaev informed the group, "that it is impossible to sell, which were dedicated, with engravings." "Why impossible?" Solomon asked. "There are names," Chutskaev replied. Krasin disagreed, proposing that the names could be sanded off, "not so much metal will be lost." But erasing the names did not erase the past. "The preparatory work of the organization must take into consideration the negative attitude," Chutskaev began, before the expert Bruk interrupted: "abroad, there will be people who say that this is all stolen, they will have to get used to it. It will be necessary to wait it out."[98] As much as it weighed on them, this past was tantalizing, too. "And there are antiquities," Chutskaev continued, "there is a sapphire of 143 karats." "I saw the clock of [the last Ottoman sultan] Abdul Hamid," Krasin countered. "A most curious thing . . . with a half-moon of red enamel, it is authentic, it was purchased at auction."[99] This was the seized bounty of the bourgeois world that would make up Gokhran's wares.

That Gokhran's wares were seized, and were thought of expressly as seized things, was, in fact, the linchpin of the enterprise, revealing a logic of arbitrage that, while not what Genzel had intended, nevertheless evinced an appreciation for the price of things at home and abroad. In the minds of Gokhran's creators, it was implausible that Gokhran could net anything other than profit. This was because, apparently, the seized valuables held at Gokhran were thought of as free—as having been extracted without cost. As a matter of administration, of course, seizure had costs, no different from any other form of extraction. The cost of taxation, for instance, preoccupied revolutionary officials debating its future in a socialized economy, who struggled to weigh whether the moral benefit of paying taxes justified the expense of collecting them.[100] Seizure, by contrast, was almost never talked about as having a cost. Perhaps this was because seized goods were collected in the course of other revolutionary labor, as by the Cheka, searching out counterrevolution. The Cheka itself had no cost in official budgets, as the government controller Ozerevsky unhappily discovered, when he found its account books entirely bare on the "expenses" side.[101] Housing authorities similarly submitted budgets covering the salaries for their staff of controllers, but they made no calculations as to how much of a controller's time was spent categorizing the population or adjudicating disputes and how much on seizing—which made sense, as it was impossible to do one without the other. Asking how much it cost to seize these things was like asking how much it cost to seize power. In the official imagination, seized goods were on a different ledger; from them there could only be gain. Now it remained only to find their price.

Secret Prices and Definite Values

Gokhran was not supposed to be a long-lasting fixture of Soviet institutional life. It was envisioned as a single-use institution, created to perform a finite task related to the transition to socialism. That task, as stated in its founding order, was to "receive valuables belonging to the RSFSR from various institutions and individuals, consisting of gold, platinum, silver, in bars and objects made of them, diamonds, colored precious stones, pearls, and coins." Upon receipt, Gokhran was to perform a rough appraisal of the "newly acquired valuables on the basis of norms set by the relevant organs," it was to store the valuables, until they were taken to a Commission on Depersonalization, where a more detailed act of "depersonalization, sorting, and assessment" would be completed. Once this procedure was finished, Gokhran's work was done. The valuables were to be packed in such a way that they could be subsequently "realized" by the relevant institutions without further physical intervention. It was anticipated that the first stage of work—receiving the valuables—would be completed within two to three months.[102] In total, Gokhran was supposed to exist for maybe a year.

The easiest thing was to house Gokhran in the building occupied at the time by the former municipal Loan Treasury, a faux-medieval confection on Nastasinsky Lane built in honor of the 300th anniversary of the Romanov dynasty, finished just a year before the dynasty fell. The old-Rus exterior had modern safes inside, which already held riches pawned before the Revolution by hard-up representatives of the bourgeoisie. As it turned out, the easiest thing was also to borrow staff from the Loan Treasury for work at Gokhran. Indeed, when Gokhran was created, "the municipal pawn office was poured right into it," in the words of Eduard Levitsky, the nobleman who ran the pawn office, and who was now installed as head of Gokhran: "not just the valuables themselves, but the people who stood among these valuables, who accounted for them and bore responsibility for their security."[103] Later on, with Gokhran in a state of collapse, there would be a flurry of debate about where the fault lay: specifically, was it with those old employees of the pawn office? Was the problem their old habits, their irrepressible capitalism, or was it that they had abandoned those capitalist habits and the discipline contained therein? But at the start, it seemed that sorting through diamonds could be left mostly to these holdovers from the old world, to be supplemented with Jewish specialists and familiar faces from the Moscow Cheka.[104]

Of course, it would be necessary to "pair each specialist with a corresponding communist, to dress them in special outfits, sit them at the table, and have communists to watch over them."[105] On this everyone agreed, except for Varlam Avanesov, the Deputy Commissar of Government Control who was responsible for naming communists to the staff of Gokhran. It turned out that Avanesov "did not share [this] view, thinking it a pity to give communists for work like that at Gokhran"—pricing Russia's past, that is, should be left to people from the past, while the communists devoted themselves to building the socialist future.[106] In any case, work at Gokhran was forced to proceed without the requisite number of communists, even after it had been revealed that the specialists were, in fact, scoundrels. Rather than communists, the new hires hailed mainly from the peasant estate—more than half of those indicted in the Gokhran case were former peasants—some of whom had worked before the Revolution as jewelers, and some of whom had been "chauffeurs," "porters," and the like. The remainder of the staff belonged to the local merchantry. When the Revolutionary Tribunal announced sentences in case No. 10069 in October 1921, staff were shot more or less in proportion to their class of origin, which meant the majority of those killed were peasants. Of the nineteen sentenced to execution, nine were peasants, five were merchants, and five were not identified by class background. None were nobility.[107]

Staffing at Gokhran was not supposed to be a problem, because Gokhran's task was not supposed to depend on its staff. This task was conceived as the objective identification of valuables, rather than their subjective interpretation, such that the people who came to work at Gokhran had to be "experts" in the same way that those building bridges had to be engineers; only people trained in the field understood the mechanics of construction. By the same token, only those trained as jewelers could distinguish a half-karat diamond from a three-quarter karat diamond, spot especially high-quality objects, and, presumably, assign prices. So what if the sales were now being made on behalf of the world's first socialist state rather than by one's own firm? A karat was still a karat, just as a bridge was still a bridge. All that was required was for the "*spetsy* [specialists] . . . to bring their specialty, and their organization of affairs," to the job at hand, which the Bolsheviks did not recognize as different in any meaningful way from what the specialists had been doing all their lives.[108] Gokhran's founders envisioned it as a "factory": "I took away the impression from yesterday's meeting," reported the trade official Solomon in February 1920, "that what was needed here was to create a whole factory, to recall the specialist-jewelers from the army" to fill out the production lines at Gokhran.[109] A year later, amid the ongoing saga of Gokhran's incompetence, it likewise appeared to Yakov Yurovsky that Gokhran's failing lay in the fact that it had not become factory enough. "What should Gokhran be and how should work be arranged? It should be a factory," he insisted, "that issues a product on the basis of a strict calculations of gold, platinum, and in weight, in bars, etc., and with a wholesale self-cost estimate . . ."[110] Like any modern factory, that is, Gokhran should be engaged in the production of a definite "commodity" (*tovar*) according to standardized measures—"strict calculations"—of output.

Some of these standardized measures were included in Gokhran's original charter, which explained that, with the aim of "systematizing valuables according to their type, quality, and price," a "commission on sorting" would be charged with "separating diamonds, precious colored stones, and pearls from metals." Once "separated," the metals were to be collected and packed into "separate packages"; the "pearls and colored stones" were to be "separated out by color and type and quality"; and finally, "with regard to diamonds, there will be adopted the following gradation," according to which the diamonds were to be sorted by size, by the quarter-karat, into groups of 100, then labeled and sealed. Accounting was to be arranged "such that at any given moment, there is a complete picture of the deposited valuables according to their type, quality, weight, and value." Future disposal of the packets would ideally require no review of their contents, nor even the opening of the packages themselves, because quality, weight, and value had already been established.[111]

Everything about Gokhran was to function just as it would at any other factory, except for one signal and never-mentioned difference: Gokhran would be a factory in reverse. Instead of making precious things out of raw materials, Gokhran's job was to make raw materials out of precious things. This process would be known as "depersonalization" (*obezlichenie*). Upon arrival at Gokhran, all objects were to undergo two rounds of sorting. Depersonalization took placed during the first, "rough" sorting of objects, to be performed by a Commission for Depersonalization, Sorting, and Appraisal of Valuables. Consisting of the director of Gokhran or his deputy, and representatives from

VSNKh, NKVT, RKI, and Narkompros, the Commission was to meet regularly to sort objects into two primary groups: the first, consisting of "valuables bearing artistic significance due to their age, craftsmanship, valuable artistic design, interest of a historical character, etc., as well as rarities and unique objects [*unikum*]," was to be "kept separately from the general mass," in a special section of the "Storage Department of Valuables of a Mixed Character." These objects would be stored in the same form in which they had been received. By contrast, the "general mass" of goods, all those not identified as valuables bearing special significance, were turned over for depersonalization, involving the "separation of diamonds, precious colored stones, and pearls from metals." The "separation" identified in this process entailed the physical removal of stones from their settings and the separation of one sort of metal from another. An informal but common synonym for depersonalization was "to break [*lomat'*]" or to be sent "to scrap [*na lom*]." In the Sovnarkom decree on Gokhran, this action was described as stripping objects of their "individuality," as in: "objects of the category [of rarities and historical valuables] should not lose their individuality and are to be stored separately, unmixed with the general mass of depersonalized stones, bits and pieces of gold, platinum, diamonds, etc."[112]

The preference for depersonalization in the handling of all but the most exceptional valuables revealed a prevalent conception that the value of precious goods inhered not in their style, beauty, or utility, but primarily in their substance as raw material. The term "depersonalization" migrated into Soviet usage from tsarist law, where it related to the treatment of bulk commodities. As Narkomiust explained in a memorandum concerning furniture, depersonalization historically described the commingling of separate parties of such commodities into a single stock, as at a rail depot. As the Narkomiust official recounted, firewood "arriving from various addresses"—that is, sellers— "being loaded onto the railways" was joined together into a common load, such that the individual parties became indistinguishable from one another. They were thus "depersonalized," unattached from their original owners as a matter of physical identification, although not ownership.[113] Sellers retained rights to a share of the wood in proportion to their original contribution; but should they have wished it, it would no longer be possible to return their actual pieces of wood to them after depersonalization had occurred.

The impossibility of return was almost certainly what attracted Soviet officials to the concept. "Depersonalization" entered usage at Gokhran through its application to safes during the nationalization of banks. It was also used colloquially in packhouses, pawns, and storage units—anywhere people stored objects of indeterminate character in individual units—to describe the moment of the facility's seizure by the state, when its diverse contents became a notional unity. Revolutionary legal officials objected to this usage on the grounds that depersonalization by definition "applied only to things that are entirely of one type, belonging to various people, things that can be measured or weighed."[114] Its application to furniture, as proposed by a local soviet, was therefore inadmissible, "because furniture is a thing of the most varied quality and purpose. Depersonalization of such things would be unacceptable from the point of view of a labor government, as a waste of the people's wealth," one justice official declared. "It would render objects of high artistic value, antique things and the like, equal to objects of the most average work, intended for kitchen work or trades." Some tables were inlaid with pearl and others bore the scars of the labor performed on them; to treat them all as equal on the basis of their common status as tables, to the exclusion of the labor and materials invested in them, "would represent a destruction of value dangerous to the people's economy."[115]

Similar objections to the new usage of depersonalization were raised and overruled at Gokhran from the very start. At its first planning meeting, the head of Glavzoloto, Bruk, warned of "things with 2,000 rubles worth of [material] while the work is worth 10,000 r. Such things cannot be scrapped," he insisted, indicating a clear appreciation for the value of the "work" as distinct from the materials embedded in precious things, even those that were not historical rarities. A similar concern cropped up in the discussion of a project favored by Chutskaev and opposed by nearly everybody else, to keep a certain quantity of mundane objects whole, "a selection for domestic sale to the countryside," consisting of wedding rings and crosses. The group was skeptical, fearing the continued circulation of precious metals in any form among the peasants: "does it make sense to provide the countryside with gold?" Krasin queried. "Perhaps it would be more profitable [*vygodno*] to melt down." Bruk sensed that "it would call up huge speculation. Gold [should be released] in absolutely no case," a concern echoed by a trade official who "insist[ed] on not sending gold things to the countryside. We think this will lead to speculation and exchange." But as Chutskaev explained, the question was one of production and labor no less than continued demand among the unenlightened. "We have a certain industrial area, like for example the Kostroma region" he observed to the group, "where tens of thousands of workers are occupied with production" of these very same objects. People "will always be looking for rings, always be looking for crosses, we must accommodate this and trade in this commodity."[116] Chutskaev left the argument there, without articulating the critical connection between his points: melting down old crosses and wedding rings even as new crosses and wedding rings were being forged effectively doubled the labor imparted in objects meant to be without value inside the Republic. The following year, when Yurovsky arrived at Gokhran, he made precisely this point, citing the example of the factory near Kostroma employing 1,600 craftsmen, who had made roughly four million silver objects for domestic sale in 1920, "including for example crosses, which at Gokhran at the very same moment are being destroyed and sent to be melted down (it is some kind of fairytale, but unfortunately a fact)."[117]

At Gokhran, much as at the grain depot, the aim of depersonalization was to create standardized products, "such that diamonds are diamonds and pearls are pearls," in Krasin's words.[118] The organizational structure of Gokhran mirrored this overarching preference for the physical separation of one substance from another. Gokhran's main duties were to be divided up among subdepartments: one for "precious stones," one for gold, one for silver, and one for "mixed objects." The latter department, "mixed objects," was likewise tasked with the enormous labor of receiving all objects entering Gokhran for the first time—naturally still "mixed"—and identifying which ones should be kept whole, and performing the physical labor of depersonalization or scrapping, after which the resulting substances would be sent along to the correct subdepartment.

Importantly, however, the substance-oriented theory of value on which this institutional organization turned was not the only one actually in effect at Gokhran. In reality, depending on the quality of workmanship embedded in an object, its life history, or its perceived utility, Gokhran's staff might send objects from the gold to the silver to the mixed subdepartment and back again, suggesting the existence of conflicting ideas about which quality should determine an object's processing. In a later interview, one Gokhran worker explained that the labor of "sorting" for some reason generally took place in the Silver Subdepartment, no matter what an object was made of. Indeed, from its initial orientation around material substance, Gokhran's institutional organization later shifted to include a "Subdepartment for Receiving Valuables" spun off from the "Subdepartment of Mixed Things." The Subdepartment for Receiving Valuables, in turn, split itself into three further subdepartments, one for "preliminary sorting," another for "household objects," and a third "economic section," which would come to perform the same function as the Economic Section of the Cheka—supplying its staff with material resources.[119]

This chaos was the product not merely of institutional disorganization and inefficiency, but of the multiple theories of value operating simultaneously at Gokhran, which conflicted with one another and unsettled the flow of work. Like a metallurgical facility, Gokhran isolated individual precious substances from composites, prying diamonds out of gold as a steel plant would pull carbon out of iron. Like a scrapyard, it salvaged reusable resources from existing objects, with the difference that the objects flowing into Gokhran, while officially worthless inside the RSFSR, did not actually enter Nastasinsky Lane as trash. Many were brand new. "There are totally new tea services that have never been in use, held in wonderful new cases," which were being "all heaped into piles . . . and thrown into the large and small boxes prepared, and judging from the objects thus transformed into trash no one needs, and the cases get torn up, these cases sometimes have two or three rows covered in suede, there are suede pillows of an arshin and a half," Yurovsky fumed. Had Gokhran been a real scrapyard, of course, it would have salvaged the suede, too. "Suede is an object that we just do not have right now, it is very hard to find, and there are thousands of these cases." But suede was neither stone, nor metal, nor mixed; there was no department for it at Gokhran, and so, flying in the face of logic and basic economy, "all this perishes for the state. Some of the cases are pilfered and the rest are burned."[120]

The final stage in Gokhran's work process was appraisal. Of course, judgments about an object's value, where it resided, and in what measure, were woven all through the work process up to this point as well—in the categorization of objects as valuables or non-valuables, art or luxury, intended for depersonalization or to be kept whole. Objects of art were to have been passed off to Narkompros; household goods lined Gokhran's hallways in bins, for distribution to staff or the neighborhoods. But appraisal was the fate of the ordinary, and thus depersonalized, valuables—broken up chunks of gold, loose diamonds, ring settings, to be graded, weighed, and finally, affixed with an expression of their economic value.

As any prerevolutionary tax assessor could have explained, appraisals are easy when the market for the object being appraised is more or less transparent. Methods of appraisal in Russia before the Revolution, as elsewhere, therefore sought to draw the object of appraisal as close to its prospective market as possible, favoring empirical prices over all other sources of information about economic value. In 1912, for instance, instructions issued by the city of

Moscow to the appraisers of its real estate directed them to base their assessments first on a building's market rent at the time; if rents at the time were for some reason not available, perhaps because owners inhabited the building and paid no rent to themselves, the assessor had to seek an alternative basis for appraisal, such as the rents collected at a nearby building of similar construction and type. If these, too, were not available, the assessor was to develop a valuation based on the component parts of the building, such as its land value, building materials, number of floors, construction costs, amortization, and the like. The act of appraisal thus became progressively more abstract and challenging as it grew more distant from empirical market price. In certain cases, where no market for a thing could be imagined, appraisal could fail: thus did officials at the Ministry of Finance in Petersburg, when asked to appraise the building they occupied on Palace Square in 1907, decline to answer on the grounds that neither they nor their neighbors paid rent, nor could there be a market price for buildings that stood at the capital's symbolic heart.[121]

At Gokhran, the task before appraisers in certain ways resembled the basic act of valuation as it had been performed before the Revolution. Beginning in the 1890s, following practices developed by the mining conglomerate De-Beers, international gem traders marketed diamonds in bulk packages of fixed price that bundled exceptional gems of high value with average ones, high prices with lower prices, in order to better control the supply pipeline. Because the value of diamonds depended on their scarcity, and because producers could not control when major discoveries of gems would be made, DeBeers and its competitors integrated the life cycle of production from extraction to marketing in order to avoid flooding the market and driving down values.[122] Per this practice, the task before Gokhran was to bundle loose stones and raw metals in bulk, so that "diamonds are diamonds and pearls are pearls," in Krasin's phrasing, according to the same basic principles of sorting and categorization in use elsewhere, in order to produce packages of a fixed expected value.

The principles by which the fixed value of the stones and raw materials was to be established, however, remained opaque. Strikingly, the question of how to arrive at such a valuation attracted almost no attention in the process of Gokhran's formation. At the initial planning meeting in February, Chutskaev reminded the group that it had yet "to set out a means for performing the valuation, there was a protocol on this topic" identifying it as unresolved. In reply, Krasin read aloud the single statement pertaining to the matter from Gokhran's charter. This statement laconically specified that "norms of valuation" would be fixed by VSNKh and automatically applied to the sorted, depersonalized raw materials at Gokhran. Providing no further insight, Krasin moved on to a separate problem, which he effectively conflated during the conversation with valuation: the question of the currency in which value would be expressed, observing that "for us, neither marks nor kroners are any good, just dollars and guldens. The mark is falling rapidly. The ruble will not exist in general. So the prices should be fixed in dollars and guldens." Those in attendance followed Krasin's lead into the topic of stable currencies, eventually agreeing that the normed prices should be expressed in "gold rubles of 1914, that is firm." They voiced concern that converting prices into gold rubles of 1914 was risky from a technical perspective: "I think this is not a good foundation for calculations," the expert Solomon warned, "mistakes are possible."[123] This was an important point, on which Solomon proved prescient; conversion between the contemporary normed prices and the 1914 gold ruble occasioned serious confusion and frequent mistakes in Gokhran's later work. But Solomon's objection was ignored, as was Chutskaev's suggestion that the group set out principles and practices of valuation. Gokhran's prices went forward in gold rubles of 1914.

All the while, Gokhran's founders evinced little awareness that the prices or values themselves might be difficult to determine, as opposed to their expression in currency. After VSNKh produced one, Krasin reviewed the table of normed prices for diamonds and pearls and casually judged them "a bit low."[124] The topic received no further consideration before work at Gokhran began, with the result, as Yurovsky later complained, that Gokhran's charter stated only that "at any given moment there should be a full picture of which valuables are being held by type, quality, weight, and value, but how this (valuation) is supposed to be done is not said. It is obvious that such a picture is supposed to be generated through accounting [schetovodstvo]"—that is, through an assessment of the different components of value poured into a given object—"[but] all the instructions say is that they will use account books."[125] The vision for valuation at Gokhran therefore involved the mechanical application of norms to interchangeable, bulk commodities. These norms were to be generated by VSNKh on an unspecified basis, and, however arrived at, it was not anticipated that they would change regularly—perhaps once every few years.[126]

In the planned economy of later decades, a chief problem with norms was that there were simply never enough of them to go around. Like the products they sought to regulate, norms were in near permanent deficit. A shortage of norms, no less than shortages in real physical produce, threatened constantly to gum up the works of Soviet production, as planners tried and failed to stay on top of changing production conditions, good harvests and bad, the many variables they could see and the many they could not.[127] The labor intensiveness of norm-setting was one reason why computers seemed to hold out such great hope for the practical execution of socialism in later decades; perhaps their processing speeds could match the sheer variety of material life that so tormented the State Planning Committee (Gosplan).[128] At Gokhran, despite Krasin and Chutskaev's best efforts to sand down the distinctiveness of material things, to depersonalize the variety of the material inheritance away, even the most stoic appraisers found themselves confronted with a diversity of goods that the norms could not swallow, either because the objects themselves were too distinctive or the norms too scarce.

Almost immediately, the staff at Gokhran began searching for ways around the norms prepared by VSNKh. Evidence of this search appeared in the very first inventories prepared by Gokhran for its first full month of activity, April 1920. As expected, this account featured a summary of depersonalized valuables in weight (karats) and value (in rubles). Between April 6 and May 1, Gokhran reported depersonalizing 1,164 karats of diamonds, valued at 9.2 million rubles, and 39 funts of gold, valued at 75,600 rubles. At the same time, however, a new column had appeared on the summary table: "silver objects with various other materials as well as religious objects." These things were not measured in value nor even in weight—they were composed of "various" substances, such that norms could not be applied, and their diversity of material meant that their weight had no meaning. Instead, they could only be measured "by the thing [shtuka]." As "things," they were extraordinarily numerous: in April, Gokhran processed 6,126 of them; in the first week of May alone, "things" numbered 5,756.[129]

At the same time, in mid-April, Gokhran's director, the former nobleman Levitsky, embarked on an effort to supply Gokhran with foreign prices, information he was sure must exist somewhere in the Soviet government, and which he believed it impossible for the institution to work without. At a meeting of a special Price Committee, called expressly on the topic, Levitsky presented a "project on the prices of precious stones for foreign trade" in which he argued that "the pricing of precious stones requires information about prices for such [stones] on the foreign market."[130] Levitsky offered no explanation for his request, but the logic was clear: as the prerevolutionary tax assessors knew, appraisal gets harder the more distant the market. Levitsky thus sought to bring foreign market prices into Gokhran, seeing little point in affixing invented norms from VSNKh to objects destined for foreign sale. The

Price Committee, he declared, should "learn whether the Commissariat of Foreign Trade is in possession of the latest information both about prices for diamonds on foreign markets and also about the course of the Russian ruble."[131] If NKVT did not have the information, he suggested immediately radioing Maxim Litvinov abroad, in his capacity as the Sovnarkom's Plenipotentiary on Currency Operations, to request it. Until it was received, Levitsky sought to use not the VSNKh norms, but, rather, "information worked up by Com. Krug on the basis of material from abroad, relating in the main to prices on the Berlin market from autumn 1919, bearing in mind the weak position of the German mark as well as that of the Russian ruble and also the fact that Berlin was never a center in the diamond trade in the view of Comrade Krasin." This data was old and German, but at least it was foreign, and with information about exchange rates, it would be possible to triangulate present prices for diamonds.

Levitsky's proposal was approved; Comrade Krug was ordered to "gather all necessary information on the foreign prices of diamonds that we have in NKVT, to contact Litvinov to learn at what [rate] pure diamonds of one to two karats are circulating on foreign markets and especially in London."[132] But Gokhran never received foreign price information from NKVT or anywhere else, and after Levitsky's attempt fizzled, official efforts in this direction were not renewed. Unofficial ones were, however, led by the jewelers Pozhamchi and Aleksandrov. According to the Cheka, which promptly opened a file on the subject, the jewelers were found to have "been in contact with abroad, for unclear purposes, with no permission to do so, concerning the present-day prices for precious stones."[133] Their search for foreign prices—together with the good breakfasts they allegedly brought to work and the mistresses they allegedly kept—was taken as evidence of speculation, which it may well have been. If so, their insistence on securing contemporary foreign prices intriguingly suggests either that speculative markets inside Soviet Russia operated with a optimistic attention to foreign prices, as an imagined tether to global markets, or that the men were smuggling diamonds abroad on their own.

Even after the Gokhran trial that convicted them, however, and after the legalization of the possession and domestic circulation of precious metals and foreign currency, which occurred deeper into the NEP, price information remained a source of powerful anxiety radiating from Gokhran. Back when Yurovsky arrived at Gokhran in the spring of 1921, he had learned that, in fact, although it refused to share them, NKVT did possess some "prices from the European market (whether good or bad)," and he begged Nikolai Basha, the

Communist Party member installed to replace Levitsky, to gain access to them. "Knowing how Com. Basha does everything," Yurosky complained to Lenin, "I prepared the paper myself and he even agreed to sign it and order the comrades I suggested to do it." But then Basha seems to have panicked, "thought better of it," and stonewalled for more than two weeks before finally pressing ahead. "This information which would have taken one hour to get was requested instead only after 15 days," during which time a shipment of diamonds to Poland was spoiled, "the Poles cursing our helplessness all the while."[134] The trade in precious metals was partially legalized in 1921, and foreign trade substantially opened with the advent of the NEP. And yet, the circulation of foreign prices remained conspiratorial and a source of both deep anxiety and considerable administrative infighting.[135]

The problem with foreign prices at the time was not simply their potential connection to economic crime. More profoundly, it was that foreign prices at the moment did not, in fact, convey what some of Gokhran's leaders thought of as the "true value" of things, a notion that referred not to their domestic market price—as it might have, had those in charge at Gokhran been interested in arbitrage—but rather to an underlying value, conceived as separate from market price in important ways.[136] Yurovsky, as noted, was in hot pursuit of foreign prices in the summer of 1921. He wanted them, however, not in order to transpose them directly onto Gokhran's wares, in the manner presumably intended by Levitsky or the jewelers Pozhamchi and Aleksandrov, but rather to learn at long last what he called "the real value [realnaya tsennost']" of Gokhran's holdings truly was—a value that, Yurovsky thought, was still "known to nobody." As he explained in his description of how Gokhran should work, its mission was not simply to release a "product with strict calculation of gold, platinum, in weight, in bars and the like"—that is, a material calculation—but also to arrive at what he called a "wholesale valuation of its self-cost [sebestoimost'], expressed in gold rubles of the prewar time, plus a percentage added for work as well as for the materials themselves, such that Vneshtorg [NKVT] or Narkomprod [People's Commissariat of Food Supply] firmly knew that it was receiving a good of definite value all ready to go, and that depending on its ability, and the market, it would receive a profit or suffer a loss, but the valuables would figure in government balances in their real value." Yurovsky thus staked out the need for a measure of value—sebestoimost'— more "real," "firm," and "definite" than what the foreign market could provide, against which the fluctuations of both the market and the behavior ("ability") of state agents at Vneshtorg and Narkomprod could be judged.[137]

FIGURE 4.2. People's Commissar of Foreign Trade
Leonid Krasin. Source: Wikipedia.

Sebestoimost' would become among the most foundational, and vexed, categories in Soviet economic calculation. But it appeared for the first time in Russian accounting literature only in 1912, and in Yurovsky's usage, was an extraordinarily novel concept.[138] It consolidated a grab bag of terms filtering through Russian accounting texts in the decade before World War I that sought to convey the German term, *preis*, with its connotations of both the price of a thing and its cost. Sebestoimost' was a direct translation of the German "self-cost," which most commonly appears in English as "prime cost."[139] In later Soviet theoretical literature, the notion of sebestoimost' was employed to impart a distinction between the real costs of production in the Marxian production framework and the unreal surplus value. Most definitions of the term included the materials and means of production consumed by production and the cost of labor paid out in wages. The notion of sebestoimost'

FIGURE 4.3. Plenipotentiary to Gokhran and executioner of the imperial family Yakov Yurovsky. Source: Wikipedia

allowed the third cost of production, the "value cost of surplus product," to be kept separate.[140] Like so many other important categories of Soviet economic calculation, then, including "surplus value," "profit," "constant capital" and "variable capital," sebestoimost' was a concept "taken directly from Marx's analysis of capitalism," filled up new and distinctive content.

These continuities in terminology, Caroline Humphrey observes, have tended to obscure "the historic difference between capitalist and socialist economies."[141] The Soviet economy owed itself a new terminology, Humphrey argues, but its theoreticians failed to create one, or to incorporate the new phenomena actually developing in economic practice, because ideological commitments to the idea of fixed laws of economic development prevented them from doing so. Sebestoimost' tormented Soviet economists and planners both as a concept and in its practical application. Debates raged over exactly what kinds of costs should be included in it, and what the existence of these costs meant for basic assumptions about socialism.[142] It proved equally intractable in practice. One Soviet accountant observed that, in its aspect as an instrument of control, sebestoimost' also appeared in the capitalist world (prime or standard costs). But where enterprises in the United States typically saw a "deviation between actual costs and standard costs in the range of 0.5 to 2 percent annually, in the Soviet setting the deviation was from 7 to 30 percent."[143] Yet despite these shortcomings, sebestoimost' was not abandoned. In contrast to the capitalist world, its usage in socialist accounting was as a vehicle for establishing an "'objective' basis for prices" rather than empirical costs; it manifested the perennial search for costs not as they were, but as they should be, once the noise of the market was stripped away.[144] It was in this aspect that it appeared at Gokhran.

At Gokhran, sebestoimost' occupied a bridge position, stretching in one direction toward a socialist future of objective value and in the other, to the immediate past of Russian economic thought. In the decades just before the First World War, as François Allisson has explained, a number of Russian economists were engaged in efforts to reconcile the classical theories of value that had long held sway in Russia, positing the source of value in intrinsic or objective factors of production and consumption such as labor, utility, or moral right, with a new, subjective theory of value emerging in continental Europe and known as marginal utility. In Europe, the classical concept of intrinsic value lost ground against theorists who argued that the question around which so much debate had turned—how to relate intrinsic value to fluctuating prices—could be done away with entirely, because intrinsic value did not exist. Theories of marginal utility held that "values in exchange are proportional" to the "last intensity of the last want satisfied," which meant, among other things, that the same object might wield a different value, commanding a different price, depending on its marginal position in the marketplace. Russian economists avidly consumed these "subjective" theories, but for the most part, they did not abandon the classical theories of objective value in which, whatever their politics, they had been steeped.[145] Instead, Russian economists sought to incorporate ideas of marginal utility into theories oriented around objective value, often in a socialist register. Only in socialism, the "legal Marxist" Mikhail Tugan-Baranovsky argued, would it become possible to align marginal utility with labor costs, through planning. Socialism would be designed to "move prices toward value, in order to follow the ethical ideal."[146] To that end, it was necessary not only to establish the "fundamental categories" of production from which value derived, but also to study historical prices, which were, according to Tugan-Baranovsky, a manifestation of intrinsic principles of value.[147]

After the Revolution, Tugan-Baranovsky became the Secretary of Finance of independent Ukraine and died of a heart attack on his way to the Paris Peace

Conference. The pursuit of a "synthesis between marginalist and classical theories, between labor and value and between value and prices," was carried on by a different economist, Leonid Yurovsky, who wrote an important treatise on prices and would become a leading theorist of Soviet monetary reform.[148] Yakov Yurovsky, the executioner of the tsar now functionally in charge of Gokhran, is unlikely to have shared Leonid Yurovsky's theoretical commitments. And yet, Yakov Yurovsky's insistence on identifying the "true [*istinnaya*] value" of Gokhran's wares had much in common with the Russian tradition attached to a classical notion of intrinsic value, less in the sense that Marx had intended, as a crystallization of labor, and more as a casual assumption that there existed an economic value distinct from market price.[149]

The Revolution, in this frame, served as an opportunity to realize true values, which would be accomplished in part by correcting the historical injustices embedded in the prices of things, prices that had been forced on Russian workers by Russian capitalists, and also on Russia by Europe (imperial capitalists). The search for true value was not limited to Gokhran. In took place in several arenas where the new Soviet economy came into direct contact with Russia's erstwhile foreign lenders and emissaries. Foreign price information played an important role in this encounter—again, not for the purpose of grafting foreign prices onto Soviet commodities, but rather, as a platform for the critical interrogation of what things were worth, what the costs of Russia's late development had been, and how value was altered by geography and time. In May 1921, at the very moment Yakov Yurovsky was seeking out the true value of things at Gokhran, another finance official took up a similar effort—valuing Soviet things for foreigners—to establish the prices to be charged to diplomatic envoys for their consumption on Soviet territory. In the absence of domestic markets, this finance official—likely A. G. Orlov, who at the time was the head of a theoretically-oriented Department of General Questions at Narkomfin—proposed two possible approaches to a new economic problem: assessing the rooms, newspapers, sofas, water, and theater tickets that would be enjoyed by the foreign envoys, who could hardly be permitted to benefit from the same subsidies as Soviet people. The first approach, identified by the Commissariat of Foreign Affairs as "mutuality," envisioned charging foreigners the exact same rents and prices that Soviet agents paid abroad. In effect, the RSFSR would mirror prices on foreign markets, "permanently fixed according to average rates in Paris and London," payable in British pounds sterling, deemed the most "reliable" currency. To set the price list, it would be necessary to send abroad for information, in particular for research relating to "rents for equivalent spaces [to those available inside the RSFSR] in different cities, vis-à-vis size, furnishings" and so forth.[150]

The "principle of mutuality," Orlov acknowledged, was "certainly the simplest solution to the problem." But he was unwilling to recommend it, due to the fact that mutuality would fail to capture the "true self-cost [*istinnaya sebestoimost'*]" of consumer goods and, especially, of built space in Russian cities. Mutuality, he argued, undervalued Russia, erasing the true costs of Russia's modernization, which the RSFSR should now strive to recoup. "It must be borne in mind," Orlov argued, "that in comparison with payments for space in Russia, apartment prices in the West were always lower, according to both prewar rates and in gold. This can be explained by the conditions of construction, thinner walls in relation to the softer climate, lower expenditures on construction in materials, and usually much lower land rents." Before the war, Orlov estimated, one would pay roughly 25 percent less in London than in Petrograd for equivalent lodgings. Moreover, he suggested, this gap would only have widened since the war—had a market for space persisted in Russian cities—due to the "enormous deterioration in our buildings, the absence of building materials, the impossibility of repairs and upkeep and so forth." Assigning the prices of space in London or Paris to Moscow was therefore "incorrect." In the same way, "there cannot be here among us a western European valuation of water, sewage, electricity, telephones, furniture, maintenance, tram tickets." Before the war, all these things cost "two and three times in Moscow what they did in Berlin."

Orlov was not a Bolshevik—according to an autobiography he wrote for his personnel file in 1923, before the Revolution he was an "administrator on special projects" for the Ministry of Finance—but he, too, was enthusiastic about extracting from Europe the unearned increment of its congenial market position and past.[151] Russia no longer had a market in space or furniture, water or sewage, but the Europeans should be made to pay for the greater costs incurred decades earlier in Russia to produce goods of the same quality and type, to rectify the historical imbalance as much as to reflect the existing difference in conditions. The absence of a free real estate market in Moscow need not prevent foreigners from paying for the scarcity that would have driven up prices. The foreigners could hardly complain at Soviet price gouging: "after all, this is how it would be if there were 'free prices for hotel rooms' in bourgeois conditions."[152]

And so, rather than adopting the technically straightforward but intrinsically unjust method of mutuality, Orlov proposed effectively resurrecting an embellished market of the prewar past, as it was in Russia and abroad, for an afterlife inside the RSFSR. No method of valuation would arrive at a truly "just valuation [*spravedlivaya otsenka*]," Orlov sighed. But an approach that took into account the historic differences between Russia and the West would get closest to that goal. Orlov proposed "taking the pre-war price in Moscow, or Petersburg, on one side, and in London or Paris on the other . . . so as to define a co-efficient of difference, then take present day foreign prices and multiply them by this co-efficient of difference. Only then will it be possible to define the true value [*istinnaya rastsenka*] of Moscow, Petersburg [*sic*], etc. buildings." Even then, "they will be significantly undervalued," due to the historical differences already noted, "but this can be lived with, provided we collect the payment in gold, as among us, gold has grown more valuable at a higher rate as compared to the West."[153]

Amid a continent-wide search for stable currency after the First World War, prewar prices carried a special appeal, stable because they were historical fact. But like fixed prices of all kinds, they were complicated to manage.[154] For one thing, it proved difficult to erect a firewall between official "1913 prices" in things or currency and those of the new world. In the RSFSR, so hungry was the population for a "firm monetary unity" that the official gold or prewar rubles fixed for state budgets leaked out into popular use, and were soon spoiled by inflationary pressures similar to those on the regular ruble.[155] An additional challenge, thrown into heightened relief at Gokhran, had to do with the effects of inflation on the relative prices of one thing to another—especially prices for precious metals, gems, and other currency surrogates, which had risen more quickly during the inflationary spiral than prices for other things. Orlov and other Soviet economists argued that gold had become more expensive in the RSFSR vis-à-vis other commodities than it had in the outside world; meanwhile the prices for precious stones were understood to have risen more rapidly in Europe than those of other things, such that adopting pre-war prices for diamonds, for instance, could lead to an effective undervaluation on European markets.[156]

Gokhran sat squarely in the crosshairs of these freighted calculations, as became immediately apparent in the fortnightly tallies of valuables it sent to Lenin, starting in August 1920. "Vladimir Ilyich! I'm sending you the first information about what has been gathered at Gokhran in preparation for shipment. We will send this every two weeks," Deputy Commissar of Finance Alsky brightly promised, "and I would add that we have already counted up diamonds of more than 9,130 karats in the first period of operation, worth more than 10 million pre-war French francs." Large quantities to the side, the inventory evinced signs of strain at Gokhran, abandoning the count by "thing" used in Gokhran's first inventories while seamlessly introducing a new category of valuation, "prices in pre-war French francs."[157] The inventory also contained a category "prices in rubles," the details of which went unexplained: which rubles? How did the prices in rubles relate to the prices in pre-war French francs? And how, for that matter, had the prices in pre-war French francs been established? One year after this inventory was made, Yurovsky demanded that Gokhran acquire "illustrated catalogs of diamonds and colored stones from before the war, during the war, and after war," both domestic and foreign, presumably in order to facilitate the painstaking translation of pre-war prices into postwar, foreign into Soviet, back into foreign again. The timing of his request suggests that, when valuation began and the first inventory was composed, Gokhran possessed no such catalogs. In all likelihood, the prices in French pre-war francs sprang not from any catalog but from the memories of the appraisers themselves; this, too, may explain why they were in francs rather than guldens, marks, pounds sterling, or any of the other foreign currencies preferred during Gokhran's planning phase. For the jewelers, knowledge of present-day foreign prices, cunningly sought out through contacts abroad, could be used against them as hard evidence of speculation. But pre-war foreign prices, pulled from the closed circuit of their memory, were hard evidence only of their expertise. Prices in pre-war French francs thus allowed access to the foreign market without risking contamination by it.

This amalgam of foreign and historical prices remained in place for more than two years, but as a metric of value, it pleased no one. It was too close to a bare replication of market prices to satisfy Yurovsky and those at Gokhran who would, through the pricing of its wares, establish benchmarks for the objective identification of "true sebestoimost." At the same time, pre-war French prices proved to be a world away from the market for precious things as it really existed in the present, a fact of which Gokhran's appraisers were acutely aware, judging from the terse "note" they appended to the inventory sent to Lenin: "at present, the prices for precious stones are much greater than before the war."[158] As Gokhran brought forth its first shipments of precious goods, largely diamonds, it immediately became clear that its valuations were severely out of sync with those of the outside world. This was partly due to some breathtaking episodes of bungling, which included Gokhran's very first shipment, "the most shamefully colossal loss-bearing transfer of valuables" to Poland, for which, rather than preparing a package worth "15 million rubles, as had been agreed," Gokhran's staff had prepared a package worth "15 million francs."

On the one hand, the mistake was honest enough, if shockingly amateurish—evidence that, as Yurovsky hissed, "it was not just the things that were poorly prepared but also the people."[159] On the other hand, this type of error was precisely the sort of mix-up that had been flagged as a risk during Gokhran's planning, the natural consequence of the decision to truck in invented pre-war currencies.[160] Gokhran's second shipment "was no less nightmarish," Yurovsky fumed, and "had it not been for the interference of Coms. Trotsky and Krasnoshchyokov"—brought in as expediters—the shipment "would never have come off." Finally, there was a party of high-quality diamonds sent to Latvia, weighing 80,000 karats, intended for sale to English buyers. After days of negotiations the buyers had walked away, perhaps because the prices were too high, or too low, or because—so the expert Pozhamchi alleged—the Soviet agents did not "speak the special language of the specialists," with its "fine distinctions" and "particular terms." Pozhamchi said that if they had let him conduct the talks, "the stones would have been sold already and not be sitting even now in Latvia." His statement was later introduced as evidence that "these spetsy of ours" were preparing parties "that could be sold only to swindlers like themselves, the sale of which is not in the power of our Vneshtorg [NKVT] spetsy, used to selling oil and manufactured goods, knowing nothing about stones."[161] As these deals came apart, so too did Gokhran.

The Afterlives of Markets

Failure at Gokhran, like failure at most other revolutionary institutions, was generally interpreted as evidence of counterrevolution. To address these suspicions, both the Central Committee and the Cheka appointed representatives to full-time work at Gokhran. The Central Committee sent Yakov Yurovsky, executioner of the tsar; the Cheka sent Gleb Bokiy, aided by Gokhran's new director, the Party member Nikolai Basha. All three men were in constant communication with Lenin, who, beginning in the spring of 1921, insisted in furious missives that "things are not alright at Gokhran [vsyo ne ladno]," veritably shouting off the page that it required "building, reorganization," and "ten times more work than you all have given." From that moment, Bokiy's updates to Lenin all began identically: "the investigation continues and uncovers more and more new criminals."[162]

Much had changed between Gokhran's founding and this new interrogation of its purpose and functioning. The advent of the New Economic Policy raised the legitimacy of hard currency and hard budgets inside Soviet officialdom, bringing with them renewed attention to these resources in the future of Soviet development and less of an excuse for the earlier bias against trucking in Gokhran's wares. The Sovnarkom's "Decree on Requisition and Confiscation" of April 1920, which established a legal footing for requisition and confiscation, opened the door to debates on the legality of possessing substances once forbidden, including precious metals (see chapter 2). New value limits on private possession appeared for the first time since 1918, fixed at twenty times the normed average salary in a given locality, rather than the flat rate of 10,000 rubles, and including a Republic-wide individual norm of precious metals.[163]

These developments spurred tentative discussion of recognizing other forms of market value of the day in official practice. The Department of General Questions, the experimental Narkomfin department helmed by Orlov, floated a proposal to return "improperly seized" money in "the currency in which it was seized," including "money of a prerevolutionary or 1917 format." Up to this moment, Narkomfin refused to recognize the fact that older monies circulated in the Republic's semi-legal currency markets and abroad at higher local courses than Soviet legal tender (*denznaki*) in its dealings with the public; when it returned seized money, it was in Soviet denznaki at a one-to-one exchange. Orlov now declared that "the official treatment of equivalent value [between old and new monies] is a fiction," writing that "we cannot close our eyes to the fact that old money has a value tens of times higher than that of the same [quantity] of Soviet issue, and that these differences have a real basis insofar as they are based on foreign currency."[164] By the end of 1921, Narkomfin had drafted decrees allowing exchange of Soviet money with foreign currency and the circulation of gold as legal tender.[165]

Even so, there remained a deep skepticism as to the legitimacy of market values and a corresponding hesitancy to integrate market prices into official use. This hesitation was not necessarily expressed as policy; often, it was expressed in the operating practice of particular agencies, even particular officials, acting to prevent the consolidation of clear channels of information and the open circulation of market prices in a way that would allow those prices to supplant the ones fixed by the state. In November 1921, for instance, the Sovnarkom directed the State Bank to issue "official exchange rates for precious metals and foreign currency," which were intended to be responsive to the "black market" in currency in urban centers. But a separate decree was necessary to allow the promulgation of the official rates, and this was not forthcoming. As a result, the rates were not permitted to circulate, and, indeed, were not even released for use among other institutions of the Soviet state.[166] "The success of the new economic politics of Soviet power in developing commercial relations inside the country as well abroad undoubtedly requires that the relevant commercial organizations and individuals be in full possession of all necessary information about market prices," the Narkomfin official Orlov insisted in December 1921. "The only way to do this is by radio," Orlov explained, but the Cheka refused to permit transmission, insisting that "all [foreign price information] is secret."[167]

While increasingly well-developed after the turn to the NEP, information about market prices thus remained jealously cloistered within particular institutions. Narkomfin relied on methods commonly employed by the police for its gathering of economic information, collecting "private rumors" circulating in Moscow and the provinces, for instance, about the usage and circulation of money.[168] With the legalization of currency exchange in late 1921, Narkomfin asked its regional offices to report on the local exchange rates for tsarist money and precious metals.[169] On the basis of these reports, Narkomfin developed "currency bulletins" for its own use, while Lenin's office at the Sovnarkom communicated directly with the editors at the newspaper *Ekonomicheskaya Zhizn'* for accurate information about foreign currency markets in Moscow; the resulting tables generally included one or two exchange rates derived from official sources, such as Gosbank, and one or two taken from what was characterized as proprietary sources, or "private information."[170] Routine currency operations remained of dubious legitimacy, as an NKVT official complained after his boss, Maxim Litvinov, blocked a resale of German marks ("arbitrage") because he claimed it was "speculative and not suitable for us as a state apparatus."[171] Even at the State Bank (successor to the People's Bank), firm knowledge of foreign currencies was so parochial that, in the midst of negotiations with the Moscow Consumer Society over a proposed purchase of tinned meat from a French merchant, the Bank director A. L. Sheinman fumed that in the future he would not negotiate with the Society "except in the presence of a notary," due to its repeated misrepresentations of the course of the French franc, also based on "private" information.[172]

The attempt to improve Gokhran bore the mark of the moment's contradictory impulses. Gokhran's problems posed questions that recurred across the revolutionary era, and for which there were no obvious answers: what was state property, how was it made, and what had the seizure of all this particular stuff—the valuables—meant? No one asked now whether its seizure had been worth it; it had been a revolutionary necessity. "Gold and silver, things made of precious stones, these are objects of luxury and, at this time, the most direct form of the bourgeoisie's appropriation of added value or, even more simply, the unpaid labor of the people for itself. Soviet power could not leave these things in the hands of their owners," a Narkomfin report subsequently explained, "without contradicting its major efforts to expropriate the means of production such as factories, machines, materials, and money from the hands of capitalists and landowners." The creation of Gokhran, of course, had not actually been an obvious outcome of the seizure of the valuables, which languished for several years without attracting serious interest from the Soviet state. With the benefit of hindsight, moreover, it had become clear that "actually, the concentration of all valuables of the republic in Gokhran in such a short period of time had turned out to be impossible," due to the "transport difficulties and the storerooms of Gokhran, despite their spaciousness," being "insufficient for all the material valuables of the republic." Nevertheless, the Narkomfin report declared in 1921, as the reforms in Gokhran got underway, the institution now represented "the brightest symbol of that sharp boundary between the old and new worlds, telling us that what was before the wealth [*dostoyanie*] of a few individuals and served as an object of their enjoyment or a means of accumulation has now become the wealth of the whole nation [*obshchenatsionalnoe* dostoyanie], concentrated in the hands of the proletarian government power for the use and good of all."[173]

And yet, if the seizure of valuable objects had been an ideological and practical necessity, their reimagination as a resource for national development seemed to have fallen short. At Lenin's behest and for his consumption, the acute dilemmas of valuation, market autonomy, and state property revealed at Gokhran were compressed and repackaged into a criminal case against Gokhran's employees. To be sure, the fact of extensive theft at Gokhran was never in question. Concrete evidence of theft was detected as early as August 1920, when Rabkrin conducted a "surprise inspection" of Gokhran workers as they headed home at the end of the work day. Searches performed at the building's exit of the departing workers and their bags resulted in the arrest of a handful of employees found to have valuables on their person. After the search was over, however, inspectors found a tiara with twenty-five diamonds, diamond earrings, rings, and assorted other valuables "scattered across the pavement," where staff had been waiting in line to be searched.[174] Ironically, those caught with valuables on their person were all later found to have plausible reason—namely that they were bringing items to the Cheka or to Narkomfin, at the special order of Alsky, Chutskaev, or senior Chekists. These were the staff who hung onto the valuables in their possession through the checkpoint, understanding their removal to be legitimate; they were arrested for it, while the presumably larger number of staff members secreting gems out illicitly dropped them on the pavement before reaching the exits and walked out free.[175] In any event, whether the actual incidence of thieving had increased or not, by the following summer it was transformed, under Lenin's watchful eye, into a full-blown crisis. When Bokiy gently introduced the possibility that "the total elimination of theft is impossible," Lenin harangued him with expressive punctuation, "(??!!)" and irate demands to hire "dozens, hundreds of reliable communists," and perform "surprise revisions, day and night, one and two times a month."[176] By June 10, following a wave of arrests two days earlier, there were no longer enough staff for work at Gokhran to go on.[177] Interrogations, however, progressed at a fabulous clip, with more than 258 completed in just six weeks.[178]

Many of the crimes they revealed were straightforward cases of theft. But many revealed improprieties that were difficult to characterize in the conventional terms of property crime, ending up under the rubric of "crime on the job" or "criminal negligence." The investigation thus reopened a series of unsettled questions about the dimensions of state property, what Gokhran's things were, and where their value lay. In particular, it uncovered a throughline of historical thinking about the valuables as things embedded in their bourgeois past, a past that included their trajectory into state possession through ambiguous acts of seizure. In interviews with inspectors, it emerged that many of Gokhran's staff understood its wares as stolen. They claimed to have arrived at this conclusion not from their own judgments about seizure and its legitimacy during socialist revolution, but rather from the officially prescribed policy of depersonalization, which did such profound damage to the economic value of seized things that it made sense to them only as an effort to cover up evidence of a crime—that is, of the state's theft of the valuables themselves. "Is it necessary to perform depersonalization?" Yurovsky asked in his report, after conducting these interviews. "That is, the destruction in storage spaces of the signs of belonging, as I was informed with regard to [depersonalization] and also as to the rough sorting performed there, that it was done in order to hide the true goal, which is a secret to no one at Gokhran, they all look at this as the Bolsheviks wanting to destroy proof and to mix up stolen valuables."[179]

Other policies at Gokhran similarly blurred the lines of state property. Like many employees of the new state, Gokhran's staff was paid partially in kind.

But where at some workplaces this meant sending workers home with produce to consume or trade, at Gokhran this meant permitting employees to select one or two items each month from the pile of seized "household things" erroneously sent to Gokhran. This allowance filled out low salaries and cleared the building's cluttered hallways. But to the extent that Gokhran's workers truly understood its wares as "stolen," then they, too, were now trucking in these ill-gotten goods.[180] Gokhran also, despite its stated mission, provided sizable quantities of valuables for official redistribution inside the RSFSR. There was particular demand for watches, which the Cheka requested and received by the hundreds.[181] Reviewing all the notes about all the requests for things from inside the Soviet state and Communist Party, Yurovsky found that in the month of May 1921 alone, Gokhran released "805 million rubles' worth of valuables," of which 622 million had gone to NKVT for its intended purpose of foreign trade, while 157 million went to the Central Committee, three million to VSNKh, four million to the Red Army, and nineteen million rubles' worth of valuables to "various" destinations.[182]

Gokhran was thus enmeshed in a program of domestic redistribution alongside its work preparing valuables for foreign trade. This program was regular and substantial, but, like so much else, it was the subject of vigilant conspiracy. The conspiracy manifested in individual interactions and as official policy. Gokhran's first director Levitsky was regularly ordered in small, handwritten notes not only to "release 10 gold rings with diamonds," "a silver tea service," and other things to various individual party and state agents, but also to do so "without demanding payment" or composing paper documentation of the transfers—the very gaps in documentation for which Gokhran was simultaneously upbraided.[183] Levitsky's boss, Alsky, was often behind these machinations, which he worked assiduously to shield from official organs of state accounting.[184] Narkomfin also relied heavily on the use of so-called unpublished decrees in its management of currency and valuables—orders that were official policy but were explicitly not promulgated publicly, distributed only inside the apparat. Such orders naturally added to the confusion around the circulation of valuables, as even well-intentioned officials could never be sure whether a given transaction, if it did not adhere to published standards, was illegal (e.g., theft or bribe), conspiratorial (e.g., Alsky's machinations), or, in fact, permissible under the terms of an unpublished order to which they were not privy (e.g., "unpublished decrees").[185]

The prevalence of conspiracy made it that much harder to detect malfeasance on the part of Gokhran's staff. The solution to this dilemma was understood to be, first and foremost, more and better conspiracy. In the spring, Basha demanded the hiring of as many undercover Chekists as possible.[186] Yurovsky was notably skeptical of the undercover staff, advocating instead for hiring "unquestionably honest communists" to work alongside a pumped-up batch of "qualified personnel."[187] But he, too, accepted the necessity of conspiracy to Gokhran's basic mission, concluding that the old nobleman Levitsky could not be renewed as Gokhran's director—not because of his impending arrest for "criminal negligence," but due to his inability to keep up with the complex conspiratorial traffic: "when and which valuables, for which sums, were to be given to the Comintern, the TsKRKP [Central Committee], and various undercover workers."[188] Levitsky could not keep it all straight.

In the wake of the criminal case and the execution of nineteen of its staff, efforts to replenish Gokhran's ranks foundered. First, the Red Army was invited to "participate in the mobilization, accounting, and appraisal of the Republic's valuables," for which soldiers were promised a 5-percent cut of whatever they succeeded in unearthing and inventorying.[189] At the same time, A. M. Krasnoshchyokov tried to woo famous tsarist jewelers to work at Gokhran, men who presumably would not have considered the prospect before the NEP. It was a hard sell: "the mood among the *spetsy* in connection to the recent events at Gokhran," Krasnoshchyokov reported, "is extremely negative, untrusting." Several, notably Agafon Karlovich Faberge, scion of the Imperial jeweler, were not long out of prison or labor camps themselves.[190] Some had "already managed to open small workshops of their own, and as far as it was possible to clarify, are in this way earning big money." By the end of his trip, "following extended negotiations," Krasnoshchyokov convinced seven jewelers, Faberge among them, to work for Gokhran. They were promised huge advances, guarantees for their apartments, and the right to continue their businesses on the side.[191]

The arrival of the experts from Petrograd accelerated the collision between clashing interpretations of value and its measurement at Gokhran, a byproduct of instability in ideas about price and value that would become a hallmark of the NEP era.[192] In whose voice did the market speak, and who could afford to listen? Faberge and his associates from Petrograd could claim as few others to command the voice of the market, not least insofar as they ran their own antiquarian businesses on the side. But they were hired not as merchants of the day—their continued activity as antiquarian traders, Krasnoshchyokov emphasized, was a painful concession—but as clearer, cleaner copies of the gem market as it had been in 1913. Meanwhile, the key methods of internal account at Gokhran were little changed. In angry meetings with the Narkomfin collegium in 1922, Basha was ordered to present "precise arithmetical accounts" of Gokhran's silver holdings, even as he himself impeded the collection and distribution of foreign price information through the apparat.[193] Faberge and the others worked under constant suspicion, in part because even their expert assessments never quite yielded what was expected.

In attempting to isolate the real value of bourgeois treasures that, officially at least, did not have value any longer within the Soviet Republic, the Bolsheviks paradoxically found themselves dependent on foreign markets and the information they produced, a dependence heightened at Gokhran thanks to the famously fickle nature of its wares. As Cecil Rhodes had discovered decades earlier, for diamonds to hold value at all, it was essential that they hold it in the same steady way over time. DeBeers tightly controlled supply in order to maintain an illusion of near-scarcity, while cultivating "orderly markets" at stable levels of demand.[194] Gokhran destabilized all of this, flooding the market with used stones precisely as their appeal grew as a hedge against inflation. In 1922, in a secret letter to Lenin's aide Nikolai Gorbunov and the Narkomfin collegium, Leonid Krasin came to a similar realization, floating a theory as to why Soviet sales never went as expected. In contrast to his own awareness of the foreign market two years earlier, and in contrast to nearly the entirety of the debate about Gokhran up to that point, Krasin now evinced curiosity not about the reliability of Soviet appraisers but instead about the interest of potential buyers. In short, Krasin explained, there was no interest in Soviet diamonds from potential buyers, not at the prices on offer, for which the Soviets had no one but themselves to blame. They had flooded the market. "We have to stop once and for all with this order, or, rather, disorder through which the build-up of our diamonds leads to losses of a dozen percent in their value."[195]

In terms of the diamonds, Krasin argued, "the only rational way of realizing the wealth that has not yet been stolen or squandered is to form a fund of some 50 million rubles' worth of valuables," and to conclude a contract with "a major firm, we had proposals from DeBeers and from Vatburg, to form a syndicate" that would give the RSFSR loans on the basis of future sales.[196] In terms of valuation at home, the only way forward was a repeat loop of the past two years: the new round of hires eventually gave way to a new round of arrests, of new appraisers unable to discern what Russia's infinity of treasures was worth. Faberge was arrested in 1924, around the same time as his official minder

Krasnoshchyokov.[197] Yakov Yurovsky, ever in search of true value, continued on as the head of Gokhran's gold department before retiring to a perch at the Polytechnical Museum, where he remained until his death in 1938—six weeks apart from that of the gold theorist Leonid Yurovsky. Leonid died on the Kommunarka shooting field outside Moscow; Yakov had a peptic ulcer. Neither solved the riddle of non-market value before his death.[198]

5

Return and the Revolution's End

Many asked, 'Is my furniture in Petersburg still all right?'

'I see, yes, I see it—your furniture,' he said to each, as he lurched about the stage in his blindfold; 'it's all right.'

—VIKTOR SHKLOVSKY

IN EARLY NOVEMBER 1917, days after the Bolsheviks seized power, a widow by the last name of Tikhobrazova was at home in Petrograd packing up her apartment.[1] Tikhobrazova was leaving for the Caucasus city of Armavir, where her grown son had been assigned to a military posting as a railway engineer. It appears Tikhobrazova intended to make the move permanent, or at least long-lasting: she packed up her entire household, and over the next several days she made every effort to have her possessions shipped by rail to Armavir. When this proved impossible—due to the chaotic condition of the railways, several agencies refused her order—she reluctantly settled for storing her possessions in a nearby warehouse, to retrieve at some future date. Soon after, she boarded a train for Armavir. She would not return to Petrograd for more than three years, as civil war raged and rail connections between the Caucasus and the Russian capitals were completely severed.

Among the many other transformations wrought by the Revolution during Tikhobrazova's time away from Petrograd, her storage unit was declared the property of the Soviet state—twice, for good measure. First, in December 1918, her possessions were "nationalized" by a local order that gave the owners of property stored in warehouses ten days to "declare their intention to remove their things." Tikhobrazova, of course, failed to do this. Tikhobrazova had not even known of the order, and indeed, how could she have? Newspapers in

Armavir could hardly be expected to print every doing in Petrograd. Then, more than a year later, the Petrograd Soviet issued a decree expressly "municipalizing" furniture and household goods located in warehouses, which it now declared to be "ownerless"—things such as those Tikhobrazova had stored. But importantly, by the time Tikhobrazova herself returned to Petrograd, on December 30, 1920, both of these orders had been superseded by the new "Decree on Requisition and Confiscation," promulgated by the Sovnarkom on April 16, 1920 and explicitly canceling all orders preceding it.[2]

Tikhobrazova was hardly alone in her peregrinations across the Republic in the three years of civil war and revolution, or in her decision toward the end of 1920, as the dust settled and the outlines of Bolshevik power solidified, to make her way home. Within days of returning, she presented herself at the warehouse where she had stored her household. Here was where her story diverged from most others, because whereas most people, upon their return, found the movable trappings of their previous lives scattered or lost, Tikhobrazova found her household intact, right where she left it, and seemingly untouched. Elated, she declared her intention to take possession of her property and bring it with her to her new living space. Just then, however, the warehouse director appeared, insisting she would do no such thing, not until she had permission from his boss, Comrade (L.) Kimber.[3]

As Tikhobrazova would shortly learn, Comrade Kimber chaired a body created by the Petrograd Soviet in October 1920 and known as the "troika for requisitions and confiscations." The troika heard all requests concerning the review of seized goods and in general it heard them all in the same way: "refuse, with no explanations given." Kimber refused Tikhobrazova's request to reclaim her possessions in the broadest possible terms. He denied her not only the right to recover her own goods, but also to receive household goods of any kind from the city stocks of seized things, even those making up the material norm regularly allotted to Petrograd residents. Tikhobrazova, in response, more or less immediately abandoned her effort to reclaim her household possessions in their entirety, setting her sights instead on securing the right to select the normed allotment of goods from among her own possessions. She petitioned all manner of city officials asking permission and eventually secured approval from the chair of the Petrograd Soviet himself, M. A. Trilisser. Yet still Kimber did not relent. Tikhobrazova next filed suit against him in the People's Court, and when he failed to show up to three separate hearings, she won the suit by default. But Kimber held fast, insisting that Tikhobrazova receive nothing—from her own goods or anyone else's. Finally, after months of her haranguing, Kimber seems to have tired of the fight. On a scrap of paper, he scrawled to an assistant, "let her have the full norm of goods for two—that is, including a samovar. It is time to be done with this matter once and for all."

This show of softness, instead of placating Tikhobrazova, seems to have energized her. She rejected this opportunity to receive the norm from the city's fund of seized goods, resuming her effort to have the People's Court ruling in her favor implemented, according to which she received not just any dining table, but her own dining table; not just any chairs, but her own chairs, in the quantity allowed by the city's "full norm." In response to this renewed campaign, the troika revealed that, in fact,—what were the chances?— sometime between Tikhobrazova's return to Petrograd in January and the People's Court ruling in February, her things had at long last been inventoried and removed from the premises of the warehouse by the municipal institution, Chrezuchyot, responsible for the management of all "ownerless" property in the city. "Ownerless" was, after all, what Tikhobrazova's property had become, if not back in December 1918, when she had failed to appear within ten days to reclaim it after the warehouse's nationalization, then certainly in October 1920, when furniture and household goods in warehouses were declared "ownerless" and made over into city property. Now, the warehouse director informed her, Tikhobrazova would have no choice but to settle for things from the common stock of seized goods.

In a last-ditch effort, Tikhobrazova arranged to visit the warehouse with her court-mandated "implementer," an officer of the People's Court charged with enforcing its decisions (so long as they did not countermand the orders of a state institution). They arrived at the warehouse together one morning in early March. At the warehouse gate, Tikhobrazova presented her court order, entitling her to select from her own possessions a quantity matching the norm for a two-person household. The warehouse director appeared, and allegedly began to shout at her, "get out of here, it is not yours, it is all the people's." The court implementer wrote a description of the encounter and departed— Tikhobrazova's court ruling, while in her favor, clearly conflicted with the orders of a state institution, the warehouse. Now all alone, Tikhobrazova lingered at the warehouse gates, poking her head this way and that, straining to get a look at the spot where her things had been. And just then, she spotted one of her own boxes, right where she had left it, intact and untouched. At this, Tikhobrazova began to cry. A young woman working inside the warehouse approached her, asking, "why are you crying so bitterly?" Tikhobrazova answered, "I have been left destitute, they have taken everything, even the remembrances of my relatives are gone, even the album." The girl asked her what her album looked like and went away. A few minutes later she returned, bearing the album of photographs Tikhobrazova had described, with a permission slip allowing her to take it home.[4]

———

Over the course of 1920, it gradually became clear to people like Tikhobrazova—people who had "gone south," as the departure of residents from the capitals after October was colloquially known—that Bolshevik rule would endure, that they would not be able to wait out the Revolution from afar. The Bolsheviks, too, faced a moment of reckoning. The Red Army was winning the civil war. Soviet power had endured successive crises on and off the battlefield. But revolution outside of Russia had not materialized, a fact that, as discussed in the previous chapter, Lenin and other revolutionary leaders understood to require new terms of engagement with foreign powers. This conjuncture—the establishment of Bolshevik power at home combined with stymied prospects for spreading revolution abroad—brought about a reorientation toward the Revolution inside Soviet Russia: namely, it raised the question of how to end it.

While the Soviet Union existed, debate over when and how the October Revolution ended, and the connection between its end and its "betrayal," was tightly bound to a search for a usable past for Marxist revolution—outside the Soviet Union, no less than within it.[5] As Sheila Fitzpatrick wrote in her definitive short history of the Revolution, for both sides in the Cold War confrontation, the timing of the Revolution's end came freighted with contemporary political meaning, obscuring the social dynamics of change that Fitzpatrick sought to recover. Fitzpatrick herself adopted a "common sense" definition of revolution as "coterminous with the period of upheaval and instability between the fall of an old regime and the firm consolidation of a new one," which allowed for a capacious narrative arc modeled on the French Revolution, spanning from the First World War to the Great Terror. This chapter employs a more restrictive concept, not to efface the Revolution, but rather to illuminate the contemporary significance of ending it as a political project, its repercussions in lived experience, and its connection to the concerted intensification of state- and party-building that began in the early 1920s in parallel with the New Economic Policy and Lenin's demise.[6] Drawing upon Dan Edelstein's study of the chronology of the French Revolution, this chapter characterizes revolution as the "temporal window between legitimate regimes," during which time the idea of the Revolution itself assumes governing authority, detached from fixed legal or constitutional order.[7]

All revolutions, Edelstein observes, begin with acts of law-breaking. Determinations about which subsequent acts of popular violence should "acquire the dignity" of recognition as acts of revolution are constitutive of the revolutionary process, up to and including the process of bringing revolution to an end. Like other episodes of mass political violence, that is, the end of revolution introduces the question of normalizing activities and practices that "would in other circumstances have been judged criminal." In France, Edelstein shows, lawmakers "devised the legislative solution of declaring amnesties 'for deeds relating to the Revolution.'"[8] But in Russia, this chapter argues, the process of closing the Revolution was considerably more complicated, and was ultimately conducted not through the declaration of amnesties but through the imposition of a forceful, official amnesia.

As earlier chapters have shown, between 1917 and 1920, one of the most essential institutions of socialist revolution—the conditions of possession and dispossession—lacked a legal and at times even a practical footing. Wielded by institutions of the revolutionary state as well as individuals and collectives acting in the name of the Revolution, the requisition and confiscation of living spaces and their contents churned through revolutionary society, giving rise to an elaborate defensive infrastructure of protections and special privileges, but nothing in the way of substantive central order—until the moment where this chapter begins, April 16, 1920, when the Sovnarkom released its first "Decree on Requisition and Confiscation." The "Decree on Requisition and Confiscation of April 16, 1920" (hereafter Decree of April 16) gave formal definition to the omnipresent act of seizure and, as compared to existing practice, dramatically limited its application. But as will be seen, rather than resolving the status of possession and dispossession in revolutionary society, the Decree of April 16 triggered both a new wave of dispossession and also a surge in claims, such as Tikhobrazova's, demanding the return of movable things that had been taken in the ambiguous circumstances of revolutionary upheaval.

The effort to contain dispossession summoned an array of anxieties about the end of the Revolution itself. Concerns that halting dispossession spelled a return to a prerevolutionary property order circulated widely in revolutionary society, driving a new explosion of conflict over the disposal of things. As this chapter shows, a "crisis of repossession" accelerated under dual pressures of resettlement: first, of people like Tikhobrazova, returning to the capital cities after months or years away; and second, of former subjects of the Russian

Empire, who, in the wake of mutual recognition agreements concluded between the RSFSR and newly independent states in the Baltics and elsewhere, declared themselves to be foreign citizens and sought to recover or liquidate their households located on what was now foreign, and socialist, soil. Inside the RSFSR, the Decree of April 16 stimulated a broad popular reappraisal of dispossession and an attempt to secure legal status for possession—something the decree did not address—forcing a series of clarifications and new orders for several years to come. The legal process of attempting to end dispossession thus illuminates the dynamism and responsiveness of revolutionary lawmaking to the lived experience of revolution, and the extent to which, as has been noted by Larissa Zakharova, individual experiences served as the basis for new law.[9]

Among the chief labors of all revolutionaries is the task of defining what constitutes "revolution."[10] The "bacchanalia" of dispossession subsequently came to appear, and has continued to appear, as an essential or natural part of socialist revolution. Yet this very naturalness was in part a legacy of the Bolsheviks' efforts to manage and constrain the practice, as it changed shape from a resource in the seizure of power to an impediment to stable governance. The crisis of repossession stimulated the construction of a retroactive legal timeline of seizure that doubled as a timeline for the socialist revolution itself, an essential, finite, and ultimately irretrievable phase of which was now understood to be "dispossession." The laws through which the Sovnarkom sought to end dispossession and consolidate state ownership of seized things were borrowed from prerevolutionary law; they drew on concepts of abandonment and ownerlessness gaining popularity at the same moment in neighboring lands with their own episodes of mass violence and dispossession to put behind them, such as the new Republic of Turkey. In Soviet Russia, however, these concepts were ill-calibrated to the condition of propertylessness in revolutionary society, as they invoked prerevolutionary legal statutes on dispossession without providing corresponding positive attributes of possession. And so while similar legal frameworks succeeded at suppressing dispossession in some of Soviet Russia's neighbors after the war, inside the Soviet Republic these decrees called forth a crisis of repossession, stimulating a deluge of petitions and legal cases on behalf of people and institutions who had lost things over the previous three years and now, using the new laws, wanted them back. Revolutionary dispossession could be neither revised nor contained through the legal process opened by the Sovnarkom. Instead, as this chapter shows, the Sovnarkom resorted to ending dispossession by forcing it to be forgotten.

Through analysis of both the personal encounters and experiences documented in legal cases and the laws that emerged from them, the chapter defines the emergence of a legal segregation around the revolutionary period—its distinctive attributes assigned variously in Soviet laws, depending on region and ethnicity—as a time apart from the regular order, to which there could truly be no return.

Law without Property: A Legal Order for Dispossession

Over the previous years, municipal governments had periodically sought to contain the requisition and confiscation of movable property in partial ways, often resorting to protections on particular classes of goods and people. (See chapter 3.) But the Sovnarkom's "Decree on Requisition and Confiscation of April 16, 1920" was the first attempt to contain dispossession itself, by endowing it with a legal footing for the first time since 1917. The Decree of April 16 invoked the reintroduction of law into the realm of dispossession in a very literal sense, by reproducing the prerevolutionary legal definitions of requisition and confiscation in full. Requisition was defined precisely as it had been before 1917 as the "forced alienation or temporary seizure by the government of property located at the disposal of private people and societies, for a payment defined by the organs of power." Confiscation was the punitive, "uncompensated forced alienation by the government of property located at the disposal of private individuals and societies."[11] The People's Commissariat of Justice (Narkomiust) borrowed these definitions almost verbatim from the orders introduced at the start of the First World War. The Decree of April 16 thus lifted a legal apparatus built before the Revolution, which assumed a surrounding infrastructure of private property law, and dropped it down into a society where this infrastructure was, still at that very moment, in the process of being effaced.

The collision engineered by the Decree between the sudden reappearance of prerevolutionary legal norms for dispossession, on the one hand, and the general postrevolutionary absence of a legal framework for possession on the other produced a startling interpretive outcome. Because the Decree of April 16 offered essentially the first commentary on the postrevolutionary property order in movable things from the Sovnarkom, in spite of the fact that its focus was dispossession, it was broadly read as a legal guide to possession. The promulgation of the Decree of April 16 on dispossession triggered a surge in petitions from people seeking the return of goods seized in years past, in ways now deemed illegal. Some individuals and even some institutions, however, went further, interpreting the Decree as a framework for positive rights to possess movable things, deduced as the inverse of the restrictions on dispossession it actually contained.

Narkomiust gave only the barest explanation for why the Decree appeared when it did, and even this emerged not in the general promulgation but in response to a query from the Petrograd Soviet, as it attempted to reason through Tikhobrazova's case. Narkomiust characterized the Decree as essential to restoring the population's psychological well-being and with it, its labor productivity. Justice officials explained that the years-long "deprivation of property" in "household goods," "furniture," and "objects of personal tastes and passions" during the Revolution had, in fact, amounted to a "violation of the regular habits of life, capable of triggering deep depression and a lowering of productive energy." Critically, this "gradual draining of productive energy" had been detected not only among so-called parasites and class enemies but in "the entire population of the RSFSR." The Decree of April 16 was therefore meant "to alienate the possibility of the incorrect and inexpedient deprivation of citizens of the worker-state of that property [which is] essential to sustain a normal ability to work and the psychological energy of a working life."[12]

Planning for the Decree began months before its promulgation, with the circulation of a draft version of the Decree among the People's Commissariats. The commissariats were instructed to report back to the Maly Sovnarkom ("Little Sovnarkom") on their proposed approaches to the "implementation of their rights of requisition and confiscation," that is, how they intended to conform to the new restrictions on requisition and confiscation. These responses attest to how heavily many institutions had come to depend on practices of requisition and confiscation as their primary "mode of acquisition" of goods. Indeed, so pervasive had "requisition-confiscation" become in institutional life that a number of institutions failed to grasp readily the distinction between the two (the compensated seizure of essential goods versus the uncompensated seizure of property as punishment) reintroduced by the Decree. Only one, the Commissariat of Foreign Trade, confidently deployed this distinction in its response, projecting that it would maintain its "use of confiscation at customs," but that it "made no use of the right to requisition" presently nor would it in the future.[13] The draft reply from the Commissariat of Enlightenment (Narkompros), by contrast, was littered with assertions of its "right to requisition," which were later crossed out by hand and replaced with claims to the more limited right to "confiscate" objects "in cases where these are being taken abroad without permission." The change accurately reflected a definition introduced by the decree linking punitive and permanent seizure to confisca-tion. But even within a single draft, this new usage did not stick, and by the end of the document, Narkompros officials had reverted to claiming broad powers to "requisition and confiscate from private people objects of scientific value, scientific museums, collections, laboratories, and equipment," with "libraries" later added in by hand.[14]

Underlying these responses was a broad confusion at what many institu-tional respondents correctly discerned was a main purpose of the Decree: to restrict the performance of seizure to a small, fixed number of official bodies. This was particularly the case in relation to "household goods," a category the Sovnarkom now formally defined as consisting of "furniture, clothing, shoes, dishes, and the like." The Decree of April 16 forbade requisition of "household goods" in its sixth article, except in cases of "special need" certified by a "spe-cial commission with representatives from the gubispolkom, gubSNKh, and gubprodkom [regional executive committee, regional council of the national economy, and regional commissar for provisions]." It likewise forbade their confiscation, except as punishment exacted by a sharply restricted set of insti-tutions listed in its fifth article as "the presidium of the VChK, revolutionary tribunals, and people's courts." Special powers over the "requisition" of food were extended to VSNKh, Narkomprod, and their local organs.

Institutions newly locked out of seizure on these terms expressed dismay at the suggestion that they perform their duties without seizing. Among many replies, only one respondent—Glavleskom, the State Timber Committee—declared that it would be unaffected by the decree's restrictions on seizure because "all materials relating to [its] action have already entered into the property of the Republic." Most institutions anticipated, to the contrary, that the decree would affect them profoundly, not because there remained signifi-cant domains of things requiring nationalization, but rather because requisi-tion and confiscation were the chief mechanisms by which they acquired *all* things. Seizure was at the core of revolutionary governance, not as a reflection of chaos or collapse, but as a basic instrument of rule. The Commissariat of Posts and Telegraphs explained that "according to current practice," it "re-ceived the right to ~~requisition~~ confiscation" of virtually everything it needed in order to operate: "spaces, fuel for those spaces, lighting, fire-starting, build-ing materials, telephone and telegraph apparatuses and their pieces, genera-tors, scales and measures, cables, switches, and other things needed for build-ing telephone apparatuses, horses for delivering mail," and "various objects" contained in the shipments it handled. Even institutions that had *not* relied on ham-fisted measures of "requisition-confiscation" to sustain routine activities found it difficult to imagine limits on their powers to seize objects related to their spheres of administration, as witnessed in the correspondence with Narkom-pros, which quickly reverted back to the muscle-memory of "requisition-confiscation" and to the expectation that it could still seize most all cultural objects with which it came into contact. So distressed was Narkompros by the Decree's proposed strictures, in fact, that it embarked on a lengthy (and unsuccessful) attempt, in 1920, to assert its claims over all the pieces of art and culture that had been inventoried in 1918 but never extracted from homes due to lack of transport. Narkomiust informed Narkompros that it could seize the objects only if it paid for them ("requisition"). Narkomfin refused to authorize the funds.[15]

The Decree of April 16 likewise prompted a broad reckoning with dispossession in localities across the RSFSR. Local governments interpreted the Decree variously, with some reading it as a confirmation of existing practice and others as a reversal. Partly this variety was due to the nature of the task that lay before the Decree: injecting elements of legal order into a sphere that had been without it for several years proved a difficult balance to strike. In Tsaritsyn, regional officials reported that the local "judicial-administrative organs," namely the Cheka, had interpreted the Decree as granting it permission "to continue to perform confiscations of clothing, linens, furniture and the like during searches, not even writing an order about this." Officials in Tsaritsyn's Regional Department of Justice, to the contrary, understood the Decree to have ordered that "requisition and confiscation of things of domestic use IS FORBIDDEN and only in cases of special, sharp civic need for these things does the right to requisition or confiscation belong to a special commission." The Regional Department of Justice therefore asked "for clarification": was the April Decree a repudiation of this revolutionary practice, or a legalization of it?[16]

Other places interpreted the Decree as a restoration of prerevolutionary property rights, down to the resurrection of individual contracts. In the Kostroma region, a district soviet inquired of Narkomiust in November 1920 "whether contracts or other obligations, having been concluded in 1916 for a period of ten years, are valid in the present day." Narkomiust replied with irritation that it was necessary to "bear in mind the article from the decree on the socialization of land, in which it says that buildings can be the object of juridical agreements only in connection with a piece of land," land that remained the property of the state. "It is obvious from this that there can be no discussion of rights to use buildings contracted before the [land] decree," the justice officials curtly explained.[17] But it seemed plausible enough in Kostroma that the Decree of April 16, though dealing with movable property, might entail a broad resumption of prerevolutionary rights, as if the intervening years had been erased. As had been the case in 1917–18 during the onset of requisition and confiscation, the absence of a full legal infrastructure led to creative extrapolation. Like officials in Kostroma, those in Tsaritsyn wondered whether the restrictions on dispossession of movable goods might reverse the seizure of buildings as well, which, they now revealed, had, in fact, continued to circulate on an illegal market, using "homemade contracts," for the previous three years.[18] Narkomiust officials replied sharply that Tsaritsyn's question betrayed the absence of "even a basic understanding of the new laws of exchange in their sphere of private possession," which were wholly unaffected by the Decree of April 16.[19]

In some places, the reckoning with dispossession prompted by the Decree of April 16 leaned toward repudiation; in others, it was interpreted to confirm and extend existing practice. That this one decree had so many readings speaks not only to the inherent lability of legal texts in general or the ambiguities of this particular Decree's construction, which were numerous. More than either of these, it speaks to the depth of the upheaval in the property order that Revolution had wrought. Revolution cleared the decks, such that people could hold all these possibilities in their minds at once, continuities and radical breaks and all.

Nowhere did the "Decree on Requisition and Confiscation" make any mention of people getting anything back; nowhere was the restoration of elements of a legal property order suggested to entail the restoration of specific properties to particular people. Nevertheless, in identifying legal forms of seizure for the first time, the Decree likewise provided concrete circumstances in which individual experiences of dispossession could be understood not as constituent of socialist revolution, but as having violated laws. This interpretation was not limited to individuals. It was also perceived by officials—leading some institutions to try to get out ahead of the Decree in order to consolidate their positions vis-à-vis things that had been up to this moment lightly regulated. On April 15, one day before the Decree's promulgation, Narkomfin issued an order declaring that from this moment forward, owners of things held in nationalized safes could not retrieve those objects under any circumstances, preemptively foreclosing the possibility of their return if laws on seizure appeared, as they did the following day.

At base, the Decree of April 16 presented a question of scale: if its purpose was the containment of dispossession, how far was this to go? Insofar as dispossession made the Revolution, was the containment of dispossession then also a retreat or a reversal in the Revolution?

Ownerless Things or the People's Property?
The Legal Status of Seized Things

Few institutions greeted the Decree of April 16 with more concern than city soviets, the institutional centers of the seizure of household goods for nearly three years. City soviets feared that the end of requisition and confiscation spelled the end of the special powers they wielded over all resources found on local terrain. More particularly, they objected to the decree because it threatened to cut off their chief pipeline of things suitable for redistribution in their Furniture and Requisition Departments—seized goods. If deprived of its regular practice of requisition and confiscation, Moscow's Gorodskoi neighborhood soviet protested, "not only will [the soviet] be unable to supply workers and the Red Army [families] with furniture, it will simply have nothing in its in-kind fund, that is just obvious."[20] In the coming months, both Petrograd and Moscow proved unwilling to accept what they understood as the implicit outcome of the Sovnarkom's decree: the ratification of property rights—cast even in the most minimal fashion, as protections from seizure. By restricting seizure, the Decree threatened to end the condition of propertylessness on which the allocative power of local soviets hinged; like a game of musical chairs at the moment when the music stopped, people would keep what they had on April 16, 1920, no matter how they had gained it and who they were. Not only would this make life hard for the Furniture Departments bombarded with requests for household goods from empty city coffers, it would imperil the authority to assign the possession of things to people that the local soviets understood to be their own.

In the wake of the April Decree, then, the soviets of both Moscow and Petrograd issued orders effectively countermanding it. The aim in each case seems not to have been to defy the Sovnarkom or restore the unrestrained practice of requisition and confiscation; indeed, the two soviets were at pains, in different ways, to avoid precisely that. Even so, both cities sought to ensure a continued supply of movable goods for the purpose of redistribution. And in order to make their cases, each city found it necessary to revisit the recent past—not in order to celebrate it or argue for the continuation of the established practice, but rather to delegitimate dispossession as it had occurred so far, in order to sever the claims that current holders of objects might make over things in their possession, claims the soviets feared would be hardened by the "Decree on Requisition and Confiscation."

On June 4, six weeks after the April Decree, the Presidium of the Mossoviet published its own "Order on the Regulation of Rights to Furniture," governing the "order by which those residents newly settled into an apartment are to be supplied with furniture." The Order directed that, if the new residents arrive to a living space without furniture of their own and "are unable to be supplied [with furniture] otherwise, they are to be supplied with the necessary furniture from the other rooms of the very same apartment"—that is, from the furniture possessed by the other *residents* of the very same apartment. The Mossoviet made efforts to couch its Order in terms that acknowledged the existence of the April Decree and its ban on the seizure of household goods, specifying that the furniture transferred to the new residents was to be understood only as "in the temporary use [*pol'zovanie*] of the newly settled residents," and thus would "remain the property [sobstvennost'] of the original possessors [vladelets]." But as local Rabkrin officials argued, "removing property from the hands of its original holders and transferring it even for temporary use to another person constitutes a legalization of requisition of that [property]," which was explicitly forbidden by the April Decree.[21] The Mossoviet Order limited the ability of the present-day "holders" of household things and furniture to dispose of them in other ways as well. It restricted "residents of Moscow wishing to sell furniture that belonged to them on a legal basis" to deals with one buyer and one buyer only, the Moscow Consumer Society (MPO), at prices fixed by the Moscow Sovnarkhoz. It forbade the free transport of furniture from one destination to another, even inside the city.[22]

The Mossoviet's package of orders on household goods elicited strong objection from the Rabkrin officials who reviewed them, and who argued that the Decree of April 16 did not merely limit dispossession, but also had to be understood to assert positive rights to the possession of household goods. "From these articles [the April Decree] forbidding the requisition and confiscation of household goods," a legal consultant at Rabkrin wrote to the Sovnarkom in protest over the Moscow orders, "it is completely clear that the HIGHEST LAWGIVING POWER recognizes the RIGHT TO POSSESS [*pravo vladeniya*] AND FREELY DISPOSE OF FURNITURE," including "the right of total or partial sale by citizens according to their own determination, as well as the right of unencumbered transport of it from one place of residence to another."[23] The Sovnarkom, however, did not sanction Moscow over its orders, and a few months later, the Presidium of the Petrograd Soviet enacted regulations of a similar character. On October 1, the Petrosoviet proclaimed what it called the "depersonalization" of furniture located within city boundaries, rights to which were assigned to the Housing Department. In a review of the order, Narkomiust rejected Petrograd's usage of the term "depersonalization" for objects so variegated as furniture (an objection also raised against the term's usage at Gokhran). Because Narkomiust did not accept this usage, its officials interpreted depersonalization instead as a synonym for dispossession, and thus, Petrograd's Order as a direct violation of the April Decree. But it seems more likely that the Petrograd Soviet's aim in using the term was, in fact, much as it had been at Gokhran, to describe not the act of seizure, but the act of severing the bonds between previous owners and already-seized things—either physically, by melting them down, or notionally, in records. Petrograd sought, through the act of depersonalizing furniture that it now called "ownerless," to establish stocks of furniture that could not become re-"personalized": that is, stocks that could not become the possession of anybody, and would instead circulate continuously in official redistribution.

"Ownerless" things had a long heritage in prerevolutionary civil law, as well as a rising profile in adjacent, nonsocialist countries after the First World War.[24] In the new Republic of Turkey, the category of ownerless property emerged at roughly the same moment as in Soviet Russia, in order to manage a different problem of return—that of Greek and Armenian former subjects of the Ottoman Empire seeking the return of properties violently seized from them during and after the First World War. In Russia, the term acquired two distinct meanings, one articulated by the Petrograd Soviet, the other by Narkomiust, which released a "Decree on Ownerless Property" defining the term only *after* the Petrograd Soviet made it the centerpiece of its own October 1 "Order on the Depersonalization of Furniture."

According to Narkomiust's usage, ownerless property could be of two types. The first related to property nominally belonging to the state. State property became ownerless when it was either "located in no one's possession [obladanie] or is in the possession of a definite organ without permission from the relevant central organ." The second type of ownerless property did not belong to the state, nominally or otherwise. Narkomiust did not specify to whom, exactly, this type of property did belong, only that its owner was not the state. This type of property, at any rate, could be considered ownerless if it had been "factually left by its owner, who is absent without having left information as to their whereabouts, as well as property the owner of which is unknown and cannot be established."[25] In both cases, "ownerless" property reverted to the state for allocation (or reallocation, if an ownerless thing was also already nominally owned by the state). The chief difference between the two sets of things, state-owned and not state-owned, was in the legal meaning of their current possession: according to Narkomiust, possession was not enough to fend off charges of ownerlessness if the nominal owner was the state. State-owned things, that is, could be classified as ownerless even if they were in the current possession of a state institution, if that institution had failed to acquire "permission from the relevant central organ." By contrast, according to Narkomiust, nonstate-owned things, so long as they were currently in *someone's* possession, could not be classified as ownerless, and were not to accede to state control for reallocation.

This difference had important implications for the fate of seized household goods. It meant that Narkomiust's definition of ownerlessness for nonstate-owned things such as furniture and other household items recognized current possession as an attribute of legal ownership. Things *in the possession of somebody* were protected against classification as ownerless and the redistribution that went along with it. The Petrosoviet, by contrast, characterized ownerless property as property that had both already been seized at some earlier date, and was at the same time currently in the possession of some specific person or household. This definition allowed for a very narrow application, more or less limited to household goods and furniture that had passed through the gauntlet of revolutionary redistribution, and were now held by new people—the beneficiaries of the Revolution—with and without official permission. Petrograd's usage targeted this specific scenario, in which the new residents of a space took possession of its contents in one way or another, and now considered those things their own. Much as Moscow had done in its order forbidding the free movement and sale of furniture, Petrograd therefore sought to ensure that the people now in possession of movable property not come to think of themselves as its owners. It declared precisely this property ownerless, and thus subject to perennial redistribution.

The dispute between Petrograd and Narkomiust therefore hinged on the meaning of possession in the revolutionary legal landscape. Before 1917, in Russia and elsewhere, possession commonly constituted one attribute of legal ownership. Other attributes would have included legal title or contract. In some cases, possession of an object could trump other attributes of ownership, as can be seen in the provisions for cases of what was commonly known as "adverse possession," in which it became necessary to allocate rights in an object when the person who held the object was not its legal owner.[26] The resolution of cases of adverse possession typically revolved around the display of proprietary behaviors, which included evidence of care for an object, adjudged through the things people did and, in particular, through the information they gave off to surrounding parties, signaling their hold on a given thing. In its definition of "ownerlessness," Narkomiust drew upon this prerevolutionary concept to argue that possession once again constituted an attribute of ownership: "property, including state property, [but] located in the use and possession of a particular person, cannot be removed from [that person's] use on the grounds of its alleged ownerlessness," it argued. Possession of a thing protected it against classification as ownerless.[27] Petrograd held the opposite: objects could be declared ownerless even when in somebody's possession, if those objects fell into the category subject to the city's "Order on Depersonalization," that is to say, if they had been already seized.

As noted above, the turn toward ownerlessness in Soviet Russia coincided with the category's take-off in neighboring Turkey, where, following the violent displacement of the Ottoman Empire's Armenian and Greek subjects, the new Turkish state sought to characterize properties seized from those subjects as "abandoned" as a means of consolidating their tenure by new Turkish owners. As Ellinor Morack and other scholars have shown, in designating the properties of Armenians and Greeks who were killed or forcibly expelled as "abandoned," the state sought to erase not only the traces of their potential claimants, but also—insofar as the new Republic wanted to preserve the legal order of private property going forward—the unsanctioned, often violent means by which those properties had passed into new hands.[28] Declaring objects to be "ownerless" mattered because, according to fundamental precepts of civil law, it determined the mode by which such things could be acquired in the future. Things with legitimate owners at the moment of their subsequent acquisition conveyed with all the "defects in the rights of the previous owner" attached to them. The unwitting purchaser of stolen goods, for instance, held no right to them, because thieves had no rights to give. Stolen goods still belonged to the person from whom they were stolen, no matter how many times they subsequently changed hands. Things that were recognized legally as being without owners, by contrast, conveyed to a new owner unconstrained by such defects in rights.

Ownerless things came in several classes: they included objects claimed on the battlefield; abandoned things, the owner of which was unknown or could not be found; and things previously not subject to property law. Ownerless things were, by definition, a clean slate.[29] This was the source of their appeal in a place like the new Republic of Turkey, which sought to maintain a system of private property law while at the same time forestalling demands from the dispossessed for their properties' return. The result, as Morack explains, was the dramatic and ubiquitous discovery of "'abandoned property,' both discursively and materially" in former Greek and Armenian settlements, by new Turkish prospective owners. In order to ensure that erstwhile owners could not return to reclaim their "abandoned" properties after the fact, the Turkish government enacted a series of passport restrictions, preventing the physical return of former owners, thereby allowing the state to maintain the fiction that the properties had truly been abandoned, and that their new Turkish owners had behaved according to the current law.

The connection between ownerlessness and a clean slate was undoubtedly what appealed to Soviet authorities, too, despite their differing aims with regard to the future of private property law. But in Soviet Russia, unlike in Turkey, ownerlessness failed to resolve the status of seized things in either law or practice. In part, this difference grew out of the differing mechanism of dispossession in the Soviet Republic. Because dispossession in Soviet Russia had been so diffuse, targeting people on an amorphous class basis and catching up many others along the way, there could be little prospect of isolating out the dispossessed and preventing them, as a group, from seeking the return of their things. This was not all. In the RSFSR, the question animating dispossession was not simply who got to bear property rights, but what property was and in what form, if any, it would continue to exist. The "Decree on Ownerless Property" did not settle this question, first and foremost because it was promulgated into a society without legal owners.

In order for a "Decree on Ownerless Property" to make any sense, there had to be some established means for judging which things *did* have owners. Deploying legal language from before the Revolution, the Decree specified that if an absent but known owner appeared, or an unknown owner was discovered, ownerless property was to be "returned or compensated" once the owner's "legal right" had been confirmed.[30] But, critically, it provided no information as to how this legal right was to be judged. What was more, and as Rabkrin officials again complained, this silence applied also to the legal rights of the state, which were laid out no more clearly than those wielded by private individuals. At a preparatory meeting held shortly before the Decree's promulgation, a Rabkrin representative asked the gathered group an essential question: was it possible, after four years of Revolution, countless nationalizations, municipalizations, requisitions, and confiscations, "to concretize the moment that property is taken over [by the state] and precisely define it." Whether because Justice officials wanted to leave room to finesse the moment of state possession in the future, or more likely, because they themselves did not know what this moment of conveyance should look like—how to draw the boundary between state things and everything else—it was decided at the meeting "not to do this, as the moment is clear enough."[31]

The difficulty of disambiguating ownerless things from the general morass was further amplified by the new meaning of the term introduced in the Decree, relating explicitly to the management of things held by state institutions. According to the Decree, ownerless things were those "not located in someone's possession or in the possession of a state institution without the permission of the central distribution organs." This was claimed as "a new understanding of ownerless property as property existing outside the control of [*nepodlezhashcheye*] the related central distribution organ." This status had to be understood "in relation to economic as opposed to its legal features." The "economic" features, more precisely, trumped the legal ones; it was in the economic rather than the legal sense that "this property was ownerless, not subject to [*nepodlezhashcheye*], not being used [*neispol'zuemoe*], not attributed [*nepriurochennoe*] and the like." As these adjectives were meant to indicate, what this property lacked was not necessarily a legal owner. Often enough, though it was not phrased in this way, its legal owner was presumed to be the state. What made a thing ownerless therefore was not legal status but rather the absence of "rational use," either because a thing was "not located in someone's possession" or because it was in the possession of "someone" or "some institution" without proper permissions to be there. Ownerless things were things out of place.[32] As in the planned economy of the future, even the state was meant to possess things, to borrow a phrase from Harold Berman, according to plan, rather than according to the tenets of property law.[33]

Coming on the heels of three years during which huge quantities of movable things and household goods had been "abandoned" in one way or another, and in the absence of positive standards for legal ownership, the "Decree on Ownerless Property" therefore had astonishing implications, opening up enormous troves of things that were no longer in the hands of their last legal owners—as of 1917—to seizure (or re-seizure) by the state. Into which category did the things already seized and redistributed inside apartments fall? Were they state property gone missing from the accounts, or nonstate property, currently held in possession, and thus made over into the property of their possessor? The Decree did not say.

Ownerlessness would therefore have to be a category defined in large part through practice, through the work of the institutions that were created to identify it locally, known as "Committees on Ownerless Property" or *kombez-khozy*. As a report prepared by Narkomiust explained, the first *kombezkhoz* appeared at the end of 1919, before the "Decree on Ownerless Property" was promulgated. Evidently it was then that the existence of ownerless property was first detected, although Russia's "encounter with ownerless property" would be later recognized to date back "to the end of the First World War, when huge quantities of this property were located at the front, on the fields, on the roads, and in various warehouses." Ownerless things had multiplied after the Revolution, the report explained, but had not initially been interpreted as belonging to a category unto themselves. Examples of such property included things "left behind on the battlefield or in an area occupied by Soviet forces," property that had been "evacuated," the term typically used to describe things (and people) displaced by the war, and property "subject to demobilization." They were managed "artisanally" by the Commissariat of War, before being taken over in 1918 by a branch of VSNKh called "Tramota" [transport-material department]. In the following year, its purview grew to include all "evacuated" property associated with the war effort and the flows of migrants it occasioned, including not only war material, but also civilian baggage left behind in train stations and other personal or household items. This nonmilitary class of things in its control continued to grow until finally, "at the end of 1919, the KOMBEZKHOZ was created," charged with funneling "ownerless" property out from the coffers of the Commissariat of War, "and putting it to rational use, in the sense of its concentration in precise distribution centers."[34]

The "Decree on Ownerless Property" empowered local soviets to form their own committees on ownerless property, which they eagerly did, adding new and different layers to the meaning of the term in the process. As the kombezkhoz in Moscow's central Gorodskoi neighborhood explained in its first annual report in 1921, the job of its kombezkhoz was to consolidate newly identified "property of the republic" for its distribution to socially worthy groups—Red Army soldiers, the demobilized, and "people suffering from accidental poverty."[35] The "Decree on Ownerless Property" specified that things in someone's possession could not be considered "ownerless," but that was not how the Gorodskoi neighborhood's kombezkhoz saw matters at all. The local search for ownerless property kicked up questions about the whirlwind of dispossession all over again. In specific, if the mission of the local kombezkhoz was to gather up of what was rightfully the "property of the republic," how could it turn a blind eye to the fact of what dispossession, in reality, had been?

Suddenly, in the wake of the center's legal efforts to put a stop to dispossession, a new narrative of it appeared in Moscow's neighborhoods. This narrative acknowledged, indeed emphasized, the many shortcomings of dispossession in the previous years. In particular, it focused on household goods as a form of state property that the state had tried and failed to physically possess. It acknowledged the condition of propertylessness, the ways in which the state had not succeeded in adequately taking possession of seized things—redefining dispossession as overtly chaotic, in order to justify the classification of seized goods as "ownerless," which would allow the neighborhood to seize them anew. "Lines to get into the warehouse," the Gorodskoi neighborhood now recalled, had made it impossible to transport seized property, with the result that "property of the republic"—that is, seized household goods—had been "left in the hands of the building committee or the residents. . . . Carried on the winds of fate, it would gradually disappear."[36] In answer to the question left unanswered in the "Decree on Ownerless Property"—whose were household things, the state's or not the state's?—the Gorodskoi neighborhood declared that of course, these things were "the property of the republic." They belonged to the state. And precisely because they were the state's, the proscription on treating seized things presently in someone's possession as "ownerless" should not apply. Because they were rightly the state's, these things had to be accounted for, taken possession of by a state institution physically, which in most instances, as we have seen, had never happened. (See chapter 3.) Because they were the state's, and on the basis of their history, these things were, in fact, "ownerless." The kombezkhoz would take physical possession at last, recovering these properties from the hands of their current holders, who were now identified explicitly as their nonowners.

To reinforce its claims, the Gorodskoi neighborhood also reconfigured the meaning of the "absence" from the capital city on the part of those who had left things behind, as well as those who gained them. Following prerevolutionary usage, the "Decree on Ownerless Property" had characterized the previous owners of ownerless things in neutral terms, as people who were now merely "absent" or "unknown"; it said nothing at all about the character or class background of the people who left, nor that of the objects' new holders. But the kombezkhozy took these neutral terms and filled them in with narrative material, judgment, and suggestive backstories from the recent revolutionary past.

As the Gorodskoi kombezkhoz explained, it purposefully sought out the things of "citizens absent from their apartments" in order to identify them as "ownerless." It identified these things as liable to state (re)seizure in two respects. First, the absence of the owners was made suspect: absent owners, the kombezkhoz explained, were, in fact, "members of the fleeing bourgeoisie [who traveled] outside the borders of the Soviet republic at various times during the revolution, or to some unknown place."[37] Absence from Moscow was thus conflated with being a class enemy at best, and a counterrevolutionary who had sought out White territory at worst.[38]

But, in fact, no one came off well in this picture of flight and attendant dispossession. The people who stayed behind were suspect, too. According to the kombezkhoz, these people allegedly took up the property of those who fled without seeking official permission to do so, an act now recast as theft—not from the people who left, but from the state. The kombezkhoz would therefore concern itself with the things of absent citizens who "at their departure, charged other citizens with this [care of their furniture], which [these new citizens] then appropriated as their own when it should have been the wealth of the republic."[39]

In the hands of the neighborhood soviets, then, the "Decree on Ownerless Property," while intended to clear the slate of the past three years, was interpreted as a new basis for extending the action of dispossession. In October 1920, six months after the April Decree restricting seizure to a few select state organs, local soviets *began* to seize property from the households of "absent" people, no matter why they were gone. In one instance, a Russian woman whose common-law husband, a Swiss citizen, traveled home for a visit that fall, was deprived of their furniture after the local soviet learned of his absence, on the grounds that because theirs was only a common-law marriage, she could not claim his property as her own: the property was all his, and he was now absent, so the property was "ownerless." In Petrograd, the Petrokommuna seized the property of a soldier sent to the front as "ownerless" and refused to give it back—or to compensate him for the loss, as he demanded—when he returned.[40]

In this wave of dispossession, two things were different from the time before the Decrees on Requisition and Confiscation, and on Ownerlessness: first, whatever the neighborhood kombezkhozy thought of them, these two significant Decrees now existed and their contents were broadly known. Their impact was felt immediately, less as a matter of careful attention to the letter of the law than as a matter of broad popular emboldening. People objected vociferously to the seizure of their household goods in violation of these orders. Local soviets reported on these objections with dismay, documenting popular engagement almost as a physical assault on their rule: a sudden ubiquity of "citizens who come in with their underlined decrees," complained the Gorodskoi neighborhood kombezkhoz, stomping about the soviet's reception rooms. Other soviets reported citizens demanding that they, the soviets, "familiarize themselves" with "what the law says." Still other citizens were found to be cagily "relying upon the latest Decrees" in an effort to revisit the property arrangements of the past, from the time before the Decrees came into effect.[41] The existence of the Decrees provided a platform for challenges of all sorts to the revolutionary property settlement.

The second difference, in at least some of these cases, lay in the people themselves, especially in Moscow and Petrograd. As 1920 wore on, these were often people who had, for whatever reason, been away over the previous three years, and now found themselves back. Russia's great cities were decimated by the economic and political dislocations of the civil war era, as people of all social classes and political inclinations fanned out across the former imperial expanse. But after losing more than 700,000 people since the civil war began, in 1920 Moscow finally stopped hemorrhaging people, and in 1921, the city gained back more than 100,000 residents.[42] This shift is well documented as a matter of demography, but it also had a profound effect on local governance. Not all of these people were the same people who had left, of course. Some were new arrivals, drawn to the new locus of state power; others came from the provinces in search of work.[43] But many of these people were returnees: Red Army soldiers; officials sent to the provinces on state or party business; the mothers, wives, and daughters of these people—all returning to find their households gone. Whatever brought them to the city, their arrival reinforced the social dynamics brewing around the attempt to end to dispossession through a process of legalization—the return of people, the return of law, and, perhaps, the return of what had been lost, all threatening to undo what the Revolution had wrought.

A Surfeit of Property Sentiments

Among other goals, the seizure and redistribution of movable things augured a new phase in the relationship between people and the objects they lived with, severing the bonds of particular owners to particular objects as a first step toward weakening the allure of material accumulation and possessive relations in society as a whole.[44] But as the crisis of repossession following the Decree of April 16 makes clear, the aftereffect of revolutionary dispossession was less the eradication of what Larissa Zakharova called the "property senti-ment" than it was that sentiment's diffusion. Zakharova writes of workers who moved into a bourgeois building in Petrograd in 1918 and who, when ques-tioned during an inspection two years later about the appropriated things in their possession, declared unambiguously that these things belonged to them.[45] The trouble, as it turned out, was that the revolutionary state felt the same way, and so, too, did the previous owners. Rather than diminishing, property sentiments after the Revolution in critical respects multiplied, clog-ging the gears of the administrative apparatus called upon to sort them out.

Stories about the lived experience of dispossession presented to revolution-ary authorities illustrate how such sentiments formed. In one such case, a caf-eteria director who returned to Moscow in 1920 after two years away raised a suit against a woman named Vasilieva, who he claimed had participated in the "appropriation" of his furniture in his absence. Before leaving, the cafeteria director, as was common at the time, entrusted his movable things to his neighbor, Klauzman. Some time later, Klauzman left the city, too; before doing so, he handed everything—his own possessions and those of the cafeteria director—over to a relative, Vasilieva, for safekeeping. The cafeteria director pieced this chain of events together upon his return, paying a visit to Vasilieva "at home," during which he somehow "saw that Klauzman had, in fact, man-aged to appropriate a big portion of my things." Before his suit against Vasilieva could even be resolved, however, Vasilieva was arrested by the Cheka (for reasons not specified in the petition). As a result, the cafeteria director's things fell into the hands of yet a third party—the porter at Vasilieva's apartment building, by the name of German, who received permission from the local housing department to move into Vasilieva's apartment and take over the fur-niture inside. Although the court eventually ruled in the cafeteria director's favor, when he and the court executor showed up at German's apartment to reclaim his furniture, they found that German had secured a competing per-mission from the Gorodskoi neighborhood Furniture Department. The con-flict culminated with the porter German, into whose hands the cafeteria direc-tor's household had fallen wholly by chance, successfully convincing the Gorodskoi Furniture Department to certify the cafeteria director's things—with their surfeit of would-be owners—as "ownerless."[46]

These conflicts reached their apex in the winter of 1921, as the waves of re-turnees continued, and as many people who had never left sought to make use of the new rules to get things back or, alternatively, to solidify their claims to things gained in the previous three years. Initially, many people brought cases to the People's Courts. To manage the surge, both Moscow and Petrograd shifted disputes over dispossession from the courts to special troikas established for the review of instances of dispossession and demands for the return of seized goods. The troikas were dubbed the highest authority for the resolution of contested instances of dispossession. But, in fact, the problem of subordination highlighted in the cafeteria director's case persisted, as people who did not like the decision of the troika continued to take their case to the city Ispolkom (which appears to have remained the functional highest instance), the People's Court, or to Rabkrin's Bureau of Complaints. Indeed, the Petrograd Rabkrin observed that, since the formation of the troika on October 1, it had received "many complaints about incorrect decisions" taken by the troika. Upon investigation, the Petrograd Rabkrin determined that the troika rarely offered any rationale for its decisions. "Usually, in fact, almost always, with rare exceptions, the order simply states: denied. No reasons for the refusal are specified, no traces of investigation are visible. Meanwhile," it concluded, "the very essence of the matter and the social position of the complainant demand careful and comprehensive investigation."[47]

Tikhobrazova launched her case in response to precisely this sort of refusal on the part of the troika, with her complaints becoming fodder for the jurisdictional battles between the local troikas, the Commissariat of Justice, and the Complaint Bureau of Rabkrin. As it circulated, however, Tikhobrazova's case consolidated principles that would be confirmed later in the year, when the Sovnarkom issued a new "Decree on Requisition and Confiscation" in October 1921. The new Decree affirmed the basic principles of the Decree of April 16, 1920, which, as it explained, had been too often ignored. Through cases like Tikhobrazova's, revolutionary authorities articulated a chronology of revolution as sequential, progressive, and irreversible, even as its fundamental precepts were being transformed. Tikhobrazova's case posed with unusual clarity the question first posed by the April Decree, undergirding virtually all the cases about return that had arisen since: to what extent was the end of dispossession a restoration—of property rights in certain kinds of things, or of certain things, to particular people? Very few people succeeded in having things they had lost during the Revolution returned to them. The crisis of repossession should therefore be understood not as a physical passage but as a discursive framework, built up toward the middle of 1920 and lasting for two more years, through which the parties to dispossession explored the new limits on possession emerging around them, reflected on the significance of dispossession, and, ultimately, developed a chronology of the revolutionary process that affirmed and erased dispossession simultaneously.

Would-be tenants and owners vied to win control over properties, much as they had sought to take it from one another over the previous three years, by telling stories about themselves and their things. Again they provided evidence of social background and careful stewardship; again they eschewed reference to positive legal rights to ownership, which still did not exist. But now, stories typically also turned on the demonstration of service to the Revolution and Soviet power, as expressed through tenure over material objects.[48] Through these stories, that is, claimants built chronologies of revolutionary development and cast their own possession of material things as a realization of revolutionary values. One case from Petrograd, involving the award of a municipal contract to rent and operate a candy shop, pitted a current employee of the municipalized shop, who had shepherded it through the tumult of revolution, against a sympathetic newcomer, who was a Red Army veteran. In the fall of 1921, the Food Section of the Petrograd Department of Communal Economy held a meeting at which both men were asked to present their claims to the space, which hinged largely on the question of renovations: who had paid for them? Who had performed the labor involved in keeping up the specialized candy-making equipment over the past four years? The Red Army veteran, Perelmitin, claimed to have performed the renovations himself, entitling him to the space and its expensive equipment; the store employee, Rivkin, angrily declared that this was not the case. All the equipment belonged to the "Food Section, to the Government," Rivkin insisted, the staff of which—-i.e., Rivkin—had repaired it. When asked by a representative from the Food Section how he was so sure the equipment belonged to the government, Rivkin declared that there had been a "witness" to its nationalization and to the nationalization of the associated production facility. The meeting chairman then asked Perelmitin and Rivkin to leave the room while the Food Section decided to whom the contract should be awarded. Once they were gone, the chairman revealed that, in fact, Rivkin was the prerevolutionary owner of the shop and the associated candy-making facility. He knew of the store's nationalization because he had witnessed it, as the former owner. The chairman included this fact "for information," before proposing that the matter be turned over to a technical commission for inspection and resolution by the Housing Department, as there were evidently too many competing variables at play for a quick decision.[49]

Episodes like this one raised a nagging question: what was the Revolution without dispossession, or, put differently, by undoing dispossession, was the Revolution itself coming undone? Another case concerned a building on Maly Kharitonovsky Lane, occupied mostly by Narkompros's Conference Department, and hardly at all by the All-Russian Association of Engineers (VAI), self-described "heirs to the Polytechnical Society" that had built the grand structure back in 1903. As a Rabkrin inspection of the conflict concluded, it was clear that the engineers, even five years after the fact, "had not in any measure made peace with the fact of the building's nationalization, viewing this nationalization as an injustice and an act of violence," a "psychological condition that explains in large measure that firmness and stubbornness that VAI has brought to its repeated efforts seeking the building's return. It is very likely that this condition likewise has led them to cram themselves (it is cramped) into the little closet of two rooms that Narkompros has left them, where it is impossible to work." Emboldened by the recent change in the atmosphere, the engineers renewed their efforts to repossess the building in the spring of 1922. The engineers' petition drew on an eclectic array of arguments to stake their claim. They emphasized that the building's construction in 1903 had been funded entirely by the engineering society's members, with absolutely no aid from the tsarist state; it could thus not be construed as having been state property before 1917. The engineers had also designed the building, and on that basis VAI cunningly claimed it not as the society's physical property but rather as its "intellectual property." Finally, VAI tossed in some anti-market rhetoric. It alleged that the current inhabitants, the Conference Department of Narkompros, which hosted all-Russian conferences in the capital for state institutions and operated a dormitory out of the building where visiting delegates could stay, sought to earn a profit off its activities, whereas they, the engineers, aimed only at popular enlightenment, with no commercial inclinations.[50]

On the one hand, as the Rabkrin review concluded, VAI's attempt to reclaim the building represented an obvious failure to come to terms with "the fact of the building's nationalization." Yet, on the other, it was equally clear that the author of VAI's petition sought to integrate key aspects of revolutionary practice in claiming a right to the building, highlighting not only the society's status as a non-profit-seeking organization, but also the fact that the engineers had funded the construction with their own moneys (albeit before the Revolution) and did not receive help from the (tsarist) state. This latter argument would have made no sense outside the revolutionary context, but it was an important one to housing departments in this period. Faced with the task of repairing decrepit buildings on the cheap, many neighborhood soviets took to rewarding residents who covered maintenance costs on their own with stable tenure in their current living spaces, a position officialized by the Mossoviet's TsZhZO around this time in 1922.[51] In its judgment on the case, Rabkrin rebutted the allegations that Narkompros profited from its activities, and ignored VAI's arguments about intellectual property. Its chief concern was with VAI's claim to have funded the construction of the building "entirely from the pittances collected from the engineers themselves, without any kind of subsidy from the Treasury." The Rabkrin report argued that, when considering the allocation of space, what mattered was not merely the fact of spending or even its amount: what mattered was its timing. Rabkrin argued that the prerevolutionary expenditure on the building—which brought it into existence— "collapses before the fact that the building, as a piece of major property, was nationalized and attached to the property of the RSFSR," an act that wiped away the earlier investment. What had to be honored instead were "all the resources spent in its time by Narkompros in order to support the building, make it fit for use, which would [be shifted] to VAI, which has spent nothing on its end to keep the building up in this time."[52] Now that money-based arguments had reappeared in the staking of claims to space, the engineers pursued those same terms—as if money were money, regardless of when exactly, before the Revolution or after, it had been spent. But Rabkrin's decision made clear this was not the case: spending had a different value (none) before the Revolution than it did during and after the Revolution, the chronology of which could not be unsettled even by new policies surrounding rental contracts and profits.

Movable goods did not generally present the same set of opportunities to revisit their disposal as did immovable ones. Still, in a surprising number of cases, former owners either found their movable goods more or less where they had left them, or traced their movement to the present. Those returning after time away avidly gathered information about the fate of their things. Sometimes they reported to local authorities on the changes they found to their old homes, with the result that new kinds of accounts began to show up in the files of local soviets: detailed descriptions of who now had what and where things may have gone, provided by returnees. One man, Voldemor Gesse, who left Moscow with his sick daughter during the civil war, returned to his five-room apartment at the end of 1920. Before he left, he had shared the apartment with two "room-renters," both of whom were still in residence.

They had been joined by three other people, all communications workers. As Gesse related, however, all his movable property now stood in the rooms of his two former room-renters, who were brothers, "such that the communications workers have next to nothing." Gesse highlighted the brothers' "appropriation" of his furniture at the expense of the communications workers in hopes of retrieving some for himself. He nearly succeeded, securing permission from the Furniture Department to retrieve furnishings from his old apartment up to the "norm," but only to the extent that the "current residents could do without." When Gesse presented the order to the brothers, they agreed to relinquish his possessions, and Gesse left to hire a truck. But by the time he returned, they had locked the door and made themselves scarce. Gesse punished the deception by complaining of their illegitimate "appropriation" of his things to the Moscow Cheka. The Cheka sent his letter back to the Gorodskoi neighborhood soviet, right where it had begun.[53]

Against this backdrop, Tikhobrazova's case was both extremely unusual—everything was exactly where she had left it—and highly suggestive. Not only were Tikhobrazova's things more or less where she left them, but also, because Tikhobrazova left Petrograd when she did—the very week of the Revolution, without an opportunity to fall into one of the population categories, without an opportunity to have gotten herself caught up in a case of speculation or a neighbor's bad luck, without an opportunity to have forged herself on the revolutionary iron in any way at all—she herself had managed to come through the period seemingly untainted. Her case distilled the problem of dispossession and repossession on the new legal landscape into unusually sharp, clear dimensions. Here she was, nominally blameless, or at least unchanged; here were her things, intact; and here were the conditions of their seizure, overturned. Here then, at last, was an opportunity to figure out what revolutionary dispossession really was.

The Return of the Dispossessed

Tikhobrazova's case hinged on three central issues: the meaning of her absence; the purpose of dispossession; and the chronology of law. These issues were heavily interdependent. In her defense, Tikhobrazova emphasized her faultlessness in leaving Petrograd, as well as the circumstances in which she left behind her possessions. The fact of absence, and how erstwhile owners comported themselves with regard to their property while they were away, was a key piece of evidence in cases of ownerless property and adverse possession in conventional law systems, which often hinged on whether owners had made provisions for their property ahead of or during their absence.[54] In this spirit, Tikhobrazova was at pains to include witness testimony from the "former senior janitor" of her apartment building and from a member of her building committee that she had tried to ship her things in 1917, as well the original receipt from the agency she hired to (unsuccessfully) ship her boxes. At the same time, she sensed that her absence was a problem not only because it evinced poor proprietorship, but also because it was politically suspect— because it suggested that she, like so many who had gone south, had done so to outrun the Revolution, returning only when the durability of Bolshevik power had become unmistakably clear. These two dimensions of her absence—whether she had been a responsible owner and whether she was politically suspect—commingled in her testimony. She emphasized that she left Petrograd only because of her son's mobilization, that she had tried to return to the city earlier, but was prevented from doing so by circumstances beyond her control—the same circumstances, she argued, that had prevented her from even knowing of the orders in Petrograd demanding that owners with things stored in warehouses appear to claim them in ten days' time, or cede them to the state, "as in the Caucasus, there were no newspapers."[55] Now that she was back, and since her things had not, in fact, been moved, only declared "ownerless," she and the Petrograd branch of Rabkrin argued, there should be no obstacle to her reclaiming them. In this view, the fact of Tikhobrazova's absence could be reversed.

The Petrograd Department of Justice rejected these arguments in the strongest possible terms, subjecting even the most basic elements of her story to radical and delegitimating suspicion. According to the Department of Justice, Tikhobrazova had failed not merely to demonstrate that she was entitled to the return of her things in the warehouse, but that the things in the warehouse had ever been hers. She had failed to prove not merely that she had followed her son to Armavir because he was drafted to serve there, but that she had a son at all, that her alleged son had been drafted to Armavir, that she herself ever went to Armavir, or that being in Armavir made it impossible to return to Petrograd.[56] On these grounds alone her case was without merit. But as the Justice Department explained, Tikhobrazova's case could not be resolved only "on the basis of formal juridical conceptions" such as these: "It must be borne in mind that precisely during those three years in which citizen Tikhobrazova was with her son in the Caucasus—so she says—the citizens of Petrograd, alongside colossal voluntary donations of things, linens, and the like, for the

Red Army, were burdened additionally with a series of forced obligations," the Justice Department recalled. "The WP [worker-peasant] government cannot allow that in the same time, the things of individual citizens, stored in a warehouse, should be somehow [protected] from all such assessments."[57] As for her objection that she could not read the Petrograd newspapers because they did not reach Armavir, the Justice Department retorted that the same was true of "all those who abandoned Petrograd after the October Revolution," a fact "the Council of People's Commissars of the Commune of the Northern Oblast undoubtedly took into account" in formulating its decrees.[58] Tikhobrazova deserved to have her things seized now, the Justice Department argued, precisely because she had left, thereby evading the original burden of dispossession. It affirmed the centrality of dispossession to the experience of revolution and membership in the present-day body politic, despite new legal orders containing the practice. Here was a dialectic concept of history at work, in which the Revolution was not erased by the transition to the New Economic Policy and its conciliatory stance toward private possession, but reinforced by it.

Tikhobrazova was back, but, according to Petrograd's Department of Justice, her absence could never be undone. This notion contravened the portion of the "Decree on Ownerless Property" providing for the return of property to owners who reappeared. But as more people sought the return of their things, more decisions appeared across institutions, confirming the principle that absence was irreversible. The following year, Narkompros asked the Commissariat of Justice to draft a new law ordering that "all objects of art or historical property taken onto account by Narkompros are national property and are not subject in any circumstances to return to their previous owners." The law was necessary, it claimed, because "at the present time, the new economic politics have given some people the idea that the artistic property left behind in the period of the mass flight of the Russian nobility and bourgeoisie from Petersburg [sic]" was "now subject to return to them." Narkompros held "the opposite view," and sought a "declaration, finally, that this property is national."[59] Asked to review the project, Narkomfin argued that a new decree was unnecessary, because, in fact, the existing "Decree on Ownerless Property" "actually said that ownerless property, including property left behind by an owner who is not known or has left no news of themselves . . . is undoubtedly subject to nationalization and not to return to its owners." By this argument, owners who went absent during the Revolution and later returned would receive nothing back, because in absenting themselves they had ceded their

"legal rights." Absence during the Revolution in and of itself erased rights to
things, a principle reinforced by Narkomfin's determination that the departure of members of the nobility and bourgeoisie from Petrograd constituted
a form of "emigration."[60] As evidence, Narkomfin's legal consultant invoked
the Roman legal principle, quoted in the original but mistranscribed in
Cyrillic, "'Kvod ab initsio defektum est, no i potest traktu temporis konva-
letsere,'" ("'*Quod ab inicio defectum est, non potest tractu temporis convales-
cere,*'"): meaning, that which is invalid in the beginning cannot gain strength
through the lapse of time. "The fact of the new economic policy does not
destroy the fact of the ownerlessness of this property up to the moment of
the person's return," in the same way that "an owner's right to property, having
been destroyed by the fact of his emigration, is not resurrected by his
re-emigration."[61]

This conclusion demanded several interpretive leaps, including the elision
of absence with wrongdoing that had by then become common. Being absent,
originally a mere circumstance of dispossession, was now made into legal
grounds for it. Narkomfin's conclusion also demanded a robust interpretation
of the progressive, irrevocable nature of the passage of time, and in so doing,
it began the work of creating the Revolution as a set of progressive and irrevocable stages through time, asserting the state's power to shape the experience
of the Revolution and its subsequent definition through the management of
revolutionary chronology. Through memorial evenings, staged reenactments,
archive-making, and a host of other projects, the Bolsheviks gradually built a
rich infrastructure of official memory of the October Revolution, all the more
resilient because it was composed of individual life stories, each one a brick in
the edifice.[62] The legalization of revolutionary chronology—the retroactive
imposition of cut-offs, periods, and turning points in revolutionary events
through an array of laws—resembled the project of official memorialization
in its capacity to elicit the many life stories like Tikhobrazova's. Beyond memorialization, however, the legalization of revolutionary chronology also functioned as an administrative resource, control over which allowed revolutionary
authorities to shape the disposal of material things in the present and to intervene directly into the trajectories of individuals and institutions.[63]

The cases brought by the dispossessed served to generate an official timeline of the Revolution, as a period with a beginning, a middle, and now, an
end. Looking back on dispossession raised a host of questions not only about
what had happened, but also about when it had happened. In the preliminary
discussions held by Narkomiust concerning the "Decree on Ownerless

Property," officials were rarely sure when things had become the state's property, or how to make that determination. The timing of dispossession mattered especially in cases like Tikhobrazova's, where the things in question bore no mark of the administrative orders successively imposed upon them. The fact of their dispossession was indiscernible, which meant that it could be erased entirely by the passage of new laws.

Timing also mattered in cases appearing with increased frequency in 1920 and 1921, as the Soviet Republic concluded peace treaties with new states carved out of the Russian Empire's territory, brought by people who had experienced the Revolution as subjects of the tsar, and were now taking their leave from it as foreigners. The peace settlements negotiated with the new Baltic states in 1920 and 1921 ambiguously promised their citizens, former Russian subjects separating from the RSFSR, "the right to real estate," as well as the right to bring their existing movable property out of the country. On this basis, many of these new foreigners demanded either compensation from the Soviet state for the prerevolutionary value of their lands upon their departure, or the right to dispose of the property in another fashion as its owner, through rent or sale.[64] Surprisingly, and as a mark of the scale of change introduced by the Decrees on Requisition and Confiscation, a host of Soviet institutions responsible for processing these demands seem to have sincerely entertained the possibility that the treaties may have effectively denationalized the properties of the new foreigners, thereby reopening a market in land and buildings.[65] Narkomiust hastened to clarify that of course, the Revolution had altered the meaning of the term "rights in real estate" inside the RSFSR, such that it now wielded "a completely different, even contrary sense for Russian citizens living in a ~~communist~~ Soviet state and for foreigners, subject in their countries to bourgeois civil law."

The key question, then, was how these two contrary legal orders would live side by side—which set of laws took precedence for whom, in which circumstances. A Narkomiust official waxed poetic about the utter novelty of this confrontation, "the resolution" of which could rely "neither on the norms nor the precedents of international law, as the relations that have developed [between the "~~communist~~ Soviet state" and "bourgeois civil law"] are appearing for the first time in history—they are connected with the most essential and principal question: how are bourgeois states to exist alongside socialist ones." He invoked the "theorists of socialism who foresaw this difficulty," among them "the first German socialist—Fichte," who resolved it through the "creation of the closed trading state," which "produced everything it needed for itself, and thus needed nothing out of foreign trade." Recent experience, "of course," had "shown this to be practicably impossible: modern humanity is drawn to mutual cooperation, and to the general division of labor among the peoples." This failure led the Narkomiust official to decidedly more traditional ground. The coexistence of socialist and bourgeois states would have to occur on the basis of the long-established principle of legal mutuality, a concession to the fact of the "transitional period, when not all states are yet socialized, and thus the bourgeois ones coexist with the ~~communist~~ socialist."[66]

But if mutuality in the financial realm meant mirroring the values assigned by capitalist markets, here in its legal sense, it meant the opposite: our laws on our territory, and your laws on your territory. As related to the promises of the Baltic peace treaties, Narkomiust argued that the peace treaties "did not speak of property rights in real estate, only of 'rights in real estate,'" by which was meant "those rights in real estate that exist and are recognized within a given state." Citizens of the Baltic states were thus subject to the "very same maximum of rights to real estate presented to Russian citizens in the RSFSR," which is to say, none. The Baltic citizens "had no right to demand the return of their lands." This was all the more true "because at the moment of their nationalization, before the conclusion of the treaties, and before the declaration [of citizenship, *optatsiya*], they were still Russian subjects, and the nationalization of real estate was applied to them as to all other Russian citizens."[67] The Baltic states, Narkomiust argued, had confused the question by introducing the "question of time frame"—which was also a question about when states began.[68] The Baltic states "sought to interpret [this question] in the widest possible sense: from the moment of the proclamation of the right of all peoples to free self-determination, made by the RSFSR on November 2, 1917." The Estonian government argued that its citizens gained foreign status, that is, not from the moment of Estonia's settlement with the RSFSR, but rather from the moment of the Provisional Government's collapse. On this basis, Estonia's citizens, no less than those of Germany or other sovereign states (as of November 2, 1917) should be shielded from the attacks on property suffered by Russian subjects. As the Narkomiust official objected, however, and quite separate from the question about states and when they started, Estonia's position naturalized property rights as universal, as if they were continuous and could be assumed in the background while states and sovereignties were transformed. In reality, these rights were discontinuous and could not be assumed; "after all, the retention of rights to movable or real property comes about as consequence of the declaration [of citizenship] and for that reason takes effect only from the very moment of the declaration ... those opting [to leave] are subject to all the same requisitions and confiscations that were required for Russian subjects."[69]

In the months that followed, a continuing barrage of petitions seeking the return of seized goods forced the Sovnarkom to revisit the legal format of dispossession again and again, culminating with the promulgation, in October 1921, of the second "Decree on Requisitions and Confiscations." The second decree emphasized requisition and compensation as "exceptional."[70] Institutions would be expected to conduct their operations by relying upon the "normal means of acquisition," a term that evidently required some clarification, as Narkomiust subsequently issued a formal instruction for the commissariats defining the "normal means of acquisition" as "the assessment of taxes, free purchase and trade."[71] In these instructions, Narkomiust also openly acknowledged the problem of return for the first time. "In connection with the publication of this decree," its statement began, "Narkomiust has been receiving many inquiries concerning on which grounds and in what legal order matters on incorrect requisitions and confiscations from the period prior to the decree should be considered." Before April 1920, the instructions observed, no legal definitions for requisition or confiscation existed. Putting the condition of propertylessness into words, Narkomiust declared that dispossession had occurred "elementally," at the instruction of any number of revolutionary authorities. "For that reason," it ordered, "it is impossible today to enter into a discussion about the evaluation of all the requisitions and confiscations that took place before April 15, 1920."[72] The whirlwind of dispossession that had gripped the Republic for the past three years—the things, the money, the effects on human and material lives—all this was to be legally ceded, "elementally," as if to a revolutionary void. Wrongs could not now be righted and questions of guilt or innocence would not be considered. Through law, the Revolution was bracketed off as an exceptional time in which exceptional, and henceforth illegal, acts had occurred. This period did not have an official start date, but it did now have an end.

The new order, Narkomiust announced, began on April 16, 1920. In the case of "requisitions and confiscations that took place after the decree came into force, after April 16, 1920," it was possible to evaluate guilt and innocence, because here, for the first time, there was a victim in whose interests wrongdoing could be prosecuted. That victim was introduced as the Soviet state. "Now that there are firmly set rules for requisition and confiscation and all forced alienations," Narkomiust explained, "violations of them should be categorized as crimes on the job." The wrongdoer, in improper cases of requisition and confiscation, was a state employee who obstructed the state from claiming material possessions from individuals that were its due. This framing left a gap: what of cases like Tikhobrazova's, and many others, complaining of an official but incorrect seizure? Of the state taking something that was not its due? Indeed, this gap in the legal treatment of dispossession was noted by the Petrograd Regional Department of Justice, in its review of Tikhobrazova's case. Although the Department sided against Tikhobrazova, it affirmed her right to bring a suit in the People's Court against Kimber in his official capacity as head of the troika, something that both the troika and the Petrograd Sovnarkhoz had opposed. These bodies had argued that the People's Court could only hear cases between two civil parties, and not between a civil party and a state official. The Petrograd Regional Department of Justice disagreed. "That was indeed the case in the old legal system," but "today, the People's Court absolutely may hear cases of citizens against administrative institutions." Bringing a suit before the People's Court was, in fact, the only avenue by which Tikhobrazova could seek a sanction against a state official for damaging her own "proprietary, personal rights and interests," as opposed to those of the state itself. But this novel interpretation did not find traction in general practice.[73]

Still, the influx of petitions for the return of seized goods did not stop, forcing the authorities to reconsider the matter again in March 1922, this time from a slightly different angle: that of "previous owners" attempting to reclaim possessions now in the hands of "current owners," whom the previous owners had taken it upon themselves to locate. The Sovnarkom issued an "Order on the Demand of Property (imushchestvo) by Previous Owners (sobstvennikami) from Current Owners (vladeltsev)" on March 29, 1922 which, in tortuous language, forbade individuals from confronting one another over dispossessed things. The order made one category of goods entirely inaccessible to the demands for return: "household goods," again defined as "furniture, clothing, linens, shoes, dishes, and the like." Insofar as these had been "received from the appropriate government (communal) organs in the fixed order" they could not, under any circumstances, be sought for repossession by their previous owners from their current ones. In cases where it was impossible to prove, however, that objects had been received in the "fixed order" from the appropriate governmental institutions, the resolution of disputes turned on a mix of social class and timing. If the "current owners belong to the laborers, they retain the objects in their possession, so long as the former owner lost possession of this property not less than two years before the publication of this decree." (Awkwardly, this date did not align with the "Decree on Requisition and

Confiscation of April 16, 1920," forcing authorities to consider what to do if they encountered a case originating in the eighteen-day window between the two.) The order allowed that some transfers of property between past and present owners might have occurred by means of "crime," but these would have to be "proven in court," which given the passage of time would have been quite difficult. Transfers that had been made by "agreement" between the two parties were also open to dispute. The March 29 Order thus completed a process of remaking the whirlwind of dispossession into something that occurred along two rails: via the seizure of property by agents of the state who might have been dishonest and taken what was not theirs, not because it belonged to the person from whom it had been seized, but because it properly belonged to the state; and via crime that occurred between two individuals, one a thief, and the other a victim, of property that should never have been seized to begin with. Both the state and its subjects could be victims, in this narrative; but subjects could never be victims of the state.

The most important achievement of the decrees on seizure had to do with timing. The March 1922 decree solidified a timeline of seizure that was simultaneously a timeline of revolution, sequential stages of progress to that moment. What happened before April 16, 1920, when the first Decree on Requisition was issued, was lost to the ages. There was no getting it back. Seizures that occurred between April 16, 1920, and October 24, 1921, were to be evaluated based on the April 1920 decree; and seizures from after October 25, 1921, on the basis of the October 1921 decree. The void of revolutionary propertylessness was thus enshrined in legal code. Nowhere was this more evident than in the explanatory note attached to the critical passage of the March order, about the "current possessors who are also laborers" being entitled to keep things in their possession that had been lost by the former owners "more than two years before the publication of this decree." This was as close to a direct statement of timeline of revolution as redistribution as you could get: workers who gained objects between October 25, 1917 and March 29, 1920 would keep what they had, as a measure of the Revolution's justice.

Emphasizing the significance of this timeline, the March "Order on the Demand of Property" altered it for application to places further afield, far away from Moscow and Petrograd, which were conquered later by the Bolsheviks and therefore might need more time to make revolutionary "mistakes." According to the Order, these places should still be permitted to experience the lawlessness of revolution—places like Siberia, where, in August 1921, a plenipotentiary reported that "the poor" were "not adopting the new course of

Soviet politics and are continuing the redistribution [*pereraspredelenie*], namely the requisitions, confiscations, and the like, events that we can call economic banditry."[74] The March order thus declared that in "Siberia, the southeast region, and the Crimea, the period specified in article two of the present decree [which closed the whirlwind of dispossession at the two-year mark, for a March 29, 1920 cutoff] is reduced to one year."[75] Siberia would be allowed an extra year's worth of disorder. The decree protected this special revolutionary era, not just for those who had experienced it in the past, but for all those who might yet experience it in the future.[76]

CONCLUSION

"There had been a world, and now that world had been killed off. There was no bringing back those years."

—MIKHAIL BULGAKOV, *WHITE GUARD*

THE ERA of the New Economic Policy (NEP), which began in 1921, ushered swift but uncertain change into the management of Soviet economic life and the trajectory of the Revolution. After painful years of violent seizure (razvyorstka), peasants were permitted once more to market grain for profit. In cities and industrial life, the NEP was characterized by a drive to adopt certain principles of profit, loss, and economic management. The official shift to self-sustaining financial operations (*khozraschyot*) triggered the creation of new inventories, meant to facilitate a search for "profitable" and "loss-bearing" state enterprises, in order to shift the latter off official balance sheets entirely—not through sale, but through long-term leases to private parties. The same principle reoriented approaches to the management and disposal of the built environment.

On August 8, 1921, the Sovnarkom released an order, "On the Review of Lists of Municipalized Buildings," directing local soviets everywhere to perform an inventory of every building in their control.[1] The inventories were to be made up of two lists: one list was to be composed of buildings that should remain in the control of the municipal government, while the other was to be composed of buildings that, for various reasons, should not. In an effort to shed dead weight and mobilize hidden reserves of capital, local soviets were encouraged to shift all but the soundest buildings—physically and financially—on to leases of twelve years or more, held by resident cooperatives or commercial enterprises. In the two weeks it took the People's Commissariat of Internal Affairs to work up instructions for the list-making, this process acquired a name:

"demunicipalization" [*demunitsipalizatsiya*]. Four years after "municipalization" burst onto the streets of Moscow, it seemed its undoing had arrived.

Much as in 1917, the changes in Russia's political economy introduced under the NEP were captured in language. Demunicipalization was soon joined by other terms of reversal, such as "denationalization," and—again as in 1917—by a host of words that previously meant one thing, and now seemed to mean another. The term "private property," for instance, reappeared in an official order issued by VTsIK granting the "rights of property" to buildings that had escaped municipalization over the previous four years, typically because they were quite small. Instructions soon clarified that VTsIK's order, in invoking the "rights of property," did not mean a return to "private property rights" in buildings as they stood before 1917—there was no bringing back those years. Instead, the rights of "private property" meant something new.[2] In similar fashion, Soviet officials explained to their counterparts outside the RSFSR that "the expression 'rights in real estate,'" when used by the Soviets in negotiations, "bears a completely different, even contrary sense for Russian citizens" as compared to its meaning for foreigners "subject in their countries to bourgeois civil law."[3]

Another old word with new meaning was the verb *zakrepit'*, meaning to fasten, consolidate, or secure, and which exploded in usage after 1921 as a noun, *zakreplenie* or "attachment." This usage related specifically to the "attachment" of buildings to a state institution, indicating a form of possession by these institutions that was somehow more secure than what they currently had. By the end of 1921, the "question of zakreplenie" had become a constant topic of discussion at meetings of the "Little Sovnarkom," the institution attached to the regular Sovnarkom where the so-called vermicelli of governance were hashed out. "Vermicelli," as T. H. Rigby long ago noted, was the preferred slang of tsarist administrators for "minor matters that for some reason required resolution at a high level," a usage carried over into the new era.[4] Of course, in both eras, the reason vermicelli required resolution at a high level was that, while small in and of themselves, they grew out of big and enduring questions. In the case of the vermicelli around zakreplenie, the big and enduring question was: what did the state own and how?

The Sovnarkom's "Order on Demunicipalization" was one in a slew of orders, instructions, and bulletins to address this question beginning in 1921, and continuing for years to come. In January 1922, the NKVD took up the problem, issuing instructions for demunicipalization to local governments.

These instructions ordered local soviets to divide the buildings under their control three ways: those buildings that would remain "municipalized," and the financial responsibility of the city; those buildings that would remain no less "municipalized," but which would be leased to nonstate parties for periods of three to twelve years; and, finally, buildings slated for outright "demunicipalization." NKVD officials anticipated that the third list would be very short, because buildings slated for outright demunicipalization had to meet a high standard regarding use, size, and prospects for capital renovation outside of municipal control. Only buildings consisting of two or fewer apartments and measuring less than twenty-five square sazhens were eligible; in Moscow and Petrograd, the number of apartments was raised to five, but with no adjustment in total area. Buildings that were occupied by state or communal institutions, inhabited by any "collective of residents wishing to take the building into their own economic administration," or with the prospect of any such use, were ineligible. Finally, the terms of outright demunicipalization were onerous: buildings could be "demunicipalized and *returned to their former owners*"—that latter clause appended only in the NKVD instructions, significantly raising the barrier to demunicipalization—only in the event that these owners existed and presented themselves. Moreover, the former owners had to sign a document promising a "total renovation of the building" within one year. If the building deteriorated in any way after the moment of transfer, it would be given to the "long-term use of another person," and the "owner" would be "called to [legal] account for the ruination of the building." Demunicipalized buildings could not be ruined, even by their owners, nor could they be sold.[5]

Like other aspects of the New Economic Policy, "demunicipalization" reflected the broad aim of recapitalizing state-owned assets with private funds. Several months after its "Order on the Conditions of Demunicipalization," the Sovnarkom reinstituted the general payment of rent.[6] Rents were fixed by local authorities according to the average cost of upkeep and a ranking assigned to each building based on its "level of repair and neighborhood." All localities fixed a base rate per square arshin of living space consumed within the norm, assessing surcharges for above-norm consumption of space and commercial use. Invalids were freed from payment. Buildings leased to tenants' associations kept the rents they collected in full, for use maintaining the building; buildings administered by the city turned the money over to it.[7] In tandem, the Sovnarkom unveiled new protections against eviction, the chief impulse of which was to restrict the power to evict to city housing departments, as opposed to restricting eviction itself. Any other party found attempting to evict without permission to do so would be "held responsible for excessive use of power." For those institutions retaining the right to evict, however, the bar was quite low: residents could be evicted for failing to pay rent, destroying living space, or making themselves "impossible to live with."[8]

These orders brought city authorities and residents into conflict in new ways. For municipal authorities, the key question in deciding which buildings to lease out to residents or private parties was their state of repair. The NKVD exhorted communal departments to face up to their "real, 'actual' abilities" to finance building upkeep in making their decisions. But few localities were eager to cede rent revenue, and fewer still even knew exactly how much caring for buildings in these new circumstances would cost.[9] An inspection of Moscow's Krasnopresnensky neighborhood revealed that the neighborhood soviet initially had planned to retain a whopping 1,000 buildings on the neighborhood accounts before "suddenly realizing that it had overestimated its abilities." The neighborhood then veered sharply in the opposite direction, shedding all but thirty-five buildings from its budget, and keeping only those buildings in the best repair. Not coincidentally, these were also the buildings whose residents had spent their own money on maintenance and repair over the previous years, in return for which the residents had been promised protection from eviction by the local soviet. This loosely formalized arrangement from the earlier era now came back to bite them, as their buildings were in such good shape that the city refused to let them go.[10]

The Sovnarkom's order characterized demunicipalization as a building's "return to the property [*vozvrat v sobstvennost'*] of the former owner [vladelets]."[11] This "return to property," however, marked less a restoration of old rights than the beginning of a process of filling "property" with new meaning. Municipalized and demunicipalized buildings shared similar encumbrances. For instance, all buildings with more than eight rooms were required to put ten percent of their total "living space" at the disposal of the communal department. Buildings freed of this requirement amounted to a small number, reduced further by an addendum declaring that *osobnyaks*, the townhouses of the former gentry, would remain state property, whatever their size.[12] Only one other category of structure could conceivably meet all of criteria for unrestricted use: summer houses (*dachas*), whose previous owners apparently jumped at the chance to reclaim their properties after the "Order on Demunicipalization" appeared—so much so that, eighteen months later, in February 1924, the Mossoviet found it necessary to proclaim that "the orders of central power regulating the possession [*vladenie*] of dachas in no way envisioned them being returned to their former owners in the course of demunicipalization." It halted dacha demunicipalization in the Moscow region and called for the creation of "an authoritative organ" to resolve the "multiple interpretations" of the Sovnarkom's order.[13]

The restored "owners" of demunicipalized buildings were also subject to city orders on rent, which was fixed in the same way for "all living spaces, in municipalized as well as in nonmunicipalized buildings" (the exception, again, being buildings with fewer than eight rooms and under five apartments). Whatever the size of their building, demunicipalized building owners were sharply restricted in what they could do to it. In 1924, the successor to the TsZhZO, the Moscow Directorate for Real Estate (MUNI) examined the "rights of property owners of demunicipalized buildings" to add floors and make new constructions on the footprint of demunicipalized buildings. It determined that, because the civil code "did not permit property rights to arise" in new buildings constructed by "private people on city land," it was also the case that owners whose demunicipalized buildings were destroyed—in a fire, for example—lost their "property right" completely. New floors could be added to demunicipalized buildings, but MUNI noted that, in making a building larger, its owners would also have to cede 10 percent of the total area to the communal fund.[14]

Demunicipalization represented the institutionalization of revolutionary mores in the allocation of space in other ways as well. Housing authorities and residents alike continued to be guided by habits of parsing people and space learned over the past four years. The residents who sought to form a tenants' association justified their right to do so on the grounds that their building was "settled almost exclusively by those belonging to the laboring elements, of whom about 20 percent [were] responsible workers," a claim they backed up with a comprehensive homemade census of their households and occupations.[15] Meanwhile, the new housing authority, MUNI, built social inventories into its review process for everything from permit approvals to housing assignments. It assessed renovation requests on the basis of three factors in equal parts: the "essence" of the renovation plan, the "makeup of the building" (number of floors, apartments, building material), and finally, the "makeup of the residents" (broken down into occupational categories: e.g., soviet employees, military, students, workers, invalids, unemployed, and artisans).[16] Struggling in the "absence of legal guidance" was a common theme of MUNI's day-to-day work—the Sovnarkom's orders still left much unresolved in this new landscape—but the underlying principles were clear: to decide matters "from the point of view of political allowability," as MUNI put it, ensuring that the usage of city buildings could not "attract a meaningful strengthening of the class of petty proprietors."[17]

The housing crisis in Moscow and other cities did not get better after the Sovnarkom's "Order on Demunicipalization." In fact, it got much worse.[18] A report presented to VTsIK in the spring of 1924 blamed the ongoing deterioration on the Order itself, which had failed to establish "housing law" on the necessary footing of "revolutionary legality." There were so "many contradictions, vestiges, and accidents" in the existing body of regulation, due as ever to the fact that "so many bodies were issuing it: VTsIK, TsIK, Sovnarkom, NKVD . . . Narkomiust, Narkompros, and local powers on top of this, in the most varied forms—decrees, orders, instructions, clarifications." The moment demanded a new approach, the report argued, guided by the "systematized publication of a housing codex" that would, at last, give people the necessary "confidence in the untouchability of the rights" to stimulate their "personal initiative in housing affairs."[19] This view made little headway, however, against the prevailing idea, expressed in repeated orders issued by Narkomiust and NKVD, that "questions of municipalization and demunicipalization" were fundamentally not meant to be understood as matters of law. Efforts by People's Courts to treat them as such after the "Order on Demunicipalization"—to decide who got what on the basis of the Order itself—were derided by the NKVD and Narkomiust alike as "interference," and sharply condemned by them in a circular explaining that these issues "are decided solely according to administrative organs, and their review does not fall under the competence of the courts."[20]

———

In Moscow, demunicipalization changed things the least for the city's most unruly occupant—the state itself. In its four years in Moscow, the central government had bent the city to its gnarled shape. A report prepared in 1921 remarked upon the "extreme incoherence in the settlement of institutions": the offices of Narkompros occupied 40 buildings; those of VSNKh 126, and the central military administration "more than 200."[21] One year before, Lenin had launched two parallel initiatives: to pare back the size of the state, and, at the same time, to "clear the city of Moscow" of excess institutions. Symptomatically, a number of new committees sprang up to manage these entwined tasks, with much correspondence dedicated to "aligning work so as to avoid paral-lelism."[22] The Mossoviet took the first stab at clearing the city of excess institu-tions, forming a commission devoted to the task, but the NKVD quickly took the process over, forming its own Commission for Clearing Moscow at the end of 1920, with the express aim, as the new head of the Sovnarkom's Admin-istrative Directorate, Nikolai Gorbunov, explained to the NKVD's M. F. Vladi-mirsky, of doing "everything possible to evict [institutions] from Moscow or to concentrate them." Moscow had to be made into a "model for all of Russia, with buildings to receive new arrivals attached to each of the People's Com-missariats, and the central institutions, in the sense of the housing question, placed on a normal footing."[23]

The process started in 1918 began anew. Within months, the Commission for Clearing Moscow, although charged with removing institutions from the "Center," came to the familiar conclusion that removing institutions from the city would be impossible. All the institutions were essential, no one should have to leave, a determination that shifted the Commission's burden entirely onto the rearrangement of space. Inspectors arrived, took measurements, counted employees, tried to fit institutions into spaces one way, then another. No one wanted to occupy the top floor of the Upper Trading Rows, despite its felicitous location near the Kremlin.[24] Everybody fought tooth and nail to hang onto their dormitories, no matter how far-flung. When the commissariats did not like the decision of one commission, they appealed to a different au-thority, or, as ever, to the Sovnarkom.

In making their complaints, the commissariats argued over the disposal of particular buildings, but underlying this was the question of how rights to buildings should be awarded, and in what they consisted. The right on offer, which the Commission on Clearing Moscow was empowered to grant, was "attachment" or zakreplenie. It was not clear on which grounds zakreplenie would be awarded, nor which powers over buildings it conferred. As a result, the disputes freely mixed claims to particular buildings with claims to the defi-nition of zakreplenie itself. For instance, was zakreplenie awarded in order to promote "expediency"? Many institutions argued as much, seeking to present their occupancy of a building as the most expedient outcome available, ac-cording to one of two different metrics. The first originated in expedient use of resources, that is, in the fit between the building and the institution; the second originated in the utility of the institution itself to the work of the state, production, or some other goal, which was often framed in specific and im-mediate terms. Narkomfin might seek to secure its hold over a dormitory—a building that many institutions could want, with no specific qualities tethering it to Narkomfin—with reference to its emergency work on rebuilding the country's tax infrastructure. If the building in question was a former bank, however, it would rely on arguments about expediency-as-fit.[25]

Much like the seizure of buildings during the early days of the Revolution, *zakreplenie* in the capital intersected with a bigger process unfolding at the same time in cities across the country. During the first waves of dispossession, cities had "nationalized" and central institutions had seized things with local meaning. The Sovnarkom's "Order on Demunicipalization" let loose renewed uproar over the proper border between national and municipal, which the NKVD sought to quell in early July 1922 with a bulletin acknowledging the recent "misunderstanding in the localities, due to a confusion between municipalized and nationalized buildings," and affirming that "as a general rule, all buildings on city territory with the exception of those in private holding, are municipalized and located at the disposal of the ispolkom."[26] But just two weeks later, at an internal meeting with representatives from all the commissariats devoted to the "attachment [zakreplenie] of rights to the properties under [the narkomats'] control to the narkomats," it emerged that, in fact, there was no "definite understanding of nationalized property" separating it from municipal property. In fact, there was no "understanding of nationalized property" at all.

For the rest of the summer, the NKVD hosted a regular meeting of the representatives, devoted no longer to zakreplenie alone but to the more fundamental problem of "fixing an understanding of nationalized property." The original "Decree on Municipalization of August 20, 1918," they determined, would be of little help, as it dealt only in the cancellation of private property rights, and did not "touch on the rights of state institutions to property in cities."[27] It ended the old order, but it did not make the new one. Without a legal platform to work from, the assembled representatives turned initially to the consideration of "principles." On what basis should institutions wield real estate? Was their authority over it a power of "disposal" (*rasporyazhenie*), "use" (pol'zovanie), or "property" (sobstvennost')? The first principle they considered was that of expedience. Expedience, they agreed, worked well as a basis for assigning rights in some circumstances, namely in the case of buildings specially outfitted for use in a distinct capacity, such as banks. On the basis of expedience, it made sense to award bank buildings, wherever they were located and whether they had been owned by the state before the Revolution or not, to Narkomfin. But in other respects, expedience was found lacking as a principle guiding the assignment of rights to buildings, as a delegate from the NKVD argued, for the simple reason that institutions, their tasks, and thus their sizes changed; fitting institutions to spaces in the present and assigning rights on that basis "failed to deal with the fact that the narkomats are not some kind of permanent entity."[28]

Another principle proposed as a basis for assigning rights was the presence of "signs of belonging" connecting a building to an institution. These signs, a draft order on nationalized property explained, could not be limited to present "signs of belonging," as the current patterns of occupation were the product of the whirlwind of dispossession, and thus lacking in rationality and order. The draft therefore proposed considering a building's prerevolutionary ownership in assessing institutional claims on it.[29] But this principle, too, was immediately dismissed. "If the definition of property rights is based on having belonged to a state organ in the prerevolutionary epoch, then the fate of property will have been pre-decided, according to principles of a totally accidental [*sluchainyi*] character," the representative from the Commissariat of Welfare objected.[30] Whatever had guided the disposal of buildings before the Revolution, whether the whims of tsarist officials or the vicissitudes of the market, it could not be allowed to dictate the allocation of space in the present day. What was needed, as a different representative argued, was rather the opposite: to find a way to recognize "that fundamental reorganization of state institutions, which was produced by the revolution and which will be continued in the further progress of its development"—to build the effects of the Revolution into the concept of nationalized property, perhaps by recognizing as "nationalized property" all things which had been "nationalized" by legal order over the past four years. But this approach was also rejected: too many things had escaped the working of law during the Revolution, the delegates realized, to rely upon it as a guide.

Unable to agree on any one of the proposed principles for defining the attributes of nationalized property and its operation, the group finally decided to use them all. Nationalized property, their final draft read, consisted of all those things, both movable and real estate, which had belonged to the state before the Revolution; all those things located in current use of state organs or connected to their work; all those things which had been nationalized according to revolutionary legal orders; and, finally, all those things, "the nationalization of which did not have legal sanction, but which, in the process of revolutionary construction, acquired an organic connection with a given state organ."[31]

Even during these discussions, skeptics in the room suggested that, whichever principles the group arrived at, it would be impossible to resolve questions of nationalized property "on the basis of general principles," due to the many "departures from the principles" forged in the course of the Revolution itself. This fundamental incompatibility between the Revolution and the idea of general principles would express itself in conflicts over the disposal of resources between state institutions, they predicted, which would require "some authoritative organ" to resolve them.[32] This was correct, as can be seen nowhere more visibly than in practical attempts to "attach" buildings to institutions in Moscow.

The authoritative organ in this endeavor was meant to be the Commission for Clearing Moscow. But it turned out the Commission was not authoritative enough to do the job. When the commissariats did not like its orders, they ignored them. Eventually, the Commission took to having its decisions formally confirmed by VTsIK. It called upon agents from the Cheka to carry out concentrations and evictions in very stubborn cases, as when the Commissariat of War flouted a series of the Commission's orders to give up space over the course of months.[33] But the appearance of the Cheka was not always enough to convince people to give up their rooms. In 1922, the Commission reported that it had "met with difficulties in freeing the Boyar's Court," a former hotel, from use as a dormitory by Narkomfin.[34] Several months earlier, the Commission had ordered Narkomfin to remove its employees from the building, so that employees affiliated with a different commissariat, the People's Commissariat of Agriculture (Narkomzem), could move in. Narkomfin waged a furious campaign, lambasting the uselessness (inexpedience) of replacing one group of state employees with another, bombarding VTsIK with reminders of its "essential state expediency," and even securing an attestation of Narkomfin's "expediency" from Vladimir Lenin.[35] But the Commission for Clearing Moscow refused to change its decision. Narkomfin workers still lived in the building when, on the appointed date of its transfer to Narkomzem, a handful Narkomzem employees appeared at the dormitory's door, announcing that they were taking it over, "by force if necessary." In response, the Narkomfin employees who lived there "stopped going out to work." Indeed, they stopped going anywhere at all, devoting themselves fulltime to squatting in their rooms. In the end, Narkomzem workers resolved to claim space as if in battle, clearing one room at a time, as individual Narkomfin workers broke down and moved out. Meanwhile "all work on the completion of budgets and the creation of a tax plan has ceased," Narkomfin's high-level collegium wrote in an urgent telegram to the Central Committee of the Communist Party and the Presidium of the Central Executive Committee.[36] Nothing would change, the collegium thundered, until these two powerful institutions intervened. And they both did—on different sides of the dispute. Before the conflict was over, Stalin had personally ordered a halt to Narkomfin's eviction; Lenin ordered that it continue.[37] It would take all of the authority concentrated at the pinnacle of the party-state to settle the dormitory at the Boyar's Court.

————

The Revolution had to end, and it had to keep going; few things better embodied this basic paradox than the problem of property. The Decree on Nationalized Property tried to let it do both at once, endowing the seizure of buildings with general principles at last, while at the same time encasing in amber the specific allocations and "organic connections" forged by the Revolution, however chaotic they had been. This kind of partial legalization had been the approach taken in the April 1920 Decree on Requisition and Confiscation as well: to put a stop to further dispossession while refusing to legitimate regular possession. In neither case was the result a firm end to the processes of redistribution set in motion by the revolutionary events. The surfeit of authority required to allocate buildings within the state would persist, while for movable goods, the way forward was not through laws on possession at all—it was through laws on forgetting dispossession.

Dispossession made itself easy to forget, by the nature of its action on buildings, their human occupants, and material contents. Eviction was a form of social dismemberment.[38] It prefigured both material loss and social erasure. As a group called the Esperanto Language Institute fretted, upon receiving its eviction notice, "this address is known as the center of Esperanto of the whole world . . . and serves as the beacon through which this movement in Russia is united with the movements around the world"—a beacon that would be lost once the Institute moved from its iconic address.[39] In some instances, the material losses of eviction and the erasure of social knowledge about it overlapped. When VSNKh's Mining Department moved to Moscow, it took over the former United Bank building on Kuznetsky Most. The bankers had departed abruptly, without clearing out the Bank's papers, and by October, the Mining Department had come to resent the clutter, demanding someone come to remove it. An inspector arrived to find the files, "important and unimportant, orders, account books, all heaped in one pile." If the papers were not taken immediately, the Mining Department director vowed to let them perish in the courtyard "under the open sky." Already, they were so "chaotic" that it was "no longer possible to make sense" of them as a meaningful record of the Bank's existence.[40]

To save other papers from this fate, the staff of the Moscow Oblast Archive spent their days rushing from one evicted household or organization to the next, seeking out records at risk of destruction. In that year, the archive saved a number of "archives that were perishing or had perished": the archives of an imperial censor, found "in a totally destroyed form"; the archives of the Moscow City Duma, "suffering from flooding." Yet to be saved were the archives of the "Moscow nobility . . . currently located in extremely unsuitable spaces and found by chance"; the archives of the prerevolutionary municipal district (*gradonachalstvo*), held up due to lack of transport; and, finally "the old files from the towers of Kitay-gorod,"— the files of the merchants—"many of which already have been stolen."[41]

Dispossession also left a scanty visual record, particularly compared to other spheres of revolutionary activity. It seems to have been rarely photographed. Trotsky brought an orchestra with him when, in November 1917, he marched over to the State Bank to demand money and the bank's subordination to the Bolsheviks, but no one brought along cameras when they seized apartments. The photograph on the cover of this book is one of three images— all made at the same time—of an apartment in the moments more or less immediately after it was unsealed, some weeks or months after the eviction of its original occupants. In straightforward, unsentimental frames, these photographs depict the chaos of dispossession: papers strewn about the floor; portraits removed from the walls, resting against the legs of a table. As an ensemble, they have a happenstance quality; there is much in the apartment that we do not see. The viewer gains no sense from the three pictures of how the space fits together, suggesting that the purpose of the images was not to document the space itself. Indeed, as an accompanying letter directly explains, the purpose of the images was not to document the space at all. It was to document the mess of objects. The apartment's evicted occupant—what were the chances?—was the Russian Photographic Society, and the person sent to inventory it was a photographer employed by the aerial photography section of the new Air Force. In desperate need of photographic equipment and supplies, the photographer had learned "through private channels that presently, there was located in the recently freed space of the former Russian Photographic Society those materials we need for work." This was the level of serendipity required to capture dispossession on film. After taking the pictures, the photographer performed an inventory of the remaining property, concluding with

FIGURE 6.1 AND FIGURE 6.2 (FACING PAGE) The Russian Photographic Society, c. spring 1921.
Photographs taken by B.N. Maklakov. Courtesy of TsAGM, photographed with permission by the author, July 13, 2017. TsAGM f. 2434, op. 1, d. 29, secured in envelope after l. 34.

disappointment that "no more than 10 percent of it was left, and all of it was in a ruined state—much already not possible to restore."[42]

Unusually, however, dispossession and its aftermath were the subjects of a large painting, made in 1936–37 by the socialist realist artist Kuzma Petrov-Vodkin. Petrov-Vodkin intended the painting, entitled "Housewarming. (Working-Class Petrograd) 1937," to be his masterpiece. He died not long after completing it. Improbable though it may seem, he chose the implicit eviction of an aristocratic household from a luxurious apartment, and the arrival of new, working-class tenants, as his final subject. Set in 1922, the painting depicts a nighttime scene inside an apartment with views across the Neva River in Petrograd, situating it in one of the city's poshest prerevolutionary neighborhoods. The interior walls are wrapped in a red, satiny jacquard; a large mirror

FIGURE 6.2

hangs between the gracious windows, which are—jarringly—cracked, as if shot through with a stone or bullet. Other elements of the scene trouble the elegant surfaces. The gilded icon frame in the corner is empty, its icon replaced with a sprig of heather. The furniture is a curious mixture, carved hardwood armchairs beside rough wooden stools. The people are a curious mixture, too: a large group of women are clustered in the foreground around a seated woman next to a jerry-rigged stove, feeding an infant. A large group of men, and one austere woman, are gathered around the table, speaking animatedly, with looks of enjoyment and optimism. Still more people fill out the enormous frame: an old peasant regaling a young soldier; a dreamy couple perched on a windowsill; a boy playing with a bird in a brass cage; a man sitting alone, lost in thought.

Socialist realism was an aesthetic famous for producing art that had to come with instruction manuals—detailed interpretive guides, conveyed to audiences through reading nights, author interviews, published in newspapers, to ensure they discerned the appropriate seeds of the revolutionary future planted in its scenes.[43] In this, Petrov-Vodkin's painting was no different. He,

FIGURE 6.3. "The Housewarming. (Working-Class Petrograd) 1937" by Kuzma Petrov-Vodkin (1937).
Source: (https://commons.wikimedia.org/wiki/File:Moving_party_(Petrov-Vodkin).jpg)

too, published lengthy explanations of it, interviews in which he explained all the stories, packed like sardines into the apartment scene: of the husband and wife, new parents, who were hosting friends at their new apartment; the dreamy young couple, hoping soon to embark on the same path; the soldier returned from the front, remembering fallen friends.[44] On and on it went, more and more stories, attached not only to the people but also to the objects crowding the frame (the brass birdcage, the empty icon frame, the cracked window). Every person and object accounted for; stories for them all. It is difficult to imagine a more accurate rendering of dispossession—a truer representation of the surfeit of stories and experiences jammed into dispossessive encounters. But this surfeit of stories was the painting's undoing. Petrov-Vodkin lived just long enough to see the critics savage his last work.[45] There were too many stories, his critics complained; too many threads to untangle, images to decipher, objects to read. And so, unlike most of the objects it depicted, "The Housewarming" was packed away for safekeeping in museum vaults.

NOTES

Introduction: An Infinity of Treasures

1. These changes were the subject of a dedicated linguistic study: Afanasy Selishchev, *Yazyk revolyutsionnoi epokhi: nablyudeniya nad russkim yazykom posklednikh let, 1917–1926* (Moscow: Rabotnik prosveshcheniya, 1928).

2. See, for instance, the jubilant mockery printed in the short-lived newspaper, *Moskovsky vecherny chas*, entitled "AOPODIOG: quasi una fantasia", a "fantasy" imagining a joint-stock company for thieves, where thieves received assignments, secretaries reminded them of their schedules, and the staff struggled with regular office problems, such as people stealing their galoshes from the coatroom. The name of the company was the nonsensical "AOPODIOG," which is revealed as an acronym, of the sort springing into existence by the dozen, for Aktsionernoe Obshchestvo po Ogrableniiu Domov i Otdelnykh Grazhdan (Joint-Stock Company for the robbery of houses and individual citizens). Although the fantasy envisioned it as a joint-stock enterprise, rather than a state institution, the suggestion of institutionalized theft was unmistakable. *Moskovsky Vecherny Chas*, Monday, March 11 [February 26 o.s.] 1918, no. 1, 3.

3. Russian State Archive of the Economy (RGAE) f. 7733, op. 1, d. 231, l. 38.

4. State Archive of the Russian Federation (GARF) f. R-130, op. 1, d. 4, l. 1.

5. Although cities occupy an important place in cultural, social, and political histories of the Revolution, there are fewer studies devoted to what might be called revolutionary urban history, or histories of the city itself—its physical environment, the routines of municipal governance, its material resources and infrastructure—through revolution. While this book does not offer a comprehensive urban history of the revolutionary city, it works more closely in that vein, stitching together the practices, routines, and, where they existed, laws governing the use and disposal of material resources in and around buildings, in order to illuminate the lived experiences of revolution and its aftermath for the people and things of the city. On the urban imaginary and attempts to realize utopian visions of daily life in urban settings after the Revolution, see Richard Stites, *Revolutionary Dreams: Utopian Vision and Experimental Life in the Russian Revolution* (Oxford: Oxford University Press, 1989); Andy Willimott, *Living the Revolution: Urban Communes & Soviet Socialism, 1917–1932* (Oxford: Oxford University Press, 2016). Roger Pethybridge offered an unusually nuanced emphasis on Petrograd as a pressure cooker and the political implications of the revolutionary geography: Roger Pethybridge, *The Spread of the Russian Revolution: Essays on 1917* (London: Palgrave Macmillan, 1972), chapter 6. The extensive historiography of the political history of Revolution in Petrograd and other cities, too large to address in entirety here, includes the series by Alexander Rabinowitch, *Prelude to Revolution:*

The Petrograd Bolsheviks and the July 1917 Uprising (Bloomington, IN: Indiana University Press, 1968), *The Bolsheviks Come to Power: The Revolution in 1917 in Petrograd* (New York: W.W. Norton and Company, 1976), and *The Bolsheviks in Power: The First Year of Soviet Rule* (Bloomington, IN: Indiana University Press, 2008); as well as Tsuyoshi Hasegawa, *The February Revolution: Petrograd, 1917* (Seattle, WA: University of Washington Press, 1981). On the cultural life of the revolutionary city, see Katerina Clark, *Petersburg: Crucible of Cultural Revolution* (Cambridge, MA: Harvard University Press, 1998). Donald Raleigh shifted the frame of analysis to the regional capital of Saratov—a shift that, due to the nature of the "Revolution" in regional capitals, also entails a chronological expansion of focus to the civil war: Donald Raleigh, *Experiencing Russia's Civil War: Politics, Society, and Revolutionary Culture in Saratov* (Princeton, NJ: Princeton University Press, 2003), work that has been continued by, among others, Liudmila Novikova, *An Anti-Bolshevik Alternative: The White Movement and the Civil War in the Russian North*, trans. Seth Bernstein (Madison, WI: University of Wisconsin Press, 2018). As Diane Koenker and others have noted, Moscow's revolution has received less attention than Petrograd's (a fact connected, since 1991 at least, to the difficulties in archival sources described below): Diane Koenker, *Moscow Workers and the 1917 Revolution* (Princeton, NJ: Princeton University Press, 1981), 366. See also D. Tolstykh, *Moskva v dvukh revoliutsiiakh: Ukreplenie mestnago gosudarstvennogo apparata v stolitse v pervoi polovine 1918 goda* (Moscow: Moskovsky rabochy, 1958); A. Ya. Grunt, V. I. Startsev, *Petrograd-Moskva Iyul' Noyabr' 1917* (Moscow: Politizdat, 1984); Timothy Colton, *Moscow: Governing the Socialist Metropolis* (Cambridge, MA: The Belknap Press of Harvard University Press, 1995).

6. As described by Orlando Figes, *Peasant Russia, Civil War: The Volga Countryside in Revolution (1917–1921)* (Oxford: Clarendon Press, 1989) esp. 48–69; and Alec Nove, *An Economic History of the USSR* (New York: Penguin, 1969), 32.

7. Eric Lohr, *Nationalizing the Russian Empire: The Campaign against Enemy Aliens in World War I* (Cambridge, MA: Harvard University Press, 2003). Peter Holquist, *Making War, Forging Revolution: Russia's Continuum of Crisis, 1914–1921* (Cambridge, MA: Harvard University Press, 2002).

8. Constantin Goschler and Philipp Ther, "Introduction," in *Robbery and Restitution: The Conflict over Jewish Property in Europe*, ed. Martin Dean, Constantin Goschler, and Philipp Ther. (New York: Berghahn Books, 2008), 5.

9. A fact remarked upon by K. V. Kharchenko, *Vlast'—Imushchestvo—Chelovek: peredel sobstvennosti v bolshevistskoi Rossii 1917–nachala 1921 gg.* (Moscow: Russky dvor, 2000), 185. For dispossession and its aftermath in World War II, see Franziska Exeler, "What Did You Do during the War? Personal Responses to the Aftermath of Nazi Occupation," *Kritika: Explorations in Russian and Eurasian History*, 17, no. 4 (2016), 805–35.

10. "Spontaneous" privatization in many instances preempted official programs, which were in any case devoted to recognizing an enterprise's current employees as prospective shareholders rather than prerevolutionary owners, as Steven Solnick describes in *Stealing the State: Control and Collapse in Soviet Institutions* (Cambridge, MA: Harvard University Press, 1998), especially 239, 252.

11. Kharchenko, *Vlast'—Imushchestvo—Chelovek*, 185. In its argument, Kharchenko's remarkable book follows the perspective articulated by Richard Pipes, among others, on the instrumental connection between the destruction of private property rights and the evisceration of

human freedom. At the same time, in his rich and nuanced treatment of the empirical phenomenon, Kharchenko transcends this framing, illuminating a vast architecture of seizure in the western lands that would become Belarus, animated not by instrumentalism alone, but rather by the perverse logics of the process itself, leading, for instance, to what Kharchenko aptly calls a "crisis of overseizure," akin to the overfulfilling of norms later on in the Soviet era. For more on the arguments of Pipes himself regarding property and freedom, see the discussion in the prologue.

12. Boris Kolonitskii, "Russian Historiography of the 1917 Revolution: New Challenges to Old Paradigms?" *History & Memory* 21, no. 2 (2009): 34–59.

13. Sheila Fitzpatrick, "What's Left?" *The London Review of Books*, 39, no. 7 (30 March 2017).

14. Carol Rose, "Property and Expropriation: Themes and Variations in American Law," *Utah Law Review*, 2000, no. 1, (Nov. 2000), 4.

15. Katherine Verdery, "Fuzzy Property: Rights, Power, and Identity in Transylvania's Decollectivization," in *Uncertain Transition: Ethnographies of Change in the Postsocialist World*, ed. Michael Burawoy and Katherine Verdery, (New York: Rowman & Littlefield, 1999), 75.

16. David Woodruff, *Money Unmade: Barter and the Fate of Russian Capitalism* (Ithaca, NY: Cornell University Press, 1999), 19.

17. Michael Heller, "The Tragedy of the Anticommons: Property in the Transition from Marx to Markets," *Harvard Law Review*, 111 (1998), 629.

18. Martin Dean, "The Seizure of Jewish Property in Europe: Comparative Aspects of Nazi Methods and Local Responses," in *Robbery and Restitution: The Conflict over Jewish Property in Europe*, ed. Martin Dean, Constantin Goschler, and Philipp Ther (New York: Berghahn Books, 2008), 22.

19. Jean-Marc Dreyfus, "The Looting of Jewish Property in Occupied Western Europe: A Comparative Study of Belgium, France, and the Netherlands," in *Robbery and Restitution: The Conflict over Jewish Property in Europe,* ed. Martin Dean, Constantin Goschler, and Philipp Ther (New York: Berghahn Books, 2008), 57.

20. The task of the liquidation commissions, later attached to the Commissariat of Finance and other commissariats, was to process prerevolutionary paperwork, and, where possible, recycle it—by sending it to an institution called Glavbum, which would pulp the rare resource for reuse. See the recycling of archives of two commercial banks to Glavbum, RGAE f. 7733, op. 1, d. 236, l. 51. Elidor Mëhilli notes a similar phenomenon in Albania in 1945–1946. Elidor Mëhilli, *From Stalin to Mao: Albania and the Socialist World* (Ithaca, NY: Cornell University Press, 2017).

21. NIOR, f. 369 (V. D. Bonch-Bruevich), carton 397, d. 14, ll. 18–19. "Recollections of A. Monisov, May 1927." Monisov's contact made the argument that, "after all, Lenin does not value these papers at all, and according to the rumors that have reached us, has even ordered that they be burned—what should stop him from receiving tens of millions of gold rubles for something that costs nothing, there is only profit in the deal on his side." According to Monisov, Lenin allegedly replied with the honesty of a good businessman and the confidence of a good revolutionary: "how could I profit on a deal when I know that all of those papers are never going to be worth anything."

22. The process of destroying the paperwork of "bourgeois credit societies" is described by the People's Commissar of Finance, N. N. Krestinsky, in his update in the Commissariat's periodical, N. N. Krestinsky, "Itogi," *Izvestia finansov* No. 10: October 25-November 7, 1919, 3.

23. Moscow typically did not require regional finance departments to send papers removed from circulation to the center, but it did demand they register such papers, a process one regional finance commissar complained was a tremendous "waste of time, as the state has no idea how many such papers were ever issued," and noted that in his district, of the estimated 2.5 million such bills in existence, his office had registered 80,000. RGAE f. 7733, op. 1, d. 120, l. 19.

24. On the efforts to build an official notarial service in 1918, see GARF f. A-353, op. 9, d. 356; on the persistence of "former notaries confirming acts of sale, purchase, gifts of houses, gardens and other real estate even after the Decree of 1917 December 17" forbidding such transfers, see l. 6.

25. The Sovnarkom decided to open a Central Bureau of Complaint, as described in chapter 2, in November 1918, when it had accumulated roughly 500 such complaints, all relating to the activity of the Cheka. As the director of the Bureau of Complaint, a lawyer named Vasily Belsky, later wrote, "in the course of time, Belsky managed to widen the task." GARF f. 4390, op. 2, d. 296, l. 189.

26. My approach here builds on Larissa Zakharova's insight, made from her beautiful study of dispossession in a single apartment building in Petrograd, that real-life scenarios and even individual experiences frequently served as the basis for revolutionary law-making. Larissa Zakharova, "Le 26–28 Kamennoostrovski, Les tribulations d'un immeuble en Revolution" in *Saint Pètersbourg Histoire, promenades, anthologie et dictionnaire* (Paris : Laffont 2003), 505.

27. On the problem of law and lawlessness in the thinking of Vladimir Lenin, see Jane Burbank, "Lenin and the Law in Revolutionary Russia." *Slavic Review*, 54, no. 1 (1995), 23–44. As Burbank notes, Lenin did not present a stable attitude toward law in his writings before 1917. In the spring of 1918, following a brief window in which he favored armed citizens enforcing justice on a class basis, he turned away from this ideal and toward the courts as a mechanism of education and discipline. Most of all, Burbank emphasizes, after 1917, Lenin governed through law—decrees, laws and courts—to defend the revolutionary state. On the dampening of Bolshevik anti-law positions over time see also Peter Solomon, *Soviet Criminal Justice under Stalin* (New York: Cambridge University Press, 1996), 18; Harold J. Berman "Soviet Property in Law and in Plan," *University of Pennsylvania Law Review*, 96, no. 324 (1948).

28. On the treatment of revolutionary decrees as source material, see V. V. Zhuravlyov, *Dekrety Sovetskoi Vlasti 1917–1920 gg. kak istorichesky istochnik* (Moscow: Izd. Nauka, 1979). Representative works on nationalization include Timothy Sosnovy, *The Soviet Housing Problem* (New York: Research Program on the USSR, 1954); *Rabochy kontrol' i natsionalizatsiya promyshlennosti v Turkestane (1917–1920 gg.): Sbornik dokumentov.* ed. E. A. Voskoboinikova (Tashkent: Gosizdat UzSSR, 1955).

29. Tsuyoshi Hasegawa, *Crime and Punishment in the Russian Revolution: Mob Justice and Police in Petrograd.* (Cambridge, MA: Harvard University Press, 2018).

30. Most commonly, the seizure of apartments and their contents appears in social and political histories of the Revolution, while histories of the revolutionary economy focus on industrial and agricultural developments and policies. The established account in the latter vein remains Silvana Malle, *The Economic Organization of War Communism, 1918–1921* (Cambridge: Cambridge University Press, 1985). Nove, *Economic History*, chapter 3, emphasizes the chaos of the period, and thus the firmness of the break with what followed. More specialized accounts include Lars T. Lih, *Bread and Authority in Russia, 1914–1921.* (Berkeley: University of California

Press, 1990). Exceptions include Kharchenko, who situates dispossession in the foundation of revolutionary governance and economy.

31. Mary McAuley, *Bread and Justice: State and Society in Petrograd 1917–1922* (Oxford: Oxford University Press, 1991), 262.

32. *Krasnaya Moskva [Red Moscow]* (Moscow: Mossoviet, 1920), 335–6. On municipal socialism and its relationship to European socialist parties see Patrizia Dogliani, "European Municipalism in the First Half of the Twentieth Century: The Socialist Network," *Contemporary European History* 11, no. 4 (2002), 578.

33. Christina Crawford, *Spatial Revolution: Architecture and Planning in the Early Soviet Union* (Ithaca, NY: Cornell University Press, 2022); Stephen Kotkin, "Shelter and Subjectivity in the Stalin Period: A Case Study in Magnitogorsk," in *Russian Housing in the Modern Age: Design and Social History, ed.* William Brumfield and Blair Ruble (Washington, D.C.: Wilson Center Press, 1993).

34. John N. Hazard, "Soviet Property Law," *Cornell Law Review*, 30, 466 (1945), 467. For "personal property" in housing in a later period, see Mark Smith, *Property of Communists: The Urban Housing Program from Stalin to Khrushchev* (DeKalb, IL: Northern Illinois University Press, 2010), 90–1.

35. I. V. Gessen, ed, *Arkhiv Russkoi Revoliutsii* (Berlin: Slovo-Verlag, 1921).

36. As Caroline Humphrey and Katherine Verdery suggest, one way of thinking about property is as a form of speech, one that "appears more in some circumstances than in others," surging at moments of "upheaval in how 'property' works in the world." Caroline Humphrey and Katherine Verdery, "Introduction," in *Property in Question: Value Transformation in the Global Economy,* ed. Humphrey and Verdery (London: Routledge, 2004), 2.

37. This approach draws from methods of historical sociology articulated by J. P. Nettl, "The State as a Conceptual Variable," *World Politics* 20, no. 4 (Jul., 1968), 559–92; Timothy Mitchell, "The Limits of the State: Beyond Statist Approaches and their Critics," *APSR*, 85: 1 (Mar. 1991), 77–96; and Venelin Ganev, *Preying on the State: The Transformation of Bulgaria after 1989* (Ithaca, NY: Cornell University Press, 2007). The core concept shared by these works, and employed in this book, is the idea that the state was, as Nettl called it, a "sociocultural" phenomenon as much as an empirical one, according to which "individuals generaliz[e] the concept and cognition of state in their perceptions and actions." Pierre Bourdieu develops a related idea, contending that the state's key power is conceptual, manifested in its ability to endow itself with an appearance of naturalness that is continuously constituted in writings about the state, especially juridical writings. Pierre Bourdieu, Loic J. D. Wacquant, and Samar Farage, "Rethinking the State: Genesis and Structure of the Bureaucratic Field." *Sociological Theory* 12, no. 1 (1994): 1–18. The direct inspiration for my approach, however, comes from Venelin Ganev, who aptly draws attention to the "fluctuation of stateness" across Soviet institutions and within them, carrying over into the post-Soviet period. As he observes, the sheer size of Soviet-style states, which blend together aspects of state administration, economy, and other institutions that elsewhere appear distinct, makes them ill-suited for analysis according to the attributes of liberal nation-states. Ganev, *Preying*, p. 11. Rather than relying on normative criteria developed for the liberal nation-state, Ganev proposes (following Charles Tilly) to examine state institutions through their "mechanics and practices," a method I also employ here. Charles Tilly, "Warmaking and

Statemaking as Organized Crime," in *Bringing the State Back In*, ed. P. Evans, D. Rueschemeyer, T. Skocpol (Cambridge: Cambridge University Press. 1985).

38. As cited and translated by Isaiah Berlin, "Russia and 1848," *The Slavonic and East European Review*, 26, no. 67 (1948), 341–60; and Claudia Verhoeven, "'Une Revolution Vraiment Scientifique': Russian Terrorism, the Escape from the European Orbit, and the Invention of a New Revolutionary Paradigm," in *Scripting Revolution: A Historical Approach to the Comparative Study of Revolutions*, ed. Keith Michael Baker and Dan Edelstein (Stanford, CA: Stanford University Press, 2015).

39. The term "state capacity" often refers to powers of fiscal and military mobilization developed by eighteenth-century states in Europe, as characterized by John Brewer in *The Sinews of Power: War, Money, and the English State, 1688–1783* (New York: Alfred A. Knopf, 1989). As Brewer and others have noted, however, precise definitions and metrics of state capacity are hard to come by, not only in the sense of the range of powers they denote but even in the range of actors they include. In the British case, the state could build its capacity through the elaboration of bureaucracies and practices that were not necessarily inside the government, including the private banking system. See also: Nafisa Akbar and Susan L. Ostermann, "Understanding, Defining, and Measuring State Capacity in India: Traditional, Modern, and Everything In Between," *Asian Survey*, 55, no. 5 (2015), 845–861.

40. My characterization of the state, and of the process of dispossession as statemaking, differs from some that maintain a Weberian characterization of it in this period, employing its normative definition of "the state as the entity wielding a monopoly on violence." As Eric Lohr and Joshua Sanborn have recently observed, the revolutionary state did not achieve this standard, not least because the February Revolution was, by its very nature, an attack that "undermined the state as that institution maintaining a monopoly on the legitimate use of violence." Eric Lohr and Joshua Sanborn, "1917: Revolution as Demobilization and State Collapse," *Slavic Review*, 76, no. 3, (2017), 703–9. Rather than concluding, however, that the resulting entity displayed "characteristics of a failed state," this book analyzes it directly as a revolutionary state, one that was, moreover, trying to make socialism a reality, with attendant consequences for the ambitions of would-be state makers. While the Bolsheviks sought to disarm people unaffiliated with themselves and resented the disordering, and at times humiliating, activity of the thieving gangs that plagued Moscow and other cities, they did not seek to protect private property as such. This feature altered the aims, operation, and structure of the revolutionary state. Among other things, it fueled tremendous growth in the state's size, even amid the disorder, a development described by Alvin Gouldner. The driver behind this immense growth, and also behind the state's basic operations, Gouldner contends, was dispossession. Dispossession was also a through-line in interwar Soviet governance, suggesting that revolutionary dispossession, while a distinctively chaotic episode, was not unique in the Soviet governing repertory. During the collectivization campaigns of the late 1920s, Gouldner observes, armed brigades stormed villages, seizing grain, collectivizing peasants, and tearing into houses. They ate whatever was at hand, grabbed hats from heads, stripped people of their clothes, took glasses from their faces. Gouldner places property transfer at the core of Stalinism, although he focuses primarily on the transfer of the means of production, particularly land. Alvin W. Gouldner, "Stalinism: A Study of Internal Colonialism," *Telos* 34, (Winter 1977–1978), 11, 29.

41. Orlando Figes and Boris Kolonitskii, *Interpreting the Russian Revolution: The Language and Symbols of 1917* (New Haven, CT: Yale University Press, 1999), 1; Boris Kolonitskii, "Anti-bourgeois Propaganda and Anti-'Burzhui' Consciousness in 1917," *Russian Review*, 53, no. 2 (1994), 183.

42. Dan Edelstein, "Do We Want a Revolution without Revolution? Reflections on Political Authority," *French Historical Studies*, 35, no. 2 (Spring 2012), 272.

43. Edelstein, "Revolution," 274; William H. Sewell, "Historical Events as Transformations of Structures: Inventing Revolution at the Bastille," *Theory and Society* 25, no. 6 (1996), 841–81.

44. Solomon, *Criminal Justice*, 19.

45. GARF f. 4085, op. 22, d. 10, l. 46.

46. As Ekaterina Pravilova notes, "the capacity of the state is often measured by its ability to enforce the security of property." E. A. Pravilova, *A Public Empire: Property and the Quest for the Common Good in Imperial Russia* (Princeton, NJ: Princeton University Press, 2014), 94, 323n, citing Douglass North, *Structure and Change in Economic History* (New York: W.W. Norton and Co., 1981), 20–32.

47. The imperative to articulate and defend a new kind of state property and the influence of this project on the operation of the Soviet state, concepts of property, and property crime is illuminated by Juliette Cadiot, *La société des voleurs: Propriété et socialisme sous Staline* (Paris: Les Éditions de l'EHESS, 2021).

48. See note 37.

49. This is the argument of T.H. Rigby, *Lenin's Government: Sovnarkom, 1917–1922* (Cambridge: Cambridge University Press, 1979), preface. Bolsheviks could be found in positions of authority throughout the hierarchy of state power, thanks to the master administrator Yakov Sverdlov's careful seeding. Still, their numbers in many institutions were minuscule, a situation that began to change—quite unmistakably—only in 1922, as this book ends. This book refers to state employees as such or as "revolutionary officials," adding in the ascription "Bolshevik" when the people concerned were party members. Narkomfin personnel files depict with striking clarity the intensification of party presence and pressure on non-party members inside Soviet institutions toward the end of 1922 and into 1923. These files grew thick with repeated surveys and autobiographies. See RGAE f. 7733, op. 18: representative files include those of a number of officials who feature in these pages, such as A. O. Alsky (d. 245), A. G. Orlov (d. 6401), and S. D. Pekarsky (d. 6644). Alsky was a Party member and one of the chief conduits between it and the Commissariat until his duties were reduced in 1922–23. Orlov and Pekarsky both served the prerevolutionary Ministry of Finance, and were "without party." Orlov had a high rank in Petrograd before 1917, while Pekarsky was a provincial accountant "invited to the center" in 1918, the latter presumably as a competent official expressing willingness to work with new authorities, gaining a higher rank in the process, although not himself a party member.

50. On the rise of the conviction that parties represented the sole "legitimate channel for political expression" see Holquist, *Making War*, 114.

51. Viktor Shklovsky, *A Sentimental Journey: Memoirs 1917–1922*, trans. Richard Sheldon, with introduction by Sidney Monas (Ithaca, NY: Cornell University Press, revised ed. 1984), 147. Shklovsky's narrative is populated almost entirely by people who changed in the crucible of revolution, writers who "later very quickly and very sincerely became staunch Bolshevik[s]";

people worth "dwelling on" in his memoir because they were "the first man [he] saw jockeying for position," followed later by "hordes of such people." Shklovsky, *Sentimental*, 12, 14.

52. Central Archive of the City of Moscow (TsAGM) f. 54, op. 1, d. 51, l. 54.

53. TsAGM f. 2382, op. 1, d. 4, l. 42.

54. Shklovsky, *Sentimental*, 177.

55. See the discussion of the state as a private owner of public goods in Pravilova, *A Public Empire*, esp. 115–116.

56. D. T. Rodgers, *Atlantic Crossings: Social Politics in a Progressive Age* (Cambridge, MA: Harvard University Press, 1998), 189.

57. Shklovsky, *Sentimental*, 182. Identical tales of spoilation fill the archives, a steady beat of spoiled sunflower seed oil and moldy leather. GARF f. 4390, op. 2, d. 204, l. 6.

58. Leora Auslander, "Coming Home? Jews in Postwar Paris," *Journal of Contemporary History* 40 no. 2, April 2005, 244.

59. Following Gregory Grossman, I take the command economy to be one in which individual firms produce and use resources "primarily by virtue of specific directives (commands, targets) received from higher authorities," with the aim of fulfilling the plan. If planning is understood as a constitutive part of economic activity in both market and non-market systems, the practice of command, Grossman suggests, made Soviet economic management distinctive. Gregory Grossman, "Gold and the Sword: Money in the Soviet Command Economy," in *Industrialization in Two Systems: Essays in Honor of Alexander Gerschenkron*, ed. Henry Rosovsky, (New York: Wiley, 1966), 204–236, here 207.

60. On currency, and the interpretation of this moment as a "revolution that did not happen," see the last chapter of the forthcoming E. A. Pravilova, *The Ruble: A Political History* (New York: Oxford University Press, 2023).

61. Caroline Humphrey, *Karl Marx Collective: Economy, Society, and Religion in a Siberian Collective Farm* (Cambridge: Cambridge University Press, 1983), 76.

62. On the long-term affiliation of Soviet practitioners with comprehensive physical accounting see Arunabh Ghosh, *Making It Count: Statistics and Statecraft in the Early People's Republic of China* (Princeton: Princeton University Press, 2020).

63. Vyacheslav Shishkov, "The Divorce," in *The Fatal Eggs and Other Satire: 1918–1963*, ed. and trans. Mirra Ginsburg (New York: Grove Press, 1987), 143–8.

64. GARF f. 130, op. 2, d. 77, l. 1.

65. GARF f. 4085, op. 22, d. 240, l. 1.

66. Svetlana Boym, *Common Places: Mythologies of Everyday Life in Russia* (Cambridge, MA: Harvard University Press, 1995), introduction, on rubber plants; Vera Dunham, *In Stalin's Time: Middleclass Values in Soviet Fiction* (Durham, NC: Duke University Press, 1990), 250, on canaries.

67. GARF f. 4390, op. 2, d. 204, l. 110b.

68. A point developed by Humphrey, *Karl Marx*, 91.

69. The status of the Mossoviet fond is conveyed in the TsAGM finding aid and was confirmed orally by archive staff to me upon repeated inquiries in 2009, 2010, and 2017.

70. Colton, *Moscow*; Yu. A. Polyakov, *Moskovskie trudiashchiesia v oborone sovetskoi stolitsy v 1919 godu.* (Moscow: Izd. Akademii nauk SSSR 1958); G. S. Ignatiev, *Moskva v pervy god proletarskoi diktatury* (Moscow: Izd. Nauka, 1974).

71. The significance of neighborhood governance is emphasized by McAuley, *Bread and Justice*.

72. See Neil Harding, *Lenin's Political Thought: Theory and Practice in the Democratic Revolution* (London: MacMillan, 1977), especially vol. 2, chs. 5 and 6. As Harding writes, in his first weeks in power, Lenin did not consider the redistribution of living space and other essentials a matter of property but rather one of "revolutionary democracy," giving as an example a "squad" of working people arriving to the apartment of a wealthy owner and taking up residence, managed administratively by a student writing orders in "revolutionary democracy"; "exactly the same procedure," he suggested "must be adopted in both town and country for the distribution of provisions, clothing, footwear, etc." Harding, *Lenin's Political Thought*, vol. 2, 133.

Prologue: Municipal Socialism

1. Pyotr Kropotkin, "Dwellings," *The Conquest of Bread* (New York, NY: New York University Press, 1972), 80.

2. Kropotkin, "Dwellings", 107.

3. GARF f. R-130, op. 2, d. 79, l. 76.

4. Milka Bliznakov, "Soviet Housing During the Experimental Years, 1918–1932," and Stephen Kotkin, "Shelter and Subjectivity in the Stalin Period: A Case Study in Magnitogorsk," both in *Russian Housing in the Modern Age: Design and Social History,* ed. William Brumfield and Blair Ruble (Washington, D.C.: Woodrow Wilson Center Press, 1993).

5. *Krasnaya Moskva* (Moscow: Mossoviet, 1920), 335–36. Later accounts of the summer of 1917 similarly emphasize that the Bolshevik platform proposed the seizure of urban land by the city government, together with the "requisition" of individual apartments in order to ease the housing crisis. Institut istorii (Akademiya nauk SSSR), *Istoriya Moskvy,* vol. 6 (Moscow: Izd-vo. Akademii nauk SSSR, 1952–1959), 53.

6. *Krasnaya Moskva*, 335–6.

7. Vladimir Trutovsky, "O munitsipal'noi programme," *Partiya sotsialistov-revoliutsionerov,* no. 25 (Petrograd: Tip. P. P. Sainina, 1917).

8. V. V. Zhuravlyov, *Dekrety Sovetskoi vlasti 1917–1920 gg. kak istorichesky istochnik Zakonodatelnye akty v sfere obobshchestvleniya kapitalisticheskoi sobstvennosti* (Moscow: Izd. Nauka, 1979), 337.

9. The definitive *Istoriya Moskvy* provides a clear statement of the seizure of the built environment as a byproduct of decades-old housing need; other emphases include the seizure of housing as spontaneous popular action; or as a conscious program of the Bolsheviks.

10. E. A. Pravilova *A Public Empire: Property and the Quest for the Common Good in Imperial Russia.* (Princeton: Princeton University Press, 2014), 5.

11. Pravilova, *A Public Empire,* 116.

12. Pravilova, *A Public Empire,* 126.

13. Eric Lohr, *Nationalizing the Russian Empire: The Campaign against Enemy Aliens in World War I* (Cambridge, MA: Harvard University Press, 2003); Peter Holquist, *Making War, Forging Revolution: Russia's Continuum of Crisis, 1914–1921* (Cambridge, MA: Harvard University Press, 2002).

14. Laura Engelstein, *Russia in Flames: War, Revolution, Civil War, 1914–1921* (New York and Oxford: Oxford University Press, 2017).

15. Michael Hamm emphasizes the political significance of deteriorating urban infrastructure in "The Breakdown of Urban Modernization: a prelude to the revolutions of 1917," in *The City in Russian History*, ed. Michael F. Hamm (Lexington: University Press of Kentucky, 1976).

16. Verdery, "Fuzzy Property", 55.

17. *Moskva Velikaya/Great Moscow: Guide* (Moscow: Moskovsky komsomolets, Exim, 1997), 28.

18. Kathleen Berton, *Moscow: An Architectural History* (London: I. B. Tauris, 1990), 185.

19. Timothy Colton, *Moscow: Governing the Socialist Metropolis* (Cambridge MA: The Belknap Press of Harvard University Press, 1995), 44, 46.

20. Colton, *Moscow*, 47.

21. *Istoriya Moskvy*, vol. 5, 695.

22. Moscow's overall density stood at 103 people per square desyatina in 1914, while in the ring of territory between the Boulevard and the Garden ring, where the newer, taller stone buildings predominated, housed 325 people per square desyatina. *Istoriya Moskvy*, vol. 5, 21.

23. Colton, *Moscow*, 52.

24. *Istoriya Moskvy*, vol. 4, 528–29; Colton, *Moscow*, 55–7.

25. A. V. Mamaev, *Gorodskoe samoupravlenie v rossii nakanune i v period fevralskoi revolyutsii 1917 g.* (Moscow: IstLit, 2017), 91.

26. *Istoriya Moskvy*, vol. 4, 528, and vol. 5, 718.

27. Colton, *Moscow*, 57.

28. Hamm, "The Breakdown," 183–4.

29. D. T. Rodgers, *Atlantic Crossings: Social Politics in a Progressive Age* (Cambridge, MA: Harvard University Press, 1998), 115, 162.

30. Rodgers, *Atlantic*, ch. 4.

31. Municipal socialists, or "municipal traders," as they were known in Great Britain, were not socialists in the eyes of the Second International. They sought to displace private property and markets from one sphere—urban infrastructure—in favor of municipal ownership and operation. M.A. Kurchinsky, *Munitsipal'ny sotsializm i razvitiya gorodskoi zhizni* (Sankt Petersburg: Brokgauz-Efron, 1907), 59, 69. Colton, *Moscow*, 52. Suffrage was limited to 21,000 property-owning Muscovites, a figure restricted in 1892 to just 7,252.

32. See Patrizia Dogliani, "European Municipalism in the First Half of the Twentieth Century: The Socialist Network," *Contemporary European History*, 11, no. 4 (2002); Malcolm Falkus, "The Development of Municipal Trading in the Nineteenth Century," *Business History*, 19, no. 2 (1977); Rodgers, *Atlantic*, 121.

33. Nicholas Bullock and James Read, *The Movement for Housing Reform in Germany and France 1840–1914* (Cambridge: Cambridge University Press, 1985), 187, 217, 223, 234. German reformers favored measuring the number of residents per "building site" because it reliably identified Berlin as the most congested city in Europe. French reformers, by contrast, preferred to measure density in volume of air per person, as they sought to convince the city to adopt standard building codes. Ann-Louise Shapiro, *Housing the Poor of Paris* (Madison, WI: University of Wisconsin Press, 1985), 144. See also "Domovoe samoupravlenie" in *Vestnik Vserossiyskago Soiuza Gorodov: Gorod.* no. 12–13, 1–15 (Dec. 1917),3, citing Adolf Damaschke, *Problems of*

City Economy, with forward by I. Kh. Ozerov, trans. V. Ya. Kanel (Moscow: Gorshkov, 1904), 23, which notes that Moscow's population tripled in the forty years before 1914, and in the census of 1912 one property in Moscow held on average 83 people, as compared to 77 in Berlin, 35 in Paris, and 8 in London. This figure reflected not the density of inhabitation but construction practices, as buildings in Berlin, like those in Moscow, commonly featured interior courtyards with multiple entryways. A different measure of density, also taken in 1912, was density per apartment: in Moscow, apartments averaged eight residents, with two to three people to a room. In London, the average to an apartment was 4.5, and in Berlin, it was four people.

34. Bullock and Read, *Movement*, 217.

35. Detailed in M. Zagriatskov, *Sotsial'naia deiatel'nost' gorodskogo samoupravleniya na Zapade* (Kyiv: Tip. Imp. Universiteta, 1906), 19.

36. Shapiro, *Housing*, 117, 136, 144.

37. Bullock and Read, *Movement*, 234; Rodgers, *Atlantic*, 180.

38. Rodgers, *Atlantic*, 188.

39. Russian experts grew interested in these ideas amid a great wave in statistical thinking fueled by the emancipation of the peasantry in the 1860s and focused on identifying the ideal allocation of land to peasant households. David Darrow shows that the search for a "modern normed entitlement" shifted attention from the peasant commune (*mir*) to the individual household as the dominant subject of study. David Darrow, *Tsardom of Sufficiency, Empire of Norms: Statistics, Land Allotments, and Agrarian Reform in Russia, 1700–1921* (Montreal: McGill-Queen's University Press, 2018). By contrast, the factory inspection movement drew on the concept of normed quantity of air—fixed by the Moscow Duma in April 1879 at one cubic sazhen' per person in both living quarters and workshops. Robert Thurston, *Liberal City, Conservative State: Moscow and Russia's Urban Crisis, 1906–1914* (New York: Oxford University Press, 1987), 142. In 1901, the *zemstvo* doctor (and the future Minister of Agriculture) Andrei Shingarev produced a report tracing "high mortality and low population growth" in a rural region to two factors: the region's relative "landlessness," and the "influence of housing." To measure the latter, Shingarev adopted the "normal" volume of air fixed by Hungarian hygienist Korosi. A.I. Shingarev, *Selo Novo-Zhivotinnoe i derevnia Mokhovatka v sanitarnom otnoshenii: Opyt san.-ekon. issled. zem. vracha A. [Sh!] Shingareva* (Saratov: 1901), 29, 189.

40. I. A. Verner, *Sovremennoe khozyaistvo goroda Moskvy* (Moscow: Gorodskaya Tip., 1913), 187.

41. Zagriatskov, *Sotsial'naia,* 17; Verner, *Sovremennoe,* 186.

42. Verner, *Sovremennoe,* 187.

43. Mamaev, *Gorodskoe,* 91, 95.

44. Pravilova, *A Public Empire,* 94. As Pravilova observes, the relative strength of a state is commonly judged by its capacity to enforce "the security of property," but, as she goes on to demonstrate, the relationship between state capacity and the defense of property rights in the Russian Empire was far more ambivalent than this simple pairing would suggest. A related point is made in a social scientific register by Kiren Aziz Chaudhry, who argued that weak states were, in fact, more likely to "nationalize" privately-held assets, whatever their ideological bent, due to the challenges they encountered in raising revenue through information-intensive tax and market systems. Kiren Aziz Chaudhry, "The Myths of the Market and the Common History of Late Developers," *Politics & Society.* 1993; 21, no. 3, 245–274, 257.

45. I.A. Verner, *Deyatel'nost' Moskovskoi Gorodskoi Dumy v 1909–1912 godakh* (Moscow: Gorodskaya Tipografiya, 1912), 36.

46. A key argument made by Pravilova, *A Public Empire*, especially 99.

47. Verner, *Deiatel'nost'*, 46; Verner, *Sovremennoe*, 295.

48. Verner, *Deiatel'nost'*, 49.

49. Verner, *Sovremennoe*, 329; see also L. F. Pisarkova, *Moskovskaya gorodskaya duma 1863–1917* (Moscow: Mosgorarkhiv, 1998), 205; Hamm, "Breakdown," 183.

50. Verner, *Deiatel'nost'*, 46; *Istoriya Moskvy*, vol. 5, 705.

51. *Istoriya Moskvy*, vol. 5, 692. These included not only powers of compulsion, such as was needed to force sewer connection, but also the generation of information about the urban environment necessary to its development. *Istoriya Moskvy*, vol. 5, 678. Plans to increase municipal revenue in Moscow by performing a new appraisal of the city's real estate based on its market valuation rather than a review of its annual income, for instance, foundered due to a sense that the new measure was beyond the capacity of the city uprava.

52. Thurston, *Liberal*, 141.

53. Verner, *Sovremennoe*, 188.

54. *Istoriya Moskvy*, vol. 5, 695. The uprava's efforts to manage the disposal of city-owned land were equally limited, here not by Duma members themselves, but by the central government's refusal to allow the city to contract leases for terms longer than 12 years without approval from the Ministry of Internal Affairs, an approval process so cumbersome that it kept prices for city-owned lands artificially low. A. Mikhailovsky, *Deiatel'nost' moskovskogo samoupravleniya*, *Izvestia Moskovskoi gorodskoi dumy*, 1917, 9; Mamaev, *Gorodskoe*, 91.

55. Verner, *Sovremennoe*, 191.

56. Russian State Historic Archives (RGIA) f. 560, op. 26, d. 1111, ll. 6, 11, 12.

57. Rents quintupled between 1901 and 1911. *Istoriya Moskvy*, vol. 5, 679.

58. Crowding persisted despite a quadrupling in the number of bunks in the Khitrovka flophouses, built privately and given to city ownership, between 1902 and 1912. (Verner, *Sovremennoe*, 179.) The city's vacancy rate fell from 5.2 percent in 1902 to 3.3 percent in 1912, a hair above the going rate of 3.0 percent considered indicative of shortage.

59. Verner, *Sovremennoe*, 179.

60. V.N. Gursky, *Kvartiranty i domovladel'tsy: Prava i obiazannosti ikh po novomu zakonu 27 avgusta 1916 goda* (Moscow: tip. T-va. I. D. Sytina, 1917), 7.

61. Kropotkin, "Dwellings," 105.

62. Kropotkin, "Dwellings," 107.

63. State Archive of the Russian Federation (GARF) f. 1788, op. 9, d. 19, l. 18.

64. Susanna Magri, "Housing," in *Capital Cities at War: Paris, London, Berlin, 1914–1919*, ed. Jay Winter and Jean-Louis Robert (Cambridge: Cambridge University Press, 1997), 378–9, 381. In mid-1915, the landlords received a concession in the form of mortgage payment suspensions, shifting the burden of relief onto the banks.

65. Magri, "Housing," 389.

66. Magri, "Housing," 410.

67. Peter Gatrell, *A Whole Empire Walking: Refugees in Russia During World War I* (Bloomington, IN: Indiana University Press, 1999), 3, 54–5.

68. *Istoriya Moskvy,* vol. 5, 698.

69. Gursky, *Kvartiranty,* 8.

70. Gursky, *Kvartiranty,* 9.

71. Gursky, *Kvartiranty,* 13.

72. Magri, "Housing," 380.

73. Hamm, "Breakdown," 191; *Krasnaya Moskva,* 332.

74. GARF f. 1788, op. 9, d. 19, l. 28.

75. Brian Goldstein, *The Roots of Urban Renaissance: Gentrification and the Struggle over Harlem* (Cambridge, MA: Harvard University Press, 2017).

76. *Krasnaya Moskva,* 334. Kuzovkov further alleged that landlords wished for the city to take over building repairs on private properties.

77. The question of whether rising real estate values should factor into the regulation of housing during the war was taken up several times by the uprava, which welcomed a landlord lobbying group to a summer 1916 meeting on the topic. The landlords insisted that the "the value of [their] real estate pays no role in the budgets of landlords," nor should it be considered in the regulation of rents, not only because they considered their real estate "only a piece of property, and not an object of trade," but also because of "the uncertain future of the general economic state of the market [*kon'yunktura*] for real estate after the end of war." GARF f. 1838, op. 1, d. 1197, l. 4.

78. TsAGM f. 179, op. 3, d. 1829, l. 6. The housing reformers included E. I. Al'brekht and I. A. Verner.

79. A. N. Voznesensky, *Moskva v 1917 godu* (Moscow: Gosizdat, 1928), 33–4.

80. See Chapter 3.

81. Voznesensky, *Moskva,* 58.

82. GARF f. 1834, op. 3, d. 595, unpaginated flyers: Tovarishchi! Partiya sotsialistov-revoliutsionerov "v borbe obretish [*sic*] ty pravo svoyo."

83. GARF f. 1789, op. 2, d. 9a, l. 12.

84. *Vestnik Vserossiyskago Soiuza Gorodov: Gorod.* no. 12–13, 1. Petrograd was in the process of embarking upon the same: GARF f. 1789, op. 2, d. 9a, l. 6.

85. N.I. Bronshtein, *Instruktsiya dlia uchreditelei DOMOVYKH ORGANIZATSII [s prilozheniem 'polozhenie o domovykh organizatsiyakh']*. (Izvestia moskovskago soveta predstavitelei raionnykh dum, Moskva, 1917), 15–6.

86. *Vestnik Vserossiyskago Soiuza Gorodov: Gorod.* no. 12–13, 1.

87. GARF f. 1788, op. 9, d. 19, l. 5.

88. GARF f. 1788, op. 9, d. 19, ll. 5, 21.

89. GARF f. 1788, op. 9, d. 19, l. 380b.

90. GARF f. 1788, op. 9, d. 19, l. 4.

91. GARF f. 1788, op. 9, d. 19, l. 380b.

92. GARF f. 1788, op. 9, d. 19, l. 6.

93. In addition to works by Bliznakov and Kotkin already cited, see Christina Crawford, *Spatial Revolution: Architecture and Planning in the Early Soviet Union* (Ithaca, NY: Cornell University Press, 2022); Steven Harris, *Communism on Tomorrow Street: Mass Housing and Everyday Life after Stalin* (Baltimore: The Woodrow Wilson Center Press and the Johns Hopkins

University Press, 2013); Christine Varga-Harris, *Stories of House and Home: Soviet Apartment Life During the Khrushchev Years* (Ithaca, NY: Cornell University Press, 2015); Susan Reid, "Communist Comfort: Socialist Modernism and the Making of Cosy Homes in the Khrushchev Era," *Gender & History* (21)3, 465; among many others.

94. Kropotkin, "Dwellings," 108.

95. *Evakuatsiya i rekvizitsiya: spravochnik deistvuyushchikh uzakonenii i rasporyazhenii po evakuatsii, rozysku evakuirovannykh gruzov i rekvizitsii* (Petrograd: Izd. Evakuatsionno-rekvizitsionnogo otdela, 1916).

96. Eric Lohr, "Patriotic Violence and the State: The Moscow Riots of May 1915," *Kritika: Explorations in Russian and Eurasian History* (4) 3, (2003), 607–26; Anne O'Donnell, "Khozyaistvennaya zhizn i vlast' v Moskve, 1914–1920," *Goroda imperii v gody Velikoi voiny i revoliutsii*, ed. A. Miller, D. Chernyi (St. Petersburg: Nestor-Istoriya, 2017), 19–51.

97. On the idea of the Revolution as a wellspring of political authority see Lynn Hunt, *Politics, Culture, and Class in the French Revolution* (Berkeley, CA: University of California Press, 1984); Dan Edelstein, "Do We Want a Revolution without Revolution? Reflections on Political Authority," *French Historical Studies*, 35, no. 2 (Spring 2012).

98. N. Sukhanov, cited by *Witnesses to the Russian Revolution*, ed. Roger Pethybridge (London: George Allen & Unwin, Ltd., 1964), 153.

99. Voznesensky, *Moskva*, 42.

100. Voznesensky, *Moskva*, 41.

101. Voznesensky, *Moskva*, 42.

102. "And that only in cases when it is crystal clear that the family is going to be located together with its head." RGIA f. 560, op. 26, d. 1413, ll. 4, 75; RGIA f. 560, op. 26, d. 1409, l. 121.

103. RGIA f. 560, op. 26, d. 1409, l. 145.

104. RGIA f. 560, op. 26, d. 1409, l. 19.

105. RGIA f. 560, op. 26, d. 1409, l. 24.

106. RGIA f. 560, op. 26, d. 1409, l. 24.

107. RGIA f. 560, op. 26, d. 1409, l. 19.

108. RGIA f. 560, op. 26, d. 1413, ll.139–142; RGIA f. 560, op. 41, d. 155. Things that could be requisitioned included "food supplies and means of transport"; things that could be "temporarily occupied" included "spaces" and "pieces of land."

109. RGIA f. 560, op. 26, d. 1413, l. 152

110. RGIA f. 560, op. 26, d. 1413, l. 5.

111. TsAGM f. 179, op. 3, d. 1831, l. 1.

112. TsAGM f. 179, op. 3, d. 1831, l. 2.

113. TsAGM f. 179, op. 3, d. 1829, ll. 8–9. With one abstention, on the grounds that the text of the measure had not been shared in advance.

114. RGIA f. 560, op. 26, d. 1413, l. 150

Chapter 1: Making Space for Revolution: Sorting People and Spaces in the Revolutionary City

1. RGAE f. 7733, op. 1, d. 120, ll. 150, 154.

2. RGAE f. 7733, op. 1, d. 120, l. 150.

3. RGAE f. 7733, op. 1, d. 120, l. 156.

4. Silvana Malle, *The Economic Organization of War Communism, 1918–1921* (Cambridge: Cambridge University Press, 1985), p. 36.

5. "Decree on Land" appearing in *Izvestia* no. 209 (Oct. 28, 1917).

6. These decrees and the conditions of their composition are treated in detail by V. V. Zhuravlyov, *Dekrety Sovetskoi vlasti 1917–1920 gg. kak istorichesky istochnik Zakonodatelnye akty v sfere obobshchestvleniya kapitalisticheskoi sobstvennosti* (Moscow: Izd. Nauka, 1979).

7. A. A. Voronetskaia, "Organizatsiya VSNKh i ego rol' v natsionalizatsii promyshlennosti," *Istoricheskie zapiski*, 1953, no. 43, 18–9.

8. RGAE f. 7733, op. 1, d. 343, l. 191. In the city of Ryazan, agents of the Commissariat of Government Control who happened to be passing through reported that the city's 65 "trading enterprises, even before the decree on the nationalization of enterprises, were given to the local 'Union of Trade-Industrial Employees,' by the order of that very same Union." The Goskon agents, referring to the transfer as "nationalization" in spite of the fact that it had been executed without the involvement of a state institution of any kind, let alone a "national" one, complained that upon seizing the firms, the Union of Trade-Industrial Employees had proceeded to disburse income and profits as it saw fit, "without waiting for general orders on the realization of sums being received for nationalized Goods [capitalization original]." GARF f. 4390, op. 2, d. 276, l. 39.

9. RGAE f. 7733, op. 1, d. 343, l. 191.

10. Verdery, "Fuzzy Property", 55.

11. Malle, *Economic*; see also Lars T. Lih, *Bread and Authority in Russia, 1914–1921* (Berkeley: University of California Press, 1990).

12. "Decree on Land" *Izvestia*, op. cit, Oct. 28, 1917.

13. A.L. Fraiman, *Forpost sotsialisticheskoi revoliutsii: Petrograd v pervye mesiatsy sovetskoi vlasti* (Leningrad: Nauka, 1969), p. 328.

14. GARF f. R-130, op. 1, d. 4, l. 1.

15. V. V. Zhuravlyov, *Dekrety Sovetskoi Vlasti 1917–1920 gg. Kak istorichesky istochnik* (Moscow: Izd. Nauka, 1979), 334–336. Zhuravlyov notably includes discussion of the seizure of real estate alongside the means of production, but does not include movable property in the analysis.

16. Zhuravlyov, *Dekrety*, 341.

17. Zhuravlyov, *Dekrety*, 343–346.

18. GARF f. 393, op. 5, d. 109a, l. 40.

19. GARF f. 393, op. 5, d. 109a, ll, 3, 5, 90b.

20. A common revolutionary phenomenon, as noted by Lynn Hunt, *Politics, Culture, and Class in the French Revolution* (Berkeley, CA: University of California Press, 1984)

21. GARF f. 393, op. 5, d. 109a, ll. 50, 51. The housing commissions were instructed to assess space by determining which residents "do not use all the rooms [in their apartments] or," conversely, "live in just one room."

22. GARF f. 393, op. 5, d. 109a, l. 44.

23. GARF f. 393, op. 5, d. 109a, l. 44

24. GARF f. 393, op. 5, d. 109a, l. 41, GARF f. 4390, op. 2, d. 281, l. 94.

25. In the Yelets proposal, municipalization was one plank of a much broader effort at city planning that would divide the city up into quadrants tiered according to location and

amenities: enterprises determined to have "wide, good storage space are to be turned into central warehouses," while shops "located in convenient places in the city's neighborhoods will be designated as municipalized." Finally, "little shops with limited quantities of goods, dull, and outside of convenient areas, are to be closed." GARF f. 4390, op. 3, d. 180, l. 1.

26. TsAGM f. 1514, op. 1, d. 5, ll. 33, 67.

27. GARF f. 393, op. 5, d. 109a, l. 90b.

28. GARF f. 4390, op. 4, d. 27, l. 60b.

29. Diane Koenker, *Moscow Workers and the 1917 Revolution* (Princeton, NJ: Princeton University Press, 1981), 366. Frederick Corney, *Telling October: Memory and the Making of the Bolshevik Revolution* (Ithaca: Cornell University Press, 2004). James von Geldern, *Bolshevik Festivals, 1917–1920* (Berkeley: University of California Press, 1993).

30. GARF 4390, op. 4, d. 44, l. 39.

31. Hubertus F. Jahn, "The Housing Revolution in Petrograd 1917–1920," *Jahrbücher Für Geschichte Osteuropas* 38, no. 2 (1990): 212–27. Citation, 217.

32. As detailed in V. F. Klementyev: *V Bolshevitskoi Moskve 1918–1920* (Moscow: Russky put', 1998), 138–40.

33. Fraiman, *Forpost*, 328–9.

34. M. N. Potekhin, *Pervyi Soviet proletarskoi diktatury* (Leningrad: Lenizdat, 1966), 170. *Pravda*, March 2 1918, no. 34, cited in Fraiman, *Forpost*, 329. Potekhin, 169, notes that the rent was to be paid by the previous bourgeois tenants.

35. NIOR, f. 369 (V. D. Bonch-Bruevich), carton 397, d. 14. "Recollections of A. Monisov, May 1927."

36. *Krasnaya Moskva (Red Moscow)*, 336. The authors of *Red Moscow* insisted that Moscow's municipalization order "arose outside of any connection with the previous battle between the population and landlords," was modeled solely on the Sovnarkom's abandoned order, and was limited to general provisions so as not to contradict any future all-Russian measure. But, in fact, the Mossoviet's order operated within the terms of the city's prerevolutionary debates, with their focus on ownership and their hesitancy to consider the redistribution of space (and its inevitable counterpart, concentration) that would soon become ubiquitous.

37. *Vestnik Vserossiyskago Soiuza Gorodov: Gorod.* Moscow, no. 12–13, 1917.

38. *Krasnaya Moskva*, 336,

39. Koenker, *Moscow Workers*, 337.

40. On the invention and application of "counterrevolution" against wide-ranging groups and political enemies, see Peter Holquist, *Making War, Forging Revolution: Russia's Continuum of Crisis, 1914–1921* (Cambridge, MA: Harvard University Press, 2002), chapter 3; Vladlen Izmozik, *Glaza i ushi rezhima: Gosudarstvenny politichesky kontrol' za naseleniem sovetskoi Rossii v 1918–1928 godakh* (St. Petersburg: Izd-vo Sankt-Peterburgskogo Universiteta ekonomiki i finansov, 1995), 63.

41. Timothy Colton, *Moscow: Governing the Socialist Metropolis* (Cambridge, MA: The Belknap Press of Harvard University Press, 1996). Yuri Aleksandrovich Poliakov, *Moskovskie trudiashchiesia v oborone sovetskoi stolitsy v 1919 godu,* (Moscow: Izd. Akademii nauk, 1958); A. Ya. Grunt and V. I. Startsev, *Petrograd-Moskva Iyul' Noyabr' 1917* (Moscow: Politizdat, 1984); G. S. Ignatiev, *Moskva v pervy god proletarskoi diktatury* (Moscow: Nauka, 1974); V. A. Klimenko, *Bor'ba s kontrrevolyutsiei v Moskve, 1917–1920* (Moscow: Nauka, 1978). S. A. Smith. "Moscow Workers and the Revolutions of 1905 and 1917." *Soviet Studies*, 36, no. 2 (1984): 282–89.

42. Tsentral'nyi Gosudarstvennyi Arkhiv Sankt-Peterburga (TsGASP) f. 1000, op. 2, d. 84, l. 17.

43. TsGASP f. 1000, op. 2, d. 84, ll. 9, 11.

44. TsGASP f. 1000, op. 2, d. 84, l. 17.

45. RGIA f. 560, op. 41, d. 159, l. 1.

46. RGAE, f. 7733, op. 1, d. 82a, ll. 27, 72, 74.

47. *Moskovsky Vechernii Chas*, March 11 [February 26 o.s.], 1918, no. 1, 2.

48. P. D. Malkov, *Zapiski komendanta Kremlya* (Moscow: Molodaya Gvardiya, Third edition, 1967), 96, 130; Colton, *Moscow*, 162.

49. The right to sell real estate was abolished separately from the abolition of private property in real estate in toto. See *VTsIK—Sbornik Dekretov* (Moscow: Gosizdat, 1920), 113. Zhuravlyov, *Dekrety*, 334.

50. Narkomfin assented to the condition, possibly because the owner held American citizenship. RGAE, f. 7733, op. 1, d. 79, ll. 19, 32.

51. RGAE, f. 7733, op. 1, d. 79, l. 32.

52. RGAE, f. 7733, op. 1, d. 79, l. 27.

53. GARF f. 4390, op. 1, d. 33, l. 18.

54. RGAE, f. 7733, op. 1, d. 79, l. 7.

55. RGAE, f. 7733, op. 1, d. 78, l. 35.

56. GARF f. 4390, op. 1, d. 33, l. 66.

57. RGAE, f. 7733, op. 1, d. 79, l. 58.

58. *Moskovsky Vechernii Chas: gazeta politicheskaya i literaturnaya.* March 11 [February 26] 1918, no. 1, 2.

59. RGAE, f. 7733, op. 1, d. 76, l. 2.

60. *Postanovleniya Moskovskogo Soveta po Zhilishchnomu i Zemelnomu Voprosam* (Moscow: 8-aya tipografiya, 1918), 55–56.

61. GARF f. 4390, op. 4, d. 44, l. 26.

62. Peter Holquist, "State Violence as Technique: The Logic of Violence in Soviet Totalitarianism," in *Landscaping the Human Garden*, ed. Amir Weiner (Palo Alto, CA: Stanford University Press, 2003), 22, 33.

63. TsGASP f. 1000, op. 2, d. 84, ll. 9, 11, 95.

64. On the connection between norms and the older subsistence minimums in land see David Darrow, *Tsardom of Sufficiency, Empire of Norms: Statistics, Land Allotments, and Agrarian Reform in Russia, 1700–1921* (Montreal: McGill-Queen's University Press, 2018), 242–4.

65. GARF f. R-130, op. 2, d. 77, l. 56.

66. TsAGM f. 2382, op. 1, d. 1, ll. 2, 3 dating from 2 June 1918.

67. GARF f. R-130, op. 2, d. 79, l. 22, 27.

68. Kolonitskii, Boris I. "Antibourgeois Propaganda and Anti-'Burzhui' Consciousness in 1917." *The Russian Review*, 53, no. 2 (1994), 193.

69. Sarah Cameron, *The Hungry Steppe: Famine, Violence, and the Making of Soviet Kazakhstan* (Ithaca, NY: Cornell University Press, 2018), 74. Moshe Lewin, "Who was the Soviet Kulak?," *Soviet Studies*, 18, no. 2 (1966), 189–212.

70. Kolonitskii, "*Antibourgeois*," 190.

71. GARF f. R-130, op. 2, d. 77, ll. 5, 6.

72. TsAGM f. 2435, op. 1, d. 85, l. 32.

73. I. S. Rat'kovsky, *Krasny terror i deyatel'nost' VChK v 1918 godu* (St. Petersburg: Izd. S. Peterburgskogo universiteta, 2006), appendix table 2.

74. GARF f. R-130, op. 2, d. 96, l. 55.

75. There was a private rental market for rooms in individual small buildings. See Klementyev, *V bolshevitskoi*, 176.

76. TsAGM f. 2435, op. 1, d. 85, l. 32.

77. GARF f. R-130, op. 2, d. 77, ll. 260b, 28.

78. GARF f. R-130, op. 3, d. 122, l. 37.

79. GARF f. R-130, op. 2, d. 77, l. 163

80. GARF f. R-130, op. 2, d. 77, l. 8.

81. GARF f. R-130, op. 3, d. 122, l. 15.

82. TsAGM f. 2435, op. 1, d. 85, l. 32.

83. For the Political Red Cross, see Stuart Finkel, "The 'Political Red Cross' and the Genealogy of Rights Discourse in Revolutionary Russia," *The Journal of Modern History*, 89, no. 1, March 2017, 79–118.

84. GARF f. R-130, op. 2, d. 77, l. 80.

85. GARF f. R-130, op. 2, d. 77, l. 79.

86. Okunev, N. P., *Dnevnik Moskvicha 1917–1924.* (Paris: YMCA Press, 1990), 216.

87. See Chapter 4.

88. GARF f. R-130, op. 2, d. 77, l. 145.

89. *Izvestia* November 29, 1918. As noted below, a clipping of the article was sent to Bonch-Bruevich by an irate transport worker, underlined to make sure he noted important passages. GARF f. R-130, op. 2, d. 77, ll. 198 199.

90. Potekhin estimates the figure to be more than double that, amounting to 65,000 worker families. Potekhin, *Pervy Soviet proletarskoi diktatury*, 169.

91. For narrative strategy in property see Carol M. Rose, "Property as Storytelling: Perspectives from Game Theory, Narrative Theory, Feminist Theory," *Yale Journal of Law & the Humanities*, 1990; Vol. 2 (37): 37–57.

92. TsGASP f. 3201, op. 1, d. 55, l. 36.

93. GARF f. R-130, op. 2, d. 77, ll. 198.

94. A. N. Voznesensky, *Moskva v 1917 godu* (Moscow: Gosizdat, 1928), 42.

95. GARF f. R-130, op. 2, d. 77, l. 2.

96. Reports made by inspectors at the First House of Soviets in the fall of 1918 suggest a fairly typical process of review, despite the prestige of the address. Controllers studied the building's account books, determined the total number of rooms and apartments in the building, how many of these were occupied, and by whom. Because residence in the First House of Soviets was a privilege afforded only to certain employees, controllers confirmed the procedure for awarding rooms—"the apartments are given to members of the Communist party or others by recommendation of active party members"—and reviewed the employment status of residents. GARF f. 4390, op. 4, d. 43, ll. 5, 13.

97. Arjun Appadurai, "Introduction: commodities and the politics of value," *The Social Life of Things: Commodities in Cultural Perspective*, ed. Appadurai (Cambridge: Cambridge University Press, 1986), 34.

98. GARF f. 4085, op. 22, d. 166, ll. 86–91.

99. GARF f. 4085, op. 22, d. 165, l. 107.

100. GARF f. R-130, op. 2, d. 77, l. 152.

101. TsAGM f. 2431, op. 1, d. 97, l. 36.

102. RGAE f. 7733, op. 1, d. 171, l. 94; RGAE f. 7733, op. 1, d. 6260, l. 87.

103. I follow here the notion of "property concepts" offered by Caroline Humphrey and Katherine Verdery, who use it to explore not a unitary definition of property but rather the ways in which the concept of property is deployed in economic, political, and other contexts. Humphrey and Verdery, *Property in Question*, 2.

104. Carol Rose argues that legibility is not merely an attribute of property but its signal characteristic—what separates property from mere "territoriality" is a shared knowledge of what belongs to whom, such that owners need not guard their territories, as animals do. Carol Rose, "Property and Expropriation: Themes and Variations in American Law," *Utah Law Review*, 2000, no. 1, (Nov. 2000), 4.

105. RGAE, f. 7733, op. 1, d. 79, ll. 5, 45, 74

106. RGAE f. 7733, op. 1, d. 79, l. 36.

107. Jeremy Adelman, *Property Rules or the Rule of Property? Carol Rose on the History, Theory, and Rhetoric of Ownership*, review essay of Carol M. Rose, *Property and Persuasion: Essays on the History, Theory, and Rhetoric of Ownership. Law & Social Inquiry*, 21, no. 4 (1996): 1041–60, 1057. See also Rose, "Property as Storytelling" (1990).

108. GARF f. R-130, op. 2, d. 77, l. 3.

109. GARF f. 4085, op. 22, d. 422, l. 15.

110. GARF f. 4085, op. 22, d. 422, ll. 7–8. Russified city name spelling original.

111. GARF f. 4085, op. 22, d. 422, l. 4.

112. GARF f. R-130, op. 2, d. 79, l. 24.

113. For the professional census of Moscow see Russian State Archive of Socio-Political History (RGASPI) f. 5, op. 1, d. 2710, l. 117. For the figures on the Mossoviet, see RGASPI f. 5, op. 1, d. 2710, l. 38. See also: S. A. Fedyukin, *Veliky Oktyabr' i intelligentsia: iz istorii vovlecheniya staroi intelligentsii v stroitelstvo sotsializma* (Moscow: Nauka, 1972). E. G. Gimpelson, *Sovetskie upravlentsy, 1917–1920 gg.* (Moscow: Institut Rossiiskoi istorii RAN, 1998). M. P. Iroshnikov, "K voprosu o slome burzhuaznoi gosudarstvennoi mashiny v Rossii," in Yu. S. Tokarev, ed., *Problemy gosudarstvennogo stroitelstva v pervye gody sovetskoi vlasti: sbornik statei* (Leningrad: Nauka, 1973).

Chapter 2: Movable People, Immovable Things: The Dispossession, Destruction, and Redistribution of Household Goods

1. This account of events at No. 3 Sadovaya-Chernogryazskaya is drawn from GARF f. 4390, op. 4, d. 44, ll. 42–48.

2. S. N. Ikonnikov, *Organizatsiia i deiatelnost RKI v 1920–1925 gg.* (Moscow: Izd. Akademii Nauk, 1960); S. N. Ikonnikov, *Sozdanie i deyatel'nost' obedinyonnykh organov TsKK-RKI v 1923–1934 gg.* (Moscow: Nauka, 1971); Thomas Remington, "Institution Building in Bolshevik Russia: The Case of 'State Kontrol,'" *Slavic Review*, 41, no. 1 (1982): 91–103.

3. GARF f. 4390, op. 2, d. 276, l. 173.

4. According to Belsky, controllers at the Bureau of Complaint approached chekists only after performing initial investigations to determine whether a complaint had merit. "[A

controller] would never allow himself to disturb an employee of the ChK." In return, Belsky claimed, "the majority of the employees of the ChK relate to the work of the Bureau with goodwill and understanding of the importance of the tasks," understanding "that the bureau was created with the special agreement of Coms. Dzerzhinsky and Mantsev," senior officials at the Cheka, "and that it was meant to improve the work of the ChK." GARF f. 4390, op. 2, d. 276, l. 175.

5. As Belsky curtly informed Stalin in writing shortly after the meeting, the number of complaints received by the Bureau was growing in direct proportion to its success in opening regional branch offices, something Belsky boldly told Stalin, "You could verify yourself if you gave yourself the trouble of reviewing even superficially the bureau's monthly reports. To make such statements on the basis of rumors, whispers, and so forth is thoughtless in the extreme for a people's commissar." GARF f. 4390, op. 2, d. 276, l. 181.

6. K. V. Kharchenko, *Vlast'—Imushchestvo—Chelovek: peredel sobstvennosti v bolshevistskoi Rossii 1917–nachala 1921 gg.* (Moscow: Russky dvor, 2000), 185. Important analysis also appears in recent histories of the Cheka, especially A. G. Teplyakov *"Nepronitsaemye nedra": VChK-OGPU v Sibiri, 1918–1929 gg.* (Moscow: AIRO-XXI, 2007).

7. Martin Dean, Constantin Goschler, and Philipp Ther, eds. *Robbery and Restitution: The Conflict over Jewish Property in Europe*, 1st ed. (New York, NY: Berghahn Books, 2008), 8.

8. Gotz Aly, *Hitler's Beneficiaries: Plunder, Racial War, and the Nazi Welfare State*, trans. Jefferson Chase (New York: Metropolitan Books, 2007). Leora Auslander, "Coming Home? Jews in Postwar Paris," *Journal of Contemporary History*, 2005; 40 (2): 237–59.

9. For a comprehensive explanation of what constituted theft with regard to different types of property in Soviet socialism and the centrality of state property to the definition, see Juliette Cadiot's important treatment of the topic, *La société des voleurs: Propriété et socialisme sous Staline* (Paris: Les Éditions de l'EHESS, 2021).

10. Nikita Okunev, *Dnevnik Moskvicha 1917–1924* (Paris: YMCA Press, 1990), 192.

11. As Mark Smith notes, "personal property" was not synonymous with movable property; small structures might also qualify as personal property, meaning they could be transferred by sale, gift, rental, or legacy, so long as "no profit accumulated." Mark Smith, *The Property of Communists: The Urban Housing Program from Stalin to Khrushchev*, (DeKalb, IL: Northern Illinois University Press, 2010), 143.

12. Richard Pipes, cited by Kharchenko, 213. Sean McMeekin's analysis of dispossession in *History's Greatest Heist: The Looting of Russia by the Bolsheviks* (New Haven, CT: Yale, 2008) shares with Pipes a focus on the instrumentalism of dispossession in Bolshevik hands, but with the wealth gained through seizure put toward the end of thuggish enrichment as opposed to political submission.

13. Tsuyoshi Hasegawa, *Crime and Punishment in the Russian Revolution: Mob Justice and Police in Petrograd* (Cambridge, MA: Harvard University Press, 2018), 15.

14. Eric Lohr and Joshua Sanborn, "1917: Revolution as Demobilization and State Collapse," *Slavic Review*, 76, no. 3, (Fall 2017), 703–9.

15. *Krasnaya Moskva*, 634. Figures presented by the Mossoviet in 1920 suggested that ordinary theft (*krazha*) in Moscow rose threefold, from 3,507 incidents in 1914 to 11,036 incidents in 1918, while robberies (*grabyozh*) rose from 49 to 421 and armed robbery from 2 incidents in 1914 to 570 in 1918. These figures only grew in 1919, leveling out in 1920 and entering decline in 1921.

16. Dan Edelstein, "Do We Want a Revolution without Revolution? Reflections on Political Authority," *French Historical Studies*, 35, no. 2 (Spring 2012), 274.

17. Alvin W. Gouldner, "Stalinism: A Study of Internal Colonialism," *Telos* 34, (Winter 1977–1978), 11, 29. As Sarah Cameron notes, "the most important consequence of the first collectivization drive was the Kazakhs' impoverishment." Sarah Cameron, *The Hungry Steppe: Famine, Violence, and the Making of Soviet Kazakhstan* (Ithaca, NY: Cornell University Press, 2018), 107.

18. Jan Gross, *Revolution from Abroad: The Soviet Conquest of Poland's Western Ukraine and Western Belorussia—Expanded Edition* (Princeton, NJ: Princeton University Press, 2002), chapter 2.

19. Cadiot, *La société des voleurs*, 13, 17–8. Railway buffet directors, for instance, were thought to benefit from a thieving background and hired on this basis.

20. Smith, *Property of Communists*, 143.

21. GARF f. A-353, op. 4, d. 317, ll. 68, 680b.

22. Decree of April 16, 1920 published in *Izvestia VTsIK* April 22, 1920, no. 85, with addendums published in *Izvestia VTsIK*, July 25, 1920, no. 163.

23. As a matter of law and recordkeeping, aryanization took sharply different forms in Western Europe, where officials sought to preserve the sanctity of property while destroying one category of owners and thus elaborated an extensive legal infrastructure for dispossession, and in Eastern Europe, in territories that had undergone Sovietization in recent years and thus a. had far less movable personal property available for seizure and b. lacked an equivalent legal infrastructure for property. Dieter Pohl, "The Robbery of Jewish Property in Eastern Europe under German Occupation, 1939–1942," in *Robbery and Restitution*, ed. Dean, Goschler, and Ther, 74.

24. See Neil Harding, *Lenin's Political Thought: Theory and Practice in the Democratic Revolution* (London: MacMillan, 1977), especially vol. 2, chapter 506.

25. *Evakuatsiya i rekvisitsiya: spravochnik deistvuyushchikh uzakonenii i rasporyazhenii po evakuatsii, rozysku evakuirovannykh gruzov i rekvizitsii.* (Petrograd: Izd. Evakuatsionno-rekvizitsionnogo otdela, 1916).

26. GARF f. 4390, op. 2, d. 281, l. 28.

27. GARF f. 4390, op. 4, d. 44, l. 38.

28. GARF f. 4085, op. 2, d. 422, l. 1.

29. If the Minister of Agriculture A. V. Krivoshein, for instance, initially asked that the Ministry receive the seized farm tools taken by the military out of conquered territories in East Prussia, later on he demanded free access to the seed produced by "enemy subject" firms within Russia itself. Eric Lohr, *Nationalizing the Russian Empire: The Campaign against Enemy Aliens during World War I* (Cambridge, MA: Harvard University Press, 2003), 63.

30. Peter Holquist, *Making War, Forging Revolution: Russia's Continuum of Crisis, 1914–1921* (Cambridge, MA: Harvard University Press, 2002).

31. RGAE f. 7733, op. 1, d. 925, l. 26.

32. RGAE f. 7733, op. 1, d. 925, l. 8

33. Hasegawa, *Crime and Punishment*, 8, 110–1.

34. Hasegawa, *Crime and Punishment*, 98–9.

35. Hasegawa, *Crime and Punishment*, 51.

36. Viktor Shklovsky, *A Sentimental Journey: Memoirs, 1917–1922*, trans. Richard Sheldon (Ithaca, NY: Cornell University Press, 1970), 146.

37. N. P. Okunev, *Dnevnik Moskvicha,* 132

38. Okunev, *Dnevnik Moskvicha,* 148.

39. A year later, neighborhood Chekas in Moscow ordered building committees to declare all weapons still held on the premises and individuals to bring their weapons in person to be registered at the Cheka's office. Notices announcing registration were routinely printed in Izvestia. MChK: Iz istorii moskovskoi chrezvychainoi komissii (1918–1921) (Moscow: Moskovsky rabochy, 1978), 14, 19, 102 (docs. 1, 6, 83).

40. Joshua Sanborn, *Imperial Apocalypse: The Great War and the Destruction of the Russian Empire.* (New York, NY: Oxford University Press, 2014), 86.

41. V. F. Klementyev, *V bolshevitskoi Moskve (1918–1920),* (Moscow: Russky put', 1998). On lethargic bourgeoisie, see 45; on searches, see 53.

42. RGAE f. 7733, op. 1, d. 120, l. 10.

43. RGAE f. 7733, op. 1, d. 120, l. 61.

44. RGAE f. 7733, op. 1, d. 120, l. 3.

45. TsGASP f. 1000, op. 2, d. 238, l. 9.

46. As described by Yanni Kotsonis, *States of Obligation: Taxes and Citizenship in the Russian Empire and Early Soviet Union* (Toronto: University of Toronto Press, 2014), 324–7.

47. RGAE f. 7733, op. 1, d. 120, l. 18.

48. On the creation of the Committees of the Poor and the postrevolutionary struggle to identify appropriate methods of assessment and collection see Kotsonis, *States of Obligation,* 322.

49. TsGASP f. 1000, op. 2, d. 238, l. 5, see the Moscow article RGAE f. 7733, op. 1, d. 171.

50. GARF f. 4390, op. 4, d. 82, l. 4.

51. GARF f. 4390, op. 4, d. 68, l. 31. Seizure continued to be performed for non-payment of the extraordinary tax. The household of Mendel Podnos, a resident of the city of Arzamas in the Nizhny Novgorod region, was seized in order to pay his one-time extraordinary revolutionary tax bill, assessed at 250,000 rubles. Podnos was known to the local Cheka as a "major timber speculator" and widely "considered a very rich man, as a railway contractor"; his bill was approved by the local Communist Party cell. His house was inventoried and goods were seized for auction after he fled. Held back from seizure were "those things necessary for the tax nonpayer and his family," though after Mendel disappeared the local police jailed his wife, Khava, and the local ispolkom embarked on the sale of "items of excess and luxury." GARF f. 4390, op. 4, d. 82, l. 4.

52. GARF f. 4390, op. 1, d. 33, l. 247.

53. GARF f. 4390, op. 1, d. 33, l. 247.

54. TsGASP f. 1000, op. 3, d. 276, ll. 46–51.

55. The VChK in Moscow routinely requisitioned motorcycles for its own use, and was occasionally admonished for doing so by the Sovnarkom. GARF f. R-130, op. 2, d. 97, l. 20.

56. TsGASP f. 1000, op. 3, d. 276, l. 45.

57. *MChK,* 19.

58. Impersonation was a problem for the Cheka in Petrograd as well. The Cheka's first official execution, performed on February 21, 1918, was of a "blackmailer and bandit" who went by the name of "Prince Eboli," and who pretended to be a Chekist during robberies. George Leggett, *The Cheka: Lenin's Political Police* (Oxford: Clarendon Press, 1981), 58; *Arkhiv VChK: sbornik*

dokumentov, eds. V. Vinogradov, A. Litvin, V. Khristoforov, N. Peremyshlennikova (Moscow: Kuchkovo pole, 2007), 168.

59. GARF f. A-353, op. 2, d. 436, l. 5. On Ya. Peters in the Cheka's early financial life, see Oleg Kapchinsky, *Gosbezopasnost' iznutri: Natsionalnyi i sotsialnyi sostav* (Moscow: EKSMO, 2005), 54–83.

60. *MChK,* 106.

61. *MChK,* 78.

62. Hannah Arendt argued that authoritarian regimes have a propensity for hiring criminals precisely in order to foster an "atmosphere of irregularity, nonrespectability, and insecurity." Hannah Arendt, *The Origins of Totalitarianism* (New York: Harcourt Brace Jovanovich, 1973), 429.

63. V. M. Chernov, *Che-ka: Materialy po deiatel'nosti chrezvychainykh komissii* (Berlin: Izd. Tsentral'nogo biuro Partii sotsialistov-revoliutsionerov, 1922), 134.

64. Gross, *Revolution,* 56.

65. A. G. Teplyakov, *"Nepronitsaemye nedra": VChK-OGPU v Sibiri, 1918–1929 gg.* (Moscow: AIRO-XXI, 2007), 83–5.

66. Teplyakov, *"Nepronitsaemye",* 79.

67. M. Ya. Latsis (Sudrabs), *Chrezvychainye komissii po borbe s kontr-revoliutsii* (Moscow: Gosizdat, 1921), 11. Due to "a whole series of technical difficulties," the text was published only in 1921, but written, Latsis claimed, in 1919. Tales of the nature of the Cheka's work breaking the men who performed it are legion. See, among others, Tepliakov, *"Nepronitsaemye",* 86; Chernov, *Che-ka,* 78.

68. Blackmail was also a common charge levied against agents of the Cheka itself. GARF f. A-353, op. 2, d. 436, l. 5.

69. Leggett, *The Cheka,* 30–1. A department to deal with speculation was added on December 11, 1917, and one on misconduct in office, or *prestuplenie po dolzhnosti,* in late January 1918.

70. GARF f. 4390, op. 2, d. 255, l. 42.

71. *Arkhiv VChK,* 158, 703.

72. *Arkhiv VChK* 165.

73. *Arkhiv VChK,* 160, 167.

74. *Arkhiv VChK,* 166.

75. GARF f. R-130, op. 2, d. 103, l. 3.

76. GARF f. 4390, op. 2, d. 255, l. 21.

77. *MChK,* 95.

78. GARF f. 4390, op. 2, d. 255, l. 24, for a teacher whose husband was wanted by the Cheka, but was away when agents came to arrest him, and arrested the teacher instead, setting up an ambush outside her door and arresting a co-worker who came to look for her the following day; GARF f. 4390, op. 2, d. 276, l. 174, for an account of a search conducted on the order of the Osoby Otdel of the VChK in November 1919, resulting in the arrest of Nikolai Tikhomirov and others who visited him, that was the result of a case of mistaken identity, as this Tikhomirov happened to have the same name as a different man wanted by the Cheka.

79. Chernov, *Che-ka,* 136.

80. GARF f. R-130, op. 2, d. 96, l. 4. Voevodsky's case suggests that the sort of perlustration described by Vladlen Izmozik that was in use in Petrograd at the time had also been adopted

by Moscow authorities. Vladlen Izmozik, *Glaza i ushi rezhima: Gosudarstvenny politichesky kontrol' za naseleniem sovetskoi Rossii v 1918–1928 godakh* (St. Petersburg: Izd-vo Sankt-Peterburgskogo Universiteta ekonomiki i finansov, 1995), chs. 3–4, 36–78. On the search of the living places of former officers conducted in late summer and early fall 1918, see GARF f. R-130, op. 2, d. 97, l. 50.

81. GARF f. 4390, op. 2, d. 255, l. 45.

82. GARF f. R-130, op. 2, d. 97, a file largely dedicated to searching for arrested people.

83. Teplyakov attests to the unwillingness of a number of Siberian Communist Party members to cooperate with the Cheka in its early years. Teplyakov, *"Nepronitsaemye"*, 81.

84. GARF f. R-130, op. 2, d. 96, l. 13.

85. GARF f. R-130, op. 2, d. 97, ll. 2–4. On the Cheka's perennial battle to control its own agents, see Kapchinsky, *Gosbezopasnost'*, 69, 84.

86. GARF f. R-130, op. 2, d. 97, l. 14.

87. *MChK*, 102.

88. GARF f. R-130, op. 2, d. 97, l. 15.

89. GARF f. R-130, op. 2, d. 96, l. 52, GARF f. R-130, op. 2, d. 97, l. 72a.

90. Shepelinsky is identified only by surname. Carr, E. H. "The Origin and Status of the Cheka." *Soviet Studies* 10, no. 1 (1958): 1–11. Peter Solomon notes the same in *Soviet Criminal Justice Under Stalin* (Cambridge: Cambridge University Press, 1996), 19. Vladimir Bonch-Bruevich's criticism of the Cheka coincided with the early portion of this campaign to rein in the Cheka, in the fall of 1918, as detailed in GARF f. R-130, op. 2, dd. 96, 97, 99, 102, 103. See also Kapchinsky, *Gosbezopasnost'*, 81; P. G. Sofinov, *Ocherki Istorii Vserossiyskoi Chrezvychainoi Komissii, 1917–1922 gg.* (Moscow: Gos. Izd-vo polit. Lit-ry, 1960); L. A. Boeva, *Osobennaya Kasta: VChK-OGPU i ukreplenie kommunisticheskogo rezhima v gody NEPa.* (Moscow: AIRO-XXI, 2009). For the development of the Cheka's role in economic life, see O. B. Mozokhin, *VChK-OGPU-NKVD na zashchite ekonomicheskoi bezopasnosti gosudarstva 1917–1941* (Moscow: Kuchkovo pole, 2016).

91. GARF f. 4390, op. 2, d. 281, l. 28.

92. GARF f. 4390, op. 2, d. 281, l. 22. Ozerevsky did not include a unit of measure, but the space most likely measured 15 × 15 arshins or sazhens.

93. GARF f. R-130, op. 2, d. 103, l. 3.

94. GARF f. 4390, op. 2, d. 281, l. 24

95. GARF f. 4390, op. 2, d. 281, l. 24.

96. GARF f. R-130, op. 2, d. 103, l. 2.

97. GARF f. 4390, op. 4, d. 45, l. 5.

98. GARF f. 4390, op. 4, d. 45, l. 7.

99. GARF f. 4390, op. 4, d. 45, l. 9.

100. GARF f. R-130, op. 2, d. 102, l. 9.

101. GARF f. A-353, op. 2, d. 441, l. 13. The agent's wife was later arrested on a train platform carrying 20 funts of sugar, 10 funts of coffee, and other goods. She was charged with speculation and brought to the Vyatka Cheka, where an agent, not her husband, took on her case. When this Cheka agent returned to work the following day, however, both the other agent's wife and the paper file charging her were gone. GARF f. A-353, op. 2, d. 441, l. 18.

102. GARF f. A-353, op. 2, d. 441, ll. 18, 78, 15, 17

103. GARF f. A-353, op. 2, d. 441, l. 3.

104. After seizing the chickens, agents released the peasant, who had been beaten. GARF f. A-353, op. 2, d. 441, ll. 18, 78, 15, 17

105. Likewise in Astrakhan, where a careful count revealed both an excess of cash and dozens more silver teaspoons than expected. GARF f. 4390, op. 4, d. 45, l. 9.

106. GARF f. 4085, op. 28, d. 20

107. The appellation became common quite soon after the Cheka's formation, and was notably durable. Yevgenia Albats, *The State Within a State: The KGB and its Hold on Russia Past, Present and Future* (New York: Farrar, Strauss and Giroux, 1994). The Lubyanka's earliest prisoners also referred to it as a city within a city, for its size and its world-like quality. *Che-ka: Materialy*, 164. Hannah Arendt observed that the "secret services have rightly been called a state within the state," not only in totalitarian regimes but in despotisms of other kinds, thanks to their possession of secret information about other parts of the state, which gave this branch "superiority over the others." Arendt further notes that the sort of financial separation seen at the Cheka, and in particular the "financing of police activities with income from its victims . . . survived all other changes" in secret policing across despotic and totalitarian states. Arendt, *Origins*, 425, 428.

108. GARF f. R-130, op. 2, d. 103, l. 3.

109. See previous section on the collection of the extraordinary tax.

110. GARF f. 4390, op. 2, d. 276, l. 73. A review of a district cheka outside of Astrakhan found that it had required a payment of 518 r. 55 k. from the soviet's economic council in return for "wool released from the warehouse of the Chrezvkom." Note that the Goskon agents' objection in this case was not that the Nikolaev cheka had demanded payment for the wool, but rather that the sovnarkhoz had indeed paid a sum of 519 r. 25 k. to the cheka, whereas the latter demanded only 518 r. 55 k., and the cheka had not made up the difference. GARF f. 4390, op. 4, d. 45, l. 7.

111. GARF f. R-130, op. 2, d. 103, l. 8. For more on the Cheka's early commercial ventures see Kapchinsky, *Gosbezopasnost'*, 74.

112. A perspective forcefully argued in McMeekin, *History's Greatest Heist*.

113. K. V. Kharchenko, *Vlast'—Imushchestvo—Chelovek: peredel sobstvennosti v bolshevistskoi Rossii 1917–nachala 1921 gg.* (Moscow: Russky dvor, 2000), 202. For more on the conflicting economic logics of seizure, see chapter 5.

114. GARF f. R-130, op. 2, d. 77, l. 138.

115. GARF f. R-130, op. 2, d. 77, l. 128.

116. *Izvestia* October 10, 1918, no. 220. See also GARF f. R-130, op. 2, d. 96, l.55.

117. TsGASP f. 3201, op. 1, d. 55, l. 66.

118. GARF f. R-130, op. 2, d. 77, l. 126.

119. GARF f. R-130, op. 2, d. 77, l. 135.

120. *Postanovleniya Moskovskogo Soveta po Zhilishchnomu i Zemelnomu Voprosam* (Moscow: 8-aya Tipografiya, 1918), 39–40.

121. TsAGM f. 2382, op. 1, d. 1, l. 10.

122. TsGASP f. 1000, op. 2, d. 136, l. 12. In the city of Kronstadt, near Petrograd, the soviet adopted a middle ground, embracing Moscow's four-tier categorization of the population, and declaring that households in the fourth category must be allowed to retain "the most essential" household goods, amounting to one single bed per person, and six chairs, one dining table, desk,

and cabinet per household. Like Petrograd, however, the city offered what it called the "norm" to residents in the third category, which consisted of the "essential" objects already listed, plus two more chairs and the right to substitute four of the chairs for a sofa if desired. GARF f. 393, op. 5, d. 109a, l. 35.

123. Acquisition of any items exceeding those specified was classified as "luxury/above the norm," and was to occur only with immediate cash payment in full and "by special order." TsGASP f. 1000, op. 2, d. 136, l. 15.

124. TsGASP f. 1000, op. 2, d. 136, l. 17.

125. Larissa Zakharova, "Le 26–28 Kamennoostrovski, Les tribulations d'un immeuble en Revolution," in *Saint Pètersbourg: Histoire, promenades, anthologie et dictionnaire* (Paris : Laffont, 2003), 486. See also chapter 6.

126. A variety of schemes were used to cover the risks associated with releasing nationalized furnishings into private households, including signed attestations of responsibility and the levying of fines.

127. GARF f. A-353, op. 4, d. 317, ll. 68, 68ob.

128. GARF f. A-353, op. 4, d. 317, ll. 68, 68ob.

129. GARF f. 4390, op. 4, d. 44, l. 38.

130. *Postanovleniya Moskovskogo Soveta po Zhilishchnomu i Zemelnomu Voprosam*, 41. Its "Instructions for the order of performing requisitions and confiscations" directed that rather than marking statization with movement to a warehouse, an inventory or receipt for the "confiscated or requisitioned property" would suffice, made in five copies: for the person being dispossessed, the building committee, the "warehouse or person" now physically in possession, the institution performing the requisition, and the local branch of Government Control. On the basis of these inventories, the Mossoviet's Economic Department further sought from the neighborhoods "weekly information about all the furniture released to institutions and private people . . . and for what sum," as well as information about "all things that might have some kind of artistic value, such as pictures, watercolors, pastels, oil paints, engravings, porcelain vases, and sculpture." TsAGM f. 54, op. 1, d. 32, l. 8.

131. The new tenants of an apartment previously occupied by the "runaway officer Khalafov," or, more accurately, "by his furniture," begged the local police to inventory the contents, which they did. But rather than taking it away, they "recorded and laid [it] out in the large room and then the room was sealed with the seal of the commissariat, also sealed were the cabinets located in the kitchen and other rooms . . . We live in fear of accidentally breaking the seals and what will happen to us, will we lose materially if this happens." TsAGM f. 54, op. 1, d. 51, l. 54.

132. TsGASP f. 1000, op. 4, d. 105, l. 58.

133. TsAGM f. 54, op. 1, d. 32, l. 7.

134. TsAGM f. 54, op. 1, d. 32, l. 41.

135. TsAGM f. 54, op. 1, d. 34, l. 68.

136. TsAGM f. 54, op. 1, d. 34, l. 68ob.

137. GARF f. 4085, op. 22, d. 381, l. 10.

138. GARF f. 4085, op. 22, d. 381, l. 9.

139. GARF f. 4085, op. 22, d. 381, l. 10

140. GARF f. 4085, op. 22, d. 381, l. 9

141. GARF f. 4085, op. 22, d. 381, l. 12. Elsewhere, they found that while the "contents of a dead citizen's apartment were recorded, there was no stamp indicating that they had indeed been given to storage. No one knew how much furniture was there or was supposed to be there, so of course widespread theft of furniture took place."

142. TsAGM f. 54, op. 1, d. 34, l. 23.

143. TsAGM f. 54, op. 1, d. 130, ll. 1,2,3,5,7,9, 11.

144. TsGASP f. 1000, op. 4, d. 105, l. 59.

145. TsGASP f. 1000, op. 4, d. 105, l. 92.

146. TsAGM f. 54, op. 1, d. 167, l. 44.

147. TsGASP f. 1000, op. 4, d. 105, l. 59.

148. GARF f. 4085, op. 22, d. 381, l. 12.

149. GARF f. 4085, op. 22, d. 381, l. 12.

150. TsAGM f. 2431, op. 1, d. 51, l. 3. In the event that citizen Zheltysheva failed to explain her typewriter she would be summoned for "an appearance before the People's Court."

151. GARF f. 4085, op. 22, d. 381, l. 12.

152. GARF f. 4085, op. 22, d. 62, l. 12.

153. GARF f. 4390, op. 2, d. 276, l. 173.

154. GARF f. 4390, op. 4, d. 44, l. 440b.

155. GARF f. 4390, op. 4, d. 44, l. 440b.

156. GARF f. 4390, op. 4, d. 44, l. 48.

Chapter 3: Accounting for Socialism: Inventories of the Built Environment

1. In August 1918, the Cheka created a Department of Strategic Concentration, tasked with seizing the upper floors of buildings deemed of "strategic interest," performing oversight of the seizure of space and things from the bourgeoisie, and fining individual residents who failed to comply with Cheka orders. Oleg Kapchinsky, *Gosbezopasnost' iznutri: Natsionalnyi i sotsialnyi sostav* (Moscow: EKSMO, 2005), 67.

2. This account is drawn from GARF f. R-130, op. 2, d. 77, ll. 33–44.

3. A process described by Robert M. Fogelson, *The Great Rent Wars: New York, 1917–1929* (New Haven: Yale University Press, 2013), chapter 1.

4. Alexia Yates, *Selling Paris: Property and Commercial Culture in the Fin-de-siecle Capital* (Cambridge: Harvard University Press, 2015), 259.

5. *Krasnaya Moskva: 1917–1920* (Moscow: Mossoviet, former co. I. D. Sytina, 1920), 335.

6. For definitions of accounting, this chapter draws on Bruce Carruthers and Wendy Nelson Espeland, "Accounting for Rationality: Double-Entry Bookkeeping and the Rhetoric of Economic Rationality," *American Journal of Sociology*, 97, no. 1 (July 1991), 31–69. Carruthers and Espeland illuminate the rhetorical function of accounts, aimed in the case of double-entry bookkeeping at projecting neutral rationality in the pursuit of efficient, "economic" decision-making. As Jonathan Levy emphasizes, accounts do not merely reflect the economic world but, in critical ways, they create it. Jonathan Levy, "Accounting for Profit and the History of Capital," *Critical Historical Studies*, 1 (2) (Fall 2014), 171–214.

7. Neil Harding, *Lenin's Political Thought: Theory and Practice in the Democratic Revolution*, vol. 2 (London: Macmillan, 1977), 42.

8. Harding, *Lenin's Political Thought*, vol. 2, 42.

9. A point made by Alec Nove, *An Economic History of the USSR* (New York, NY: Penguin, 1969), 44.

10. Harding, *Lenin's Political Thought*, vol. 2, 76.

11. Harding, *Lenin's Political Thought*, vol. 2, 129, quoting Vladimir Lenin, *State and Revolution*.

12. Richard Sakwa, "The Commune State in Moscow in 1918," *Slavic Review*, 46, no. 3–4 (1987), 429–49.

13. TsAGM f. 2435, op. 1, d. 60, l. 3.

14. TsAGM f. 2435, op. 1, d. 60, l. 9.

15. RGAE, f. 7733, op. 1, d. 62, ll. 4, 10–12.

16. V. A. Mazdorov, *Istoriya razvitiya bukhgalterskogo uchyota v SSSR (1917–1972)* (Moscow: Finansy, 1972), 43.

17. Mazdorov, *Istoriya*, 28.

18. Mazdorov, *Istoriya*, 53.

19. A. M. Galagan, *Kurs schetovedeniya*, 2nd ed. (Moscow, Vysshaya shkola, 1918); *Obshcheye schetovedenie: konspektivny kurs* (Moscow: Ekonomicheskaya zhizn', 1921); *Spravochnik bukhgaltera i schetovoda* (Moscow: Izd. V.S.N.Kh., 1924). See also M. Kuter, M. Gurskaia, and A. Kuznetsov, "Alexander Galagan: Russian Titan of the Enlightenment in the History of Accounting," *Accounting History*, 24, no. 2 (2019), 293–316.

20. Mazdorov, *Istoriya*, 54.

21. A. M. Galagan, *Osnovy obshchego schetovedeniya* (Moscow: Izd-vo Narkomtorga SSSR i RSFSR, 1928), 77.

22. City soviets similarly created separate subdepartments for "municipal" and "soviet" buildings, the former devoted to properties owned by the city for public use before the Revolution and the latter devoted to properties seized after it.

23. TsAGM f. 2435, op. 1, d. 3, l. 8.

24. TsAGM f. 2435, op. 1, d. 3, l. 7.

25. TsAGM f. 2435, op. 1, d. 3, l. 7.

26. GARF f. 4390, op. 1, d. 33, l. 247.

27. TsAGM f. 1514, op. 1, d. 5, l. 37.

28. TsAGM f. 1514, op. 1, d. 5, l. 38.

29. TsAGM f. 1514, op. 1, d. 5, l. 33.

30. The Commission counted the "bourgeois consultant" D. Kuzovkov and the head of the TsZhZO (and future Commissar of Internal Affairs) M. F. Vladimirsky among its members. GARF f. 4085, op. 22, d. 381, l. 145.

GARF f. R-130, op. 3, d. 122, ll. 95, 91.

31. TsAGM f. 2382, op. 1, d. 1, l. 10.

32. TsAGM f. 2382, op. 1, d. 1, l. 10.

33. TsAGM f. 2435, op. 1, d. 85, l. 32. By early 1921, Gelbras had risen to director of the TsZhZO, his path cleared by the arrests of his predecessors in the job. He narrowly dodged the same fate. GARF f. 4085, op. 22, d. 381, l. 97.

34. TsAGM f. 2382, op. 1, d. 1, l. 10.

35. TsGASP f. 3201, op. 1, d. 113, l. 4.

36. TsGASP f. 3201, op. 1, d. 113, l. 4.

37. GARF f. 4085, op. 22, d. 381, l. 145.

38. GARF f. 4085, op. 22, d. 381, l. 145.

39. TsGASP f. 3201, op. 1, d. 115, l. 1.

40. GARF f. 4390, op. 4, d. 44, l. 26.

41. In the spring of 1919, Larin's Commission turned its attention to the "cost of the resettle-ment of the bourgeoisie" and the proposed cancellation of rent payments in cities of more than 100,000 residents. Up until this point, policies on rents varied from one city to the next. Moscow continued to collect rents through the building committees, generally at the tariffs fixed in 1918, which—given the inflation—had rendered them a generally insignificant burden on most households; some buildings, however, had seen meaningful increases in their charges, including in "worker buildings," residents of which complained of increases in January 1919. TsAGM f. 2434, op. 1, d. 36, l. 27. In Petrograd, only the original tenant or resident of a concentrated apart-ment was responsible for the rent, with new residents living without payment. Some petitions indicate this was a hardship for the affected households—these petitions, notably, were in-cluded in the files of officials considering whether to cancel rent. GARF f. R-130, op. 3, d. 122, l. 77. When Larin's Commission considered the topic, it determined through loose calculation that up until the spring of 1919, despite inflation, the rents collected by the city roughly covered its expenses on the maintenance of the city's housing stock—due to the fact that nearly two-thirds of prerevolutionary rent payments, the Commission argued, was devoted to the "pure profit" of former landlords. This figure began to change, however, in the winter of 1919, as build-ings deteriorated, demanding either a steep increase in rents—or a cancellation of rent entirely, and the dedication of the savings, purportedly on rent collection, to maintenance. These estima-tions involved calculations of the buildings' current "value" that were difficult to untangle. GARF f. R-130, op. 3, d. 122, ll. 92–94. The economist Pavel Genzel, whose opinion on the matter was solicited by Narkomfin, argued sharply against cancelling rent, but the opposing position won the day. RGAE f. 7733, op. 1, d. 6302, ll. 19–24, on the cancellation of payment for services, a report which makes reference to Genzel's opposition to cancelling rent as well.

42. GARF f. 4390, op. 4, d. 43, ll. 3–5.

43. TsAGM f. 2435, op. 1, d. 85, l. 9.

44. TsAGM f. 2435, op. 1, d. 85, l. 5.

45. TsAGM f. 2435, op. 1, d. 85, ll. 9, 13, 14.

46. *Krasnaya Moskva*, 352.

47. TsAGM f. 2435, op. 1, d. 85, ll. 3, 14.

48. *Krasnaya Moskva*, 54.

49. *Krasnaya Moskva*, 352.

50. TsAGM f. 2433, op. 1, d. 118, l. 21. In his own work, Kuzovkov decided to ignore both the population census and the aborted building census, relying instead on an employment census held by the city on April 21, 1918. *Krasnaya Moskva*, 356 and TsAGM f. 2435, op. 1, d. 85, l. 14.

51. TsAGM f. 1514, op. 1, d. 5, l. 51.

52. TsGASP f. 3201, op. 1, d. 115, ll. 1, 3.

53. GARF f. 4390, op. 3, d. 80, l. 3.

54. See above, GARF f. 4390, op. 4, d. 44, l. 26.

55. GARF f. 4085, op. 1a, d. 231, l. 4. GARF f. 4390, op. 4, d. 44, l. 29.

56. *Izvestia VTsIK,* July 3, 1918, no. 136, 4; *Izvestia VTsIK,* July 16, 1918, no. 148, 3.

57. The existence of two distinct modes of gathering information about built space in the same institution is not unique to this case, as the work of anthropologist Matthew Hull makes clear. Indeed, the parallels between the efforts of the TsZhZO in revolutionary Moscow and the housing bureaucrats in the would-be planned city of Islamabad are quite striking. In Hull's case study, government officials in Islamabad's Capital Development Authority unwittingly developed two land-reckoning systems, one rooted in metric measurement, the other in inherited "revenue record," developed by the British from the Mughal system. Formal acknowledgment of this duality was more forthcoming in Islamabad than in Moscow, but in both cities, local actors proved adept at mobilizing one or the other logic of space according to their interests. As Hull notes, it was up to residents, bureaucrats, and petitioners to "enact two different sorts of objects. . . . that must be 'coordinated.'" Matthew Hull, *Government of Paper: The Materiality of Bureaucracy in Urban Pakistan* (Berkeley: the University of California Press, 2012), 181.

58. Stephen Kotkin, "The State—Is It Us? Memoirs, Archives, and Kremlinologists," *Russian Review,* 61, no. 1, (2002), 35–51, here 35.

59. TsAGM f. 2435, op. 1, d. 85, l. 32.

60. GARF f. R-130, op. 2, d. 79, l. 27. This attitude became entrenched across the various levels of Moscow's government, encouraged by negative attention toward the building committees in the local party press as well as the building committees' own behavior. When a workers' inspection inquired into the progress of the Sokol ZhZO on "taking apartments onto account" in the summer of 1919, it found that "it was not possible to fulfill the work through the domkoms, which do not come to the aid of the Housing-Land Department." (TsAGM f. 54, op. 1, d. 34, l. 52.) The following year, the Moscow Communal Economic agency tried to abolish the building committees due to their "alienation from the general Soviet system," self-dealing, and "unreliability in implementation of general communist politics." But the Mossoviet blocked the action. "Even their opponents allow that there is no institution that, gathering information or data of one kind or another [*sobiraya te ili inye svedeniya i dannye*], does not depend on the domkoms," a Rabkrin inspector explained. (GARF f. 4085, op. 22, d. 381, l. 165.)

61. GARF f. 4085, op. 22, d. 381, ll. 8, 113, 114. TsAGM f. 2435, op. 1, d. 85, l. 4. See also *Krasnaya Moskva,* 339.

62. Their trustworthiness was secured by the manner of their election to their positions: Kuzovkov proposed that voting rights in *kvartkhoz* elections would be limited to residents belonging to the Communist Party or to categories 1 or 2 of the bread ration (workers), and others who could personally vouched for by senior officials. TsAGM f. 54, op. 1, d. 22, l. 2.

63. TsAGM f. 2434, op. 1, d. 41, l. 48; GARF f. 4085, op. 22, d. 381, l. 7.

64. TsAGM f. 54/2431, op. 1, d. 19, l. 6.

65. GARF f. 4085, op. 22, d. 381, l. 14.

66. TsAGM f. 54/2431, op. 1, d. 19, l. 41.

67. TsAGM f. 1514, op. 1, d. 113, l. 15.

68. GARF f. 4085, op. 22, d. 381, ll. 6, 10.

69. TsAGM f. 1514, op. 1, d. 113, l. 20.

70. TsAGM f. 1514, op. 1, d. 113, l. 15.

71. TsAGM f. 2434, op. 1, d. 66, l. 1690b.

72. GARF f. 4085, op. 22, d. 381, l. 112.

73. TsAGM f. 2434, op. 1, d. 29, l. 173.

74. TsAGM f. 2434, op. 1, d. 36, l. 137; GARF f. 4085, op. 22, d. 381, l. 97.

75. GARF f. 4085, op. 22, d. 381, l. 6.

76. GARF f. 4085, op. 22, d. 381, l. 6.

77. GARF f. 4085, op. 22, d. 381, l. 112.

78. GARF f. 4085, op. 22, d. 381, l. 18.

79. GARF f. 4085, op. 22, d. 381, l. 11.

80. GARF f. 4085, op. 22, d. 381, l. 8.

81. GARF f. 4085, op. 22, d. 381, l. 114.

82. GARF f. 4085, op. 22, d. 381, l. 18.

83. GARF f. 4085, op. 22, d. 381, ll. 11, 12.

84. GARF f. 4085, op. 22, d. 381, l. 18.

85. GARF f. 4085, op. 22, d. 381, l. 14.

86. GARF f. 4085, op. 22, d. 381, l. 14.

87. GARF f. 4085, op. 22, d. 381, l. 11.

88. GARF f. 4085, op. 22, d. 381, l. 7.

89. GARF f. 4085, op. 22, d. 381, l. 7.

90. GARF f. 4085, op. 22, d. 381, l.12.

91. GARF f. 4085, op. 22, d. 381.

92. GARF f. R-130, op. 2, d. 77, ll. 197–198.

93. *Izvestia VTsIK*, Nov. 29, 1918, no. 261.

94. Levy, "Accounting for Profit."

95. Caroline Humphrey, *Karl Marx Collective: Economy, Society, and Religion in a Siberian Collective Farm* (Cambridge: Cambridge University Press, 1983), 197.

96. Humphrey, *Karl Marx*, 199.

97. The concept of "excess" as a basis for dispossession, and its subjective application, had a long history, including in the Russian colonial setting, as Maya Peterson described in her treatment of the Ministry of Agriculture's Steppe Statute of 1895, allowing the Ministry "explicit permission to take possession of any lands deemed in 'excess' of nomadic use," a provision extended in 1910 to Turkestan. Maya Peterson, *Pipe Dreams: Water and Empire in Central Asia's Aral Sea Basin* (Cambridge: Cambridge University Press, 2019), 167.

98. TsAGM f. 2434, op. 1, d. 66, l. 171.

99. TsAGM f. 2434, op. 1, d. 29, l. 27.

100. TsAGM f. 2434, op. 1, d. 66, ll. 171. 170.

101. TsGASP f. 3201, op. 1, d. 55, l. 17.

102. TsGASP f. 3201, op. 1, d. 55, ll. 21, 19, 41, 46, 76.

103. TsGASP f. 3201, op. 1, d. 55, l. 66.

104. GARF f. 4085, op. 22, d. 165, l. 239.

105. The targeting of households headed by women was observed by Provisional Government officials in the seizure of settler-farms in the summer of 1917. C. E. Vulliamy, ed. *The Red Archives: Russian State Papers and Other Documents Relating to the Years 1915–1918*, trans. A. L. Hynes (London: G. Bles, 1929), 257.

106. GARF f. 4085, op. 22, d. 165, ll. 19, 5.

107. GARF f. 4085, op. 22, d. 166, ll. 36–37.

108. TsAGM f. 1514, op. 1, d. 113, l. 10.

109. TsAGM f. 1514, op. 1, d. 113, l. 12.

110. GARF f. 4085, op. 22, d. 165, l. 134.

111. GARF f. 4085, op. 22, d. 165, l.135.

112. GARF f. 4085, op. 22, d. 165, l.135.

113. GARF f. 4085, op. 22, d. 381, l. 7.

114. GARF f. 4085, op. 22, d. 381, l. 8.

115. GARF f. 4085, op. 22, d. 381, l. 20.

116. GARF f. R-130, op. 2, d. 79, l. 50.

117. RGASPI f. 5, op. 1, d. 45, ll. 1, 2.

118. Humphrey, *Karl Marx*, 226.

119. TsAGM f. 2434, op. 1, d. 66, ll. 157, 153.

120. TsAGM f. 2434, op. 1, d. 66, l. 172.

121. TsAGM f. 2434, op. 1, d. 66, l. 157.

122. Michael Heller, "The Tragedy of the Anticommons: Property in the Transition from Marx to Markets" *Harv. L. Rev.* 111 (1998), 629.

Chapter 4: The Wealth of the Whole Nation: Searching for Value at Gokhran

1. RGAE f. 7733, op. 1, d. 343, l. 231.

2. Vladimir Lenin, *Polnoe sobranie sochinenii*, tom 36 (Mar.-July 1918), 270, responding to complaints that his insistence on "counting and distributing correctly" constituted a dictatorship not of the proletariat but of Napoleon III; "let them know in each factory, in each village, . . . that we are giving all our might to organizing calculation, control, and correct distribution."

3. RGAE f. 7733, op. 1, d. 343, l. 232. Nickel silver, or "German nickel," as it was sometimes known, is a copper alloy that contains no silver but was frequently used in the production of decorative housewares at the turn of the century.

4. RGASPI f. 5, op. 1, d. 127, l. 109.

5. RGASPI f. 5, op. 1, d. 127, l. 103.

6. RGASPI f. 5, op. 1, d. 127, ll. 116, 94.

7. RGASPI f. 5, op. 1, d. 127, l. 103.

8. RGASPI f. 5, op. 1, d. 127, l. 105.

9. RGAE f. 7733, op. 1, d. 231, l. 40.

10. RGAE f. 7733, op. 1, d. 231, l. 39.

11. GARF f. 4085, op. 1a, d. 123, ll. 34, 35. Aleksandrov was sentenced to five years of forced labor, while Pozhamchi miraculously disappeared shortly before sentencing. RGASPI f. 5, op. 1, d. 127, l. 109. It was not just the jewelers whom Gokhran pried away from the honest path. The services of a cipher clerk named Vera Zarkhi were specially requested by a trade envoy assigned to coordinate diamond transfers between Moscow and Latvia in Riga. "Finding a suitable employee for the task is extremely difficult," the envoy reported; thankfully he had "suddenly remembered that in the Gokhran department there was a certain Vera

Matveevna Zarkhi who would be suitable for the job," also for "conspiratorial reasons." Zarkhi
left for Riga immediately, but within months the Cheka was searching for her in connection
with case No. 10069, as she was evidently not conspiratorial enough. GARF f. 4085, op. 28,
d. 20, ll. 26, 112.

12. Francois Allisson, *Value and Prices in Russian Economic Thought: A Journey Inside the
Russian Synthesis* (New York: Routledge, 2015), 14.

13. Allisson, *Value*, 14; David Woodruff, "Profits Now, Costs Later," *The London Review of
Books*, 40, no. 22 (22 Nov. 2018), 17.

14. As cited by Woodruff, 17. See Philip Mirowski, "Learning the Meaning of a Dollar: Conservation Principles and the Social Theory of Value in Economic Theory," *Social Research*, 57
(3), (1990), 689–717.

15. Allisson, *Value*, 15.

16. Woodruff, "Profits," 17

17. Allisson, *Value*, chapter 1.

18. Caroline Humphrey, *Karl Marx Collective: Economy, Society, and Religion in a Siberian
Collective Farm* (Cambridge: Cambridge University Press, 1983), 91.

19. Humphrey, *Karl Marx*, 74.

20. Yuri Slezkine, *The House of Government: A Saga of the Russian Revolution* (Princeton, NJ:
Princeton University Press, 2017), 149. "Once in power," Slezkine observes, "the Bolsheviks did
what all millenarians do: waited for the inevitable while working to bring it about."

21. Humphrey, *Karl Marx*, 91.

22. Alfred Zauberman argued that the question of value was nearly fully suppressed under
Stalin; recent work by Giovanni Cadioli suggests that value was never as dead as it seemed, and
that postwar economists began to engage with it more directly in the late 1940s. Alfred Zauberman, "The Law of Value and Price Formation," *Value and Plan: Economic Calculation and
Organization in Eastern Europe*, ed. and intro by Gregory Grossman (Berkeley, CA: the University of California Press, 1960). Giovanni Cadioli, "Economic Levers in the Soviet Union in the
late 1940s," *Cahiers du monde russe*, 64 (1), 2023: 135–170.

23. As characterized by William Rosenberg, "The Problem of Market Relations and the State
in Revolutionary Russia," *Comparative Studies in Society and History*, 36 (2), (1994), 377.

24. Elena Osokina, *Zoloto dlya industrializatsii: TORGSIN* (Moscow: Rosspen, 2009); also
Elena Osokina, *Ierarkhiya potrebleniya: o zhizni lyudei v usloviyakh stalinskogo snabzheniya* (Moscow: MGOU, 1993), chapter 4.

25. Osokina, *Ierarkhiya*, 108.

26. As described by Humphrey, *Karl Marx* (1983), as well as Alan Abouchar, "The Time
Factor and Soviet Investment Methodology," *Soviet Studies*, 37, no. 3 (1985): 417–27; Alec Nove
and Alfred Zauberman, "A Resurrected Russian Economist of 1900," *Soviet Studies*, 13, no. 1
(1961): 96–101; Maurice Dobb, "The Revival of Theoretical Discussion among Soviet Economists," *Science & Society*, 24, no. 4 (1960): 289–311; and Naum Jasny, "A Note on Rationality and
Efficiency in the Soviet Economy. I," *Soviet Studies*, 12, no. 4 (1961): 353–75.

27. Osokina, *Zoloto*, and Alan Ball, "Lenin and the Question of Private Trade in Soviet Russia," *Slavic Review*, 43, no. 3 (1984): 399–412.

28. Yaroslav Sokolov, *Bukhgaltersky uchyot: ot istokov do nashikh dnei* (Moscow: Yuniti, 1996),
446. See also chapter 3.

29. Mark Harrison, "Prices in the Politburo, 1927: market equilibrium versus the use of force," *The lost Politburo Transcripts: From Collective Rule to Stalin's Dictatorship.* Ed. Paul R. Gregory and Norman Naimark, (New Haven, CT; Yale University Press, 2008), 233.

30. Sokolov, *Bukhgaltersky*, 452.

31. RGAE f. 7733, op, 1, d. 343, l. 275 ob.

32. RGAE f. 7733, op. 1, d. 120, ll., 26, 61, 75 for value limits in Shenkursky uezd, Penza, Mstislavl, and Vyatka.

33. RGAE f. 7733, op. 1, d. 187, ll. 6, 9, 18 for the 10,000-ruble value limit on inheritance and safe-deposit boxes.

34. RGAE f. 7733, op. 1, d. 187, l. 18, for the extensions of the 10,000-ruble limit on withdrawal from safes to all holdings of silver coinage in the absence of a "corresponding directive" on the topic.

35. RGAE f. 7733, op. 1, d. 343, l. 17.

36. RGAE f. 7733, op. 1, d. 343, l. 229; RGAE f. 7733, op. 1, d. 242, l. 22. For the ruling on speculative origins, see GARF f. A-353, op. 4, d. 317, l. 55.

37. RGAE f. 7733, op. 1, d. 120, ll. 3, 33. Yanni Kotsonis provides a valuable distinction between the prerevolutionary assessment commissions formed to implement the 1916 income tax and the postrevolutionary variety, including the Committees of the Poor, which aimed explicitly at waging class war, in "'No Place to Go': Taxation and State Transformation in Late Imperial and Early Soviet Russia," *The Journal of Modern History*, 76, no. 3 (Sept. 2004), 531–77, here 566. See also Linda Bowman, "Russia's First Income Taxes: The Effects of Modernized Taxes on Commerce and Industry, 1885–1914," *Slavic Review*, 52 (Summer 1993), 256–82.

38. Z. S. Katsenelenbaum, *Russian Currency and Banking* (London: P.S. King, 1925), 10.

39. RGAE f. 7733, op. 1, d. 120, l. 3.

40. Harrison, "Prices in the Politburo," 230.

41. GARF f. 4390, op. 4, d. 68, l. 31.

42. Humphrey, *Karl Marx*, 91.

43. GARF f. 4390, op. 4, d. 41, l. 13.

44. See RGASPI f. 5, op. 1, d. 341, l. 15.

45. TsGASP f. 1000, op. 4, d. 105, l. 89.

46. TsGASP f. 1000, op. 4, d. 105, l. 101–102.

47. TsGASP f. 1000, op. 4, d. 105, l. 103.

48. TsGASP f. 1000, op. 4, d. 105, l. 89. On the distribution of nonvaluables, see chapter 3.

49. TsGASP f. 1000, op. 4, d. 105, l. 59.

50. RGASPI f. 5, op. 1, d. 127, l. 135.

51. GARF A-2306, op. 1, d. 777, l. 72.

52. As a result, those 7,000 objects were removed from Glavmuzei's ledgers and returned to the possession of their owners (often a purely nominal change, as Glavmuzei had lacked the ability to remove them from owners' apartments physically back in 1918). Their further disposal depended on whether Glavmuzei judged them as "presenting artistic-historical meaning as the national wealth of the republic." If they remained meaningful, the owners had to pay a two-percent tax on the basis of the object's present "market value," as assessed by Glavmuzei, and the object itself remained under an "order of protection," blocking it from sale. If an object was no longer meaningful, the owner was required to pay a tax of 10 percent on the market value of

the day, in exchange for which he or she received the right to sell. GARF A-2306, op. 1, d. 777, ll. 27, 38, 38ob.

53. TsGASP f. 1000, op. 4, d. 105, l. 60.

54. See chapter 3.

55. RGAE f. 7733, op. 1, d. 6302, l. 20. Water was paid for in two ways, according to Genzel: first, through inflation, and second, by a kind of labor tax on all those who lived in buildings without running water—51.1 percent of the Moscow population—and who would suffer from both inflation and the labor of "carting water with their own hands."

56. RGAE f. 7733, op. 1, d. 6258, ll. 41; RGAE f. 7733, op. 1, d. 343, ll. 143–145 on the internal history of budgeting since the revolution up to 1921.

57. RGAE f. 7733, op. 1, d. 37, l. 77.

58. TsGASP f. 1000, op. 4, d. 105, ll. 90–91.

59. Other documents indicate the presence of a fairly refined sensitivity to the different brands of typewriters in use at the time, with office workers requesting typewriters by specific make or model. GARF f. 4085, op. 22, d. 10, l. 6.

60. TsAGM f. 54, op. 1, d. 34, l. 68ob.

61. And with them an economic logic of amortization, which would find a place in pricing practice of later decades, in the form of what Alfred Zauberman called the "subconscious marginalist calculus" expected of plant managers who were made to calculate their real "prime costs of production," distinct from the officially stated ones, and maximize resource allocation accordingly. Zauberman, "The Law of Value," 20.

62. TsAGM f. 54/2431, op. 1, d. 144, ll. 11, 12.

63. GARF f. 4390, op. 4, d. 45, l. 12; GARF f. 4390, op. 2, d. 276, l. 104.

64. RGAE f. 7733, op. 1, d. 6260, l. 84.

65. See chapter 3.

66. GARF f. 4390, op. 11, d. 41, l. 30b. The matter was resolved, although it required interrogating the man who traveled with the gems from Petrograd to Moscow; the former aide to the Director of the *Kameralnaya Chast'*; the former Commissar of the People's Property; the former controller of the former Ministry of the Court, who was "today the Director of the Finance Department of Commissariat of People's Property"; and a host of other men involved in the evacuation of the jewels, on the basis of which, after three months of inquiry, "the question about the absence of inventories evacuated to Moscow on July 24, 1917, together with the valuables from the diamond room may be considered clarified," the inventories found, and the gems secured. GARF f. 4390, op. 11, d. 41, l. 4

67. GARF f. 4390, op. 11, d. 41, l. 7.

68. TsGASP f. 3201, op. 1, d. 55, l. 105.

69. RGAE f. 7733, op. 1, d. 231, l. 39.

70. RGASPI f. 5, op. 1, d. 127, l. 132.

71. RGAE f. 7733, op. 1, d. 343, l. 229.

72. GARF f. 4085, op. 28, d. 259, l. 65.

73. RGASPI f. 5, op. 1, d. 127, l. 132.

74. RGASPI f. 5, op. 1, d. 127, l. 132.

75. RGAE f. 7733, op. 1, d. 242, l. 69. Around the same time, Commissar of Foreign Trade Krasin introduced a similar project to search for papers in European currencies "that could be

sold abroad," while talk in Narkomfin's "Liquidation Department," responsible for closing out the accounts of prerevolutionary public and private credit institutions, turned to the question of whether it would be possible to establish what one party official called "the indebtedness to us of foreign governments, enterprises, banks, and individuals," rephrased by his Narkomfin interlocutor as "our mutual indebtedness abroad." RGASPI f. 5, op. 1, d. 127, l. 5; RGAE f. 7733, op. 1, d. 1926, l. 64.

76. After Versailles, Narkomfin's research unit eagerly studied the principles of indebtedness and reparation established in the peace treaties, looking for concepts that could be of use in this new geopolitical environment. RGAE f. 7733, op. 1, d. 6260, ll. 68–70.

77. GARF f. R-130, op. 3, d. 122, l. 74, with M. F. Vladimirsky, Kuzovkov, and the head of the NKVD's section on municipalization, Yeltsin.

78. GARF f. R-130, op. 3, d. 122, l. 94.

79. RGAE f. 7733, op. 1, d. 6302, l. 19.

80. RGAE f. 7733, op. 1, d. 231, ll. 37, 38.

81. Although commonly known as Natalya Ivanovna Sedova, in official correspondence (authored by Anatoly Lunarcharsky among others) in 1918, Natalya Ivanovna was identified as "Trotskaya" or even "Com. Bronshtein-Trotskaya". GARF f. 4390, op. 11, d. 24, l. 9.

82. RGASPI f. 5, op. 1, d. 341, ll. 20–21.

83. RGASPI f. 5, op. 1, d. 341, l. 21.

84. RGASPI f. 5, op. 1, d. 341, l. 21.

85. David M. Woodruff, "The Politburo on Gold, Industrialization, and the International Economy, 1925–1926," *The lost Politburo transcripts: from collective rule to Stalin's dictatorship*, ed. Paul R. Gregory and Norman Naimark, (New Haven, CT; Yale University Press, 2008), 200.

86. RGAE f. 7733, op. 1, d. 6302, l. 66.

87. Woodruff, "Politburo," pp. 202, 218.

88. RGASPI f. 5, op. 1, d. 127, l. 135.

89. RGAE f. 7733, op. 1, d. 6302, l. 66.

90. RGAE f. 7733, op. 1, d. 231, l. 39.

91. RGAE f. 7733, op. 1, d. 231, l. 38.

92. RGAE f. 7733, op. 1, d. 231, l. 51.

93. RGAE f. 7733, op. 1, d. 231, l. 37.

94. RGAE f. 7733, op. 1, d. 231, l. 39.

95. RGAE f. 7733, op. 1, d. 231, l. 39.

96. RGASPI f. 5, op. 1, d. 127, l. 132.

97. Igor Kopytoff, "The cultural biography of things: Commoditization as process," in *The Social Life of Things: Commodities in Cultural Perspective*, ed. Arjun Appadurai (Cambridge: Cambridge University Press, 1986), 64–92.

98. RGAE f. 7733, op. 1, d. 231, l. 38.

99. RGAE f. 7733, op. 1, d. 231, l. 39.

100. RGAE f. 7733, op. 1, d. 187, l. 334.

101. As discussed in chapter 3.

102. RGAE f. 7733, op. 1, d. 231, ll. 1–5, 10.

103. RGAE f. 7733, op. 1, d. 1926, l. 115.

104. RGAE f. 7733, op. 1, d. 231, l. 38

105. RGAE f. 7733, op. 1, d. 231, l. 37

106. RGASPI f. 5, op. 1, d. 127, l. 6.

107. RGASPI f. 5, op. 1, d. 127, l. 103.

108. RGASPI f. 5, op. 1, d. 127, l. 122.

109. RGAE f. 7733, op. 1, d. 231, l. 38.

110. RGASPI f. 5, op. 1, d. 127, l. 134.

111. RGAE f. 7733, op. 1, d. 231, l. 4.

112. RGAE f. 7733, op. 1, d. 231, l. 2. See also Osokina, *Torgsin*, 84–9.

113. GARF f. 4085, op. 22, d. 10, l. 46.

114. GARF f. 4085, op. 22, d. 10, l. 46.

115. GARF f. 4085, op. 22, d. 10, l. 46.

116. RGAE f. 7733, op. 1, d. 231, l. 37.

117. RGASPI f. 5, op. 1, d. 127, l. 133.

118. RGAE f. 7733, op. 1, d. 231, l. 38.

119. RGASPI f. 5, op. 1, d. 127, l. 19.

120. RGASPI f. 5, op. 1, d. 127, l. 133.

121. RGIA f. 560, op. 22, d. 528, l. 91. The Ministry of Finance officials, of course, could have hazarded an estimate of the building's replacement value, but did not do so.

122. Debora L. Spar, "Markets: Continuity and Change in the International Diamond Market," *The Journal of Economic Perspectives*, 20, no. 3, (2006), 195–208.

123. RGAE f. 7733, op. 1, d. 231, l. 40.

124. RGAE f. 7733, op. 1, d. 231, ll. 39–40.

125. RGASPI f. 5, op. 1, d. 127, l. 19.

126. RGAE f. 7733, op. 1, d. 231, l. 39.

127. A point made by Sokolov, *Bukhgaltersky*, 504.

128. Sokolov, *Bukhgaltersky*, 483.

129. Paper money was recorded on the inventories not by value—different currencies circulated at different prices inside the RSFSR and on foreign markets—but by container: in the first week of May, Gokhran registered 33 "boxes" of paper money, plus 12 "bags." The following week, another new category appeared, entitled "deposits in private pawns, evacuated from various cities," of which Gokhran processed "47 boxes." RGAE f. 7733, op. 1, d. 231, ll. 52, 56, 61, 65.

130. The Sovnarkom created a Price Committee attached to Narkomfin on August 5, 1921, with the aim of "defining prices for many goods guided not just by their prices on the domestic markets but also on foreign markets." As preparatory materials for a congress of financial workers explained, each price was to derive from the "sebestoimost' of each object, but it also must be recognized as necessary to consider market prices, as valuations set higher than the so-called market prices will result either in the reduction of demand for a given object or in the lowering of the market price, with extremely negative effects in the course of the ruble as a result." The aim was to identify a price that was "not lower than the sebestoimost' and not higher than the market." RGAE f. 7733, op. 1, d. 380, l. 23. By contrast, Levitsky referred here to a price committee specially formed more than a year earlier, in April 1920, with representatives from VSNKh, Gokhran, NKVT, and Goskon in order to set prices "for precious stones [intended for] trade

abroad." On this special committee, see RGAE f. 7733, op. 1, d. 231, l. 51. On the Price Committee attached to Narkomfin of the following year, see also RGAE f. 7733, op. 1, d. 386, l. 8.

131. RGAE f. 7733, op. 1, d. 231, l. 51.

132. RGAE f. 7733, op. 1, d. 231, l. 51.

133. RGASPI f. 5, op. 1, d. 127, l. 77.

134. RGASPI f. 5, op. 1, d. 127, l. 121.

135. RGAE f. 7733, op. 1, d. 386, 8.

136. Famously, Eugene Fama, "Random Walks in Stock Market Prices," *Financial Analysts Journal*, 21, no. 5 (1965): 55–59.

137. RGASPI f. 5, op. 1, d. 127, l. 134. Emphasis original.

138. Sokolov, *Bukhgaltersky*, 499.

139. Sokolov, *Bukhgaltersky*, 499. Alan Abouchar, "The Time Factor," 423.

140. Abouchar, "The Time Factor," 423.

141. Humphrey, *Karl Marx*, 76.

142. Abouchar, "The Time Factor," 425.

143. In fact, sebestoimost' and the concept of self-costing it reflected shared certain features across the socialist-capitalist divide in later years, most notably the connection to control. In capitalist firms, "standard costs" were calculated alongside "actual costs" as a gauge of waste and productivity, much in the way that Soviet firms were instructed to calculate actual and normed sebestoimost' in production. As cited by Sokolov, *Bukhgaltersky*, 504.

144. Humphrey, *Karl Marx*, 96.

145. Allisson, *Value*, 62.

146. Allisson, *Value*, 124.

147. Allisson, *Value*, 120.

148. See the excellent study of Siberian monetary history in A. V. Aliamkin and A. G. Baranov, *Istoriya denezhnogo obrashcheniya v 1914–1924 gg. (po materialam Zauralya)* (Yekaterinburg: Izd. UGGU, 2005), chapter 5. See also Allisson, *Value*, ch. 6; Osokina, *Torgsin*, 30; Vincent Barnett, *A History of Russian Economic Thought* (London: Routledge, 2005), 97–8; *Denezhnaya reforma 1921–1924 gg.: Sozdanie tvyordoi valyuty (dokumenty i materialy)*, ed. L. N. Dobrokhotov, V. N. Kolodezhnyi, V. S. Pushkarev (Moscow: ROSSPEN, 2008); Yu. M. Goland, *Diskussii ob ekonomicheskoi politike v gody denezhnoi reformy 1921–1924* (Moscow: Ekonomika, 2006).

149. Allisson, *Value*, 120.

150. RGAE f. 7733, op. 1, d. 377, l. 71.

151. RGAE f. 7733, op. 18, d. 6401, l. 12.

152. RGAE f. 7733, op. 1, d. 377, l. 75.

153. RGAE f. 7733, op. 1, d. 377, l. 71.

154. As described for Germany by Gerald Feldman, *The Great Disorder: Politics, Economics, and Society in the German Inflation, 1914–1924* (New York: Oxford University Press, 1993), chapter 2.

155. Goland, *Diskussii*; RGASPI f. 5, op. 1, d. 2765, l. 1.

156. RGAE f. 7733, op. 1, d. 377, l. 71, RGASPI f. 5, op. 1, d. 127, l. 2.

157. RGASPI f. 5, op. 1, d. 127, l. 2.

158. RGASPI f. 5, op. 1, d. 127, l. 2.

159. RGASPI f. 5, op. 1, d. 127, l. 116.

160. RGASPI f. 5, op. 1, d. 127, l. 39.

161. RGASPI f. 5, op. 1, d. 127, ll. 134, 133.

162. RGASPI f. 5, op. 1, d. 127, ll. 70, 75.

163. GARF f. R-130, missing file number, l. 48. Photographed by author, July 2017.

164. RGAE f. 7733, op. 1, d. 343, ll. 14–17.

165. RGASPI f. 5, op. 1, d. 2763, l. 36; RGAE f. 7733, op. 1, d. 472, l. 11a.

166. RGAE f. 7733, op. 1, d. 386, l. 8.

167. RGAE f. 7733, op. 1, d. 386, l. 8. Conspiratorial attitudes were not confined to the Cheka: Orlov himself cautioned that price information must not circulate to "small radio stations" for fear that they would encourage people to make "incorrect use of prices."

168. RGAE f. 7733, op. 1, d. 1932, l. 8.

169. Chelyabinsk reported that it had "noticed almost open trade in Romanov and kerenki, gold and silver," toward summer 1921, a development which the office in Barnaul reported as well, in late fall. RGAE F. 7733, op. 1, d. 1932, ll. 12, 24, 34, 35.

170. RGASPI f. 5, op. 1, d. 341, l. 4.

171. RGAE f. 413, op. 2, d. 1604, l. 17.

172. RGASPI f. 5, op. 1, d. 75, l. 2.

173. RGAE f. 7733, op. 1, d. 343, ll. 230–231.

174. RGAE f. 7733, op. 1, d. 242, l. 18.

175. RGAE f. 7733, op. 1, d. 242, ll. 44–47.

176. RGASPI f. 5, op. 1, d. 127, l. 4, published in Lenin, *PSS*, 5th ed. Vol. 52, 207–208.

177. RGAE f. 7733, op. 1, d. 5925, l. 17.

178. RGASPI f. 5, op. 1, d. 127, l. 73.

179. RGASPI f. 5, op. 1, d. 127, l. 135. Gokhran's workers were not alone in asking the question: Narkomfin's office in charge of newspaper clippings carefully followed the foreign financial press on whether a shipment of Russian gold melted down in Revel and stamped by the Swedish mint, obscuring its origins, would be seized upon arrival in New York. RGAE f. 7733, op. 1, d. 343, l. 294.

180. RGASPI f. 5, op. 1, d. 127, l. 133; RGAE f. 7733, op. 1, d. 242, l. 75.

181. RGASPI f. 5, op. 1, d. 127, l. 27.

182. RGASPI f. 5, op. 1, d. 127, l. 30.

183. RGASPI f. 5, op. 1, d. 127, l. 66; RGAE f. 7733, op. 1, d. 231, l. 101.

184. RGAE f. 7733, op. 1, d. 2166, ll. 4, 12. Alsky sternly ordered Rabrkin to keep its nose out of Party finances.

185. "Secret" or "unpublished" decrees permitted Narkomfin officials to break rules pertaining, for instance, to the ban on releasing pre-1917 currency notes, returning items in safe deposit boxes after the period for such requests had elapsed, and the like. RGAE f. 7733, op. 1, d. 386, l. 2; RGAE f. 7733, op. 1, d. 231, l. 166.

186. RGASPI f. 5, op. 1, d. 127, l. 5.

187. RGASPI f. 5, op. 1, d. 127, l. 136.

188. "There was one instance when an undercover worker, receiving diamonds, was asked 'for which country he needed them, and he responded for Austria,' and when he later returned with a request to exchange the diamonds and was asked for what, he answered that he needed

them not for Austria but for Ukraine, then he was told, you deceived us, no we will not exchange them." This story was recounted to Yurovsky by the appraiser Pozhamchi as evidence of the fact that Levitsky kept things above board at Gokhran; what it really signified, Yurovsky lamented, was how far out of the loop Levitsky was. RGASPI f. 5, op. 1, d. 127, l. 132.

189. RGAE f. 7733, op. 1, d. 472, l. 6.

190. RGASPI f. 5, op. 1, d. 127, l. 97.

191. Faberge, it is noted, "will be getting a higher salary," possibly a reference to the promised return of his stamp collection, reputedly authorized by Trotsky. RGASPI f. 5, op. 1, d. 127, l. 152.

192. Gregory Grossman, "Gold and the Sword: Money in the Soviet Command Economy" in *Industrialization in Two Systems: Essays in Honor of Alexander Gerschenkron*, ed. Henry Rosovsky, (New York: Wiley, 1966), 209.

193. RGAE f. 7733, op. 1, d. 472, l. 10; RGASPI f. 5, op. 1, d. 127, l. 121.

194. Spar, "Markets," 198.

195. RGASPI f. 5, op. 1, d. 127, l. 145.

196. The USSR eventually concluded an agreement with DeBeers, in 1959, lasting five years.

197. Natalya Golitsina, Robert Coalson, "A Century Later, Faberge Still Dazzles," RFE/RL Feb. 5, 2017. https://www.rferl.org/a/russia-faberge-eggs-century-later/28280309.html

198. Zauberman, "Law of Value," 23.

Chapter 5: Return and Revolution's End

1. Tikhobrazova is identified only by her last name throughout her case file. My account is drawn from GARF f. 4085, op. 22, d. 630, ll. 4–5.

2. GARF f. 4085, op. 22, d. 630, ll. 16–18.

3. Kimber is occasionally rendered as "Kimberg" in the file; he is most commonly identified as "Comrade" and only once given a first initial, L.

4. GARF f. 4085, op. 22, d. 630, ll. 8, 9, 13, 18, 19, and 40.

5. Sheila Fitzpatrick, *The Russian Revolution* 2nd ed., (New York: Oxford University Press, 1994), 4.

6. T.H. Rigby, *Lenin's Government: Sovnarkom, 1917–1922* (Cambridge: Cambridge University Press, 1979). Niels Erik Rosenfeldt, *The "Special" World: Stalin's Power Apparatus and the Soviet System's Secret Structures of Communication*, vols. 1, 2. (Copenhagen: Museum Tusculanum Press, 2009).

7. I use "legitimate" here not to sanction the Bolshevik seizure of power or its aftermath, but rather in the sense suggested by Edelstein: as a political order with fixed legal, constitutional, or institutional foundations—the point being to emphasize the transition from a period in which the idea of revolution wields its own authority to one in which political authority is vested externally in regular order.

8. Dan Edelstein, "Do We Want a Revolution without Revolution? Reflections on Political Authority," *French Historical Studies*, 35, no. 2 (Spring 2012), 275.

9. Larissa Zakharova, "Le 26–28 Kamennoostrovski, Les tribulations d'un immeuble en Revolution," in *Saint Pètersbourg: Histoire, promenades, anthologie et dictionnaire* (Paris: Laffont, 2003), 505.

10. William H. Sewell Jr., "Historical Events as Transformations of Structures: Inventing Revolution at the Bastille," republished in *Logics of History: Social Theory and Social Transformation* (Chicago: University of Chicago Press, 2005), 225–270.

11. "Decree on Requisition and Confiscation," published in *Izvestia VTsIK*, Apr. 22, 1920, no. 85, from which this account is drawn.

12. GARF f. 4085, op. 22, d. 10, l. 46.

13. GARF f. R-130, missing file number, l. 32. Photographed by author, July 2017.

14. GARF f. R-130, missing file number, ll. 34, 35. Photographed by author, July 2017.

15. GARF A-2306, op. 1, d. 777, ll. 23, 24, 38, 380b.

16. GARF f. A-353 op. 4, d. 325, l. 121.

17. GARF f. A-353 op. 4, d. 302, ll. 71, 710b.

18. GARF f. A-353 op. 4, d. 325, l. 123. For the previous three years, non-municipalized buildings in the region had continued to be "sold through homemade contracts/the majority according to bills of sale or covered by purchase-sale agreements or long-term rents," which had even gone through "judicial processes"—that is, the agreements were certified by Tsaritsyn's local courts, in violation of the Sovnarkom's very first order on real estate, forbidding the sale of buildings in November 1917.

19. GARF f. A-353 op. 4, d. 325, l. 118.

20. TsAGM f. 2434, op. 1, d. 60, l. 126.

21. GARF f. 4085, op. 22, d. 62, l. 23. Note the profusion of terms used to suggest property or possession, as well as Rabkrin's avoidance of these terms in its characterization of people who possess furniture only as its "original holders."

22. GARF f. 4085, op. 22, d. 62, l. 24.

23. GARF f. 4085, op. 22, d. 62, l. 24. Emphasis original.

24. Craig Anderson, *Roman Law* (Dundee: Dundee University Press, 2009), 51.

25. GARF f. 4085, op. 22, d. 10, l. 47.

26. Carol Rose, "Property and Expropriation: Themes and Variations in American Law," *Utah Law Review*, 2000, no. 1, (Nov. 2000), 8–9.

27. GARF f. 4085, op. 22, d. 10, l. 47.

28. Ceyda Karamursel, "Shiny Things and Sovereign Legalities: Expropriation of Dynastic Property in the Late Ottoman Empire and Early Turkish Republic," *International Journal of Middle East Studies*, 51 (2019), 447, 454. Ellinor Morack, *The Dowry of the State? The Politics of Abandoned Property and the Population Exchange in Turkey, 1921–1945* (Bamberg: University of Bamberg Press, 2017), 42.

29. Anderson, *Roman Law*, 51.

30. *Izvestia*, November 21, 1920.

31. GARF f. A-353 op. 4, d. 297, l. 38.

32. *Izvestia*, November 21, 1920.

33. Harold J. Berman "Soviet Property in Law and in Plan," *University of Pennsylvania Law Review*, 96, no. 324 (1948).

34. GARF f. A-353 op. 4, d. 297, l. 35.

35. TsAGM f. 2434, op. 1, d. 60, l. 1260b; TsAGM f. 2434, op. 1, d. 66, l. 48.

36. TsAGM f. 2434, op. 1, d. 66, l. 48.

37. TsAGM f. 2434, op. 1, d. 60, l. 1260b.

38. GARF f. 4085, op. 22, d. 166, l. 122.

39. TsAGM f. 2434, op. 1, d. 60, l. 1290b.

40. GARF f. A-353 op. 4, d. 318, l. 5.

41. TsAGM f. 2434, op. 1, d. 94, l. 63; GARF f. 4085, op. 22, d. 166, l. 164.

42. Timothy Colton, *Moscow: Governing the Socialist Metropolis* (Cambridge, MA: The Belknap Press of Harvard University Press, 1995), 757.

43. David L. Hoffmann, *Peasant Metropolis: Social Identities in Moscow* (Ithaca, NY: Cornell University Press, 2000).

44. Christina Kiaer, *Imagine No Possessions: The Socialist Objects of Russian Constructivism* (Cambridge, MA: MIT Press, 2008); Andy Willimott, *Living the Revolution: Urban Communes & Soviet Socialism, 1917–1932* (Oxford: Oxford University Press, 2016).

45. Zakharkova, "Le 26–28 Kamennoostrovski," 505.

46. TsAGM f. 2434, op. 1, d. 94, l. 56.

47. GARF f. 4085, op. 22, d. 630, l. 4.

48. A useful comparative from the aftermath of the Second World War is described by Franziska Exeler, "What Did You Do during the War?: Personal Responses to the Aftermath of Nazi Occupation," *Kritika: Explorations in Russian and Eurasian History* 17, no. 4, 805–35.

49. Regrettably, I have been unable to document the outcome of the case. TsGASP f. 3201, op. 1, d. 157, l. 42.

50. GARF f. 4085, op. 1a, d. 368, ll. 15–17.

51. GARF f. 4085, op. 22, d. 243, l. 16; *Sistematichesky sbornik dekretov postanovlenii M.S. i rasporyazhenii pravitesltvennoi vlasti PO ZHILISHCHNOMU VOPROSU* (Moscow: Moskovskoe Kommunal'noe Khozyaistvo, 1923), 18.

52. GARF f. 4085, op. 1a, d. 368, l. 17.

53. TsAGM f. 2434, op. 1, d. 94, ll. 62, 620b.

54. Rose, "Property and Expropriation," 8–9.

55. GARF f. 4085, op. 1a, d. 368, l. 16.

56. GARF f. 4085, op. 1a, d. 368, l. 17.

57. GARF f. 4085, op. 1a, d. 368, l. 18.

58. GARF f. 4085, op. 1a, d. 368, l. 18.

59. GARF A-2306, op. 1, d. 777, l. 10.

60. Some justice officials even sought to unite the framework of ownerless property in the capitals with the treatment of property abandoned by owners fleeing with the Whites. Legally, the two situations remained separate, but functionally, it was common to conflate "absence" with having traveled willfully "outside the borders of the RSFSR," so much so that a common defense of people trying to get back things seized as "ownerless" on account of their absence was to demonstrate that, although they had left the capitals, they had remained continuously inside the borders of Bolshevik-controlled territory. GARF f. A-353 op. 4, d. 297, l. 41. In September 1921, the Commissariat of Justice informed Narkomfin that it could apply neither the "Decree on Ownerless Property" nor the instructions on seizing property of citizens who fled with the Whites to the movable property of a certain Saburov, accidentally left behind in a closet of the Yelets People's Bank, due to the fact that "[Saburov] was from the time of the October Revolution not only located on the territory of the RSFSR but even, without stop, in soviet service." GARF f. A-353 op. 4, d. 317, l. 84.

61. GARF A-2306, op. 1, d. 777, l. 17.

62. Frederick Corney, *Telling October: Memory and the Making of the Bolshevik Revolution* (Ithaca, NY: Cornell University Press, 2004).

63. Karen Barkey, "In Different Times: Scheduling and Social Control in the Ottoman Empire, 1550 to 1650," *Comparative Studies in Society and History*, 38, no. 3 (1996): 460–83.

64. GARF f. A-353 op. 4, d. 306, l. 65.

65. A legacy of the months immediately after the Revolution, when dispossession was first getting underway, during which Germans, Dutch, and other foreign citizens—such as the Lithuanian Rekets—had been allowed various protections against the seizure of their properties by local authorities. See chapter 3.

66. GARF f. A-353 op. 4, d. 306, l. 65. All strikethroughs original.

67. GARF f. A-353 op. 4, d. 306, l. 66. Emphasis original.

68. A problem outlined by Natasha Wheatley, *The Life and Death of States: Central Europe and the Transformation of Modern Sovereignty* (Princeton, NJ: Princeton University Press, 2023).

69. GARF f. A-353 op. 4, d. 306, l. 66ob.

70. New to the October 1921 decree was the stipulation of a protocol or "act" to be composed "at the moment of requisition or confiscation," in recognition of the state's presence in the process, that listed the names of those performing the seizure, those from whom property was being seized, and those accepting the seized goods into storage, as well as "detailed and precise information about the property itself." The act was to be signed by all three parties, as well as two additional witnesses. *Izvestia*, Oct. 26, 1921, no. 240.

71. RGAE f. 7733, op. 1, d. 343, l. 332.

72. GARF f. 4085, op. 22, d. 10, l. 39.

73. GARF f. 4085, op. 22, d.630, ll. 31–32.

74. RGASPI f. 5, op. 1, d. 2560, l. 93.

75. *Izvestia*, Mar. 29, 1922, No. 71.

76. Significant as this shift was for the conceptualization of seizure, in practice the punctuated thrust of the decree was likely lost. When the decree was published in *Izvestia*, the second article read clearly that current possessors retained their rights so long as the former ones lost possession more than two years *before* the publication of the decree. Due to a typography error, the version of the decree disseminated in the *Sobranie uzakoneniya*—the publication of record for all government organs—read instead that current owners could keep their objects so long as the previous owners had lost them at some point *since* March 29, 1920. A wave of new queries swept in, and rather than closing the door on the past, the disseminated version of the text thus opened it up to new scrutiny, and a plethora of cases wanting to revisit past mistakes.

Conclusion

1. *Sistematichesky sbornik dekretov postanovlenii M.S. i rasporyazhenii pravitesltvennoi vlasti PO ZHILISHCHNOMU VOPROSU* (Moscow: MKKh, 1923), 18.

2. *Sistematichesky sbornik*, 22.

3. GARF f. A-353, op. 4, d. 306, l. 65.

4. T.H. Rigby, *Lenin's Government: Sovnarkom* (Cambridge: Cambridge University Press, 1979), 36. For "zakreplenie" in the Maly Sovnarkom, see TsAGM f. 2433, op. 1, d. 28.

5. *Sistematichesky sbornik*, 21.

6. Rents were reinstated as of May 1, 1922, overturning the Decree abolishing rent of January 27, 1921. *Sistematichesky sbornik*, 61.

7. *Sistematichesky sbornik*, 61.

8. The same order affirmed the right of residents to "self-concentrate" in the event that local authorities deemed this necessary. *Sistematichesky sbornik*, 57. "Postanovlenie SNK," Apr. 27, 1922, published *Izvestia VTsIK*, May 3, 1922, no. 96.

9. *Sistematichesky sbornik*, 19.

10. GARF f. 4085, op. 22, d. 243, l. 16. These expenditures had protected them from eviction—staying put had been their reward (see chapter 2).

11. Ambiguity was built even into the title of this document, the "Order on the Conditions for the Demunicipalization of Buildings," which was not a "Decree on Demunicipalization," which would have made it equivalent to the "Decree on Municipalization of August 1918," but rather an order "developing the Sovnarkom's order of August 8, 1921, on the review of lists of municipalized buildings."

12. *Sistematichesky sbornik*, 19.

13. TsAGM f. 2433, op. 1, d. 205, l. 7.

14. TsAGM f. 2433, op. 1, d. 205, ll. 2, 3.

15. GARF f. 4085, op. 22, d. 243, l. 24.

16. TsAGM f. 2433, op. 1, d. 120, l. 1.

17. TsAGM f. 2433, op. 1, d. 205, l. 3.

18. MUNI traced the decline in an annual report prepared at the end of 1925. TsAGM f. 2433, op. 1, d. 118, l. 21.

19. TsAGM f. 2433, op. 1, d. 106, l. 3

20. *Sistematichesky sbornik*, 26.

21. GARF f. 4085, op. 1a, d. 231, l. 20.

22. RGASPI f. 5, op. 1, d. 123, l. 6.

23. RGASPI f. 5, op. 1, d. 123, l. 10.

24. GARF f. 4085, op. 1a, d. 231, l. 2.

25. RGAE f. 7733, op. 1, d. 690, l. 41.

26. *Sistematichesky sbornik*, 25.

27. RGAE f. 7733, op. 1, d. 690, l. 13.

28. RGAE f. 7733, op. 1, d. 690, l. 14.

29. RGAE f. 7733, op. 1, d. 690, l. 170b.

30. RGAE f. 7733, op. 1, d. 690, l. 13.

31. RGAE f. 7733, op. 1, d. 690, l. 24.

32. RGAE f. 7733, op. 1, d. 690, l. 150b.

33. GARF f. 4085, op. 1a, d. 231, ll. 5, 8.

34. GARF f. 4085, op. 1a, d. 231, l. 23; RGAE f. 7733, op. 1, d. 694.

35. GARF f. 4085, op. 1a, d. 231, l. 43.

36. RGAE f. 7733, op. 1, d. 472, l. 3.

37. RGAE f. 7733, op. 1, d. 472, l. 3 to Lenin; RGAE f. 7733, op. 1, d. 550, l. 20 to Stalin and Politburo.

38. A point Matthew Desmond makes in *Evicted: Poverty and Profit in the American City* (New York: Broadway Books, 2016).

39. GARF f. R-130, op. 2, d. 77, l. 129.

40. GARF f. 4390, op. 2, d. 204, l. 8. GARF f. R-130, op. 2, d. 77, l. 144.

41. GARF f. R-130, op. 3, d. 122, l. 50.

42. TsAGM f. 2434, op. 1, d. 29, in an envelope after l. 34. Photographs of the images taken with permission by this author, July 13, 2017.

43. An argument of Thomas Lahusen, *How Life Writes the Book: Real Socialism and Socialist Realism in Stalin's Russia* (Ithaca, NY: Cornell University Press, 1997); as well as, for a later period, Denis Kozlov, *The Readers of* Novy Mir: *Coming to Terms with the Stalinist Past* (Cambridge, MA: Harvard University Press, 2013).

44. Like the other artists participating in the All-Union 20th Anniversary of Socialist Industry exhibition, Petrov-Vodkin published a text to explain his painting in *Pravda*, 21 October, 1936, no. 291, 4.

45. Petrov-Vodkin's stories in "Housewarming," the critique that there were too many, and the painting's critical failure are described by the Soviet art historian V. I. Kostin, *Kuzma Petrov-Vodkin* (Moscow: Sovetsky khudozhnik, 1966).

SELECT BIBLIOGRAPHY

Periodicals Consulted

Ekonomicheskaya Zhizn'
Ekonomist
Izvestia VTsIK
Izvestia finansov
Kommunistichesky Trud. Mossovet/MKRKP
Moskovsky vecherny chas
Pravda
Vechernie izvestia Mossoveta
Vechernyaya Krasnaya Gazeta. Moscow.
Vechernyaya Moskva
Vestnik finansov
Vestnik Vserossiyskago Soiuza Gorodov: Gorod.

Other Published Works

Abouchar, Alan. "The Time Factor and Soviet Investment Methodology," *Soviet Studies*, 37, no. 3 (1985).

Adelman, Jeremy. "Property Rules or the Rule of Property? Carol Rose on the History, Theory, and Rhetoric of Ownership," *Law & Social Inquiry*, 21, no. 4 (1996): 1041–60.

Akbar, Nafisa and Susan L. Ostermann. "Understanding, Defining, and Measuring State Capacity in India: Traditional, Modern, and Everything In Between" *Asian Survey*, 55, no. 5 (2015): 845–81.

Akcam, Taner and Umit Kurt. *The Spirit of the Laws: The Plunder of Wealth in the Armenian Genocide*, trans. Aram Arkun (New York, NY: Berghahn, 2015).

Aliamkin, A. V. and A. G. Baranov. *Istoriya denezhnogo obrashcheniya v 1914–1924 gg. (po materialam Zauralya)* (Yekaterinburg: Izd. UGGU, 2005).

Allisson, Francois. *Value and Prices in Russian Economic Thought: A Journey Inside the Russian Synthesis* (New York: Routledge, 2015).

Aly, Gotz. *Hitler's Beneficiaries: Plunder, Racial War, and the Nazi Welfare State*, trans. Jefferson Chase (New York: Metropolitan Books, 2007).

Anderson, Craig. *Roman Law* (Dundee: Dundee University Press, 2009).

Appadurai, Arjun. "Introduction: commodities and the politics of value," in *The Social Life of Things: Commodities in Cultural Perspective*, ed. Appadurai (Cambridge: Cambridge University Press, 1986).

Arendt, Hannah. *The Origins of Totalitarianism* (New York: Harcourt Brace Jovanovich, 1973).

Armstrong, George M., Jr. *The Soviet Law of Property: The Right to Control Property and the Construction of Communism* (The Hague: Martinus Nijhoff, 1983).

Atlas, Z. V. *Sotsialisticheskaya denezhnaya sistema*. (Moscow: Finansy, 1969).

Auslander, Leora. "Beyond Words," *American Historical Review*, 110, no. 4. (2005).

———. "Coming home? Jews in Postwar Paris," *Journal of Contemporary History*, 40, no. 2, (2005), 237–259.

Bailey, Derek. "Accounting in the Shadow of Stalinism," *Accounting, Organizations and Society* 15, no. 6 (1990), 513–25.

Baker, Keith Michael and Dan Edelstein, eds. *Scripting Revolution: A Historical Approach to the Comparative Study of Revolutions* (Stanford, CA: Stanford University Press, 2015).

Ball, Alan M. *Russia's Last Capitalists the Nepmen, 1921–1929* (Berkeley, CA: University of California Press, 1987).

Ball, Alan. "Lenin and the Question of Private Trade in Soviet Russia," *Slavic Review* 43, no. 3 (1984), 399–412.

Banerji, Arup. *Merchants and Markets in Revolutionary Russia, 1917–1930* (New York: St. Martin's Press, 1997).

Barkey, Karen. "In Different Times: Scheduling and Social Control in the Ottoman Empire, 1550 to 1650," *Comparative Studies in Society and History*, 38, no. 3 (1996), 460–83.

Baransky, N. *Rol' i zadachi raboche-krest'yanskoi inspektsii v sviazi s novoi ekon. politikoi (tezisy priniatye kollegiei NKRKI v zasedanii 2 sent. 1921 g.* (Moscow: 7-aya tip. M.S.N.Kh., 1921).

Barnett, Vincent. *A History of Russian Economic Thought* (New York, NY: Routledge, 2005).

Berman, Harold J. "Soviet Property in Law and in Plan," *University of Pennsylvania Law Review*, 96, (1948), 324.

Berton, Kathleen. *Moscow: An Architectural History* (London: I.B. Tauris, 1990).

Bliznakov, Milka. "Soviet Housing During the Experimental Years, 1918–1932," in *Russian Housing in the Modern Age: Design and Social History*, ed. William Brumfield and Blair Ruble (Washington, D.C.: Woodrow Wilson Center Press, 1993).

Blum, Alain, and Martine Mespoulet. "Le Passe Au Service Du Present. L'administration Statistique de l'Etat Sovietique Entre 1918 et 1930," *Cahiers Du Monde Russe*, 44, no. 2/3 (September 2003), 343–68.

Boeva, L.A. *Osobennaya kasta: VChK-OGPU i ukreplenie kommunisticheskogo rezhima v gody NEPa* (Moscow: AIRO-XXI, 2009).

Bourdieu, Pierre. Loïc J. D. Wacquant, and Samar Farage. "Rethinking the State: Genesis and Structure of the Bureaucratic Field," *Sociological Theory*,12, no. 1 (1994), 1–18.

Bowman, Linda. "Russia's First Income Taxes: The Effects of Modernized Taxes on Commerce and Industry, 1885–1914," *Slavic Review*, 52 (Summer 1993), 256–82.

Boym, Svetlana. *Common Places: Mythologies of Everyday Life in Russia* (Cambridge, MA: Harvard University Press, 1995).

Brewer, John. *The Sinews of Power: War, Money, and the English State, 1688–1783* (New York: Alfred A. Knopf, 1989).

Broner, D. L. *Ocherki ekonomiki zhilishchnogo khozyaistva Moskvy* (Moscow: Izdat. Narkomkhoza RSFSR, 1946).

Bronshtein, N. I. *Instruktsiya dlya uchreditelei DOMOVYKH ORGANIZATSII [s prilozheniem 'polozhenie o domovykh organizatsiiakh'].* (Moscow: Izvestia moskovskago soveta predstavitelei raionnykh dum, 1917).

Bullock, Nicholas, and James Read. *The Movement for Housing Reform in Germany and France 1840–1914* (Cambridge: Cambridge University Press, 1985).

Burbank, Jane. "Lenin and the Law in Revolutionary Russia," *Slavic Review*, 54, no. 1 (1995), 23–44.

Cadioli, Giovanni. "Economic Levers in the Soviet Union in the late 1940s," *Cahiers du monde russe*, 64 (1), 2023: 135–170.

Cadiot, Juliette. *La société des voleurs: Propriété et socialisme sous Staline* (Paris: Les Éditions de l'EHESS, 2021).

Cameron, Sarah. *The Hungry Steppe: Famine, Violence, and the Making of Soviet Kazakhstan* (Ithaca, NY: Cornell University Press, 2018).

Carr, E. H. "The Origin and Status of the Cheka." *Soviet Studies*, 10, no. 1 (1958).

Carr, E. H. and R. W. Davies. *Foundations of a Planned Economy* (New York: Macmillan, 1969).

Carruthers, Bruce, and Wendy Nelson Espeland. "Accounting for Rationality: Double-Entry Bookkeeping and the Rhetoric of Economic Rationality," *American Journal of Sociology*, 97, no. 1 (July 1991).

Chaigneau, Aurore. *Le droit de propriété en mutation: Essai à la lumière du droit russe* (Paris: Dalloz, 2008).

Chaudhry, Kiren Aziz. "The Myths of the Market and the Common History of Late Developers," *Politics & Society*, 21, no. 3, (1993), 245–74.

Chermensky V. D. and M. N. Smit, eds. *Statistika v rabotakh V.I. Lenina* (Moscow: Gos. Sotsial'noe-ekonomicheskoe Izd. 1933).

Chernov, V. M. *Che-Ka: Materialy po deiatelnosti chrezvychainykh komissii* (Izd. Tsentral'nogo biuro Partii sotsialistov-revoliutsionerov, 1922).

Clark, Katerina. *Petersburg: Crucible of Cultural Revolution* (Cambridge, MA: Harvard University Press, 1998).

Colton, Timothy. *Moscow: Governing the Socialist Metropolis* (Cambridge, MA: The Belknap Press of Harvard University Press, 1995).

Corney, Frederick. *Telling October: Memory and the Making of the Bolshevik Revolution* (Ithaca, NY: Cornell University Press, 2004).

Crawford, Christina. *Spatial Revolution: Architecture and Planning in the Early Soviet Union* (Ithaca, NY: Cornell University Press, 2022).

Darrow, David. *Tsardom of Sufficiency, Empire of Norms: Statistics, Land Allotments, and Agrarian Reform in Russia, 1700–1921* (Montreal: McGill-Queen's University Press, 2018).

Dean, Martin. "The Seizure of Jewish Property in Europe: Comparative Aspects of Nazi Methods and Local Responses," in *Robbery and Restitution: The Conflict over Jewish Property in Europe*, ed. Martin Dean, Constantin Goschler, and Philipp Ther, (New York: Berghahn Books, 2008).

Desmond, Matthew. *Evicted: Poverty and Profit in the American City* (New York: Broadway Books, 2016).

Dyachenko, V. P. and Kosyachenko, G. *50 let sovetskikh finansov* (Moscow: Finansy, 1967).

Dobb, Maurice. "The Revival of Theoretical Discussion among Soviet Economists," *Science & Society*, 24, no. 4 (Fall, 1960), 289–311.

Dobrokhotov, L. N., V. N. Kolodezhnyi, V. S. Pushkarev, eds., *Denezhnaya reforma 1921–1924 gg.: Sozdanie tvyordoi valiuty (dokumenty i materialy)* (Moscow: ROSSPEN, 2008).

Dogliani, Patrizia. "European Municipalism in the First Half of the Twentieth Century: The Socialist Network," *Contemporary European History* 11, no. 4 (2002).

Domovladenie i gorodskoe khozyaistvo: delovoi organ dlya domovladel'tsev, stroitelei, i gorodskikh obshchestvennykh upravlenii, ed. S. A. Prosbin (Petersburg: S. A. Prosbin, 1911–1915).

Dreyfus, Jean-Marc. "The Looting of Jewish Property in Occupied Western Europe: A Comparative Study of Belgium, France, and the Netherlands," in *Robbery and Restitution: The Conflict over Jewish Property in Europe*, ed. Martin Dean, Constantin Goschler, and Philipp Ther (New York: Berghahn Books, 2008).

Dunham, Vera. *In Stalin's Time: Middleclass Values in Soviet Fiction* (Durham, NC: Duke University Press, 1990).

Edelstein, Dan. "Do We Want a Revolution without Revolution? Reflections on Political Authority," *French Historical Studies*, 35, no. 2 (Spring 2012), 269–289.

Engelstein, Laura. *Russia in Flames: War, Revolution, Civil War, 1914–1921* (New York, NY: Oxford University Press, 2017).

Epikhin, A. Yu., and O. B. Mozhokhin. *VChK-OGPU-NKVD na zashchite ekonomicheskoi bezopasnosti gosudarstva 1917–1941* (Moscow: Kuchkovo pole, 2016).

Ertman, Thomas. *Birth of the Leviathan: Building States and Regimes in Medieval and Early Modern Europe* (Cambridge: Cambridge University Press, 1997).

Evakuatsiya i rekvizitsiya: spravochnik deistvuyushchikh uzakonenii i rasporyazhenii po evakuatsii, rozysku evakuirovanykh gruzov i rekvizitsii (Petrograd: Izd. Evakuatsionno-rekvizitsionnogo otdela, 1916).

Evzlin, Z. P. *Dengi; pod redaktsiei i s predisloviem prof. M. I. Bogolepova.* (Petrograd: Glavlit; PEPO, 1923).

Exeler, Franziska. "What Did You Do during the War?: Personal Responses to the Aftermath of Nazi Occupation," *Kritika: Explorations in Russian and Eurasian History*, 17, no. 4 (2016), 805–835.

Falkus, Malcolm. "The Development of Municipal Trading in the Nineteenth Century," *Business History*, 19, no. 2, (1977), 134–161.

Fedyukin, S. A. *Veliky Oktiabr' i intelligentsia: iz istorii vovlecheniya staroi intelligentsii v stroitelstvo sotsializma.* (Moscow: Nauka, 1972).

Feldman, Gerald. *The Great Disorder: Politics, Economics, and Society in the German Inflation, 1914–1924* (New York: Oxford University Press, 1993).

Figes, Orlando. *Peasant Russia, Civil War: The Volga Countryside in Revolution (1917–1921)* (Oxford: Clarendon Press, 1989).

Figes, Orlando, and Boris Kolonitskii. *Interpreting the Russian Revolution: The Language and Symbols of 1917* (New Haven, CT: Yale University Press, 1999).

Finkel, Stuart. "The 'Political Red Cross' and the Genealogy of Rights Discourse in Revolutionary Russia," *The Journal of Modern History*, 89, no. 1 (March 2017).

Fitzpatrick, Sheila. "Ordzhonikidze's Takeover of Vesenka: A Case Study in Soviet Bureaucratic Politics," *Soviet Studies*, 37, no. 2 (1985), 153–172.

———. "What's Left?" *The London Review of Books*, 39, no. 7 (30 March 2017).

———. *The Russian Revolution* 2nd ed., (New York: Oxford University Press, 1994).

Fogelson, Robert M. *The Great Rent Wars: New York, 1917–1929* (New Haven: Yale University Press, 2013).

Fraiman, A. L. *Forpost sotsialisticheskoi revoliutsii: Petrograd v pervye mesiatsy sovetskoi vlasti* (Leningrad: Izd. Nauka, 1969).

Galagan, A. M. *Kurs schetovedeniia*, 2nd ed. (Moscow, Vysshaya shkola, 1918).

———. *Osnovy obshchego schetovedeniya* (Moscow: Izd-vo Narkomtorga SSSR i RSFSR, 1928).

Ganev, Venelin. *Preying on the State: the transformation of Bulgaria after 1989* (Ithaca, NY: Cornell University Press, 2007).

Gatrell, Peter. *A Whole Empire Walking: Refugees in Russia During World War I* (Bloomington, IN: Indiana University Press, 1999).

Geldern, James von. *Bolshevik Festivals, 1917–1920* (Berkeley: University of California Press, 1993).

Gessen, I. V., ed. *Arkhiv russkoi revoliutsii* (Berlin: Slovo-Verlag, 1922).

Ghosh, Arunabh. *Making it Count: Statistics and Statecraft in the Early People's Republic of China* (Princeton, NJ: Princeton University Press, 2020).

Gimpelson, E. G. *Sovetskie upravlentsy, 1917–1920 gg.* (Moscow: Institut Rossiiskoi istorii RAN, 1998).

Gindin, A. *Kak bolsheviki ovladeli gosudarstvennym bankom.* (Moscow: Gosizdat, 1961).

Glenny, M. "Leonid Krasin: The Years Before 1917, an Outline," *Soviet Studies*, 22, no. 2 (1970).

Goland, Yu. M. *Diskussii ob ekonomicheskoi politike v gody denezhnoi reformy 1921–1924* (Moscow: Ekonomika, 2006).

Goldstein, Brian. *The Roots of Urban Renaissance: Gentrification and the Struggle over Harlem* (Cambridge, MA: Harvard University Press, 2017).

Goschler, Constantin, and Philipp Ther. "Introduction," in *Robbery and Restitution: The Conflict over Jewish Property in Europe*, ed. Martin Dean, Constantin Goschler, and Philipp Ther (New York, NY: Berghahn Books, 2008).

Gosudarstvennyi kontrol', 1811–1911 (St. Petersburg: Gos. Tip., 1911).

Gouldner, Alvin. "Stalinism: A Study of Internal Colonialism," *Telos*, no. 34 (1977–8), 5–48.

Grabar, Igor. "Rynki v staroi Moskve," *Stroitelstvo Moskvy*, no. 5 (May 1925), 11–4.

———. "Slomka zdanii i gorodskoe blagoustroistvo." *Stroitelstvo Moskvy*, no. 7 (July 1925).

Gronsky Pavel P. (Pavel Pavlovich), and N. I. (Nikolai Ivanovich) Astrov. *The War and the Russian Government: The Central Government, by Paul P. Gronsky. The Municipal Government and the All-Russian Union of Towns, by Nicholas J. Astrov.* (New Haven, Yale University Press; London, Oxford University Press, for the Carnegie Endowment for International Peace, Division of Economics and History, 1929).

Gross, Jan. *Revolution from Abroad: The Soviet Conquest of Poland's Western Ukraine and Western Belorussia—Expanded Edition* (Princeton, NJ: Princeton University Press, 2002).

Grossman, Gregory. "Gold and the Sword: Money in the Soviet Command Economy," in *Industrialization in Two Systems: Essays in Honor of Alexander Gerschenkron*, ed. Henry Rosovsky (New York: Wiley, 1966).

———. "Introduction," *Money and Plan: Financial Aspects of East European Economic Reforms*. ed. and intro. by Gregory Grossman (Berkeley: University of California Press, 1968).

Grunt, A. Ya., and V. I. Startsev. *Petrograd-Moskva Iyul' Noyabr'1917*. (Moscow, Politizdat, 1984).

Gursky, V. N. *Kvartiranty i domovladel'tsy: Prava i obiazannosti ikh po novomu zakonu 27 avg. 1916 g.* (Moscow: tip. T-va I. D. Sytina, 1917).

Hamm, Michael. "The Breakdown of Urban Modernization: a prelude to the revolutions of 1917," in *The City in Russian History*, ed. Michael F. Hamm (Lexington: University Press of Kentucky, 1976).

Harding, Neil, and Political Studies Association of the United Kingdom. Communist Politics Group. *The State in Socialist Society* (Albany: State University of New York Press, 1984).

Harding, Neil. *Lenin's Political Thought: Theory and Practice in the Democratic Revolution* (London: MacMillan, 1977).

Harris, Steven. *Communism on Tomorrow Street: Mass Housing and Everyday Life after Stalin* (Baltimore: The Woodrow Wilson Center Press and the Johns Hopkins University Press, 2013).

Harrison, Mark. "Prices in the Politburo, 1927: market equilibrium versus the use of force," in *The lost Politburo transcripts: from collective rule to Stalin's dictatorship*, ed. Paul R. Gregory and Norman Naimark (New Haven, CT: Yale University Press, 2008).

Hasegawa, Tsuyoshi. *Crime and Punishment in the Russian Revolution: Mob Justice and Police in Petrograd* (Cambridge, MA: Harvard University Press, 2018).

———. *The February Revolution: Petrograd, 1917* (Seattle, WA: University of Washington Press, 1981).

Hazard, John N. "Soviet Property Law," *Cornell Law Review*, 30, no. 466 (1945).

———. *Soviet Housing Law* (New Haven, CT: Yale University Press, 1939).

Heller, Michael. "The Tragedy of the Anticommons: Property in the Transition from Marx to Markets," *Harvard Law Review*, 111 (1998).

Hoffmann, David L. *Peasant Metropolis: Social Identities in Moscow* (Ithaca, NY: Cornell University Press, 2000).

Holquist, Peter. "'In Accord with State Interests and the People's Wishes': The Technocratic Ideology of Imperial Russia's Resettlement Administration." *Slavic Review* 69, no. 1 (Spring 2010), 151–79.

———. "State Violence as Technique: The Logic of Violence in Soviet Totalitarianism," in *Landscaping the Human Garden*, ed. Amir Weiner (Stanford, CA: Stanford University Press, 2003).

———. *Making War, Forging Revolution: Russia's Continuum of Crisis, 1914–1921* (Cambridge, MA: Harvard University Press, 2002).

Hubbard, L. E. *Soviet Money and Finance* (London: Macmillan, 1936).

Hull, Matthew. *Government of Paper: The Materiality of Bureaucracy in Urban Pakistan* (Berkeley, CA: The University of California Press, 2012).

Humphrey, Caroline. "Ideology in Infrastructure: Architecture and Soviet Imagination," *Journal of the Royal Anthropological Institute*, 11, no. 1 (2005), 39–58.

——. *Karl Marx Collective: Economy, Society, and Religion in a Siberian Collective Farm* (Cambridge: Cambridge University Press, 1983).

Humphrey, Caroline. and Katherine Verdery, "Introduction," in *Property in Question: Value Transformation in the Global Economy,* Humphrey and Verdery, eds., (New York: Routledge, 2004).

Hunt, Lynn. *Politics, Culture, and Class in the French Revolution* (Berkeley: University of California Press, 1984).

Iakovlev, V. "Malo-Vishersky epizod (Pereezd Sovnarkoma v Moskvu v 1918 g.)." *Krasnaya letopis',* 1, no.58 (1934), 94–102.

Ignatiev, G. S. *Moskva v pervyi god proletarskoi diktatury* (Moscow: Nauka, 1974).

Ikonnikov, S. N. (Sergei Nikolaevich). *Sozdanie i deyatel'nost' obedinyonnykh organov TsKK-RKI v 1923–1934 gg.* (Moscow: Nauka, 1971).

——. *Organizatsiia i deyatel'nost' RKI v 1920–1925 gg.* (Moscow: Izd-vo Akademii nauk SSSR, 1960).

Ilyin-Zhenevsky, A. F. *The Bolsheviks in Power: Reminiscences of the Year 1918,* trans. Brian Pearce (London: New Park Publications, 1984).

Iroshnikov, M. P. *Sozdanie sovetskogo tsentral'nogo gosudarstvennogo apparata: Sovet Narodnykh Komissarov i narodnye komissariaty, okyabr' 1917 g.–yanvar' 1918 g.* (Leningrad: Nauka, 1967).

——. "K voprosu o slome burzhuaznoi gosudarstvennoi mashiny v Rossii," in *Problemy gosudarstvennogo stroitelstva v pervye gody sovetskoi vlasti: sbornik statei,* ed. Yu. S. Tokarev. (Leningrad: Nauka, 1973).

Istoriya Moskvy: period postreniia sotsializma (1917–June 1941), Vols. 4, 5, 6. (Moscow: Izd. Akademii nauk SSSR, 1952–1957).

Izmozik, V. S. *Glaza i ushi rezhima: gosudarstvennyi politichesky kontrol' za naseleniem Sovetskoi Rossii v 1918–1928 godakh* (St. Petersburg: Izd-vo Sankt-Peterburgskogo universiteta ekonomiki i finansov, 1995).

Jahn, Hubertus F. "The Housing Revolution in Petrograd 1917–1920," *Jahrbücher Für Geschichte Osteuropas,* 38, no. 2 (1990), 212–27.

Jasny, Naum. "A Note on Rationality and Efficiency in the Soviet Economy. I," *Soviet Studies,* 12, no. 4 (1961).

Kapchinsky, Oleg. *Gosbezopasnost' iznutri: Natsionalnyi i sotsialnyi sostav* (Moscow: EKSMO, 2005).

Karamursel, Ceyda. "Shiny Things and Sovereign Legalities: Expropriation of Dynastic Property in the Late Ottoman Empire and Early Turkish Republic," *International Journal of Middle East Studies,* 51 (2019).

Katsenelenbaum, Z. S. *Russian Currency and Banking* (London: P.S. King, 1925).

Kenez, Peter. *The Birth of the Propaganda State: Soviet Methods of Mass Mobilization, 1917–1929* (New York: Cambridge University Press, 1985).

Kharchenko, K. V. *Vlast'—Imushchestvo—Chelovek: peredel sobstvennosti v bolshevistskoi Rossii 1917–nachala 1921 gg.* (Moscow, 2000).

Kiaer, Christina. *Imagine No Possessions: The Socialist Objects of Russian Constructivism* (Cambridge, MA: MIT Press, 2008).

Klementyev, V. F. *V bolshevitskoi Moskve (1918–1920)* (Moscow: Russky put', 1998).

Klimenko, V. A. *Bor'ba s kontrrevolyutsiei v Moskve, 1917–1920.* (Moscow, 1978).

Koenker, Diane. *Moscow Workers and the 1917 Revolution* (Princeton, NJ: Princeton University Press, 1981).

Kolonitskii, Boris I. "Antibourgeois Propaganda and Anti-"Burzhui" Consciousness in 1917," *The Russian Review*, 53, no. 2 (1994), 183–96.

———. "Russian Historiography of the 1917 Revolution: New Challenges to Old Paradigms?" *History & Memory*, 21, no. 2 (2009), 34–59.

Kopytoff, Igor. "The cultural biography of things: Commoditization as process," in Arjun Appadurai, ed., *The Social Life of Things: Commodities in Cultural Perspective* (Cambridge: Cambridge University Press, 1986).

Kosomarov, G. D., ed. *Uprochenie Sovetskoi vlasti v Moskve i Moskovskoi gubernii: dokumenty i materialy* (Moscow: Moskovsky rabochy, 1958).

Kotkin, Stephen. "Shelter and Subjectivity in the Stalin Period: A Case Study in Magnitogorsk," in *Russian Housing in the Modern Age: Design and Social History*, ed. William Brumfield and Blair Ruble (Washington, D.C.: Wilson Center Press, 1993).

———. "The State—Is It Us? Memoirs, Archives, and Kremlinologists," *Russian Review*, 61, no. 1 (2002), 35–51.

Kotsonis, Yanni. *States of Obligation: Taxes and Citizenship in the Russian Empire and Early Soviet Union* (Toronto: University of Toronto Press, 2014).

———. "'No Place to Go': Taxation and State Transformation in Late Imperial and Early Soviet Russia," *The Journal of Modern History*, 76, no. 3 (2004), 531–57.

Kozlov, Denis. *The Readers of* Novyi Mir: *Coming to Terms with the Stalinist Past* (Cambridge, MA: Harvard University Press, 2013).

Krasnaya Moskva: 1917–1920 (Moscow: Mossoviet, former I. D. Sytina, 1920).

Kudrin, A. L. ed. *Istoriya ministerstva finansov v chetyrekh tomakh* (Moscow, 2002).

Kurchinsky, M.A. *Munitsipal'nyi sotsializm i razvitiya gorodskoi zhizni* (St. Petersburg: Brokgauz-Efron, 1907).

Kuter, M., M. Gurskaia, and A. Kuznetsov, "Alexander Galagan: Russian Titan of the Enlightenment in the History of Accounting," *Accounting History*, 24, no. 2 (2019), 293–316.

Lahusen, Thomas. *How Life Writes the Book: Real Socialism and Socialist Realism in Stalin's Russia* (Ithaca, NY: Cornell University Press, 1997).

Larsons, M. J. *An Expert in the Service of the Soviet*, trans. Angelo Rappoport. (London: Ernest Benn Ltd., 1929).

Latsis (Diadia), M. *V poslednei skhvatke s tsarizmom: vospominaniya o rabote moskovskikh bolshevikov v gody imperialisticheskoi voiny* (Moscow: Mosk. rabochii, 1935).

Latsis, M. Ya. (Sudrabs). *Chrezvychainye komissii po bor'be s kontr-revolyutsiyei* (Moscow: Gosizdat, 1921).

Lefebvre, Georges. *Coming of the French Revolution*, trans. R. R. Palmer (Princeton, NJ: Princeton University Press, 2005).

Leggett, George. *The Cheka: Lenin's Political Police* (Oxford: Clarendon Press, 1981).

Lenin, V. I. *Polnoe sobranie sochinenii*, 5th ed., (Moscow, 1958–1965).

Levy, Jonathan. "Accounting for Profit and the History of Capital," *Critical Historical Studies*, 1, no. 2 (Fall 2014).

Lewin, Moshe. "Who was the Soviet Kulak?," *Soviet Studies*, 18, no. 2 (1966), 189–212.

Lih, Lars T. *Bread and Authority in Russia, 1914–1921* (Berkeley, CA: University of California Press, 1990).

Lohr, Eric. "Patriotic Violence and the State: The Moscow Riots of May 1915," *Kritika: Explorations in Russian and Eurasian History*, 4, no. 3, (2003), 607–26.

———. *Nationalizing the Russian Empire: The Campaign against Enemy Aliens during World War I* (Cambridge, MA: Harvard University Press, 2003).

Lohr, Eric and Joshua Sanborn, "1917: Revolution as Demobilization and State Collapse," *Slavic Review*, 76, no. 3, (2017), 703–9.

MChK: Iz istorii moskovskoi chrezvychainoi komissii (1918–1921) (Moscow: Moskovsky rabochy, 1978).

Magri, Susanna. "Housing," in *Capital Cities at War: Paris, London, Berlin, 1914–1919*, ed. Jay Winter and Jean-Louis Robert (Cambridge: Cambridge University Press, 1997).

Malkov, Pavel. *Zapisiki komendanta Moskovskogo Kremlya* (Moscow: Molodaya gvardiya, 1967).

Malle, Silvana. *The Economic Organization of War Communism, 1918–1921* (Cambridge: Cambridge University Press, 1985).

Mamaev, A. V. *Gorodskoe samoupravlenie v rossii nakanune i v period fevralskoi revoliutsii 1917 g.* (Moscow: IstLit, 2017).

Mazdorov, V. A. *Istoriya razvitiya bukhgalterskogo ucheta v SSSR (1917–1972)* (Moscow: Finansy, 1972).

McAuley, Mary. *Bread and Justice: State and Society in Petrograd, 1917–1922* (Oxford: Oxford University Press, 1991).

McKeon, Michael. *The Secret History of Domesticity: Public, Private, and the Division of Knowledge* (Baltimore: Johns Hopkins University Press, 2006).

McMeekin, Sean. *History's Greatest Heist: The Looting of Russia by the Bolsheviks* (New Haven, CT: Yale, 2008).

Mëhilli, Elidor. *From Stalin to Mao: Albania and the Socialist World* (Ithaca, NY: Cornell University Press, 2017).

Melgunov, Sergei. *Red Terror in Russia* (New York, NY: Hyperion, 1975).

Mikhailovsky, A. *Deiatel'nost' moskovskogo samoupravleniya, Izvestia Moskovskoi gorodskoi dumy* (Moscow, 1917).

Mirowski, Philip. "Learning the Meaning of a Dollar: Conservation Principles and the Social Theory of Value in Economic Theory," *Social Research*, 57, no. 3, (1990), 689–717.

Mitchell, Timothy. "The Limits of the State: Beyond Statist Approaches and Their Critics," *The American Political Science Review*, 85, no. 1, (1991), 77–96.

Morack, Ellinor. *The Dowry of the State? The Politics of Abandoned Property and the Population Exchange in Turkey, 1921–1945* (Bamberg: University of Bamberg Press, 2017).

Moskovskaya gorodskaya duma 1913–1916: [ocherk deyatel'nosti] Mosk. Gor. Duma: Kom. gruppy progres. glasnykh (Moscow: Gor. Tip., 1916).

Moskva Velikaya/Great Moscow: Guide (Moscow: Moskovsky komsomolets', Exim, 1997).

Muldrew, Craig. "'Hard Food for Midas': Cash and its social value in Early Modern England," *Past and Present*, no. 170, (Feb. 2001), 78–120.

Narodnyi Komissariat Finansov 1917–1922. (Moscow: Krasny proletariat, 1922).

Narsky, I. V. *Zhizn' v katastrofe: budni naseleniya Urala v 1917–1922 gg.* (Moscow: Rosspen, 2001).

Nettl, J. P. "The State as a Conceptual Variable," *World Politics*, 20, no. 4 (Jul. 1968), 559–92.

Normy dlya otsenki gorodskikh nedvizhimykh imushchestv po zakonu 8 iyunya 1893 (Moscow: Vys. utverzh. t-stvo "pechatnia S.P. Yakovleva," 1898).

Nove, Alec. *An Economic History of the USSR* (New York, NY: Penguin, 1969).

Nove, Alec, and Alfred Zauberman. "A Resurrected Russian Economist of 1900," in *Soviet Studies*, 13, no. 1 (1961).

Novikova, Liudmila. *Provintsial'naya 'kontrrevolyutsiya': beloe dvizhenie i grazhdanskaya voina na russkom severe 1917–1920* (Moscow: Novoe Literaturnoe Obozrenie, 2011).

O'Donnell, Anne. "Khozyaistvennaya zhizn' i vlast' v Moskve, 1914–1920," in *Goroda imperii v gody Velikoi voiny i revoliutsii*, ed. A. Miller, D. Chernyi (St. Petersburg: Nestor-Istoriya, 2017), 19–51.

Okunev, N. P. *Dnevnik Moskvicha 1917–1924* (Paris: YMCA Press 1990).

Orlovsky, Daniel T. "State Building in the Civil War Era: The Role of the Lower-Middle Strata," in *Party, State, and Society in the Russian Civil War: Explorations in Social History,* ed. Koenker, Diane, William G. Rosenberg, and Ronald Grigor Suny. (Bloomington: Indiana University Press, 1989).

Osokina, Elena. *Ierarkhiya potrebleniya: o zhizni lyudei v usloviyakh stalinskogo snabzheniya* (Moscow: Izd. MGOU, 1993).

———. *Zoloto dlya industrializatsii: TORGSIN* (Moscow: Rosspen, 2009).

Pavlov, P. M. *Dengi v period stroitelstva kommunizma* (Moscow: Gosfinizdat, 1962).

Peterson, Maya. *Pipe Dreams: Water and Empire in Central Asia's Aral Sea Basin* (Cambridge: Cambridge University Press, 2019).

Pethybridge, R. W. *The Spread of the Russian Revolution: Essays on 1917* (London: Palgrave Macmillan, 1972).

———. "The Bolsheviks and Technical Disorder, 1917–1918," *The Slavonic and East European Review*, 49, no. 116 (1971), 410–24.

Pethybridge, Roger. ed., *Witnesses to the Russian Revolution* (London: George Allen & Unwin, Ltd., 1964).

Petrograd Soviet Otdel Upravlenie. *Instruktsiya domovym komitetam bednoty i komendantam domov.* (Petrograd: Petrograd Soviet Otdel Upravlenie, 1920).

Pisarkova, L. F. Moskovskaya gorodskaya duma 1863–1917 (Moscow: Mosgorarkhiv, 1998).

Pohl, Dieter. "The robbery of Jewish property in eastern Europe under German occupation, 1939–1942," in Martin Dean, Constantin Goschler, and Philipp Ther, eds. *Robbery and Restitution: The Conflict over Jewish Property in Europe* (New York, NY: Berghahn Books, 2008).

Poliakov, Yu. A. *Moskovskie trudyashchiyesya v oborone sovetskoi stolitsy v 1919 godu* (Moscow, 1957).

Postanovleniya Moskovskogo Soveta po Zhilishchnomu i Zemelnomu Voprosam (Moscow: 8-aya Tipografiya, 1918).

Potekhin, M. N. *Pervyi Soviet proletarskoi diktatury* (Leningrad: Lenizdat, 1966).

Pravilova, E. A. *The Ruble: A Political History* (New York: Oxford University Press, 2023).

———. *A Public Empire: Property and the Quest for the Common Good in Imperial Russia* (Princeton, NJ: Princeton University Press, 2014).

Programmy russkikh politicheskikh partii 1. Partii narodnoi svobody 2. Narodnykh sotsialistov 3. Sotsialistov revoliutsionerov 4. Yevreiskaya sotsialisticheskaia 5. Sotsial-demokratov (Stavropol: Trud i znanie, 1917).

Rabinowitch, Alexander. *The Bolsheviks in Power: The First Year of Soviet Rule* (Bloomington, IN: Indiana University Press, 2008).

———. *The Bolsheviks Come to Power: The Revolution in 1917 in Petrograd* (New York: W.W. Norton and Company, 1976).

———. *Prelude to Revolution: The Petrograd Bolsheviks and the July 1917 Uprising* (Bloomington, IN: Indiana University Press, 1968).

Raleigh, Donald. *Experiencing Russia's Civil War: Politics, Society, and Revolutionary Culture in Saratov 1917–1922* (Princeton, NJ: Princeton University Press, 2003).

Ratkovsky, I. S. *Krasnyi terror i deyatel'nost' VChK v 1918 godu* (St. Petersburg: Izd. SPb. Univ, 2006).

Reid, Susan. "Communist Comfort: Socialist Modernism and the Making of Cosy Homes in the Khrushchev Era," *Gender & History*, 21, no. 3 (2009).

Remington, Thomas. "Institution building in Bolshevik Russia: The Case of 'State Kontrol,'" *Slavic Review*, 41, no. 1 (1982), 91–103.

Rigby, T. H. *Communist Party Membership in the U.S.S.R. 1917–1967* (Princeton, NJ: Princeton University Press, 1968).

———. *Lenin's Government: Sovnarkom, 1917–1922* (Cambridge: Cambridge University Press, 1979).

Rodgers, D. T. *Atlantic Crossings: Social Politics in a Progressive Age* (Cambridge, MA: Harvard University Press, 1998).

Rose, C. M. *Property and Persuasion: Essays On The History, Theory, And Rhetoric Of Ownership* (New York: Routledge, 1995).

———. "Property and Expropriation: Themes and Variations in American Law," *Utah Law Review*, 2000, no. 1, (November 2000).

———. "Property as Storytelling: Perspectives from Game Theory, Narrative Theory, Feminist Theory," *Yale Journal of Law & the Humanities*, Vol. 2, 37, 1990: 37–57.

Rosenberg, William. "The Problem of Market Relations and the State in Revolutionary Russia." *Comparative Studies in Society and History*, 36, no. 2 (April 1994), 356–96.

Rosenfeldt, Niels Erik. *The "Special" World: Stalin's Power Apparatus and the Soviet System's Secret Structures of Communication*, vols. 1, 2. (Copenhagen: Museum Tusculanum Press, 2009).

Sakwa, Richard. "The Commune State in Moscow in 1918," *Slavic Review*, 46, no. 3–4 (1987), 429–49.

Sanborn, Joshua. *Imperial Apocalypse: The Great War and the Destruction of the Russian Empire* (New York, NY: Oxford University Press, 2014).

Sanchez-Sibony, Oscar. "Global Money and Bolshevik Authority: The NEP as the First Socialist Project," *Slavic Review*, 78, no. 3 (2019), 694–716.

Selishchev, Afanasy. *Yazyk revolyutsionnoi epokhi: nablyudeniya nad russkim yazykom posklednikh let, 1917–1926* (Moscow: Rabotnik prosveshcheniia, 1928).

Sewell, William H. "Historical Events as Transformations of Structures: Inventing Revolution at the Bastille," *Theory and Society*, 25, no. 6 (1996).

Shapiro, Ann-Louise. *Housing the Poor of Paris* (Madison, WI: University of Wisconsin Press, 1985).

Shingarev, A. I. *Selo Novo-Zhivotinnoe i derevnya Mokhovatka v sanitarnom otnoshenii: Opyt san.-ekon. issled. zem. vracha A. [Sh!] Shingareva* (Saratov: 1901).

Shishkov, Vyacheslav. "The Divorce," in *The Fatal Eggs and Other Satire: 1918–1963*, Mirra Ginsburg, ed. and trans. (New York: Grove Press, 1987).

Shklovsky, Viktor. *A Sentimental Journey: Memoirs 1917–1922*, trans. Richard Sheldon, with introduction by Sidney Monas (Ithaca, NY: Cornell University Press, 1984).

Sistematichesky sbornik dekretov postanovlenii M.S. i rasporaizhenii pravitesltvennoi vlasti PO ZHILISHCHNOMU VOPROSU (Moscow: M.K.Kh., 1923).

Slezkine, Yuri. *The House of Government: A Saga of the Russian Revolution* (Princeton, NJ: Princeton University Press, 2017).

Smail, Daniel Lord. *Imaginary Cartographies: Possession and Identity in Late Medieval Marseille* (Ithaca, NY: Cornell University Press, 1999).

Smele, Jonathan D. *Civil war in Siberia: The Anti-Bolshevik government of Admiral Kolchak* (Cambridge: Cambridge University Press, 1996).

Smith, Mark. *Property of Communists: The Urban Housing Program from Stalin to Khrushchev* (DeKalb, IL: Northern Illinois University Press, 2010).

Sobranie uzakoneniy i rasporyazheniy, 1917–1949 (Moscow: Iuridicheskoe izd. N.K.Iu. RSFSR, 1920–1950).

Sofinov, P. G. *Ocherki Istorii vserossiiskoi chrezvychainoi komissii 1917–1922* (Moscow: 1959).

Sokolov, Iaroslav. *Bukhgaltersky uchyot: ot istokov do nashikh dnei* (Moscow: Yuniti, 1996).

Soll, Jacob. *The Reckoning: Financial Accountability and the Rise and Fall of Nations* (New York: Basic Books, 2014).

Solnick, Steven L. *Stealing the State: Control and Collapse in Soviet Institutions* (Cambridge, MA: Harvard University Press, 1998).

Solomon, Peter. *Soviet Criminal Justice under Stalin* (New York, NY: Cambridge University Press, 1996).

Sosnovy, Timothy. *The Soviet Housing Problem* (New York: Research Program on the USSR, 1954).

Spang, Rebecca. *Stuff and Money in the Time of the French Revolution* (Cambridge, MA: Harvard University Press, 2017).

Spar, Debora L. "Markets: Continuity and Change in the International Diamond Market," *The Journal of Economic Perspectives*, 20, no. 3, (2006).

Stites, Richard. *Revolutionary Dreams: Utopian Vision and Experimental Life in the Russian Revolution* (Oxford: Oxford University Press, 1989).

Strumilin, S. G. *Na planovom fronte, 1920–1920 gg.* (Moscow: Gosizdat. pol. literatury, 1958).

Teplyakov, A. G. *"Nepronitsaemye nedra": VChK-OGPU v Sibiri, 1918–1929 gg.* (Moscow: AIRO-XXI, 2007).

Thurston, Robert. *Liberal City, Conservative State: Moscow and Russia's Urban Crisis, 1906–1914* (New York: Oxford University Press, 1987).

Tilly, Charles. "Warmaking and Statemaking as Organized Crime," in *Bringing the State Back In*, ed. P. Evans, D. Rueschemeyer, T. Skocpol. (Cambridge: Cambridge University Press. 1985).

Timasheff, N. S. "The Impact of the Penal Law of Imperial Russia on Soviet Penal Law," *American Slavic and East European Review*, 12, no. 4 (1953), 441–462.

Tolstykh, D. "Ukreplenie mestnago gosudarstvennogo apparata v stolitse v pervoi polovine 1918 goda," in *Moskva v dvukh revolyutsiyakh. Fevral'—oktyabr' 1917g. (Sbornik statei)* (Moscow: Moskovsky rabochy, 1958).

Trutovsky, Vladimir. "O munitsipal'noi programme" (Partiia sotsialistov-revoliutsionerov, no. 25) (Petrograd: Tip. P. P. Sainina, 1917).

Valentinov (Volsky), N. Novaya Ekonomicheskaia politika i krizis partii posle smerti Lenina: gody raboty v VSNKh vo vremya NEPa. Vospominaniya. (Moscow: Sovremennik, 1991).

Varga-Harris, Christine. Stories of House and Home: Soviet Apartment Life During the Khrushchev Years (Ithaca, NY: Cornell University Press, 2015).

Velychenko, Stephen. State Building in Revolutionary Ukraine: A Comparative Study of Governments and Bureaucrats, 1917–1922 (Toronto: University of Toronto Press, 2011).

Verdery, Katherine, What Was Socialism, and What Comes Next? (Princeton, NJ: Princeton University Press, 1996).

———. "Fuzzy Property: Rights, Power, and Identity in Transylvania's Decollectivization," in Uncertain Transition: Ethnographies of Change in the Postsocialist World, ed. Michael Burawoy and Katherine Verdery (New York, NY: Rowman & Littlefield, 1999).

Verner, I. A. Sovremennoe khozyaistvo goroda Moskvy (Moscow: Gorodskaya Tip., 1913).

———. Deiatel'nost' Moskovskoi Gorodskoi Dumy v 1909–1912 godakh (Moscow: Gorodskaya Tip., 1912).

Vinogradov, V., A. Litvin, V. Khristoforov, N. Peremyshlennikova, ed., Arkhiv VChK: sbornik dokumentov (Moscow: Kuchkovo pole, 2007).

Voronetskaya, A.A. "Organizatsiya VSNKh i ego rol' v natsionalizatsii promyshlennosti," Istoricheskie zapiski, no. 43. (1953).

Voskoboinikova, E. A. ed. Rabochii kontrol' i natsionalizatsiya promyshlennosti v Turkestane (1917–1920 gg.: Sbornik dokumentov.) (Tashkent: Gosizdat UzSSR, 1955).

Voznesensky, A. N. Moskva v 1917 godu (Moscow: Gosizdat, 1928).

Vulliamy, C. E. ed. The Red Archives: Russian State Papers and Other Documents Relating to the Years 1915–1918, trans. A.L. Hynes (London: G. Bles, 1929).

Wheatley, Natasha. The Life and Death of States: Central Europe and the Transformation of Modern Sovereignty (Princeton, NJ: Princeton University Press, 2023).

Willimott, Andy. Living the Revolution: Urban Communes & Soviet Socialism, 1917–1932 (Oxford: Oxford University Press, 2016).

Woloch, Isser. The New Regime: Transformations of the French Civic Order, 1789–1820s (New York, NY: W.W. Norton & Co., 1994).

Woodruff, David M. "The Politburo on Gold, Industrialization, and the International Economy, 1925–1926," in The Lost Politburo transcripts: From Collective Rule to Stalin's Dictatorship, ed. Paul R. Gregory and Norman Naimark (New Haven, CT; Yale University Press, 2008).

———. Money Unmade: Barter and the Fate of Russian Capitalism (Ithaca, NY: Cornell University Press, 1999).

———. "Profits Now, Costs Later" in London Review of Books, 40, no. 22 (Nov. 2018).

Yates, Alexia. Selling Paris: Property and Commercial Culture in the Fin-de-siecle Capital (Cambridge, MA: Harvard University Press, 2015).

Yurovsky, Leonid Naumovich. Denezhnaya politika sovetskoi vlasti (1917–1927) (Moscow, 1996).

Zagriatskov, M. Sotsial'naia deyatel'nost' gorodskogo samoupravleniya na Zapade (Kyiv: Tip. Imp. Universiteta, 1906).

Zakharova, Larissa. "Le 26–28 Kamennoostrovski, Les tribulations d'un immeuble en Revolution" in Saint Pétersbourg: Histoire, promenades, anthologie et dictionnaire (Paris: Laffont, 2003).

Zauberman, Alfred. "The Law of Value and Price Formation," in *Value and Plan: Economic Calculation and Organization in Eastern Europe*, ed. and with introduction by Gregory Grossman (Berkeley, CA: University of California Press, 1960).

Zheleznov, V. Ya., Z. S. Katsenelenbaum, A. A. Sokolov, and K. F. Shmelyov. *K teorii deneg i uchyota* (Petrograd-Moscow: b.i. [bez izdatel'stva], 1922).

Zhizhilenko A. A. *Dolzhnostnye [sluzhebnye] prestupleniya (st.st 105–118 ugolovnogo kodeksa).* (Moscow: "Pravo i zhizn'", 1923).

Zhizhilenko, A. A. *Imushchestvennye prestupleniya.* (Leningrad: Nauka i shkola, 1925).

Zhuravlev, V. V. *Dekrety Sovetskoi Vlasti 1917–1920 gg. kak istorichesky istochnik* (Moscow: Izd. Nauka, 1979).

INDEX

Note: page numbers given in *italics* indicate a figure

accidental holders: dispossession and, 95–96, 120–34; official owners and, 120–34; resettlement and, 120–23

accounting: apartments and, 138–40, 143, 150–79, 315n41, 316n60; audits, 11–12, 97, 112–13, 117, 130–33; banks and, 80, 144–45; black lists and, 175–76; Bolsheviks and, 138–39, 142–44, 149–50, 153, 177; Bonch-Bruevich and, 139–41, 158, 165; bookkeeping practice and, 166–79; bourgeoisie and, 142, 144, 153, 155, 163, 166, 174–78, 313n1, 314n30, 315n41; building committees and, 138–43, 157–63, 171–76, 315n41, 316n60; capitalism and, 142, 144, 149; Central Bureau of Complaint and, 175; Central Committee and, 171, 178; Chekas and, 138–41, 145, 165, 173–74, 313n1; class warfare and, 153, 159; communism and, 144–45, 151, 158, 316n60, 316n62; concentrations and, 138, 162, 165, 174, 176; confiscation and, 157; corruption and, 145; crime and, 162, 177; "Decree on the Accounting and Distribution of Space," 156–57; destruction of records and, 145, 157, 161, 175–76; eviction and, 138–41, 151, 153, 165–66, 173–76; expropriation and, 144; factories and, 147, 151, 174–75; furniture and, 150, 172; Goskon and, 139–40, 146–49, 155–69, 173; housing and, 138, 141–43, 150–79, 315n41, 316n57, 316n60; industry and, 144; inflation and, 141, 147, 315n41;

inventories and, 138, 142, 161, 163, 168, 245–47; Krasin and, 176; Kuzovkov and, 153–56, 158, 161, 163, 168, 177, 314n30, 315n50, 316n62; kvartkhoz and, 158–64, 171, 174, 316n60; labor and, 140–41, 144–46, 150–51, 154–55, 158–68, 171, 174–79, 315n41, 316n60, 316n62; landlords and, 141–42; Lenin and, 142–46, 176, 318n2; Marx and, 144, 172; Moscow and, 138, 141–42, 145, 148–57, 164–65, 171–78; Mossoviet and, 139, 150–53, 157–58, 316n60; MUNI and, 150, 154; Narkomfin and, 145, 315n41; nationalization and, 148; New Economic Policy (NEP) and, 150; No. 29 Povarskaya Street and, 138–42, 164–66; nonmarket, 166–70; October Revolution and, 1, 138, 142–45; off-book registration and, 177; "Order on the Accounting and Distribution of Living and Non-living Space in the City of Moscow," 157; parasites and, 151, 157–58, 165; petitions and, 139–40, 156, 165, 172, 175, 178, 315n41, 316n57; Petrograd and, 138, 150–55, 171–74, 315n41; police and, 173; prices and, 147; private property and, 142–44, 147–48, 179; production units and, 166–67; property rights and, 140, 144; Provisional Government and, 317n105; Rabkrin and, 173–78, 316n60; railroads and, 165; requisition and, 138–41, 148–49, 153, 156–57, 176; resettlement and, 155, 161, 165, 173–75, 178, 315n41;

347